TOP
SECRET

INFORMATION

THE

GOVERNMENT,

BANKS,

AND

RETAILERS

DON'T WANT
YOU TO KNOW

PUBLISHER'S NOTE

This book is intended for general information only. It does not constitute medical, legal, or financial advice or practice. We cannot guarantee the safety or effectiveness of any treatment or advice mentioned. Readers are urged to consult with their personal financial advisors, lawyers, and health-care professionals.

Fear not, for I am with you; be not dismayed, for I am your God. I will strengthen you, yes, I will help you, I will uphold you with My righteous right hand.

Isaiah 41:10

Contents

Tax Strategies 175

Money and the People You Love 209

Security and Safer Living 351

Travel Dollars and Sense 359

Index 373

INTRODUCTION

Hundreds of America's best-kept secrets are now in your hands. To bring you the inside scoop, we've interviewed experts from finances to fashion and discovered what they've been keeping in the dark. And we've searched through bookstores, magazines, and computer databases to find the most useful information that's in print. We hope our lists of consumer tips will leave you with more money in your pocket at the end of the month.

Here are some of the vital secrets you'll find in our new book:

17 best values in used cars

You can cut your search time for a used car dramatically if you stick with cars that have proven themselves over the years. Nationwide automotive expert Jim Mateja offers these suggestions:

- ► Toyota Mr-2
- ► Toyota Celica (Post-1986 models)
- ► Toyota Cressida/ Nissan Maxima
- ► Dodge Shelby Charger
- ► Ford LTD/ Mercury Marquis
- ► Ford Mustang (Post-1979 models)
- ► Chevy Cavalier
- ► Any Chevy Camaro or Pontiac Firebird
- ► Any Chevy Corvette
- ► Chevrolet Celebrity (provided it was made after 1983)
- ► Chevy Impala/Caprice
- ► Pontiac Grand Am (post-1985 models)
- ► Buick Century/Olds Ciera (but don't get one with a 3 liter carbureted engine)
- ► Any pre-1986 Buick Riviera/ Olds Toronado/ Cadillac Eldorado
- ► Any pre-1986 Buick LeSabre/ Olds 88
- ► Oldsmobile Cutlass Supreme/ Buick Regal
- ► Cadillac Sevilles built between 1980 and 1985

Source:
Best Buys in Used Cars by Jim Mateja, Bonus Books, Chicago, 1995

6 signs of designer quality without designer price tags

Unless you're a tailor, it's hard to tell which clothes are quality and which are junk. That's one reason so many people pay top dollar for a designer label. Save your money, and use this checklist instead:

- ► Seams: Do they pucker? Is the thread the right color?
- ► Collars: Do they lie flat? Are both sides the same?
- ► Pockets: Are they sewn properly? Do they bulk at all?

▶ Buttonholes: Are they the right size for the buttons? Is the stitching frazzled?
▶ Prints: Do they match at the seams?
▶ Shoulder pads: Are they lumpy? Are they too big for the shoulders?
Source:
Looking, Working, Living Terrific 24 Hours a Day by Emily Cho, G.P. Putnam's Sons, New York, 1982

Bathing suits that flatter any figure

Who cares about fashion when so much of your body is exposed? You'll save money on bathing suits if you take the time to find one that works for you, then wear it for years.

▶ Full-breasted? Search out square necklines and wide straps. Look for a bathing suit with a built-in bra that encircles your entire torso.
▶ Heavy upper body? Find a V-necked suit. It will slenderize your shoulder area.
▶ Pear-shaped? Search for two-colored suits that feature light colors or a pattern on top and dark colors on the bottom.
▶ Thick thighs or varicose veins? Look for low-cut legs. Turn a large scarf into a sarong and tie it around your waist or hips.
▶ Saggy bottom? Stay away from skimpy suits with high-cut legs.
Source:
New Choices (34,4:17)

8 cheap household products that clean almost anything

Advertisers say you need a different cleaner for every household chore. Don't believe it. You can clean almost anything with ammonia and bleach.

Besides whitening clothes, bleach will kill mildew in the bath. Put bleach down your drains to keep them unclogged. It's faster and cheaper than drain cleaners. Ammonia is a great glass cleaner and can be used to clean stoves, counters, floors, etc. Be sure to follow the dilution instructions on the label.

Caution: Never mix ammonia and bleach. The fumes are toxic.

More cleaning supplies for those strapped for cash:

▶ Shampoo can clean ring around the collar.
▶ Vinegar and lemon juice will get out grease and clean glass. Combined with hot water, they'll help clean out the drains. Freeze them into ice cubes and they can clean the garbage disposal.
▶ Hair spray will get out ink marks on clothing. Peanut butter may get gum off clothes.
▶ Sponges and rags are cheaper than paper towels. Turn old towels into cleaning rags.
Source:
How to Pinch a Penny 'Til It Screams by Rochelle LaMotte McDonald, Avery Publishing Group, Garden City Park, N.Y., 1994

For more big secrets the government doesn't want you to know, the banks don't want you to know, and secrets that retailers would rather not tell you either, keep reading!

SMARTER SHOPPING

Garage sale secrets

Rummage, yard, garage, or tag sales. No matter what you call them, they are great opportunities for sellers to make extra cash while cleaning out clutter — and for buyers to find bargains.

Sellers, your rummage sale will be more successful if you follow these tips from Steven Ellingboe, editor of *Today's Collector*:

Price items low. After all, you want to sell the stuff you don't need! Don't make this mistake: "People read that a comic book or baseball card they have is worth a certain amount of money, and they try to get that same price," notes Ellingboe. "Remember, price guides list retail prices for items in mint condition. Sure, a like-new baseball card may sell at a collectors show for $15, but your used one is really worth only about $1.50."

Expect buyers to bargain. Even if you've priced your items fairly, don't be offended if your customers ask if you'll take less. Garage sale regulars often expect to haggle over prices a little — it's part of the fun. Consider offering a discount when someone buys several items.

Use removable stickers. Never, *never*, use tape or write the price on an object with a marker. Why? Because it lowers the value of some items. "For example, board games and toys are very popular with collectors right now. They'll pay more money if you have the original boxes," Ellingboe explains. "But so many people write on the box or use stickers that won't come off, and that ruins the collectible value of a lot of objects."

Buyers, be patient. You never now what you'll find at rummage sales, from trash to treasures. But, if you are patient, you can find just about anything you need — including books, plants, tools, clothes, and dishes — often at rock bottom prices. Wood furniture especially is likely to be far cheaper, and much better made, than the modern fiberboard variety.

Find unique decorating ideas. Don't pass by old magazines. "You can often find old *Looks*, *Lifes*, and *Saturday Evening Posts* for a dime to a quarter," says antiques and collectibles expert Ellingboe. "The ones with Marilyn Monroe or John Kennedy on well-preserved covers might obviously be worth a little more money. However, don't ignore the ones with damaged or even missing covers."

He explains that what's inside — vintage advertisements for Coca Cola or Cadillac, for example— can be framed to make great nostalgic pictures. Antiques dealers often do just that. "It's possible to buy an old magazine for a quarter and have advertisements in it worth $30," Ellingboe relates.

Spin some tunes. Interested in a still cheap collectible that might hold investment potential? Consider record albums — not for the vinyl, but for the cover art.

"I think record albums are going to become valuable as display pieces," says Ellenboe, an avid collector himself. "Particularly albums of the 1950s, 1960s and even some of the psychedelic record covers of the 1970s."

Albums are still cheap — usually priced from a dime to a dollar at rummage sales and thrift stores.

Source:
Interview with Steve Ellingboe, Editor, *Today's Collector*, published monthly by Krause Publications, Iola, Wis.

Recalls: How to find out about free car repairs and more

We've all seen consumer alerts in the newspaper or heard about them on TV news. Cars, toys, coffee makers, and more have been found to have serious flaws. Sometimes, they are even life-threatening. Remember the case of the car with an easy-to-explode gas tank?

Manufacturers "recall" these items. Recently recalled items in the news include miniblinds tainted with lead, possibly dangerous hot tubs, and malfunctioning bread machines.

"Companies usually have to replace or repair an item if it's recalled at no cost to the consumer," says Carol Reeves, public affairs officer of the U.S. Consumer Product Safety Commission's Atlanta office.

That can add up to big savings when cars are repaired for free. For example, a few years ago, when a particular car model's paint began turning bumpy and mottled, car owners got a new paint job for free.

"In other cases, companies may offer a credit. For example, if you had a coffee maker for 10 years, and it was recalled, the manufacturer might offer you a $10 credit toward a new machine," explains Reeves.

How do you know if something you bought has been recalled? You may receive a letter from the manufacturer or from the dealership where you bought your car, if you sent in a warranty card.

But what happens if you think an item you have has been recalled — maybe you heard it mentioned on the news — and no one has contacted you? Or maybe you bought the item used, or lost your receipt?

To learn about specific problems with cars and car-related items (like car seats), contact the National Highway Traffic and Safety Administration. The toll-free number is 1-800-424-9393. Staff members are available to help consumers Monday through Friday, from 8 a.m. to 10 p.m.

Call the U.S. Product Safety Commission toll-free at 1-800-638-2772 for questions you have about other recalled items. That 24-hour hot line provides access to a host of information about all kinds of products — ranging from recalled hair dryers to food and cosmetics. Moreover, if you believe you have an unsafe product, you can use the number to report the problem. Your information could help prevent injury to others.

If you need additional help, check the phone book to see if your city has a local office of the U.S. Product Safety Commission listed. In Atlanta, for instance, the office will help consumers track down recall information going all the way back to 1974.

Source:
Interview with Carol Reeves, public affairs officer, U.S. Product Safety Commission, Atlanta

How to fight retailers' powers of persuasion

You may have heard of people freezing desserts in single-size portions so they won't eat the whole thing at once. Ginger Applegarth in *The Money Diet* describes a woman who put her credit cards in a plastic bag and froze the bag in a container of water. If she wants to use the cards, she has to wait several hours. By then, the spending urge has usually passed.

Retailers don't want you to control your spending habits, and they'll try to sabotage your efforts to stay on a money diet with enticing ads and sales. But if you're trying to save money or get debt under control, you need to build in an automatic "spending stopper" like the ones below:

► At the beginning of every week, figure out how much cash you will need for the next seven days. Go to the bank and withdraw the money, then put your ATM card in a safe place at home. Take the credit cards out of your wallet, too, except for the one with a zero balance that you must pay off every month.

► Before you go shopping, decide how much you want to spend. Take that amount of cash and leave the credit cards behind. (If you find something extra you "must have," put it on hold. You may find it's not worth it to go back to the store. Children who really needed a certain item often lose interest later, especially if they have to go shopping with their parents again to get it.)

► Shopping for the fun of it is a bad idea. If you really enjoy walking through malls, leave all your money behind or allow yourself to make only one small purchase.

► Don't take credit cards on vacation. The feeling of freedom you get at the seaside can wreak havoc on your finances. Set a budget before traveling and take that amount in cash or traveler's checks.

Whatever it takes to make you face reality the minute you are tempted to spend, do it. Reality will slap you in the face when you get your credit card bill, but by then, it's often too late.

Source:
The Money Diet by Ginger Applegarth, personal finance correspondent for *The Today Show*, Viking, New York, 1995

How to buy other people's lost luggage

Ever lost your luggage and never found it? It probably made its way to a new home in Scottsboro, Ala.

Approximately 2 million bags are handled by the nation's airlines each day. Roughly 10,000 to 20,000 are misplaced.

Of those, 200 or so per day are never returned to their owners. Those are the suitcases that find their way to the Unclaimed Baggage Center.

This store buys the lost, abandoned, and forgotten luggage from the airlines and — after checking for cash — puts the contents and suitcases up for sale.

Virtually anything you can imagine can be found on the company's showroom (or in one of its three satellite stores) and all of it goes for a song.

London Fog raincoats will cost you $25 or so. Armani suits are only $50. Cameras start at about $25. Also hidden in the nooks and crannies of the huge store are trombones, tools, toys, and toasters.

People flock to the store from all over the country. New merchandise hits the racks daily, so locals say the best time to shop is early in the morning.

Source:
The Wall Street Journal (March 15, 1994)

How to find a package lost in the mail

Do you remember the package you sent your cousins last Christmas? The one they never received. What happened to it? Despite what most people think, there is not a postal heaven where all undeliverable packages go to rest. There are, however, three mail recovery centers in the United States.

If you mail a package or a letter and it is never delivered, you can go to the post office that you mailed it from and fill out search form 1510 for the mail piece to be traced. Or you can call your local post office branch, and they will fill out the form for you.

Letters and packages that don't have postage or packages that have an incorrect address are considered undeliverable if they also have no return address. Packages determined to be undeliverable are sent to the closest of the three mail recovery centers. The centers are located in St. Paul, Minn.; Atlanta, Ga.; and San Francisco, Calif.

Once the package or letter arrives at the mail recovery center, it is opened and inspected for an invoice or any type of address. When addresses can't be found, postal employees enter the name and contents of the package into the computer. Each package or letter is held for a minimum of 90 days. Express Mail is held for six months, while other accountable mail such as registered, COD, or numbered insured (a fancy kind of insurance) is held for one year.

So remember, the next time you think something was lost in the mail, it could be only a phone call away.

Source:
Interview with Ray Long, manager of the Mail Recovery Center in Atlanta

How to buy other people's mail

Looking for a bargain on anything from new clothes to television sets? Attend an auction given by the U.S. Postal Service.

If no inquiries are made about a lost package or letter within 90 days, postal employees pull the mail piece to determine if it has value. Packages with value are auctioned and packages determined to be of no value are thrown away.

The items that are auctioned are as varied as the different items people mail. You'll find computers, radios, plates, silverware, promotional items, and books. Items are sold in lots, which usually include several items. Big items, ~uch as televisions, are often sold separately as one lot.

Auctions are held at mail recovery centers every four to six weeks. The ꞁost office notifies the public in various ways. They run an ad in the city's ꞁajor newspaper and advertise in local post office branches.

Also, if you are on the mailing list, you receive notification through the ꞁail 10 to 14 days in advance. If you want to receive notice of upcoming auc-ꞁons, all you have to do is call or write one of the three centers and ask to be ꞁn the list.

Before each auction, you can buy a catalog that describes the contents of ꞁch lot and the minimum bid for each particular lot. Minimum bids range ꞁom $10 to $500. Also, you can view the lots for approximately two hours ꞁefore the auction begins.

Postal employees conduct the auctions, so you won't hear the traditional ꞁuctioneer language — great news for those inexperienced in "auctionese." The auctions are usually three-to-four hour events in the middle of the week.

Right now, credit cards are not accepted but should be in the near future. Personal checks are accepted with two forms of identification, usually a driver's license and major credit card. You can use cashier's checks, postal money orders, and, of course, cash.

Auctions can be fun and a good place to find bargains. But make sure you really want to own what you buy because you can't return it.

Source:
Interview with Ray Long, manager of the Mail Recovery Center in Atlanta

Driving home in a government car (and other GSA bargains)

Looking for a good deal on a used car? Forget the dealers. Try Uncle Sam.

Government Service Administration auctions help the folks in Washington make back some of the money they spend on equipment. After an "official government vehicle" is driven for a few years, it's sold to the highest bidder.

And because the GSA is in charge of the government's auto fleet, it's responsible for finding buyers.

The auctions are held on an irregular basis around the country, depending on how much the GSA has to get rid of. Even if you're not in the market for a car, you may still want to check out these sales, since office equipment and real estate are put up for bid, too.

To find out when the GSA will hold its next auction in your part of the country, call the nearest regional office. If you don't know where that is, call the Federal Information Center at 1-800-688-9889. Or, if you happen to have a government printing office in your town, you can buy the Federal Sales Guide for $1.75. This booklet lists the 13 government agencies that put property up for bids, tells you what they typically sell, and lists upcoming auctions.

Source:
Interview with Government Service Administration

Crime does pay — for you!

We've all seen the spoils of a busted drug dealer or counterfeiter: furs, jewels, yachts. But once the criminals are convicted, they lose these belongings. If you know where to go, you can pick them up — often dirt cheap.

Every month or so, the vault at the U.S. Marshals Service overflows, and seized items go up for sale. Because the Marshals are too busy arresting criminals, though, the auction duties are contracted out to private companies. Cars are usually sold by local auction firms. Collectible items like fur coats, jewels, and paintings are sold by Manheim Auctions (call 1-800-222-9885 for up-to-the-minute auction information). Planes are sold in Texas by Aero-Mod Services every three to four months. Real estate is forfeited to the General Services Administration.

Typically, the vendors are responsible for advertising the auction, but every Wednesday in *USA Today*, the Marshals Service posts a classified ad for upcoming sales.

Sources:
Interviews with U.S. Marshals Service, Manheim Auctions, Aero-Mod Services

Who needs department stores?

The U.S. Marshals Office isn't the only clearinghouse of criminal property. The U.S. Customs Service has plenty of ill-gotten gain in its possession, too.

Cars, planes, boats, stereos, televisions, and jewelry are all common items at Customs auctions. To attend one, you may have to be willing to travel. Unlike other agencies, which hold auctions all over the country, Customs keeps its sales in one of eight cities: Miami/Fort Lauderdale, Fla.; El Paso, Texas; Laredo, Texas; Annenberg, Texas; Edison, N.J.; Los Angeles, Calif.; Nogales, Ariz.; and Chula Vista, Calif.

Sales are typically held every nine weeks. Cars, however, are sold every four weeks — and only in Chula Vista.

The local papers in and around these cities carry ads for the sales. An easier way for you to hear about them, though, is to subscribe to the agency's sales flyers. The prices range from $25 to $50 per year, depending on how much information you want. Call 1-703-273-7373.

Source:
Interview with U.S. Customs Service

Government freebies

The government collects thousands of dollars from you each year in taxes, but you can actually get some of that back — in merchandise.

For example, need some firewood? Where there's a surplus, you can cart off free timber from public lands. Simply call your local forest ranger.

If you're planning to do some gardening, Uncle Sam will be happy to supply you with free fertilizer, too. It's going to stink, though. Most extension service offices offer free manure by the barrel or truckload. (Also, if the circus comes to town, they often give away manure their last day in town. Just bring a shovel and a container — airtight might be a smart idea.)

Washington loves a party as much as any town. If you know someone about to reach their 80th birthday or their 50th (or better) wedding anniversary, you can arrange for a signed card from the President. Send a written request at least one month in advance to:

> Presidential Correspondence
> Chief Executive Office Building, Room 94
> Washington, DC 20500

If you want a picture included, be sure to mention that.

Source:
Lesko's Info-Power by Matthew Lesko, Visible Ink Press, Detroit, 1994

Little-known bargain shopping tips

► Most stores will gladly match a competitor's price on the same item. All you have to do is ask. If you know one store sells an item for $19, but you are shopping in a store that sells the item for $24, don't be ashamed to ask at the customer service desk for the lower price.

► Be sure to ask for a discount when you're making a major cash purchase. If you don't get one, talk to the manager.

► Ask retailers when sales are planned. The item you want to buy may be going on sale next week.

Sources:
Interview with a professional bargain shopper, Peachtree City, Ga.
Life After Debt by Bob Hammond, Career Press, Franklin Lakes, N.J., 1995

Save up to 80 percent on furniture

Every time you turn on the radio or look in your newspaper, you're bombarded with ads for huge sales at your local furniture store: "Prices Slashed 50, 60, even 75 Percent."

All that price slashing should make you suspicious. Retail furniture stores are charging far too much for their merchandise. A normal markup on furniture at a local store is 200 or 300 percent.

So, don't even think about refurnishing your living room until you read this news: You can save 30 to 80 percent on your next furniture purchase by taking a trip to North Carolina. And those savings include the cost of traveling to the Furniture Capital of America and having your purchases shipped home.

North Carolina's 600 factories make most of the furniture sold in the United States, and you don't have to be a furniture retailer to shop the showrooms and outlets lining the streets in the North Carolina towns of Hickory and High Point. Any consumer can shop the discount stores. You'll find incredible bargains and excellent customer service, too.

So why haven't you heard more about this? Furniture retailers are in cahoots to keep you in the dark. They put pressure on the furniture manufacturers, who in turn threaten to withhold their furniture from the discounters unless they keep a low profile. No big advertising campaigns are allowed.

If you really don't want to make the trip to North Carolina, you may be able to order from the discounters by phone. About 15 percent of the discounters aren't allowed by manufacturers to take phone orders, but you can place a phone order with the rest of them.

You'll need to find the furniture you want at a local store and get the exact model number of the furniture and the fabric. Most retailers will make it difficult for you to get that information, but you may be in luck.

For more information on shopping the North Carolina discounters, call the High Point and Hickory Convention and Visitors Bureaus:

High Point Convention and Visitors Bureau
300 Main Street
P.O. Box 2273
High Point, NC 27261
1-910-884–5255

Greater Hickory Convention and Visitors Bureau
470 Highway 70 S.W.
P.O. Box 1828
Hickory, NC 28603
1-800-849-5093 or 1-704-322–1335

Source:
Greater Hickory Convention and Visitors Bureau, Hickory, N.C.

How to buy surplus property from the government

When the U.S. Department of Defense has property it no longer needs, it sells or auctions it off to the general public. As you would expect, ships, aircraft, electronic manufacturing equipment, and machine tools make up a large part of the sales, but you can also get excellent deals on vehicles, clothing, hand tools, hardware, musical instruments, and furniture.

To find out about local sales and auctions, all you have to do is call the Defense Reutilization and Marketing Office nearest you to be placed on their local mailing list. Most states have several DRMOs.

When you're placed on the mailing list, you'll receive a sales catalog describing the property for sale, a date when you can come to inspect the property, and the sale location and date. If you don't participate in a sale after you've received three catalogs, you'll usually be taken off the mailing list.

To participate in these sales, you have to be over 18 and you can't be a federal government employee. And, in case you were wondering, arms, ammunition, and combat aircraft and vehicles aren't sold in their original form. They are "demilitarized" so that you and your neighbors can't start a war against a nearby neighborhood.

Joking aside, you will find good prices on hand tool sets, cameras, film, household furniture, mattresses, blankets, carpets, tile, draperies, awnings, kitchen equipment and appliances, tableware, office supplies, stationery, books, maps, televisions, athletic equipment, toys, fishing equipment, tents, tarpaulins, luggage, clothes for men, women's clothes, children's wear, and more.

Items are sold both by auction and by cash-and-carry sales.

Source:
How to Buy Surplus Personal Property From the Department of Defense, Defense Reutilization and Marketing Service, National Sales Office, P.O. Box 5275 DDRC, 2163 Airways Blvd., Memphis, TN 38114–5210, Phone: 1-800-222-DRMS (3767)

Saving money at the post office

Next time you send out party invitations, make them postcards instead of letters. You'll save 12 cents on every invitation. Remember to make your card no bigger than 4 1/4 inches by 6 inches. Ralph Schiller, an Atlanta customer service representative for the United States Postal Service, says to pay attention to those dimensions. "A lot of people think when they print a card they should get postcard rate, even if the card is 8 1/4 inches by 3 3/4 inches. The International Postal Union set the 4 1/4 by 6 inch dimensions."

Don't buy insurance. It costs 75 cents to insure a package worth $50 or less, $1.60 for a package worth $100 or less, and $2.40 for a package worth $200 or less. If you're mailing a wedding present of Tiffany china, you may want to insure it. Otherwise, skip the insurance, especially if you're shipping a manuscript you have another copy of, perishable items, or inexpensive books.

If you are mailing something valuable, you may find United Parcel Service to be a better choice. UPS automatically insures everything up to $100.

Choose certified mail plus insurance over registered mail. If you're shipping a family heirloom or expensive jewelry, registered mail with insurance is the best security you can buy. Registered mail is signed for every time it's turned over to another delivery person. At night, the postal driver turns the package over to a post office to be locked up. Registered mail is not cheap.

Certified mail is a record of delivery. The person who receives the package must sign for it, and the post office sends the signed card back to you. Certified mail only costs $1.

To send a package worth $50 by registered mail costs $4.50 with postal insurance and $4.40 without postal insurance. Instead, you could send it by certified mail with postal insurance for $1.75. Unless your package is irreplaceable, certified mail is probably the best choice.

Pick Priority Mail instead of overnight delivery. You may be one of those who is helping the overnight carriers — Airborne Express, DHL Worldwide Express, Emery Worldwide, Federal Express, and United Parcel Service — earn close to $20 billion in annual sales. Most packages that are sent by overnight mail do not absolutely have to be there the next day.

Usually, Priority Mail is a wiser choice than an overnight carrier or the post office's Express Mail. With Priority Mail, you can ship a 2-pound package for $3.00 and get it there in two days. Priority Mail is any first-class mail that weighs over 11 oz. and under 70 pounds. (Although you probably won't beat the Priority Mail price, other carriers such as UPS and Federal Express also offer two-day services.)

Get free envelopes and boxes. Most people don't know it, but the post office provides Priority Mail envelopes and boxes for free. Some companies get whole pallets of Priority Mail envelopes at once. These envelopes cost the post office about 45 cents apiece, so getting them for free is quite a bargain.

Plus, you don't even have to weigh whatever you can stuff into a cardboard Priority Mail envelope. You automatically pay the 2-pound postage rate ($3.00) regardless of weight. For instance, you come out way ahead if you can manage to fit 3 pounds worth of papers into the cardboard envelope.

Save money by sending it "Standard Mail." If you have a week or two before a package needs to be at its destination, don't send it first-class. What used to be called third- and fourth-class mail is now called "Standard Mail." It's much less expensive than first-class mail.

Source:
Interview with Ralph Schiller, Atlanta customer service representative, United States Postal Service, Atlanta

How to buy a chair that will baby your back

If you've ever suffered the agony of a backache, you know the value of babying your back. And if you know that sitting places one and a half times more pressure on your back than standing or walking, you know the value of picking the proper chair for your back. Here are some tips to help you choose a chair that will do just that:

► Select a chair with a firm seat that is low enough for your feet to rest comfortably on the floor. Shun soft chairs as comfy as they may seem. They're generally unsupportive and can cause your back muscles to tighten up and go into spasms.

► Look for a chair with a back that fits the curves of your spine and does not cause your back to sway or be overly rounded. Don't pick a chair that has an open space where your lower back will be. Select a chair that is big enough to completely support your thighs.

► Choose a chair that will rock back. This will ease pressure on your spine. Relaxing in a regular rocking chair is very helpful for an aching back. The rocking motion helps relieve back pain by changing your muscle positions and removing some of the strain caused by gravity.

► Make sure your chosen chair has armrests and use them. They will reduce the amount of pressure on your spine while you're sitting. Don't forget to use the armrests to shift your weight now and then and to help push yourself out of the chair.

► Find yourself a footrest to go with your chair. A footrest will help reduce pressure from your thighs as you sit. If you aren't using a footrest, your feet should rest flat on the floor so the weight of your legs is not supported completely by the front of your thighs.

Source:
The Better Back Book by Constance A. Bean, William Morrow and Company, New York, 1989

Don't get ripped off in the jewelry store

Do you remember the last time you purchased jewelry? Was it an overwhelming experience? All the choices and different prices can make buying jewelry an ordeal. Saving money on jewelry almost seems like an oxymoron.

You'll save money on jewelry if you buy quality merchandise, even if the price is higher. Quality jewelry will last longer and need fewer repairs.

The biggest mistake consumers make is being misled by jewelers. Some dishonest jewelers misrepresent their products. That's easy to do because prices vary so much depending on the shape, quality, number of flaws, and rarity of a gemstone. Make sure you know the jeweler or have checked the reliability of the jewelry store.

It's also easy to get confused when jewelers start discussing the different types of gold, such as 14-karat, gold-filled, or gold-plated. Here are the basics:

► 24-karat gold — This is pure gold. All gold adds up to 24 parts. The karat weight tells you how much of the metal is gold. So if a piece of jewelry is 14-karat gold, it is 14 parts gold and 10 parts other metal.

▶ Gold-filled — Jewelry that is gold-filled doesn't have enough gold to qualify as 10-karat gold. Gold-filled jewelry should not change colors because the gold is mixed in with the other metals.

▶ Gold-plated — A piece of jewelry that does not contain gold can be plated, or covered, in gold. The jewelry can change colors when the gold wears off.

When buying jewelry, remember two rules: You get what you pay for, and if it sounds too good to be true, it probably is.

Your jewelry will last longer and look nicer if you clean it every night. Jewelers recommend bringing your jewelry into the store to be cleaned at least four times a year. Store your jewelry in a box with a soft lining and a separate compartment for each piece. Jewelry should never be stored in extreme heat or extreme cold.

If you aren't sure of your jewelry's value but think it's more than the deductible on your homeowner's insurance policy, have it appraised. Once again, make sure you trust the jeweler performing the appraisal.

Source:
Interview with Sherrell Campbell, Brown Jewelers, Peachtree City, Ga.

How to buy a diamond

Whether you're buying a diamond as an investment or to announce your engagement, you need to know the 4 C's to make a good choice.

Cut. The precision of a diamond's cut determines how much light the diamond will refract and reflect. The better a diamond is cut, the greater its brilliance and sparkle. Ask a reputable jeweler to show you a diamond cut with good proportions.

Color. Many diamonds look colorless, but most actually have a hint of yellow or brown due to traces of nitrogen in the gem. The closer a diamond is to truly having no color, the more valuable it is. However, those diamonds that do have a distinctive red, pink, or blue color (although they may come in all colors) are also very rare and valuable.

Clarity. Clarity refers to the number of a diamond's naturally occurring inclusions or flaws, which are often created by minerals trapped during the diamond's crystallization process. The fewer the inclusions, the more light the diamond will reflect, and the more valuable it will be.

Carat weight. This unit of measure was derived from early diamond traders who used seed from pods of the carob tree to determine diamond weight. A one-carat diamond equaled the weight of one carob seed.

Today, carats are measured in metric terms. One carat is 0.2 grams or about 1/42 of an ounce. Each carat is divided into 100 points. For example, if you bought a half-carat diamond, it should have 50 points. A diamond's weight does not affect its cut, color, or clarity.

For more details on buying a diamond, talk with a jeweler you trust or call the American Gem Society at 1-800-341-6214 and request their brochure "How to Buy Diamonds You'll Be Proud to Give."

Source:
How to Buy Diamonds You'll Be Proud to Give, American Gem Society, 8881 West Sahara Avenue, Las Vegas, NV 89117

Self-defrosting refrigerators: Why it's better to stick with old Frosty

Almost all owners of refrigerators that have to be manually defrosted look forward to the day when they own a refrigerator that defrosts itself.

And with good reason, you say.

Well, maybe not — not if you want to save money, that is.

If the only problem with your old refrigerator is that it won't defrost itself, you may want to reconsider your decision to buy a new, self-defrosting one. Here are two good reasons why:

Not only are you going to have to spend a sizable chunk of money to get one, anywhere from $500 upwards, a frost-free model will cost you 40 to 60 percent more in electricity just to run.

Plus, your new refrigerator will probably also have more complicated parts, such as complex circuitry, fans, and heaters, all of which present potential breakdown problems and repair bills.

Whatever you decide about that new refrigerator, here are some ways to keep cooling costs down:

▶ Don't keep your refrigerator cooler than 40 degrees Fahrenheit. You can buy relatively inexpensive freezer/refrigerator thermometers to hang in your refrigerator that will give you a constant temperature reading. You can also check the temperature by leaving an ordinary household thermometer in the fridge for 10 to 15 minutes.

▶ Make sure the rubber gasket around the door is keeping the cold air inside the fridge. Here's an easy way to test your gasket's effectiveness: Open the refrigerator door, place a piece of paper against the gasket and shut the door. If the paper slips out, you need a new gasket. Take care to keep the gasket clean of crusted food particles; otherwise it may not make a proper seal, and cold air will still be able to slip out.

▶ If you do decide to buy a new refrigerator, make sure it's not bigger than what you really need. Big refrigerators lose more cold air than small ones. You're also more likely to let food go to waste in a big fridge than a small one.

Source:
Living Cheaply With Style by Ernest Callenbach, Ronin Publishing, Berkeley, Calif., 1993

How to pick a fresh Christmas tree every time

$50 to $150 is about the price you'll pay these days for a fresh Christmas tree. While the fragrance and fun alone make choosing a live tree a worthwhile experience, you'll enjoy this purchase more if you know how to choose wisely and keep your tree fresh and fragrant for the entire season.

If you aren't growing your own or going to a tree farm to choose and cut your Christmas tree, you at least need to know what to look for on a lot. Don't depend on the tree sellers to tell you. They're there to sell trees, not to please picky purchasers.

► Buy early in the season so your tree will be at its freshest — early December is your best bet.

► Look for loose needles. A tree with loose needles is probably not as fresh as it could be. Bounce the tree stump on the ground a few times to see if green needles fall off easily or not. Pine trees are an exception to this rule. Since these trees shed their inside needles every fall, it's normal for a few yellow needles to fall off when bounced.

► Feel for flexible needles. Take a needle between your thumb and forefinger and gently try to bend the ends together. If the tree is fresh, the needle should bend, not break. However, if you're testing a tree in below-freezing temperatures, even a needle from a fresh tree is likely to break.

► Let your nose be your guide. Fresh trees smell good.

Besides a better appearance, a well-cared for tree is much less likely to fuel a fire in case you have an electrical short in some of your Christmas tree lights. Here are some helpful tree-care tips.

► Get a good, sturdy stand for your tree; this stand should be able to hold about two gallons of water. Saw one inch off your tree trunk once you get it home so that it will more quickly absorb water. Then place the tree in the stand and fill it with warm water. Keep a close eye on the amount of water in the stand, and make sure to refill it at least every other day to ensure tree freshness. A fresh tree may drink from a quart to a gallon of water a day. A well-watered tree will not catch fire easily.

► If the water level falls below the bottom of the trunk, the tree may develop a resin seal or an air block, both of which can prevent the tree from absorbing water. To enable the tree to continue to drink water, you will need to trim another inch off the bottom of the tree. When a tree will no longer drink water, it becomes a potential fire hazard, and you should remove it from the house.

► Position your tree so that it is not near a fireplace or other heat sources or major appliances.

▶ Check light sets you plan to use to decorate the tree to make sure no cords are worn or frayed. If you find any damaged cords, either replace them or throw them away.

▶ Remember to always unplug tree lights when you leave the house and when you go to bed.

After the holidays, you can make good use of your Christmas tree by grinding it up to use as mulch in your yard. If you don't have a way of grinding your tree, many recycling centers offer this service. Azaleas, blueberry bushes, mountain laurels, and rhododendrons all like the acidic evergreen mulch produced by Christmas trees.

A used Christmas tree also makes a great natural bird feeder. Set the tree up in some location birds seem to like, then hang pine or spruce cones rolled in peanut butter and birdseed on it. If you don't want to go to the trouble of making special cones, commercial seed/suet hangers also work well.
Source:
Conservationist (49,12:16)

Purchasing the perfect pooch

All puppies are cute, but not every one's the right one for you and your family. Choosing the wrong dog will mean problems for you and your pet down the road.

Before getting a puppy, take him to a quiet place and put him on the floor. Chances are the dog will freeze at first. That's normal. Before too long, though, he should begin to explore and get friendly. If the animal never moves from its initial spot, tries to hide or tries to run you down, keep looking.

Your personal interaction is also very important. Bend down and call the puppy, whistling, clapping, and making unusual noises. If he comes, praise him promptly. After he does it once, move to another spot in the room and try again. Each time you call, the puppy should be more responsive.

After you've called him a few times, start petting the puppy gently. (Don't force him to stay near you.) The ideal response, of course, is for the dog to lick you or roll over. If he nips you or shows some other sign of dominance, firmly say *"no"* then try again.

Gentle biting is normal for puppies and it's easy to train them not to do this, but if the dog is too dominant or aggressive, he will be hard (if not impossible) to train. If you've got a family around, very aggressive dogs are certainly not for you.

If the dog wanders off as you pet him or is only friendly for a second, he may be too aloof.

After stroking the dog some, stand up and walk around the room. A friendly dog will follow you.

If you're picking your puppy at the standard age of eight to 12 weeks old, it's really too early to begin teaching him tricks. Try, however, working on the simple task: "Sit."

Jingle a set of keys above his head while you give the command. Some puppies will lose their balance and fall to a sitting position. If this doesn't work, raise the dog's chin and push gently on his hind legs. If the dog is sitting after a few tries, you've got a *very* trainable pup.

Gauge how active the puppy is in your time with him. If you're exhausted when you get in from work, you probably don't want a bundle of energy. If, however, you like taking numerous walks or jogs each day, an ultrafrisky pet may be right for you.

Source:
The Chosen Puppy: How to Select and Raise a Great Puppy From an Animal Shelter by Carol Lea Benjamin, Howell Book House, New York, 1990

Expensive dog food has drawbacks

Are you in the doghouse with your pooch because you've picked the wrong kind of dog food? There are hundreds of brands, but here are the pros and cons of the three basic types:

Dry foods are the cheapest, the easiest to feed your dog, and the easiest to store.

Semi-moist foods apparently taste a bit better to dogs and also require no refrigeration. If you're on the road, they're very convenient. These brands tend to be more expensive, and some dogs begin overeating because of the good taste.

Moist (or canned) foods seem to taste the best. They are expensive, and they must be kept in a refrigerator. If left in a bowl, they will spoil. The good taste of canned foods may also lead to overeating, but the biggest problem comes with clean-up. Most canned foods have a high concentration of water. When your dog digests the food and expels the waste, he or she will have very soft stool, which is absolutely no fun to clean up.

Source:
The Dog Care Book by Sheldon L. Gerstenfeld, Addison-Wesley Publishing, Reading, Mass., 1989

How to buy a healthy rabbit

It's tempting to snap up the first cute and fuzzy bunny rabbit with big ears that you see. But don't do it!

Make sure the rabbit is alert and active. The rabbit should come to the front of the cage when you open the door.

Beware of a listless look. The eyes should be bright, the nose dry. The front paws shouldn't be matted — that's a sign the rabbit has a cold.

Rabbit droppings should be hard and round. If not, the rabbit may have stomach problems. Rabbit ears should be clean.

Stroke the fur from the rump toward the head. The fur should quickly return to its original position.

Examine the teeth. Upper front teeth should barely overlap the tips of the lower front teeth. If the teeth overlap too much the rabbit will have trouble eating.

Source:
Raising Rabbits Successfully by Bob Bennett, Williamson Publishing, Charlotte, Vt., 1984

Grocery store penny pinching

Buy in bulk. Lee and Barbara Simmons, authors of *Penny Pinching*, give a new twist to this old advice. They've discovered that store managers will quietly give discounts to regular customers who buy by the case. They suggest politely mentioning to the manager that you'll shop elsewhere if they don't accommodate you.

Bend and stretch. Shop the bottom shelves. The most popular and expensive items are at eye level. Plus, clerks tired of bending may "forget" to reprice the items on the low shelves (repricing usually means higher pricing).

Avoid end-of-aisle items in bins. Most people assume these items are on sale. They're usually not.

Avoid shopping at the first of the month. Supermarkets sometimes raise prices in anticipation of social security and welfare checks coming out.

Try to do your shopping on Tuesday or Wednesday. That's when supermarkets run most of their specials. An added bonus is that stores are least crowded on these days.

Take a calculator. Most stores post unit prices, but not always comparable unit prices. How do you compare price per toilet paper sheet to price per roll, or price per popcorn ounce to price per each microwave popcorn bag? You use a calculator.

Shop once a week. You'll save time, gasoline, and beat the great enemy — impulse buying.

Buy in season. Don't pay more for less tasty, frozen items when they are out of season. If you want to enjoy strawberries year-round, buy them while they are in season and freeze them yourself.

Don't buy "convenience" products. Some aren't all that convenient anyway. Buy dry pasta instead of fresh, and fresh vegetables instead of frozen. Buy blocks of cheese instead of shredded. Avoid "boil in the bag" rice and prepackaged macaroni and cheese. Buy oats by the pound instead of in packages. Add your own raisins, dried apples, or fresh fruit to cereal instead of buying cereal with fruit in the box.

For brans, cereals, and grains, check prices at a health food store. These stores sometimes have better deals.

Buy bread by weight, not size. Bread sizes can be deceiving. You may think you're getting more bread, but you're probably just paying a premium price for air. If you want the most nutritious bread, buy whole wheat.

Don't think all your protein has to come from beef. Beans, milk, cheese, eggs, peanut butter, turkey, and chicken are all good sources of protein and they cost less, too.

Don't buy frozen foods with ice crystals on them. That means the food has thawed, then been refrozen. The food probably won't hurt you, but it might taste bad.

Finally, avoid supermarkets for nonfood items, don't trust the checkout scanner, leave the kids at home if possible, experiment with generics, cook ahead instead of taking out, don't shop when you're hungry, and, if you think preparing food is hard, invest in a good, basic cookbook.

Sources:
Penny Pinching by Lee and Barbara Simmons, Bantam Publishing, New York, 1995
Shopping Smart by John Stossel, G.P. Putnam's Sons, New York, 1980

Homemade solutions to everyday problems

Loose buttons. Use dental floss to sew on buttons that refuse to stay put. Use colored markers to tint floss the same shade as the garment. To keep buttons on longer, reinforce the thread with a drop of clear nail polish in the center of the button.

Scummy glasses. Tired of scrubbing out scum stuck in the bottom of a glass? Let denture tablets do the dirty work. Use hot water to dissolve one denture tablet into the dirty glass. Let stand several hours, then rinse.

Slippery shoes. For shoe bottoms that are too slippery, use an old emery board to rough up the bottoms slightly.

Useless erasers. Emery boards are also good for removing oil and gunk from a pencil eraser too covered with grime to erase well anymore.

Stinky sneakers. Stuff a sheet of fabric softener into each shoe for a sweeter smell the next morning.

Static in your hair? Rub a sheet of fabric softener through it. You'll smell sweet, and your hair will stay in place.

Squeaky hinges. Stop squeaks with a squirt of nonstick vegetable oil.

Painful splinters. Whether you're 9 or 90, removing stubborn splinters is often a painful ordeal. An easier solution is to numb the area with ice or teething pain reliever. Then, dab a drop of glue over affected area. Let dry; peel off glue. The splinter often comes out as you peel off the dried glue.

Droopy plants. Give plants the greenhouse treatment indoors; run a vaporizer or a humidifier in the same room as you keep your plants.

Flimsy rubber bands. Turn worn out rubber gloves into heavy-duty rubber bands. Simply cut horizontal strips from the finger, palm, and wrist parts and tie ends together.

Messy microwave. When cooking in the microwave, cover bowls or dishes with a coffee basket filter. The filters are perfect covers when a paper towel just won't do.

Rusty screws or shaving cream cans. Paint the screw or can bottom with clear nail polish to keep it from rusting.

Scratched glass. Polish out scratches with toothpaste.

Corroded car battery. Bubble away the corrosion with a can of Coca-Cola.

Barking dogs. Squirt lemon juice into dog's mouth and say, "Quiet."

Dusty refrigerator. When dust collects under the refrigerator, put an old pair of pantyhose over a broomstick, and slide the dust catcher back and forth.
Sources:
Don't Throw That Out!: A Pennywise Guide to Creative Uses for Over 200 Household Items by Vicki Lansky, The Book Peddlers, Deephaven, Minn., 1994
Polish Your Furniture with Panty Hose by Joey Green, Hyperion, New York, 1995

Bartering: The secret to getting what you need without spending money or paying taxes

Using money to buy what you want seems as natural as breathing to most of us.

However, there's another way to obtain certain services and goods that's perfectly legal, if you know the rules. It's bartering — the ancient practice of exchanging one commodity for another.

For example, say an accountant does the books for a lawyer who in turn handles some legal matters for the bookkeeper's business. Both receive services that would add up to quite a lot of money — if they paid for them out of their pockets. By exchanging a service for a service, the balance paid through bartering is zero.

And, says Neil Galanti, CPA, "There is no taxable income involved."

The Internal Revenue Service provides a line on tax forms for bartered income. "They are looking for people receiving personal services in exchange for business services — a situation that can create income," notes Galanti. "For all practical purposes, many cases of bartering are not reported."

He cautions, however, that if you join a bartering club or organization and barter frequently, you are more likely to come up with swaps that involve a profit — and you need to report those transactions to the IRS.
Source:
Interview with Neil Galanti, CPA, Atlanta

Don't get stuck with something you don't want

"There's no law that says someone can't pressure you into purchasing something," says consumer rights advocate Betty Lipshutz. "But when the pressure to buy is intense, it should trigger caution."

What to consider before you sign on the dotted line:

▶ It's your money. Don't let anyone pressure you into making a quick decision. Never sign a contract just to get rid of a persistent salesperson.

▶ Read the contract, *every word of it*, before you sign.

▶ Were any oral promises made about the goods or services you are buying?
Have them written into the contract.

▶ Are there blank spaces in the contract an unscrupulous salesperson could
fill in later? Cross them out or fill them in before you sign. Make sure no
parts of the contract are covered or hidden and no pages are stuck together.

▶ Make a check or money order payable to the merchant, not the salesperson.

▶ Make sure your copy of the contract is the same as the merchant's.

When can you legally get out of a contract?

"Few contracts can be canceled after they have been signed," notes
Lipshutz. "But under Federal Trade Commission law, you have a three-day
'cooling off' period that allows you to cancel some contracts."

A contract that can be canceled within three business days must:

▶ Be for a total of $25 or more (including interest, handling charges, postage,
and any other charges related to the purchase).

▶ Have been entered into in some place other than a regular place of
business — for example, your home, a sales party, or a hotel room. It
cannot have been made by mail or telephone.

▶ Involve the sale, lease, or rental of services or goods for your personal,
family, or household use. It can't involve real estate, securities, insurance,
or emergency home repairs.

Want to cancel a contract that meets these conditions?

▶ Read the contract and make sure the cancellation period hasn't passed.
(Remember: You have three business days to cancel — Sundays and holidays don't count.)

▶ Sign and date both copies of a Notice of Cancellation form (supplied by the
merchant) and mail or hand-deliver one copy to the merchant by midnight
of the third business day after signing the contract. You can also cancel the
contract with a letter or telegraph. Make a copy for your records.

▶ Keep proof of when you canceled. If you mail the notice, send it certified,
return receipt requested. If hand-delivered, get a signed and dated receipt.

▶ Within 10 days of receiving your notice of cancellation, the merchant must
refund your money, cancel and return any papers you signed, arrange for
the return of any product you received, and return to you any trade-in you
gave as part of the sale.

▶ If the merchant doesn't pick up any merchandise you have within 20 days,
you can keep it without further obligation.

▶ The merchant must reimburse you, within 20 days of the contract's cancellation, for any money you spent to return a product.

Don't assume you're "stuck" without checking your rights. Betty Lipshutz points out that certain contracts have longer cancellation periods, depending on the state you live in.

For example, the Georgia Fair Business Practices Act allows consumers to cancel campground, marine, and health spa memberships up to seven days after signing a contract. Check with your Office of Consumer Affairs to find out what the law is in your state.

Source:
Interview with Betty Lipshutz, former special assistant to the administrator for the Governor's Office of Consumer of Affairs, Atlanta

Everything's negotiable

If you're paying full retail without thinking twice, you're costing yourself money. With a little haggling, you can get a better price on almost anything. And when bargaining won't work, smart shopping will.

The trick is to remain in control of the situation. Stay cool. No matter how eager you are to buy, don't let it show. Don't let cranky store owners or managers draw you into an argument. The easiest way to ruin a haggling session is to call merchandise "cheap" or "inferior."

No matter what the store's original offer is, refuse it. Flinch or make some other visible reaction to point out to the salesperson that the price is too high. Be sure to offer a fair price. If you start too low, the merchant won't bother talking to you.

Offer to pay for the item in cash. This alone should net you a 10 percent discount since merchants save money when you use greenbacks. (Stores lose up to 15 percent on purchases made with credit cards.)

When you make your counteroffer, consider removing some of the features you don't need.

Make sure you're talking to the right person before you start haggling in earnest. A floor sales associate probably doesn't have the authority to cut prices, but a manager does. (This is especially true at department stores.) If you're asked to wait while the flunky gets the boss, move around some. Show them that you're not someone who takes orders from salespeople.

Let the manager or owner know what he'll get in return for lowering the price — steady business, positive word-of-mouth, referrals, etc. None of these cost you anything, but all can dramatically increase a store's bottom line.

Always walk into a negotiation prepared. Know what other stores are charging and have it in writing to show the merchant. If you're just starting to look, have the store put its best price in writing. (That will give you leverage if you return and can't find the same manager.)

Occasionally, your haggling will be in vain. This is where smart shopping comes into play. If you can't talk the store into discounting a certain item, offer to buy the floor model or a recently discontinued version. This can often save you anywhere from 15 to 30 percent. Be sure to check for scratches.

Should this fail, shop seasonally. Freezers are a lot cheaper in January and June. Air conditioner prices plummet in February and September. And end-of-season clothing sales can save you up to 50 percent.

Sources:
Everything's Negotiable (When You Know How to Play the Game) by Eric Skopec and Laree S. Kiely, American Management Association, New York, 1994
The Money Book of Personal Finance by Richard Eisenberg, Warner Books, New York, 1996

AT-HOME SHOPPING: TELEMARKETING AND DIRECT MAIL

Unordered goodies in the mail

Your mail carrier delivers a mysterious package addressed to you. It's from a well-known mail order company. You have placed orders in the past with the company — but you know you didn't order this purple down comforter.

Are you stuck with paying to return it?

No. In fact, federal law forbids a company from sending unordered goods in the mail.

That means you don't have to return the goods or pay for them. You can consider the merchandise a free gift.

Source:
U.S. Federal Law (39 U.S.C. Section 3009)

Better catalog shopping

Buying from catalogs is like a new store arriving at your doorstep every day. No worry about lines, parking spaces, or running into people you don't want to see at the shopping mall.

However, even while shopping from your easy chair, you're still prey to scams and sorry service. Here's how to make the best of your at-home shopping:

▶ Ask if any of the merchandise is on sale. Oftentimes it is, but you must ask.

▶ Check the return policy. Most reputable catalogs have a no-questions-asked policy. Many even pay for the return shipping. Don't buy underwear or swimsuits unless they can be returned.

▶ Don't be afraid to ask for advice on size, wearability and washing. Sometimes the salesperson will even say whether or not she likes the purchase.

▶ Ask about exchanges, refunds, and warranties. If you aren't satisfied with the answers or advertising claims seem outrageous, don't deal.

▶ Check out unfamiliar companies through the Better Business Bureau (BBB) office located nearest the mail order firm. To get the correct BBB number, call the Council of Better Business Bureaus at 1-703-276-0100.

▶ Pay by credit card only. This way you'll have a record of your purchase, and you'll simply get a credit on your bill if you return the item. An additional benefit: You can request the credit card company to withhold payment if there is a problem with your order.

Most banks will also stop payment on a check for a fee. If you order by C.O.D. (cash on delivery), make the check out to the seller instead of the post office so you can stop payment if you need to.

▶ Keep a copy of the ad you responded to and the order form you used. If there is no order form, make your own notes about the company's name, address, and phone number. Keep these records handy in the event of a problem.

▶ Don't pay sales tax unless you're in the same state as the store.

▶ If mail orders are not shipped by the promised date, you can cancel and request a full refund. You should receive a full refund within seven working days or one credit card billing cycle.

▶ If the company states no shipping date, your right to cancel begins 30 days after the mail order firm received your order and payment.

▶ If there's a problem with your order, write to the company, explaining the problem and requesting a specific solution, such as a full refund or a product exchange. Include your name, telephone number, order number, copy of canceled check, and any other helpful information.

Send a copy of the letter to your credit card company or bank. Ask that the financial institution withhold payment until the problem is resolved. Credit card companies must respond to your complaint within 30 days although they have up to 90 days to resolve the problem.

Sources:
At-Home Shopping Rights, American Express
Chic on a Shoestring by Annette Swanberg and Leigh Charlton, Doubleday & Co., New York, 1984

Don't be fooled by phone fraud

Be sure to stay on your guard when talking to telemarketers. Experts estimate that one in 10 telemarketing calls is a scam. These schemers walk away with about $40 billion a year from unsuspecting victims.

Don't think it can't happen to you. The typical victim is a well-educated, financially secure, active, and able homeowner. He or she usually has a good stock of worldly wisdom to draw on.

The problem is dishonest telemarketers are practically impossible to detect. Plus, they're persistent and really put on the pressure. In the past, it was not unusual for people to receive three or four calls a day from the same telemarketer, trying different tactics. New laws make unwanted repeat calls from telemarketers illegal.

New federal rules also make it harder for scam artists to operate by limiting the sales tactics that telemarketers can legally use. In addition, the new laws expand the rights of people trying to defend themselves against phone fraud.

Now, telemarketers

▶ can't call you before 8 a.m. or after 9 p.m.

▶ can't call you back if you tell them not to.

▶ can't mislead you about the product or service they're selling.

▶ can't take money from your bank account without proof that you've authorized them to do so. The proof may be in writing or a taped conversation in which you give your permission.

What to do when you receive a call from a telemarketer:

▶ Ask who's calling.

▶ Ask for the name of the company they represent.

▶ Keep a list of telemarketers you tell not to call back. Also, be sure to note the date of your discussion.

▶ Let your state attorney general know if you receive another call from a telemarketer you have requested not call you. They can be fined $10,000 if they call you back after you've requested they stop. You should also contact your state attorney general if you think you've been scammed by a telemarketer.

Just play it safe and say goodbye to telemarketers who want to

▶ send a courier service for your money.

▶ have you send money by wire.

▶ automatically withdraw money from your checking account.

▶ offer you a free prize, but charge handling and shipping fees.

▶ ask for your credit card number, checking or savings account number, social security number, or other personal information.

▶ get payment in advance, especially for employment referrals, credit repair, or providing a loan or credit card.

It's your time, your life, and your money. Hang up on telemarketers who won't take no for an answer. And if you receive a suspicious telemarketing call, contact the National Fraud Information Center hot line at 1-800-876-7060.

Sources:
AARP Bulletin (37,2:1)
1994 Consumer's Resource Handbook, United States Office of Consumer Affairs, Washington, D.C.

Getting rid of that pesky salesperson

Persistence is a virtue for salespeople, but if you're the person they're trying to sell something to, it's a pain in the neck.

The trick to getting an overzealous seller to leave you alone is to either convince them you're not worth their time or tell them firmly but politely to go away. If the pitch comes over the phone, say that you're in the middle of something and ask them to call you back.

Occasionally, you'll encounter a salesperson who refuses to listen to your objections. The best way to get rid of this type is to let them keep their dignity. Tell them you appreciate their information, but you have no need for their product. Mention that you have their name and number and will call them if you have need of their services. It may sound like you're stringing them along, but a professional salesperson will recognize what you're saying.

Source:
Interview with Jeffrey Gitomer, president, Business Marketing Services, Charlotte, N.C.

Sweepstakes savvy

Can you really win a prize through a sweepstakes? You bet, and sometimes it can be a big one.

Sweepstakes persuade people to buy products and generate lots of money for the companies who sponsor them. So, they're indeed on the up and up, and you really can win.

You don't even have to buy to win. Believe it or not, buying something won't increase your chances of winning. Even though separate "yes" and "no" envelopes are provided for you to indicate whether you're ordering or not, both envelopes receive equal treatment. The division of envelopes simply helps speed up order processing.

Before you take the time and trouble to enter a sweepstakes, be sure it's not a scam or a prize of such small price it won't be worth it to win.

What to look for in a sweepstakes

▶ Play only if you see the words "No purchase necessary to win." Otherwise, you may end up spending money for a very tacky prize.

▶ Check to see who's sponsoring the sweepstakes. Sometimes disreputable companies use a variation of the name of a well-known sweepstakes sponsor to suck in unwary consumers. Usually, any prize you receive from these people won't be what you expected.

A company may claim to represent a well-known sweepstakes company and request a "refundable deposit" or a "pre-payment of taxes." Before you pay a refundable deposit to anybody, call the real sweepstakes sponsor (not the number provided in the mailing — get the number from the operator) to find out what's going on. And never, never pay sweepstakes taxes to anyone but the Internal Revenue Service.

▶ Look for clear and easy-to-understand rules and instructions.

▶ Find out if there is only one grand prize winner or if the grand prize is divided among many people. A grand prize shared by many people may be worth only a few cents.

► Check out your chances of winning. If the odds of winning some award are 1:1, it means everyone who enters will get that award, so it's obviously not going to be worth very much.

How to increase your chances of winning

► Enter as often as you receive the sweepstakes. Check the rules to make sure this is allowed. Otherwise, you'll be wasting your time.

► Read through the rules to see if the sweepstakes will allow write-in entries. If they will, by all means send some in. The more you enter, the more likely you are to win.

► Follow instructions carefully. If your entry form isn't filled out correctly, it may be thrown out.

Are you really a big winner?

► If the sweepstakes says you must pay a fee to claim your prize, you're not a big winner. An offer which says you've won a prize, but you must pay shipping or handling or other fees to receive it is not a sweepstakes, and it may be a scam.

► If the postmark on your envelope which says "Big Winner" has a postal permit number, you're not a big winner. A postal permit number indicates that the same piece of mail you've just received was mailed to many other people, too. If you've won anything, it is probably a small prize.

Other mail offers sometimes confused with sweepstakes

Lottery — Sometimes lotteries come through the mail disguised as sweepstakes. Although prizes are awarded by chance like they are in sweepstakes, you must pay to play a lottery. However, lotteries are illegal unless they are conducted by states or certain charitable organizations.

Skill contest — Unlike sweepstakes, a fee may be required to enter a skill contest. Also, winners are determined by skill, not chance. Be sure you know what a skill contest costs and what prizes will be awarded before you decide to play.

Premium offer — Premium offers are often made to look like sweepstakes, but they are not the same. A premium is a gift you will receive if you act according to a company's instructions. There is no element of chance here. Everyone who follows instructions receives the same gift. However, you often have to buy something else from the company before you can receive your premium.

Postcard prize announcement — These mailings congratulate you for winning a valuable prize, such as cash, a car, or an expensive vacation. Many have a 900 number for you to call to learn what prize your have won. Before you dial, just remember that 900 numbers are *not* free calls.

Ask your local phone operator how much the 900 call will cost. If you don't want to call, but still want to participate, request the information by mail instead. Calling doesn't improve your chances of winning.

And remember that these prize promotional mailings almost never deliver what they seem to promise. You'll usually win the prize of lowest value, not the one promoted in big print. You'll also often find that the processing fee you have to pay to claim your prize will be worth more than the prize itself. In some cases, you have to buy another extremely overpriced item in order to get your prize. Throw any offers like this in the trash. You won't save any money and you're likely to lose some.

Source:
Direct Marketing Association, 1111 19th Street N.W., Suite 1100, Washington, D.C., 1995

Getting rid of unwanted mail

Tired of seller's unwanted mail? Here's one easy way out of the trash heap that's in your mail box every day.

Use the change of address cards that come in some of the regular mailings you get to delete your address from their mailing list.

Just cut out your mailing label and cut out the address of the mailer. Tape the mailer's address on the card, and tape your mailing label on the back of the card. Check the delete box.

Do this as often as you can, and you'll see a big difference in the amount of unwanted mail you get.

Source:
From Nine to Five, The Dartnell Corporation, Chicago (Sept. 18, 1995)

Charitable donations

Before you donate any of your hard-earned cash to a charity, make sure the organization is on the up and up. Since charities are required to disclose information to contributors, it is in your best interest to ask these vital questions to find out if you're giving to a charity or being conned:

When you get a phone call, ask who's calling. All volunteers collecting for charity must offer the name and location of their charity. Also, if the caller is a professional telemarketer, he should tell you this at the time of the call. Consider this when making a decision to give — after all, if a charity hires an outside individual to make a call, a chunk of your donation will no doubt go towards the caller's salary.

Have you heard of the charity before? Don't be confused by a charity that has a name similar to that of an established organization. If there's any doubt in your mind, ask to look over any information — booklets, pamphlets, and press releases — that the charity will provide. Don't give unless you are completely satisfied with what you read about the group.

Where is the money going? If a caller can't or won't give you this information, think twice before giving. Charities must tell you how much (what percentage) of your donation will benefit specific programs and how much is being channeled into fundraising. If you're not satisfied with the answer you're given, use your own best judgment, but don't be taken in by a questionable "cause." Look for a charity that gives a large percentage (80 percent is good) of its donations to the needy.

Did you order this complimentary merchandise? Many charities try to play on your sense of guilt by sending greeting cards or personalized mailing labels along with a donation request. This is because such groups know that many people will feel obliged to give money in return for "free" gifts.

Be on the lookout for emotional language or photos that are provided to provoke a certain response. Many fake charities will try to trick you into giving by stamping their envelopes with the words "extremely important," "urgent," or "immediate aid is needed!" Don't fall for such appeals. Also, be wary of any mailings that include photos of people — especially children — suffering. Ask yourself if a legitimate charity would blatantly exploit the people it is trying to help.

Beware of charities collecting door-to-door. Most charities don't collect this way. One popular scam is for two sturdy-looking men, dressed in blue uniforms and wearing badges, to collect for the Police Relief Fund or another official-sounding organization. Many people give because they feel intimidated seeing police standing at their front door, but many times these people aren't police. They'll just take your money and run. Don't be fooled by the badges. They're often phony.

Find out more by contacting an organization that specializes in policing charities. The NCIB Charity Catalog provides interested parties with a selection of over 350 charities that meet certain criteria. For a copy, write to:

NCIB
Department 296
19 Union Square West
New York, NY 10003–3395
Be sure to include a self-addressed, stamped envelope.

The Annual Charity Index from The Council of Business Bureau/ Philanthropic Advisory Service gives information on organizations and the amounts they spend on fundraising, management, and charitable services. This guide is available for $12.95. Write to:

The Council of Business Bureau
Philanthropic Advisory Service
4200 Wilson Blvd.
Arlington, VA 22203

Keep in mind that both these groups also publish reports on various specific national charities. Contact your state's attorney general to find out whether or not a local charity is credible.

Sources:
National Charities Information Bureau Wise Giving Guide (Winter 1995-1996)
Shopping Smart by John Stossel, G.P. Putnam's Sons, New York, 1980

Red flags of fraud

"A fool and his money are soon parted." Be wise, know the red flags of fraud, and no schemer will be able to make a fool out of you. Walk away, toss out the mail, or hang up the phone when you hear someone say:

► "Sign now, or the price will increase."
► "You have been specially selected ..."
► "You have won ..."
► "All we need is your credit card (or bank account) number — for identification only."
► "All you pay for is postage, handling, taxes ..."
► "Make money in your spare time — guaranteed income ..."
► "We really need you to buy magazines (a water purifier, a vacation package, office products) from us because we can earn 15 extra credits..."
► "I just happen to have some leftover paving material from a job down the street ..."
► "Be your own boss! Never work for anyone else again. Just send in $50 for your supplies and ..."
► "A new car! A trip to Hawaii! $2,500 in cash! Yours, absolutely free! Take a look at our ..."
► "Your special claim number entitles you to join our sweepstakes ..."
► "We just happen to be in your area and have toner for your machine at a reduced price."

And last, but not least, stay away from pyramid schemes and multi-level sales scams. They sound super, but they quickly separate you from your money and give you little or nothing in return — not a good investment option.

Remember, the smart consumer always looks at the total price before deciding, and checks out the company and product before buying.

Source:
1994 Consumer's Resource Handbook, United States Office of Consumer Affairs, Washington, D.C.

CREDIT CARD SAVVY

How to erase the month you blew it

You know you're supposed to pay your credit cards off every month. But what happens when you get a bill you can't pay (in January, for instance)?

Don't let one bad month force you into financial ruin. The first month you are not able to pay, evaluate what happened. Then set up a plan for yourself to pay it off. You may need to put aside an extra $50 or $100 a month.

This is the month you'll be thankful you've found that credit card with a really low interest rate. You should have a card with an interest rate around 12 percent. Some banks offer around 7 percent, but that's usually a teaser rate that's going to go up eventually.

While you're paying off a credit card bill, don't allow yourself to put any more debt on that card. If you're just paying your minimum balance, the card company will start charging you interest by the date of purchase. You're no longer getting a 30-day interest-free grace period. At this point, if you can't write a check for the item you want, you're just borrowing money to pay for it.

Remember, you'll be less likely to have bills you can't pay if you limit the number of cards you carry. The fewer cards you have the less likely you are to use them.

If you feel in over your head, get free help from the Consumer Credit Counseling Service. This government service can help you contact your creditors and work out a debt repayment plan. To find the office nearest you, check the Yellow Pages or call 1-800-388-CCCS (2227).

Losing debt is like losing weight. You can't take care of it in just a few days. If you aim too high, you will get frustrated and give up. Instead, set minigoals and reward yourself slightly when you reach them.

Sources:
Interview with Tim Anders, CPA, Peachtree City, Ga.
Interview with Suzanne Boas, president, Consumer Credit Counseling Service of Greater Atlanta

Hidden credit card interest

Does your credit card company sneak in extra finance charges when you carry a balance? If they do, you may not even know it. You may think you're using a card with an 18 percent interest rate when you're really paying 24 percent.

Let's say you usually pay in full every month, but one month you decide to carry a balance. Normally, you get a 25-day grace period before the card company starts charging interest on your purchases, but some companies pile on retroactive finance charges. The grace period just disappears, and you start paying interest from the day you made your purchases.

Card companies can legally do this — it's called the two-cycle method. The company charges you interest based on your average daily balance for two monthly billing periods — the previous month (the one you didn't pay off) and the current month. Find out if your credit card uses this formula by reading the fine print on the back of one of your statements. Look for the words "two-cycle average daily balance including new purchases."

If you always carry a balance, the two-cycle billing method doesn't affect you much. You don't have an interest-free grace period anyway. And if you never carry a balance, interest and finance charges certainly don't affect you. But if you occasionally carry a balance, make sure your credit card company isn't getting more of your money than you think.

Sources:
Ninety Days to Financial Fitness by Joan German-Grapes, Collier Books/Macmillan Publishing, New York, 1993
The Wall Street Journal (Dec. 14, 1995, C1)

Withholding payment on a credit card purchase

It's smart to make big purchases with your credit card. That way, if you aren't happy with the merchandise or service, you simply subtract the charge from your credit card bill. You can subtract any finance or related charges, too. That's your right under the Fair Credit Billing Act.

You do have to meet these conditions:

▶ You must make a good faith effort to work out the problem with the seller.
▶ The purchase must exceed $50 (unless you are using a store-issued card).
▶ The purchase must occur in your home state or within 100 miles of your billing address (unless it's a store-issued card).

If you don't meet these conditions, you may have to go to small claims court to get your money back. If you do meet the conditions, you don't have to pay for that television with a fuzzy picture or the sofa with the wobbly leg, and don't let the merchant convince you that you do.

Source:
Choosing and Using Credit Cards, Bureau of Consumer Protection, Federal Trade Commission, Washington, D.C. 20580

How to get cash instead of credit for your returned merchandise

It happens all the time with department store credit cards. You return clothes or other merchandise you bought with your card, and the clerk insists on crediting your card instead of giving you the cash for the returns. You've already paid your credit card bill, and you want the cash. Legally, you can get it.

If the clerk won't give it to you, write a short letter to the card issuer asking for a refund. The card issuer must send you the refund within seven business days. (Also, if a credit balance has remained on your account for more than six months, the card issuer must make a good faith effort to refund the balance to you.)

Of course, the store doesn't want you to write for a refund. It would rather you feel forced to return quickly and buy something with your credit card to get rid of the balance. Don't fall into this trap. Jotting a short letter only takes a few minutes. Even better, since you're already writing, go ahead and cancel the store-issued card.

Source:
Choosing and Using Credit Cards, Bureau of Consumer Protection, Federal Trade Commission, Washinᵔton, D.C. 20580

New credit card law

You have an unauthorized charge on your bill, and the credit card company tells you that you are responsible for it because you didn't file a police report on time. Once upon a time, this scenario could have happened, but a new federal law says clearly that credit card companies can't hold you liable solely because you didn't follow a particular requirement.

The new law also says that credit card issuers can't dismiss a claim of an unauthorized charge out of hand. They must conduct a "reasonable investigation."

Source:
The Wall Street Journal (Feb. 14, 1996, C1)

How to correct errors on your bill

Month after month, Charles Wilson was billed for an exercise machine he never ordered and never received. Finally, he tore up his bill and mailed the pieces back to the company.

There's a better way to fix errors, and one that will protect your credit rating. If you think anything is wrong with your bill, including math errors, failure to show a payment, an item you need more information about, or a charge for something you didn't accept on delivery, follow these steps:

1) Write to the company within 60 days of receiving your bill. Include your name and account number, tell why you think the bill is wrong, and the date and amount of the error or the item you want explained.

2) Pay the parts of the bill that aren't in dispute, but don't pay any finance charges that apply to the amount in dispute. You must receive a response within 30 days. Within 90 days, your bill must be corrected or you must be told why the creditor believes the bill is correct. If no error is found, the company must send you an explanation and a statement of what you owe (which may include finance charges that have accumulated). You have at least 10 days to pay.

3) If you're still not satisfied, write the company again before your bill is due.

4) During this dispute, the creditor may not threaten your credit rating, may not give out information to anyone that would hurt your credit reputation, and may not take any action to collect the disputed amount.

5) If the creditor breaks any of these rules, you can take legal action. You can sue for actual damages plus twice the amount of any finance charges (not less than $100 or more than $1,000). You can also get court costs and attorney's fees if you win. Even if your bill was correct, a creditor who breaks the rules must automatically pay you the amount owed on the item in question and any finance charges on it, up to a combined total of $50.

Source:
Consumer Handbook to Credit Protection Laws, Board of Governors of the Federal Reserve System, Washington, D.C. 20551

Complaining effectively to your credit card company

Credit card companies are notoriously stubborn. Once they make a mistake, they hate to admit it. And getting them to correct the error can be a trying process.

Complaining effectively is an acquired art. First off, persistence is crucial. If you don't get what you want, keep on complaining. Otherwise, you're wasting your time.

No matter how mad you are, keep a tight rein on your temper. Shouting and cursing at people will get you nowhere. If anything, it will hurt your chances of getting the problem solved.

"Hi, I have a problem and I need your help" will get you a lot further than "You numskulls screwed up my bill!"

If anything, blame the problem on some faceless corporate entity. It's easier for the customer service representative (or manager) to fault an invisible bad guy than himself.

Follow the chain of command. If you start at the top, you have nowhere to go should your complaint be rejected.

Define your goals before you start complaining. Know exactly what you want and what you will settle for. Keep things in perspective. If the problem is insignificant, consider whether it's worth the time and effort you will have to put into it.

Submit your complaints in a brief, one-page, typed letter. Handwritten complaints don't get the same respect.

Finally, never, *ever*, send the company original documents — receipts, statements, etc. The chances of the paperwork getting "lost" are simply too great.

Source:
Credit Card Secrets That You Will Surely Profit From by Howard Strong, editor in chief, The Boswell Corp., Beverly Hills, Calif., 1989

How to get more out of your credit card

It's a buyer's market in the credit card business. Credit card companies have gotten so competitive that they are offering incentives and deals to keep you as a customer.

If you are paying an annual fee, simply call the bank or card company and threaten to leave them for a no-fee card. If you have a good credit history, the card company is likely to drop their fees for you.

Now, however, shopping for a credit card means more than looking for low annual fees and interest rates. You can get more out of your credit card with special deals like these:

The GE Rewards Card gives savings coupons worth up to $1,000 a year plus 2 percent back in reward checks for purchases you make with the card. Those coupons can be used for buying products and services from up to 27 companies.

The GTE MasterCard is made for people with a high phone bill. This card will give you 10 percent off the value of the calls you make.

The Ford Citybank Card is for you if you like Ford cars or trucks and you buy a new vehicle every five years. This card will accumulate up to $3,500 in credits over five years toward the purchase of a Ford vehicle.

The AT&T Universal Card is an example of an incentive card without an annual fee. Transfer $1,000 or more from one or more cards, and they'll waive your annual fee for life.

The GM Corporate Card lets you accumulate $3,500 over seven years toward the purchase of a GM car. This card will also give you credits for using specific hotels, long-distance companies, gasoline companies, etc.

Many airlines have frequent flyer programs connected with credit cards. If you fly American Airlines, Delta, or others, you might get frequent flyer points for using Visa, MasterCard, American Express, etc. Ask the individual airline or credit card of your choice.

One incentive program to avoid is a credit card that gives donations to a particular organization based on your purchases. You'll save money by shopping for a better card deal for yourself and giving money directly to the charity. You'll also be able to make tax deductions on your charitable giving, which you couldn't make on the use of that card.

Source:
365 Ways to Save Money by Lucy H. Hedrick, William Morrow & Co., New York, 1994

Best credit card deals

To get a list of credit cards with low fees and low interest rates, send $5 to:

RAN Research
PO Box 1700
Frederick, MD 21702

You can also reach this group by phone at 1-301-695-4660.

You'll also find a column on the best cards available in the United States in *Money* magazine.

To get a low-rate card, you may need to wait to apply at least 12 months after you've changed jobs or your address. Also, check your credit report to make sure everything is accurate before you apply.

Source:
365 Ways to Save Money by Lucy H. Hedrick, William Morrow & Co., New York, 1994

Credit card fraud — it's costing you big bucks

Let's say you're an average American, with eight credit cards in your wallet. You leave your wallet at a store, someone steals it, and the spending spree begins. If you don't notice the loss and report it before the spending begins, you're liable for up to $50 of charges for each one of your cards.

Savvy clerks could prevent some of this fraud by comparing signatures on the card with the credit card slip, but often clerks don't wish to antagonize customers by challenging them.

As soon as you realize your card is missing, follow these steps to minimize your loss:

▶ Call the company immediately to report your loss.

▶ Follow up your call with a letter that notes the card number, the day you missed the card, and the time you called to report the loss.

▶ Review your monthly statement carefully. If you find phony charges on your statement, call the card company immediately and then write them a letter detailing the incorrect charges.

Even if you've never had your credit cards stolen, credit card scams cost you money each year in the form of higher interest rates and annual fees.

One credit card company has been able to cut fraudulent use by two-thirds simply by adding card owners' pictures to the front of their cards. Another strategy being considered is requiring card users to enter a personal identification number (PIN) on a keypad when they use a card.

Tougher to crack than the problem of lost or stolen cards is the endless variety of counterfeiting schemes. Some counterfeiters steal or manufacture blank cards, then obtain real card numbers by bribing clerks in stores or stealing receipts.

Once they have this data, the crooks use encoders to record the necessary information on a magnetic strip and affix the strip on a blank or stolen card. Store clerks can prevent much of this type of theft by comparing the information contained in the magnetic strip with the information on the front of the card. That's if they have a good scanner that can read the magnetic strips.

You can prevent fraud by staying alert. Don't throw away the hundreds of documents that contain your credit card number without tearing them up first.

Tear up all those credit card applications you get, too. Crooks can send them in and get a new card in your name.

Sources:
Business Week (Jan. 17, 1994; April 4, 1994)
Money (April 1994)

Protect your credit cards

▶ Be cautious about disclosing your account number over the phone unless you know you are dealing with a reputable company.

▶ Never put your account number on the outside of an envelope or on a postcard.

▶ Draw a line through blank spaces above the total on charge slips so the amount cannot be changed.

▶ Rip up carbons and save receipts to check against your bill every month.

▶ Keep in a safe place a record of your card numbers, expiration dates, and the telephone numbers of each credit card company in case you lose your card.

Source:
Lost or Stolen: Credit and ATM Cards, Federal Trade Commission, Bureau of Consumer Protection, Washington, D.C. 20580

MANAGING YOUR MONEY

When paying late isn't your fault

Paying a bill late almost always means paying a finance charge. But before you pay the penalty, make sure the creditor is following the rules.

Prompt billing rule. When you get your statement, look at the date on the postmark. If the creditor will charge you a finance charge for paying late, then the company must mail your statement at least 14 days before payment is due.

Prompt crediting rule. Also look at the payment date on the statement. Your payment must be credited on the day it arrived (as long as you followed all the instructions, like sending your payment to the correct address).
Source:
Consumer Handbook to Credit Protection Laws, Board of Governors of the Federal Reserve System, Washington, D.C. 20551

Hang up on high phone bills

Did you know that each month, your phone company collects thousands of dollars that it doesn't deserve? Some of that money could be yours. Getting it back isn't that hard. You just have to know how. A few tips:

Call your local phone company and ask for a detailed bill. (What you typically receive is just a summary.) Examine it closely to see what you're being charged for. It could be full of surprises, such as features, like call waiting or call forwarding, that you didn't order.

Don't rent your phone, buy it! Believe it or not, more than 6 million AT&T customers still lease their phones. Instead of paying $5 or $6 dollars a month in rental fees, you can buy one that will do just as good a job for $20.

Slip around local long distance charges. Many companies have local toll call programs that offer fixed rates for popular calling destinations. If you make regular calls to someone in the same area code, but still have to dial 10 numbers, you might save a bundle by purchasing a program.

Curb daytime long distance calls. You'll save by calling on weekends or between 11 p.m. and 8 a.m. on weekdays.

Threaten to switch long distance companies. The competition in the long distance industry is fierce. If you tell your provider that you're about to move to a different company, you're sure to be offered an incentive package. And when that package expires (usually in about six months), call back and threaten to switch again.

Read your cellular phone bill closely. Did you make three calls to the same number in a 10-minute period? You were probably caught in a bad cell at some point. You shouldn't have to pay for calls you can't complete. Most companies will credit your account if you point this out to them.

Keep track of your calls. Someone may have pressed the wrong button when entering their calling card number, and you got stuck with the bill.

Computers put the bills together, but once they make a mistake, they keep making it. If you find an error, go back and check previous account statements. Instead of just being owed a dollar or two, you could have been overcharged by hundreds. Never ask for just a one month refund when you may have been ripped off for years.

Source:
Interview with Jeffrey Kagan, president, Telechoice Consulting, Marietta, Ga.

Pay phone rip-offs

Long distance companies can be sneaky, especially if you're away from home. Consider Tammy Upson, a writer and part-time student who recently found $9 worth of charges on her phone bill for several long distance calls she made from a pay phone. She was astounded — because none of the calls had ever connected.

Apparently, with some long distance carriers, your unanswered calls will sometimes register as billed calls. If you call and complain, the company must remove those charges.

To protect yourself against unreasonable charges, especially ones you can't remove later, make sure you use your own long distance company when you're using a pay phone. Don't follow the instructions on the phone. If you dial 0 before you dial any other number, you may be routed through a long distance company you've never heard of.

Instead, dial the access code or 800 number of your long distance company (listed on your calling card), then enter your personal card number, then dial the number you'd like to reach.

If you don't have a calling card, call your long distance company before you leave home to get pay phone instructions. They'll give you an 800 number, or a local number that begins with 950, or a five-digit access code to use at pay phones.

To make sure you've accessed your own long distance carrier, listen after you dial the number. The carrier must identify itself before charging you anything. If you don't recognize the name of the carrier, hang up before your call goes through.

Source:
Federal Communications Commission, Common Carrier Bureau, Consumer Complaints, Washington, D.C. 20554

Calling card warnings

Not all calling cards are equal. The best cards use your entire telephone number as part of the calling card number. If your entire phone number is on the card, you should be able to use it from any location and be billed through your card.

Otherwise, you may only be able to use your card when you're at a phone that is hooked up to the long distance company that issued the card.

If you have a card that doesn't include your entire phone number, make sure you know how to call your long distance company before you leave home. You don't want to find outrageous charges on your phone bill because you used a long distance company you've never heard of.

Source:
Federal Communications Commission, Common Carrier Bureau, Consumer Complaints, Washington, D.C. 20554

Free long distance phone calls with your computer

If you're hooked into the Internet, you need never pay a long distance phone bill again.

With the right equipment and software, you can use your computer as a telephone to call friends around the country and around the world. And all you pay is your regular bill for accessing the information superhighway.

Several programs have become available in recent months that will let you speak to someone sitting at another computer. Some cost hundreds of dollars, but just as many quality versions are available for free over the Net. Your computer should be fairly new (i.e., purchased within the last five years) and be equipped with a sound card, speakers, and a microphone. You'll also need a fast modem. One with 14,400 bps per second is OK, but 28,800 bps is preferable.

The software will compress and digitize your voice and send it over the Internet. The person you're talking to will hear you almost instantaneously. (Occasionally, there is a slight delay, but nothing more than you would experience on a typical overseas call.) The audio quality is a little less clear than a standard phone line, but you'll still be able to hear every word.

It may not be long before you can use your computer to call regular phones, too. A test program for this is under way, but apparently has a way to go before it becomes common.

Source:
Frequently Asked Questions: How can I use the Internet as a telephone?, http://www.northcoast.com/savetz/voice-faq.html

How's your credit rating?

Don't let errors sit for years on your credit report. Someday, you may need an emergency loan. You don't want an old credit report mistake you never cleared up to stand in your way.

You should check your credit report once a year to make sure it is correct and complete. Just call one of the national credit bureaus:

▶ TRW 1-800-392-1122

▶ Equifax 1-800-685-1111
▶ Trans Union 1-800-916-8800

You can get a free copy of your report if you've been denied credit. If you are just checking, your report will cost you around $8 in most states. But TRW will send you an easy-to-read report once a year for free.

If you find a mistake, you should file a dispute form, then wait for a reply. The mailing address is on the report. The credit bureau must look into your problem and get back to you, usually within 30 days.

If you find an error on one credit bureau's report, it's probably on the other two credit bureaus' reports, too. You should clear up the mistake with all three credit bureaus.

Your credit report will also show you all the credit cards you own. Lenders recognize the dangers of temptation, so they may refuse to give you a loan if you have too much credit available to you. You should cancel any credit cards you don't use.

Ask the credit card company to put the line "account closed due to consumer request" on your report. You want everyone to know that you canceled your card; they didn't take it away from you.

By the way, you can sue any credit reporting agency or creditor who doesn't properly correct errors in your file or who breaks the rules about who may see your credit records. You can get actual damages, court costs, and attorney's fees, plus punitive damages if the violation was intentional. Anyone who gets your credit report without proper authorization, or an employee of a credit reporting agency who improperly gives your credit report out, may face a year in prison or a fine of $5,000, or both.

Source:
Consumer Handbook to Credit Protection Laws, Board of Governors of the Federal Reserve System, Washington, D.C. 20551

9 questions to ask yourself before you buy on credit

1) Will the item that you are purchasing still be usable after you've finished making the payments?
2) Have you read and understood everything in the contract? Are there any blank spaces? Do you get a copy of the contract?
3) Can you handle the added amount of debt without jeopardizing other commitments?
4) What will happen if you can't make the payments? Will it be repossessed? If it is repossessed, will you still be required to pay for it? Will you lose something else you own because you've used it as collateral?
5) Do you have the guarantee, the agreements, and the promises all in writing?
6) If married, have you discussed this with your spouse?
7) Was this a planned purchase, or was it impulsive?
8) Would you buy this same thing if you were paying cash?

9) Have you compared interest charges?
Source:
Bonnie's Household Budget Book by Bonnie Runyan McCullough, St. Martin's Griffin Publisher, New York, 1995

15 simple money savers

▶ Plan your meals for the entire week so you don't end up throwing away ruined food.

▶ Clip coupons, but only use them if you would have bought the item before you saw the coupon.

▶ Make a shopping list for the grocery store and stick to it. (Hint: Make a master list of food categories, make copies of it, and leave a copy on the refrigerator so you can note quickly when you're out of an item.)

▶ Buy store brands instead of name brand items, especially on staples. You may save 20 cents on a five-pound bag of sugar or 50 cents on two quarts of bleach.

▶ Don't pay for trash service you don't need. If your service charges you by the bag or for extra bags, get into recycling. Take your aluminum cans to the recycling center, and you'll actually make money instead of paying out more.

▶ Instead of eating at fancy restaurants once a month, try cheaper restaurants twice a month.

▶ Eat in with friends instead of eating out.

▶ Instead of paying for a baby sitter when you go out, arrange with a neighbor to trade off baby sitting nights.

▶ Instead of eating dinner then going to a 7 p.m. or 9 p.m. movie, go to a matinee show and eat dinner afterward.

▶ Brown bag your lunch to work.

▶ Ask yourself: Do I really need this? Think about how many hours you'd have to work to pay for that new coat. To figure out approximately how much an item costs in "before tax" dollars, multiply the purchase price by 1.65. That's how much you had to earn to pay for the item.

▶ If you need a specialty item (such as heavy digging equipment), but will only be using it once or twice, rent rather than buy. You'll save hundreds of dollars.

▶ Make a list of things that are free: libraries, parks, your city's recreation department, museums, or municipally supported concerts.

▶ Instead of buying a gift or sending flowers, try making something for others — bake bread or cookies, grow flowers or potted plants, or take a free craft class and give handmade ceramics, baskets, or stained glass.

▶ Don't buy lottery tickets — unless you know you'll win.
Source:
Where Does All The Money Go? Taking Control of Your Personal Expenses by Andy Mayer, W.W. Norton & Company, New York, 1992

Keep more of your money with 5 budget basics

Ever noticed that paydays at work are big-spending, cash-collecting days? People run around paying co-workers back for yesterday's lunch, collecting money for the boss's present or for Girl Scout cookies, and cashing in on IOUs. By Monday, everyone is broke again and nobody knows where the money went.

Most of us are in the midst of a personal budget crisis. To get control of your money, take these basic steps:

▶ First, estimate all your regular monthly or weekly expenses: mortgage payments, food, car payments, monthly bills, recreation, etc. Write down your estimates.

Then estimate all the nonmonthly "surprise" expenses that come up during the year: insurance payments, license renewals, tax preparation, subscriptions, utilities, gifts, vacations, major medical and auto expenses, clothes, home improvements, etc. Add up all the nonmonthly expenses and divide by 12. That's how much you need to have available every month to cover the "surprises."

▶ Don't overlook how much you spend on gifts. Gift giving is one of the most underestimated budget categories. Create a list of friends and family members and decide how much you'll spend on each person on special occasions. Don't forget anniversaries, weddings, showers, Mother's Day, graduation, and religious events. Include costs of flowers and celebration dinners, too.

▶ Now for the tried-and-true method for keeping track of your expenses: Go on a dollar diet. Carry a notebook around with you and write down every dime you spend and what you spend it on. At the end of the month (or even better, at the end of every week), you can add up your purchases and find out what's really happening to your money. You'll be amazed.

▶ Keep a savings account for your big-ticket goals — cars, stereos, or a home. Getting rid of a debt can be a goal, too. Budget a certain monthly amount for your goals.

▶ Give yourself an allowance every month. You'll just get frustrated with a budget that doesn't give you any wiggle room for fun.

▶ Make a needs/wants list. When you see something you'd like to have, write it down on your list. Use your list to help you decide what you really do want when you have extra allowance money. That way, you won't impulsively buy the first thing that catches your eye. Having a written list of needs and wants will also help you remember to watch for sales and list gift ideas.

For a complete set of easy-to-use budget worksheets, buy *The Budget Kit: The Common Cent$ Money Management Workbook* by Judy Lawrence. Many computer programs are available to make budgeting easier, too.

Source:
The Budget Kit: The Common Cent$ Money Management Workbook by Judy Lawrence, Dearborn Financial Publishing, Chicago, 1993. To order by phone, call 1–800–283–4380.

Saving a piece of your paycheck

If a financial emergency were to happen, would you be prepared? If your answer is no, you're not alone. Most people's saving habits are horrendous. Putting a little cash aside every payday is actually not that difficult, but you have to have enough self-control to leave it alone.

If your employer offers a direct deposit program, divert 10 percent of your paycheck into a savings account each month. Once it's there, don't touch it unless you're in a true cash emergency. (Leaky roofs and lost jobs qualify as emergencies. The designer gown that was just out of your price range does not.) If direct deposit isn't an option, write yourself a check every month when you sit down to pay your bills. Pay yourself first and deposit it fast.

While it's a good idea to keep some of your savings liquid in case of an emergency, put as much as you can into areas where it's harder to get your hands on the cash. If it's inaccessible, you're less tempted to spend it. Some banks and savings and loans offer what's called an *add-to CD*. This is much like any other certificate of deposit, except that you divert a portion of your weekly income directly into it.

Lighten your pockets, too. Put all your change in a jar or piggy bank. When it fills up, deposit the money. Or, even better, don't spend $1 bills. Instead, pay for everything with a $5, $10, or $20. When you get single dollars back as change, put them in the bank. If you know a candy bar is going to take $5 out of your pocket, it will be easier to resist the impulse.

While adults have trouble starting a savings program, children often find it easy and enjoyable. A number of banks offer school-based programs for elementary and junior high school students. On "banking day," the kids deposit a portion of their allowance into accounts, which sometimes earn higher interest than the average savings account. They, too, may have to pass on that candy bar, but they're well-positioned for the future.

Sources:
Interview with Charles Pinkerton, consumer lending officer/branch manager, Tucker Federal Savings and Loan, Tucker, Ga.
Life After Debt by Bob Hammond, Career Press, Franklin Lakes, N.J., 1995

How to become a millionaire in only 20 steps

Multimillionaires amass their riches by putting their money to work. They say all you need is $1 to start. To become a millionaire, you only have to double that dollar 20 times. Once you've doubled your dollar 20 times, you will have $1,048,576.

The trick is learning how to double your dollars. This probably won't be as easy as winning the lottery, but it's a lot more likely.

Don't attempt to rush things by starting out with $1,000 instead of $1, the experts say. The experience you gain doubling your initial dollar into $1,000 will be invaluable in your later investments.

Source:
The Thirteen Secrets of Power Performance by Roger Dawson, Prentice Hall, Englewood Cliffs, N.J., 1994

The 'Rule of 72'

Want to know how fast your savings will double? There's an easy way to find out.

Divide 72 by the percent of interest you're earning. The resulting number is how many years it will take to double your money. For instance, if you're earning 8 percent interest, you'll have twice as much in nine years (72/8 = 9). Simple!

Source:
Life After Debt by Bob Hammond, Career Press, Franklin Lakes, N.J. 1995

How much will you be worth?

Do you want to know how much that money you have stashed away will be worth in a few years? Let's say your money is in a certificate of deposit that earns interest and is compounded monthly.

First, choose the number in the years column that shows the length of time you plan to invest. Now, slide your finger over to the column that shows the interest rate you earn. Multiply the amount of money you have now by the number your finger is pointing to.

	Annual Interest Rates:					
Years	**5%**	**6%**	**7%**	**8%**	**9%**	**10%**
1	1.0511	1.0616	1.0722	1.0829	1.0938	1.1047
2	1.1049	1.1271	1.1498	1.1728	1.1964	1.2203
5	1.2833	1.3488	1.4176	1.4898	1.5656	1.6453
10	1.6470	1.8193	2.0096	2.2196	2.4513	2.7070

Source:
Personal Budget Planner by Eric P. Gelb, Career Advancement Center, Woodmere, N.Y., 1995 (To order the Personal Budget Planner complete with worksheets, call the publisher at 1–800–295–1325.)

How to avoid saving too much

How much would you have to save every month to reach a financial goal? Let's say you want to save $2,000 over two years to build a new porch. Because your certificate of deposit will earn interest and that interest will be compounded monthly, you'll save too much if you simply divide $2,000 by 24 months.

Instead, multiply the amount of money you want to accumulate ($2,000, for instance) by the correct number from the chart below. Here's how to find that number: First, locate the number in the years column that shows the length of time you have to invest. Now, slide your finger over to the column that shows the interest rate you can earn. Now, multiply the amount of money you want to save by the number your finger is pointing to. That will give you what your monthly deposit should be.

Years	**Annual Interest Rates**					
	5%	**6%**	**7%**	**8%**	**9%**	**10%**
1	0.815	0.0811	0.0807	0.0804	0.0800	0.0796
2	0.0398	0.0394	0.0390	0.0386	0.0382	0.0379
5	0.0148	0.0144	0.0140	0.0137	0.0133	0.0130
10	0.0065	0.0062	0.0058	0.0055	0.0052	0.0049

Source:
Personal Budget Planner by Eric P. Gelb, Career Advancement Center, Woodmere, N.Y., 1995 (To order the *Personal Budget Planner* complete with worksheets, call the publisher at 1–800–295–1325.)

Build easy savings with 'found' money

You have to live off your regular salary, but any unexpected windfalls or "found" money should go straight to your savings account. Money that you don't count on getting includes:

Tax refunds. This money should be unexpected, so send it immediately to your savings account.

Loose change. Wrap the coins and deposit them. Pocket change can turn into $100 or more a year.

Product rebates. Take those $2 and $10 checks to the bank and watch them grow.

Annual bonus. Most people spend their bonus before they get it. This extra money should go to savings.

Gifts. Do you get Christmas money from a relative every year? Stash the cash.

Salary from a second job or a special project. A Saturday afternoon job can build a big savings account, especially if you take on tough work like waiting tables. Plus, a second job takes up your time and keeps you from spending money.

Source:
Personal Budget Planner by Eric P. Gelb, Career Advancement Center, Woodmere, N.Y., 1995

A dozen freebies but goodies

Free vacations, free books, free decorations, free phone calls — the woman who can pinch a penny 'til it screams is at it again. Look at these freebies ferreted out by *Tightwad Gazette* author Amy Dacyczyn, the expert of living on a shoestring budget.

▶ See your credit report for free. You can get one free copy by writing TRW Complimentary Credit Report, PO Box 8030, Layton, UT 84041–8030. Send in your full name, current address plus all addresses used in the past five years, social security number, year of birth, and spouse's name. You'll also need a proof of address document that contains your name and current address — a major creditor billing statement, a utility bill, or a driver's license. Finally, sign and date your request.

▶ Call *Consumer Reports* for a subscription at 1-800-234-1645 and get a free issue plus a free copy of their latest buying guide. If you don't want to subscribe, write "cancel" on the bill. You get to keep the freebies.

▶ Check the calendar section of your newspaper for free local attractions, like museums, gardens, and historical buildings.

▶ The federal government has dozens of free consumer books, from *Student Guide to Financial Aid* to *Social Security*. For a complete catalog of available publications, write to S. James, Consumer Information Center, 2D, Box 100, Pueblo, CO 81002.

▶ Let the postal service decorate your child's room for free. The U.S. Postal Service sends out attractive posters promoting new lines of stamps to local post offices around the country. You'll find posters of wild animals, flowers, birds, trains, etc. Look at the post office for a nice poster, then ask your postmaster if you can have it when they no longer need it.

▶ Get free tax guides from the government. Call 1-800-829-3676. The guides cover everything from how to report real estate transactions to the IRS to how to deduct the business use of your home.

▶ If your flight is overbooked, you can usually get a free round trip ticket if you give up your seat for a seat on a later flight. Ms. Tightwad herself suggests that you casually strike up a conversation with a flight attendant over soda and peanuts and ask what time of the day, week, and month flights tend to be overbooked. Fly at those times.
Always arrive at the airport early and tell the gate ticket agent that you are willing to be bumped if need be. Over a 12-week period, one Atlanta business traveler who took two flights a week had received three free round-trip tickets. He simply offered to be bumped each time a flight was overbooked.

▶ If you need to contact a large organization or company, make the phone call for free. Most large companies have toll-free numbers. Find the number by calling toll-free directory assistance at 1-800-555-1212.

▶ Newspaper classified ads or swap publications usually list "for the taking" items. For instance, you can get free firewood if you cut it or haul it away yourself or free kittens because someone has too many.

▶ If you own a small business or want to start one, you can get free advice from the Service Corps of Retired Executives (SCORE). The Small Business Administration has put together this group of former executives, most of whom are retired.

▶ Get free calendars from your congressional representative. Most of these calendars list a significant historical event for each day of the year. Don't forget to visit your congressional representative when you travel to Washington, D.C. He or she can give you free passes to the House and Senate and VIP tour tickets to the White House. The VIP tours usually have shorter lines.

▶ Get free admission to events by doing volunteer work. For example, Maine's Common Ground Country Fair offers you free admission, an attractive T-shirt, and a free meal for four hours of work. Many theaters, like Atlanta's premier Fox Theater, offer free admission if you usher.

Sources:
Interview with Todd Shapiro, business traveler, Atlanta
The Tightwad Gazette, II by Amy Dacyczyn, Villard Books, New York, 1995

Trash or stash — which financial records are keepers?

Unless you own no property and pay no taxes, you're going to have to keep up with certain financial records. But you don't have to hang on to every receipt and check stub forever.

Unless the IRS has reason to suspect fraud, they must audit a person's return within three years of filing. After three years have passed, you can trash these items:

▶ Dividend reinvestment statements and trade confirmations (Exception: If your tax return shows that you lost or gained from selling stocks or bonds, keep these statements indefinitely.)

▶ Paycheck stubs

▶ Supporting tax documents

▶ Credit card statements and cancelled checks

Certain records should stay with you forever. The must-have list includes

▶ Tax returns

▶ IRA statements

▶ Annual statements for mutual funds

▶ Brokerage statements

▶ All real estate documents: deeds, titles, mortgage contracts, receipts for repairs and improvements to your real estate.

To save yourself hours (and accountant's fees) at tax time, you can use a ledger book and an accordion file to organize your tax information. Look at what you deducted on your last tax return, then label your ledger book and your file with those deductible categories.

When you pay a bill in one of these categories, write down the date, the amount, the check number, and the total paid to date in that category. Then you can file the bills and cancelled checks in your accordion file. When tax time rolls around again, you'll have everything already organized.

Source:
Money (April 1994)

Organizing your financial life

If you ever feel overwhelmed when you look at your financial records, imagine how your family is going to feel after you've passed away. You can make life a lot easier for them at a difficult time, and you can make sure none of your assets gets lost in the clutter.

Get a clean folder and label it "My Personal Finances," "My Financial Diary," or something more imaginative. (Many insurance companies, lawyers, and funeral directors can provide forms for you to fill out, but most are designed to make you feel you need to buy the product they are offering.)

In the folder, list your date of birth, your social security number, and your legal state of residence. Tell where you've stored your birth, citizenship, passports, and marriage and divorce information. List all the people who are dependent on you for care or financial support.

Next, list your attorney's name if you have one. If you have given someone power of attorney (which authorizes someone to control your assets when you are unable) or named a health care power of attorney (which allows someone to make health care decisions for you when you can't), list these names and addresses.

Tell how to locate your safe deposit box or home safe and who is authorized to open it. Include where your will is located.

If you have created any trusts, write the names, phone numbers, and addresses of the trustees. List where your titles, deeds, registrations, and insurance papers can be found on your home, your car, and any property you own.

Include where your tax records are located and the name of your tax accountant if you have one. Also include a list of companies, agent names, and phone numbers for all your insurance policies: life, accident, home, auto, and medical.

List the institutions, along with the account numbers, where you maintain savings and checking accounts, stock and mutual fund investments, bonds, IRAs, SEPs, Keoghs, and 401k funds.

List the names and phone numbers of the people who handle your employee benefits.

List any loans or mortgages you have. If you have mortgage life insurance, write down who should be contacted about it, along with a phone number.

If any bills are paid automatically by your bank, include that information. Include information on all your credit cards.

If you'd like anyone notified of your death, include the names here. People who run their own small business should create a list of customers, accountant, attorney, suppliers, or others who need to be notified.

An excellent workbook for serious organizers is *One of These Days We'll Have to Get Organized* by Donald Upp. Taking a few hours to complete the workbook or to prepare your own homemade folder is one of the nicest things you can do for your family. And it's one of the smartest ways to put order in your financial life.

Source:
One of These Days We'll Have to Get Organized by Donald Upp, Jadlu Press, Jenison, Mich.

Protecting your money against fraud

Fools aren't the only ones soon parted from their money. Even cautious consumers can fall victim to fraud.

Professional financial advisors are, for the most part, reputable individuals. But there are those who don't think twice about dashing off with your dollars.

How do you protect yourself? The International Association for Financial Planning offers this advice:

► Whatever advice you get, remember that it's still your money at stake. If you're not comfortable with the investment or account, say no.

► Meet possible advisors in person. Make sure your personalities are compatible. Does the advisor listen to you? Are his responses candid? Does he or she volunteer information?

► Remember, if a deal sounds too good to be true, it probably is. Your advisor should tell you all the risks involved before investing your money. Take notes. Ask questions.

► Verify that your advisor is a registered investment advisor. You can verify this information by calling the Office of Filings, Information, and Consumer Services division of the Securities and Exchange Commission at 1-202-942-8090. In addition, you may want to check and see if any disciplinary action has been taken against an advisor by calling the National Association of Security Dealers at 1-800-289-9999. It also never hurts to ask for references.

► Understand how you will be charged. Some advisors ask for a commission. Others demand either an hourly or flat fee. This should all be discussed upfront.

► Don't sign anything before you've thoroughly read it. If someone's hurrying you through the paperwork, walk away.

► Make sure you get regular statements from the investment or insurance company as well as from the advisor. If you have questions, demand answers and keep following up until you're satisfied.

► It might be smart to choose an advisor with liability insurance.

► Don't just glance at the statements you get from your advisor. They may be boring, but they're your best link to your money.

Source:
International Association for Financial Planning, Atlanta

6 easy roads to riches

Never worry about money again with these six New Year's resolutions offered by James Jorgensen, a San Francisco talk show host and the author of *It's Never Too Late to Get Rich: Secrets of Building a Nest Egg at Any Age.*

▶ Put 10 percent of your gross income (before taxes) into savings every year. You can start with 5 percent and take several months to work your way to 10 percent.

▶ Pay off personal debt. Think there's no way you can save 10 percent a year? Pay off credit card debt, and you'll find it's easy.

▶ Double your savings power by taking advantage of your company's retirement plan. Tax-deferred compounding plus your employer matching the money you put in will make your savings add up fast.

▶ Insure yourself against loss of income with life and disability insurance.

▶ Get out of some of those safe, safe investments. When you consider inflation and taxes, you're actually losing money in some bank savings accounts. Get into the stock market. Jorgensen says to use this formula to figure out what percentage of your long-term savings should be in the stock market: 100 minus your age.

▶ Refuse to play the market. For the most part, once you've made an investment in the stock market, you need to leave it alone. Most of a stock's yearly growth can occur in just a few days. If you've pulled your money out, you're out of luck.

Sources:
It's Never Too Late to Get Rich: Secrets of Building a Nest Egg at Any Age by James Jorgensen, Dearborn Financial Publishing, Chicago, 1995

Financial scams: Don't be duped

Swindlers swarm all over this earth. But you don't have to be a victim if you are aware of some of the most common scams:

Switching health care insurance companies. Protect yourself from high pressure salespeople by thoroughly reading any policy before signing on the dotted line. Find out first who fills out the reimbursement forms, how long you must wait for coverage, and whether there are any upfront fees.

Medical "cures." Talk with your doctor, pharmacist, or other health care provider before spending a cent on what's touted as a "cure-all for what ails you."

Living trusts. If you want to set up a living trust, ask a friend or relative for the name of a reputable attorney who knows your state's trust laws. Don't be fooled by a fast-talking huckster who will likely misinform, deceive, and overcharge you.

Credit card fraud. Never, ever give your credit card number to any unknown person who calls you or sends you "official-sounding" mail. No legitimate "sweepstakes" sponsor will ask for your credit card number. Nor will the IRS.

Organizations offering help with Social Security benefits. You don't need them. Instead, make an appointment with your local Social Security Office. You'll learn everything you need to know about applying for your benefits.

Retirement planning seminars. While you can gain valuable information at these seminars, be wary of sponsors who try to sell you investments and financial services you may not need. Don't be intimidated by claims that you won't have enough money for retirement. Instead, before investing a penny, insist on seeing prospectuses and other types of credible information.

Franchises. You may be tempted to invest in "your own business," but do your homework before you put pen to paper. Speak with other franchisees and ask if you can visit their sites. Review the company's financial statements, preferably with your attorney or accountant. Have an attorney knowledgeable in franchise law review the agreement.

Schemes that sound too good to be true usually are. Caveat emptor (let the buyer beware)!

Source:
Managing Your Money in Retirement: A Guide for Investors 50 and Older, AARP Investment Program from Scudder, Boston, 1994

BETTER BANKING

Is the bank's mistake your gain?

Your bank's automated teller machine is apparently in love with you. You took $100 out of your account, but the machine malfunctioned and kept spitting out hundred dollar bills — until you had ten of them!

A malfunctioning banking machine doesn't automatically turn into a slot machine where the winner takes all. In fact, if you try to keep the extra money — or if the teller gives you more than she's supposed to when you cash a check — you had better turn it back in. If you don't, you can face criminal charges for keeping it.

Source:
The Court TV. Cradle-to-Grave Legal Survival Guide: A Complete Resource for Any Question You May Have About the Law by American Lawyer Media; Little, Brown, and Company, New York, 1995

11 ways to sidestep sneaky bank fees

The cost of banking is higher than ever, with banks inventing sneaky new fees and raising minimum required balances. But the smart consumer can pay less to keep a bank account, says the U.S. Public Interest Research Group (PIRG), a national consumer and environmental lobbying organization. Take a close look at your bank statement and figure out exactly what fees you are paying.

► The most slippery fees are checking account charges. Look for a bank that offers free checking and doesn't require a minimum balance. They are hard to find. Credit unions and small banks usually have the best deals. If you can't find free checking, look for a bank that lets you pool the balances in your savings and checking accounts, counting all of your balances against the minimum.

► If you can, direct deposit your paycheck or your government check. Many banks offer lower fees for customers who use direct deposit.

► Steer clear of checking accounts that earn interest if you won't be able to maintain the required minimum balance. The interest you earn, usually less than 2 percent, is pennies compared with the fees you pay. The minimum balance is usually a much higher minimum than required for a regular checking account.

► Consider a no-frills account with lower fees, available at many banks, if you write only a few checks a month.

► Watch out for bank fees on uncollected or unavailable funds. When a check you deposited hasn't yet cleared, the bank won't bounce checks but it will charge a fee for uncollected or unavailable funds. Manage your money so you don't have to pay bounced check penalty fees. When banks do charge for uncollected funds, complain. Change banks if they continue charging you those fees.

▶ You can be charged twice for a single ATM transaction. Many banks now charge a fee for using another bank's ATM machine. And the bank whose ATM you use also charges a surcharge. Use your own bank's machines as much as possible.

▶ Don't pay annual fees for your bank credit cards. With all the competition in credit cards today, few banks try to charge a fee. If you do pay an annual fee, your credit card is a dinosaur. Get rid of it, or tell your bank you just got an offer from another bank and ask them to drop the fee.

▶ Demand lower interest rates on your credit cards if you are paying more than 15 percent, or even 12 percent, as long as you have good credit. Threaten to transfer your balance to a bank with a lower credit card interest rate.

▶ Pay more than the minimum on your credit card balance. Because the banks request such a tiny monthly payment, the amount of money consumers pay in interest is unbelievable. Don't carry a balance on high interest rate credit cards. If you have two credit cards, try to transfer all your debt to the one with the lower interest rate.

▶ Keep an eye on due dates. Banks are shortening grace periods and are playing fast and loose with the way they calculate interest. Pay your bill when you get it, not the day before it is due.

Remember, you can vote with your feet. If your bank is charging too many fees, walk away.

Send complaints or inquiries to the U.S. Public Interest Research Group. Write to U.S. PIRG, 218 D St. S.E., Washington, D.C. 20003. The e-mail address is USPIRG@PIRG.org or contact the group on its web page address at www.pirg.org/pirg, which features a consumer tip guide.

They may not be able to handle every case, but they do find it helpful to know about your problem.
Source:
Interview with Ed Mierzwinksi, consumer program director, U.S. PIRG, Washington, D.C.

How to check up on your bank

Banks are constantly merging or being liquidated. Over 1,000 commercial and savings banks are on the Federal Deposit Insurance Corporation's trouble list.

Should you tuck your money under the mattress to keep it safe? No, but you do need to protect your assets, mainly by getting some information about your bank.

First, make sure your bank is insured by the Federal Deposit Insurance Corporation (FDIC). The FDIC stands behind all deposits up to $100,000. (You should never put more than $100,000 in one bank.)

Next, ask for a copy of your bank's annual report and financial statements. Your banker probably didn't offer these to you when you signed up for an account, but it's your right to see them.

Also request the *call report* on your bank from the FDIC. This report is available for main banks only, not branches. Here you'll find information like how much money your bank makes and whether your bank is making risky loans. The report costs $6.00. To receive a report, call 1-800-945-2186.

Now here's what to look for in those financial statements:

▶ You want to determine if your bank is making risky loans. Compare the *nonperforming assets* (the loans that are more than 90 days overdue and unlikely to ever be paid) to *total loans*. The FDIC standard for a solid loan portfolio is 1 percent.

▶ If your bank has a large number of problem loans (look in the section called *past due and nonaccrual loans*), they should have plenty of money on hand to cover the loans. Look at the *loan-loss reserve balance*. Your bank could be headed for trouble if problem loans are greater than loan-loss reserves.

▶ Make sure your bank could handle a run. You should see a *loan-deposit ratio* of less than 70 percent and at least five percent in *cash* or *short-term investments*.

▶ The bank should have a large *shareholder's equity*. That gives it a cash cushion to cover a big loss. Divide assets into equity to come up with a percentage. Equity should not be below 5 percent of assets.

▶ Is your bank profitable? Its *net income* (found in the call report) should be positive.

▶ You shouldn't see drastic changes in equity and liquidity from quarter to quarter.

If you want more information, you can get a *uniform bank performance report*. These reports cost $45, and they compare banks within a certain state or county. To receive an order form for a uniform bank performance report, call 1-800-945-2186.

Source:
Dun & Bradstreet Guide to $Your Investments$ 1992 by Nancy Dunnan, HarperCollins Publishers, New York, 1992

Safer banking

▶ Keep all of your bank records — deposit slips, statements, and all other records. If a bank is going to fail, its records are likely to be sloppy.

▶ You may be surprised to hear that smaller banks tend to be safer than large multibillion-dollar banks.

▶ Safe banks don't offer unusually high interest rates on deposits. Their regular customers bring them all the business they need.

Source:
Dun & Bradstreet Guide to $Your Investments$ 1992 by Nancy Dunnan, HarperCollins Publishers, New York, 1992

Automatic payments can be risky

When you let a company make automatic deductions from your checking account for a monthly payment, you're taking a risk. That flow of money from your account can be out of your control.

There are two kinds of automatic payments — bank transfers and credit transfers. It's important to understand the difference. The automatic bill-paying service offered by your bank to pay monthly bills is known as a bank transfer.

With bank transfers, you have direct control. You can stop payment on a bill or stop using the service altogether, just by notifying the bank.

Credit transfers are another story. Depending on the kind of agreement you sign with a creditor, such as a furniture store or health club, you could have a hard time stopping those automatic deductions from your checking account. Here's why:

While bank transfers are regulated by the Federal Reserve Board, credit transfers operate under the rules of the National Automated Clearing House Association. The NACHA says you have the right to cancel automatic payments, but lets the companies decide how and when. (Each company's cancellation rules, incidentally, must be clearly stated in the authorization agreement you signed. Be sure to read the fine print.)

Some companies let you cancel by phone three to five days before a payment is due. Other require 30 days notice in writing. Unless you follow their rules to the letter, they can — and will — continue to debit your account.

Of course, even when you do cancel the credit transfer, you still have to make the payments you agreed to.

Sources:
Interview with Linda Garvelink, senior director of marketing, NACHA, Herndon, Va.
Interviews with Harold McCoy, branch manager, NationsBank, Newnan, Ga., and John Waller, personal banker, NationsBank, Alpharetta, Ga.

What to keep in a safe-deposit box

If you're using your safe-deposit box to hide money or jewels, you've got the wrong idea. There's nothing really wrong with squirreling away your valuables (unless you're trying to hide them from the IRS), but that's not what the boxes were designed for.

Instead, it's best to keep your valuable documents stored in the bank vaults. You — and your heirs — will always know where to find insurance policies, title papers, birth certificates, or stock certificates. Plus, there's the added advantage of knowing the papers are secure in a fireproof box.

The security of safe-deposit boxes is a dual-edged sword. If you're the only person with access, you never have to worry about theft. Should you die suddenly, though, it could create a world of headaches for your family. If a safe-deposit box contains your will, but you have not set up a joint account, then your heirs must go before a probate judge and get a court order to enter the box.

Even then, your survivors have to know the will is in the box, and they are allowed to take nothing but the will out. Bank personnel will watch them every moment to ensure nothing else is taken. For a person in mourning, those restrictions can be as painful as the loss.

Keep a copy of your will in your safe deposit box, but keep the original at your attorney's office.

Source:
Interview with Charles Pinkerton, consumer lending officer/branch manager, Tucker Federal Savings and Loan, Tucker, Ga.

Getting a loan when your credit stinks

Those lean times when you forgot to pay the credit card bill may not have seemed like a big deal, but to banks, they're a warning sign. If you've got a bad credit history, your odds of securing a loan with a major financial institution are low.

That doesn't mean you won't be able to get the money. Secondary markets exist for people whose credit is tarnished but showing signs of improvement. However, before you explore them, ask yourself some questions.

Do you have any collateral? A company won't lend you money unless it has some guarantee it's going to get it back in one form or another. Also, do you have enough income to pay the debt? The greater your income and the lower your debt, the better. If you don't have much left over after your bills are paid, you won't get a loan.

Finance companies are the best places for people with poor credit to turn, but they have several disadvantages. Expect a substantially higher interest rate — maybe twice as much as a primary lender (such as a bank) would charge. You may also have to agree to prepayment penalties. That means if you pay your debt off early, you still have to pay at least a portion of the interest the finance company would have collected.

If you're trying to buy a house, call a mortgage broker. These professionals are listed in the yellow pages, and they will put you in touch with groups that extend mortgages to people considered high risk. Again, be prepared to pay more in interest.

Don't borrow from your friends and family if you can help it. It's a bad idea for both sides. For the lender, there's a good chance that the debt will not be repaid. And you risk alienating someone close.

Persistence pays when searching for a high-risk loan. As long as your cash flow sufficiently outweighs your debts, you can probably find someone to lend you money.

Source:
Interview with John Carpentier, CPA, Tarpley and Underwood, Atlanta

Finding hidden cash

Banks aren't the only place to go when you need money, especially when you're already swimming in debt. If you're lucky, you can tap into cash you have stashed away.

Your 401k plan. Certain retirement plans let you borrow back some of the money you've been contributing for years. Exactly how much you can get depends on the plan, but generally, you can borrow as much as $50,000 or half the vested value of your account (whichever is less).

401k loans are considered one of the worst ways to borrow from yourself. First of all, you must repay the money plus interest within five years, making payments at least once per quarter. And, you are actually taking away from the capital, not just borrowing against the money you have in the plan. That means you limit the earnings potential of the account, which may force you to work longer before retiring.

Life insurance policies. You can get your hands on quick cash by borrowing against the cash value of your life insurance policy. Even better, you don't necessarily have to repay the loan. It's a good idea to do so, of course, since the more you borrow, the less your heirs will get when you die.

On the other hand, loans from life insurance policies tend to pay themselves back. If you leave some cash value in the policy, the interest earned from that will be applied to the loan. That means the amount you owe yourself will slowly decrease over time.

Stock portfolio. If you've got a portfolio to borrow against, your cash crisis isn't all that bad. If you're borrowing on margin to reinvest in the stock market, the interest you pay is deductible. However, if you're taking money out of the stock market to buy a new car or boat or the like, you get no tax advantages.

Home equity loans. Talk about tax advantages! If you are planning to buy a car or boat, this is where you should go for the money. Your interest rate is generally equal to or better than a standard bank loan and the interest is completely deductible, no matter what you use the money for. Be aware that you're putting your home up as collateral. If you think you might have trouble repaying this loan at some point, don't take the risk.

Sources:
Interview with Don Flower, vice president, Pension Financial Services, Atlanta
Interview with John Carpentier, CPA, Tarpley and Underwood, Atlanta

Pay less in interest

Borrow a little. Pay a lot. If you're not careful, interest payments on credit cards, car loans, and mortgages can add up to a lot more than you expected. The trick to avoiding a credit crisis is to take control of the situation before you make any sort of commitment.

The chief villains in outrageous interest charges are credit cards. The market is saturated these days, however, which gives you power. Shop around and read those offers that come in the mail. Then call your credit card company and mention the best deal you find. More often than not, they will match or better the rate in order to keep you as a customer.

Interest on bigger loans, such as for a car or house, can be kept under control by getting the financing underway before you begin looking for the car or house. It's hard to be objective about a financing offer when you already have your eye — or heart — set on something.

Also, if you're buying a car, you'll be able to compare the dealer's financing offer to what you've already secured. If it's better, you can sign immediately. If not, you're still getting the best rate in town.

Source:
Interview with Suzanne Boas, president, Consumer Credit Counseling Service of Greater Atlanta

Establishing good credit

The college years are crucial to your credit history. Preapproved applications flood your mailbox, making it too easy to stretch a lean budget.

College students need to handle checking accounts delicately. One bounced check could put you in the financial doghouse. Also keep a savings account. If you can successfully manage both, potential lenders will see that you are a responsible person.

Arrange to get a secured credit card from your bank. Most people carry around unsecured cards. With a secured card, a bank will offer you a loan as long as you maintain an account balance equal to or greater than the value of that loan. If you default, the bank knows it can get its money back.

A secured credit card is different from a debit card. With a debit card, you're taking money directly from your savings account. Secured credit cards send you a monthly bill, which you repay.

Source:
Interview with Suzanne Boas, president, Consumer Credit Counseling Service of Greater Atlanta

One fast loan and one low-cost loan

A bank isn't doing you a favor when it gives you a loan. It's making money. So quit feeling grateful to your lenders, and start searching for good deals on loans.

For a very quick loan (and one you should use only in emergency situations), open a checking or NOW account that has an overdraft privilege. When you open the account, fill out the credit application and ask for a credit limit of $2,000 or more. Then, when an emergency arises, you have an automatic loan. All you have to do is write a check and overdraw your account. Of course, this kind of loan is expensive, especially if you don't pay it off very quickly.

A cheap way to borrow money is to get a one-payment loan. With this type of loan, you don't pay monthly installments. Instead, you pay the entire balance when the loan period is up.

Take the sum of money you'll owe when the loan comes due, and divide it by the number of months you have until the due date. Put that amount into a savings account every month, or into another type of account that earns even more interest. The interest you earn will help pay off the loan at the end.

The one-payment loan is not a lender's favorite, so you may have to look hard for a lender willing to do it. You should be able to find one if you have a good credit record.

Source:
Ninety Days to Financial Fitness by Joan German-Grapes, Collier Books, New York, 1993

Cheaper checking

You can often avoid paying a monthly service charge on a checking account by maintaining a minimum balance. But parking too much extra money in a checking account usually means you aren't driving the road to riches. Get out your calculator to figure out if the minimum balance/free checking deal your bank is offering is a good one.

Suppose your bank will waive a $9 monthly service charge if you keep a minimum balance of $500. That's a deal you should consider. $9 multiplied by 12 equals $108. $108 is almost 22 percent of $500. (Divide 108 by 500 to get the percentage.) You probably can't earn 22 percent by investing your $500.

On the other hand, suppose your bank will waive a $5 monthly charge for keeping a minimum balance of $2,000. $5 multiplied by 12 equals $60. $60 is 3 percent of $2,000. You are better off paying the service charge and putting your $2,000 into an investment that earns more than 3 percent.

Source:
Money and the Mature Woman: How to Hold On to Your Income, Keep Your Home, Plan Your Estate by Frances Leonard, Addison-Wesley Publishing, Reading, Mass., 1993

How to spot a bad check

One of the easiest ways for a thief to steal your property is to pay for it — with a rubber check. There are plenty of warning signs to watch for, however, that will help you avoid being ripped off.

Low-numbered checks are one of your best alert signals. Scam artists will open legitimate bank accounts and write numerous checks far exceeding their balance before fleeing town. When you see checks numbered from 101 to 150 and 1001 to 1050, you should be on your guard.

Get a good look at the person writing the check, too. If he or she can't make eye contact or seems overly nervous, you may be dealing with a criminal. Always demand photo identification and don't be afraid to photocopy it. In cases where you can't shake your suspicions, call the phone number listed on the check and ask whoever answers if they've had their checkbook stolen recently.

The check itself should have a distinctive feel. At least one side should be perforated. If not, it's probably a phony that came from a laser printer. Also, the numbers and letters on the check shouldn't reflect light. Magnetic ink, which is used by check-making companies, is dull.

Above all, listen to your instincts. If something seems wrong, it probably is. For example, if the buyer pulls out a partially written check, that should send up a red flag. If you're in a business setting, beware of the person who's in a hurry to buy a big ticket item or insists on carrying out something that's usually delivered.

Source:
Interview with Captain Cecil Goodroe, DeKalb County Sheriff's Office, Decatur, Ga.

Hidden dangers of debit cards

Credit cards are convenient, but the monthly bills can be shocking. Another option: debit cards.

With debit cards, instead of borrowing money from a company like Visa or MasterCard, you simply make a withdrawal from your checking account. That means no interest charges. Plus, it helps you resist making impulse buys with your plastic.

Debit cards come in two varieties: on-line and off-line. On-line cards are the kind you use at an ATM. Off-line cards look more like traditional credit cards (sometimes even carrying the Visa or MasterCard logo). Your purchases are deducted from your checking account one to three days later.

The problem: less protection. Debit cards don't offer you the same protection as credit cards. Because the cards essentially act as a check, it's the merchant's option whether or not to give you a refund if you ask. If he's not willing to return your money, you can't appeal to a higher power, except the courts.

Also, if you use a debit card to purchase something via mail order and it arrives damaged, you have no legal protection to get it replaced. (Some banks, however, do offer coverage beyond what is legally required.)

Most importantly, if your card is lost or stolen, your liabilities are much higher than if you were to lose a credit card. If you report the problem within two business days, you're only responsible for up to $50. Wait longer and your liability jumps to $500. If you don't report a loss or theft within 60 days from the date you are sent a statement, you are completely responsible for the charges, whether they are yours or not. Your liability for a lost or stolen credit card is just $50.

And the fees. While you won't have to pay interest charges, you may have to pay some sort of fee for using a debit card. Charges vary from bank to bank. Some demand up to 75 cents per transaction. Others ask just $1 per month. Some have no fees.

Source:
Interview with Ruth Susswein, executive director, Bankcard Holders of America, Herndon, Va.

Smart shopping with your ATM card

No doubt, you already know the advantages of having an ATM (automated teller machine) card. Not only do they let you withdraw or deposit money at your bank or credit union at whatever hour of the day or night you wish, you can get cash quickly almost anywhere in the world, from your local bank all the way to Bangkok.

Pay for purchases with your ATM card. Many gas stations and grocery stores have PIN pads that let you directly deduct your purchases from your checking account. You can also get ATM cards that carry the logo of MasterCard or Visa, enabling you to use your ATM card at more retail locations than ever before.

If you want to know whether a particular store accepts your ATM card, look at the logo on your card to see if it matches any of those displayed at the entrance of the store or at the cash register. If you don't want to take time to look, just ask whether or not the store accepts your ATM card.

Depending on which logos you have on your card and whether or not the store has PIN pads, you'll either have to punch in your PIN (personal identification number), or you'll have to sign for your purchase (just like when you use a credit card).

Either way, the amount of your purchase will be deducted immediately from your checking account. This will save you money in interest, especially if you don't always pay your credit card bills off at the end of the month.

Beware of bank fees. Some banks charge high fees when you use your card to withdraw money or make a purchase. Ask your bank these questions:

▶ What are the monthly or annual fees for your card?

▶ What are the "per use" fees when using your own bank's ATM or an ATM at another bank or credit union?

▶ What are the "per use" fees when using the ATM card to shop?

▶ How can you avoid any of these fees?

Be picky with pin numbers. Pick a PIN you can remember, but don't choose a number that someone else might easily associate with you like your birth date, social security number, street address, or telephone number. Never write your PIN number on your ATM card.

Protect your card. Don't let it get scratched, bent, or overheated. It's especially important to protect the magnetic strip on the back of your card. Don't let that strip come in contact with other magnetic cardkeys, which can erase all information from your ATM card.

Check receipts for accuracy. Compare receipts against your monthly statement. If you notice any suspicious transactions, report them to your bank immediately. You must show your statement with the questionable transactions to your bank or credit union within 60 days. Otherwise, you may be responsible for all the funds the unauthorized user withdrew from your account. Federal regulations protect you against errors that may occur during electronic fund transfer.

Watch out. The convenience of quick cash often causes people to lose track of how much they're spending. Deduct the purchase or withdrawal amount from your account immediately. This will help you keep a correct balance.

ATM cards are a type of debit card, so see the previous story for more information on how to protect yourself when your card is stolen.

Source:
Shopping With Your ATM Card, Consumer Information Center, U.S. General Services Administration, 1994

Earn more interest on your bank CDs

Do you keep most of your money in low-risk bank CDs? Respected investment advisor William Donoghue has a secret he's willing to share with you. You can dramatically increase the interest you earn on your CDs and similar investments by following a number published in many major newspapers. It's called the *average maturity* of taxable money funds.

Every once in a while, your bank asks you to decide if you want to roll over your certificate of deposit. You can either reinvest in a CD, or you can put your money in a place where you can get to it easily – a money market mutual fund or money market deposit account.

You can usually earn higher interest rates on CDs, but if the interest rates are about to go up, you've lost out. You're stuck with the current rate until your CD matures. You need to know what interest rates are about to do, and, according to Donoghue, that's no longer a secret to small-time investors.

When professional money fund managers think interest rates are rising, they invest money in securities that mature in a day or a week. That's so they can quickly reinvest the money at the new, higher interest rates. Therefore, the *average maturity* of taxable money funds is an excellent signal of future interest rates.

When the average maturity is short – 39 days or less – interest rates are on the rise. Do not invest in a long-term CD. Put your money in a bank money market account or a money fund and wait for your chance to buy a long-term CD when interest rates are higher.

When the average maturity is long — 46 days or more — and it hasn't gone down in the past three weeks, the pros think interest rates are falling. Buy a one-year or longer CD.

When the average maturity stays between 40 and 45 days for three weeks, the pros aren't sure, but they think the interest rates are likely to remain stable or fall. Consider buying a six-month CD.

You can find Donoghue's Money Market Funds table in the financial section of many newspapers. Find the column marked *average maturity (days).*

Even in easy, low-risk investments such as bank CDs, you can earn more money by watching the Wall Street crowd and doing not what they say, but what they do.

Source:
The Donoghue Strategies by William E. Donoghue with Robert Chapman Wood, Bantam Books, New York, 1989

Watch out for fake CDs

If you see an ad for a CD with an exceptional interest rate, don't be fooled. Many finance companies are trying to get your money by offering fake CD accounts. The only difference is, your money isn't insured.

Don't even think about buying CDs or similar accounts offered by anyone other than a federally insured bank or thrift institution, an SEC-regulated money fund, a Treasury bill, or other obligation of the federal government.

Watch out for state-insured savings and loan associations, uninsured credit unions, and other finance companies offering fake CDs. The extra interest isn't worth the risk.

Source:
The Donoghue Strategies by William E. Donoghue with Robert Chapman Wood, Bantam Books, New York, 1989

The future of banking

Remember when you had to go inside the bank to withdraw money and transfer funds? Banking has been a challenge for working Americans, who go to work before banks open and don't get off until they close. Within the last few years, the automated teller machine (ATM) has allowed us to complete almost all our banking needs at any hour of the day. In the not-too-distant future, you'll be able to cash checks at ATMs.

In 10 years, you won't have to visit your local bank to apply for a loan. Instead, you will simply enter a booth and apply at an automated loan machine. Within approximately 10 minutes, you'll know whether or not you were approved. No more long nights wondering if you qualify for the loan.

Banking technology is constantly changing. Even now, some banks offer telephone banking services. You can check the balance of your account, check your most recent withdrawals, and even transfer money from one account to another from your own phone. Enhanced services through telephone banking will also be a wave of the future.

One of the newest areas of banking technology is on-line banking. From your personal computer, you can perform similar tasks to telephone banking and more. One possibility for the future is banking on the Internet. As more and more people become computer literate, banks will enhance these services as well.

Banking may always be a hassle, but changes are coming that will make it easier and more consumer-oriented.

Source:
Interview with Ellison Clary, Senior Vice President in Corporate Affairs, NationsBank, Charlotte, N.C.

WISE INVESTING

The future of your investments

You don't need magical powers and a crystal ball to know that some investors are in for a big surprise over the next few years. Just look at the facts, say data analysts like Gerald Perritt.

Right now, many people are making the mistake of counting on the 15 percent or better return they've made on their mutual funds and stocks in the last decade. That return isn't likely to last.

You can figure that out by looking at a number that everybody forgets about — the *compounded annual rate of return for large blue-chip stocks*. This number is very stable; it may not change for years and years. (That's why everybody forgets about it.)

Over the last 50 years, the compounded annual rate of return for large blue-chip stocks has averaged 12.5 percent. Since 1982, it's averaged 16.2 percent — way more than the long-term average.

Soon, we should see a dip in the interest we earn on our mutual funds and stocks. It could go far below that average of 12.5 percent.

All this doesn't mean you should rush to get out of the stock market. You can still make money there, especially if you're in for the long haul.

People planning to retire on the interest from their investments and parents who are counting on a certain return to send their children to college may need to rethink. If it's possible to put a little more aside, do so.
Source:
John Cunniff, AP Business Analyst, New York, writing in *The Newnan Times-Herald* (Oct. 18, 1995, 11C)

Trade secrets of nosy brokers

Nosy brokers can be an investor's dream come true or his worst nightmare. Some simply want to know your net worth to help make appropriate recommendations. Others want to get their hands on your cash.

Even keeping quiet about your financial secrets doesn't keep a persistent broker from learning what you're worth. Some will drive by your home to give it the once-over. Others will ask for a copy of your tax return (if you've got a lot of interest income, you've probably got a sizable savings account).

If your broker starts to complain about low interest rates on certificates of deposit, clam up. He's probably trying to get you to talk about your savings.

A broker may say he will act as your financial planner. Keep in mind that by agreeing to the offer, you're giving him full access to all your financial records.
Source:
Money (January 1994)

Suing your broker

Brokers make their money by charging a commission every time you buy or sell a stock. Unscrupulous stockbrokers handling your brokerage account may try to earn extra cash by buying and selling stocks and bonds for you more often than you'd really like. Making lots of unnecessary purchases and sales is called *churning* your account, and people, especially women, who put too much faith in their broker's recommendations are vulnerable to it.

If you think your account has been churned, complain to the Securities and Exchange Commission. They will help you determine if you need a lawyer or if you can take your case to small claims court. You may be able to collect thousands in damages.

You may also be able to sue your broker for losing your money. Under the *know your client rule*, the broker is liable if he knows your financial history and needs and he recommends unreasonably risky investments.

Most investors don't need a broker's services. You can avoid paying commissions by buying mutual funds directly from fund companies and government securities directly from the federal reserve bank.

If you want a brokerage account, consider using a *discount broker*. They don't give you advice; they only buy and sell when you say so. And, they charge a lower commission.

A broker can also call himself an "account executive" or a "financial adviser." Don't be fooled — they're all stockbrokers who'd love to manage your money. Make sure anyone who handles your investments comes well-recommended.

Source:
Money and the Mature Woman: How to Hold On to Your Income, Keep Your Home, Plan Your Estate by Frances Leonard, Addison-Wesley Publishing, Reading, Mass., 1993

Why use a full-service stockbroker?

Why pay nearly twice as much in commissions to a full-service broker when you can buy the same stocks through a discount broker?

Because most discount brokers only buy and sell according to your instructions. Few provide investment advice and even fewer offer other services.

Full-service brokers have easy access to the information you need to make wise investment decisions. Within minutes, they can access a company's earnings, earnings estimate, and management compensation. They can tell you about insider buying and selling and sentiment buying (people buying a stock because they read about it in a magazine or they like the company's product or they got a "hot" tip). They can tell you whether there are scads of buyers, indicating that a stock's price is close to peaking, or there are scads of sellers, indicating the stock is bottoming out. All this is information hard to come by if you don't know where to look.

Besides being a direct path to sophisticated research, full-service stock-brokers also recommend investments, offer advice on allocating assets, and manage your portfolio. Full-service brokers are handholders as well. When stock prices fall during a market "correction," or in reaction to economic forecasts, inexperienced investors often scramble to sell their stocks. Full-service brokers help you to realistically review your options rather than emotionally react to the situation.

Even with a full-service broker, you ultimately give the order to buy and/or sell stocks, but you may find their services worth the extra cost.
Source:
Interview with Kenny Brandt, CFP, executive vice-president, WSB Advisors in Birmingham, Mich.

Keep your eye on the insiders

Want to know which stocks are winners? If you've taken a look at the records of most Wall Street stockbrokers and money managers, you may have decided you'd be better off picking your stocks yourself than trusting your money to a stranger.

One way to know where to put your money is to watch the ones who are really in the know — the officers, directors, and major shareholders of the thousands of public companies in America. After all, if an executive of a big soft drink company or a major airline is buying his company's stock, he is sure to believe that the future of the company looks bright.

Keeping up with the insiders is easy. Every company executive and shareholder who owns more than 10 percent of a company's stock is required by law to report any trading he does to the Securities and Exchange Commission every month. Many publications and major newspapers regularly report this information, often once a week. Check your local paper to see if they include insider trading data.

History says this method really works. Nine of the 10 top-performing stocks on the New York Stock Exchange in 1993 showed lots of insider buying in the last half of 1992.

Once you see what the company insiders are buying, make sure you research the company so you won't be in for any surprises. Then you'll be on your way to putting some winners in your portfolio.
Sources:
The Atlanta Journal/Constitution (Oct. 10, 1994, E1)
Winning on Wall Street by Martin Zweig, Warner Books, New York, 1995

Warning: the dangers of illegal insider trading

You don't have to be an executive to get in trouble. It's perfectly legal for executives or employees to buy or sell stock in their company. They just have to file their transactions with the Securities and Exchange Commission, so the public knows what they're doing.

Insider trading becomes illegal when someone buys or sells stock based on information kept from the public — like the company is going bankrupt or about to be sold for a big profit. People trading stock with info like that can reap enormous profits and cause stock prices to fluctuate wildly.

The SEC says this is a kind of fraud. Illegal insider trading can land folks hefty fines and hard jail time. We've all heard of the billionaire executive who bilked the public out of millions with his insider trading schemes and ended up in prison.

What you may not know is that it's not just the rich and powerful who can get in trouble using insider information. So can secretaries, human resource directors, or any other employee or independent contractor.

If you find out information about your company's financial dealings that could affect stock prices — information the public doesn't have access to — and you use that information to buy or sell stock, you could land in legal hot water.

It's rare for the "small fry" to be prosecuted, but it does happen, says business attorney Edward Greenblatt. A case in point: A typesetter worked for a printer who produced annual reports for a large company. He read the copy he was working on and used that information, before it was published, to make a killing in the stock market. He was prosecuted for insider trading.

As a stockholder, illegal insider trading can cost you money, notes Edward Greenblatt. "You can buy stock in good faith. But if hot shots in the company use insider information to manipulate either the price or the market for their own benefit, you can be hurt financially."

What can you do if you think that's happened to you? "Sue them," answers attorney Greenblatt. "Most of these lawsuits are class action securities cases. Contact a lawyer who handles securities cases to see if that's the course of action you should take."

Source:
Interview with Edward Greenblatt, attorney-at-law, Lipshutz, Greenblatt, and King, Atlanta

How to research stocks like a pro

A group of women from a small town in Illinois — farmers' wives, schoolteachers, homemakers, and retired secretaries — with an average age of 63 1/2, got together over 10 years ago and formed an investment club that ranks among the top 10 in the nation. They now have a portfolio worth more than $90,000 and an average return of 23 percent — outperforming mutual funds and professional money managers 3 to 1.

What's their secret? Investing regularly (each woman puts in $25 a month) and doing their own homework, instead of relying on the advice of the pros, they say. Their most valuable research tool is available to you, too, for free. It's called *Value Line's Investment Survey*, and you can find it at most large public libraries.

Value Line tells you what you need to know about more than 1,700 companies trading on the stock exchange. You won't be overwhelmed because they cram all the information about a company onto one sheet of paper.

You'll find out what the company does, who runs it, and where it spends its money. A Value Line analyst writes his opinion of the company's prospects. Then you'll find charts and figures that tell you about the company's performance for the past 15 years and its projected performance for the next two or three. You'll find out if the company's earnings, sales, and profits are increasing; how much debt the company has; and whether it regularly pays dividends.

Finally, Value Line ranks the company for you on several scales and grades its financial strength (from A++ down to C). You'll also find grades for the company's price stability, its price growth persistence, and its earnings predictability (the top grade is 100).

The Beardstown, Ill., ladies say that reading these company descriptions can become addicting. If something doesn't look right about one company, flip the page to the next. With over 1,700 companies, you can afford to be choosy.

Source:
The Beardstown Ladies' Common-Sense Investment Guide: How We Beat the Stock Market — And How You Can, Too by the Beardstown Ladies Investment Club with Leslie Whitaker, Hyperion, New York, 1994

Beardstown ladies' top 10 investment tips

The Beardstown ladies call these 10 hot tips their "recipe for successful stock picking."

1. Stock is in the top third of its industry (according to Value Line). Even better, pick a stock in the top 25 for its industry.
2. Timeliness rating of stock is 1 or 2 (according to Value Line). Timeliness means how fast a stock will probably grow compared with other stocks. The Value Line rating goes up to 5.
3. Safety rating of stock is 1 or 2 (according to Value Line). A safe stock is one whose price is fairly steady rather than constantly rising and falling.
4. Total debt is less than one third of total assets. A company with little debt makes for a sounder investment.
5. Beta (a number that shows how much a stock's price moves compared with the rest of the market) is between .90 and 1.10. A beta of 1 means the stock's price moves along with the moves of the market. A beta of 2 means the stock's price usually moves twice as much as the rest of the market. For instance, if the stock market went up or down 10 percent, the individual stock is likely to go up or down 20 percent.
6. Sales and earnings have been growing for five years, and they are expected to grow 12 to 15 percent in the next few years. For a very large, established company, a growth of 7 to 10 percent isn't bad.
7. The stock's price per share is no more than $25. This isn't a hard-and-fast rule for the Beardstown ladies, but they point out that the cheaper stocks are easier to buy in even lots. Buying even lots (e.g., 100 shares at once) reduces brokers' fees.

8. The company's price-earnings ratio is below the average p/e ratio for the last five years. The price-earnings ratio is the price of a stock divided by the earnings per share. Of course, you'd like that ratio to be low. You can find the average p/e ratio for the last 15 years in *Value Line*.

9. The stock's upside-down ratio is at least 3 to 1. A ratio of 5 to 1 is even better. A good upside-down ratio means the stock's price is more likely to rise than fall. To figure this ratio, you need to look in *Value Line* for their projected high price of the stock and the projected low price.

    Suppose the stock costs $15 now with a projected high price of $40 and a projected low price of $10. Subtract the present cost of $15 from $40 to get the upside potential ($25), and subtract $10 from the present cost of $15 to get the downside risk ($5). The upside-down ratio is 25 to 5, or (divide 25 by 5) 5 to 1. 5 to 1 is a good buy.

10. The company's management is experienced and competent. The worth of a stock all depends on who's running the show. Read the *Value Line* analysis, and keep your eyes and ears open for news of the management's performance.

These tips are valuable ingredients, but never leave your common sense out of the mix, either. For instance, don't buy stock in a restaurant chain when the franchise near you is always empty.

Source:
The Beardstown Ladies' Common-Sense Investment Guide: How We Beat the Stock Market — And How You Can, Too by the Beardstown Ladies Investment Club with Leslie Whitaker, Hyperion, New York, 1994

How to float when the market takes a plunge

In October 1987, many people panicked when the market dropped 500 points in one day. As the ticker tape tumbled, they couldn't sell their stock and stock mutual funds fast enough. Those who held on, though, weathered the short-term decline and within a few months watched stock prices recover and reach record highs.

Market corrections occur every so often. As you watch money that you plan to use for your retirement or your kid's education evaporate, you may be tempted to get out of the market. Relax. Before you sell your stocks consider:

▶ Stocks recover. Over time, stock prices recover and go on to outperform other investments. Sell at this time and the next sure-to-come upswing will pass you by. If, for example, you were in the market for just 90 of its best days between 1963 to 1993, your investments would have grown a startling 95 percent.

▶ It's a bargain hunter's market. Low prices enable you to add high-quality stocks to your portfolio. Because of a correction in the market, an excellent company with good management and strong earnings can have low stock prices.

▶ Taxes bite. Before you rush to sell, think about how much you'll actually net. Sell a stock you've held less than a year and a day, and your profits will be taxed as ordinary income, up to 39.6 percent. Hold that stock beyond a year and your profits will be taxed as capital gains, no more than 28 percent.

Prepare for the plunge. Not all sectors are affected in a bad market. U.S. stock prices may fall, while global stocks rise. Value stocks may be down while growth stock prices stay steady. Bonds may be up as stocks fall.

The best way to reduce risk and boost returns is to diversify. Put your assets in different types of investments and only a portion of them are likely to be hit at any one time.

If, for example, you're 50 years old, you could divvy up your assets like this:

Type of Investment	Percentage of Portfolio
Large Company Growth Stocks	10-15%
Large Company Value Stocks	10-15%
Small Company Growth Stocks	10–15%
Small Company Value Stocks	10–15%
Income-like Bonds	15–20%
Foreign Growth Companies	20%
Emerging Markets	10%

Source:
Interview with Kenny Brandt, CFP, executive vice-president, WSB Advisors in Birmingham, Mich.

Signs of a budding bull market

You don't want to be left out in the cold when the market is about to rally. Here are some economic indicators that signal an upswing in the market:

Interest rates. When interest rates are low, stocks provide a better return than other investments, so stock prices go up. Conversely, when interest rates are high, people sell stocks and prices plunge.

Inflation. Falling interest rates usually follow lower inflation figures. So, low inflation can signal a strong stock market.

Employment numbers. Low employment figures, in theory, are inflationary. More people working means more money spent on goods and services. Higher inflation and higher interest rates lead to lower stock prices. High unemployment figures, on the other hand, are deflationary. During these times, interest rates fall and stock prices rise.

The *odd-lot* theory. People who buy less than 100 shares of a company's stock are called *odd-lotters*. Records kept of these trades suggest that when odd-lotters are buying stock, the market is on the way down. When odd-lotters sell, the market is usually on the way up. Publications such as the *Davis Digest* provide information on odd-lotters. So do stockbrokers.

Mutual fund trading. When people pour money into mutual funds, stock prices rise because fund managers are out buying stocks. When money invested in mutual funds dries up, stock prices tend to fall.
Source:
Interview with Kenny Brandt, CFP, executive vice-president, WSB Advisors in Birmingham, Mich.

Dow down? Don't panic

As fast as the stock market is moving these days, a 100-point shift for the Dow Jones industrial average isn't as rare as it used to be. Don't let a sharp drop like that scare you. Unless your portfolio is filled exclusively with shares of the 30 companies that make up the Dow, the closing number won't affect you as much as you think.

At the end of the day, the market is only what you own. The closing numbers of companies like Coke, AT&T, and IBM don't necessarily reflect how your holdings are performing, especially if you focus on newer, hotter stocks like Microsoft and Hewlett Packard. Call your broker to get more specific numbers. If your money is spread out over several companies and you want a general idea of how they are performing, ask about the average price per share. That will give you a better idea of what kind of day it was on Wall Street.

Don't ignore the Dow completely. While it may not reflect your investments, people view it as a good yardstick. Wall Street investors have a herd mentality. If they see the Dow start to decline, they will often sell their holdings at a lower price, which could start to affect you after a while.
Source:
Interview with Gary Alexander, broker, Interstate/Johnson Lane, Atlanta

Signs of a staggering stock

Look beyond the profit line when reading a financial report to discover when a company's stock price is likely to plummet. If you know what to look for in financial documents, you can predict when a stock is on its way down. Every number you need is in the company's detailed annual 10-K and quarterly 10-Q reports available from its investor relations office.

So, which figures should you study? Stock analysts suggest:

Inventories. A rising supply of unsold goods might be a positive sign if customer demand for the company's products is on the upswing or a negative sign if company sales are dwindling. You can tell the difference between robust inventory growth and slipping sales by tracking the company's inventory-to-sales ratio.

All you need are the inventory numbers found in the quarterly 10-Q report's consolidated balance sheet and the sales numbers printed in the report's income statement. Then, to get the inventory-to-sales ratio, divide inventory by the dollar amount of sales.

Compare one quarter's ratio with the same from the previous year to spot a company with large inventory heading into trouble. (You'd want the inventory-to-sales ratio to stay the same or get smaller.)

Accounts receivable. Receivables, the money owed to a company for products or services, can foretell falling prices. If receivables grow faster than sales, the stock's price is likely to fall during the following quarter.

Let's say that receivables are up by 50 percent over the previous quarter and sales are up by 5 percent. The company may be so anxious to sell its goods that it is extending payment deadlines. Or, the company may be recording sales before its customers return unsold goods for refunds. Accounts receivable numbers are on the report's balance sheet.

Cash flow. The net flow of real money in or out of the firm reflects the financial health of a company. Unlike earnings or profits, cash flow doesn't address items such as depreciation, a charge against earnings without spending actual dollars. Instead, cash flow figures include items such as new factories and new equipment, expenses immediately taken rather than charged against future earnings. Compare cash flow figures to net income. Be wary of a stock when the cash flow is falling while the net income is rising. If cash flow doesn't increase, the company may have trouble financing future growth.

Expenses. Companies can either *expense* a cost (charge it against this year's profits) or *capitalize* it (charge it against future profits). Expenses are recorded on the income statement. Sometimes, companies capitalize costs that should be expensed to pad the bottom line.

For example: A company spends $1 million in 1996 on direct mail to find subscribers to its on-line service. That $1 million could be shown as an expense charged against current earnings. Or, it could be capitalized on the premise that it was money spent to acquire future revenue. By capitalizing the $1 million over several years, the company can show higher earnings for the current year. If a company is capitalizing costs it should be expensing, the stock may be heading for a fall.

Profit margins. Profit margins reveal how much money is made per dollar of sales. Margins can be stated as *gross profit* (total sales minus product cost) or *net profit* (total sales minus product cost, general and administrative costs, research and development, and interest and taxes).

Watch out when gross profit margins fall. Oftentimes, net profit margins fall with them. Also be wary when gross profit margins drop and net profit margins rise (companies can easily manipulate costs to improve net profits. However, it's a good sign when gross profit margins are up and net profit margins are down. This indicates that the company is investing in its future.

Source:
Worth (June 1996)

Making money the contrarian way

Like to swim against the tide? Consider investing the *contrarian* way. Contrarians do the opposite of what most other investors do. They invest for the long term in out-of-favor stocks that are at or near their 52-week lows.

Contrarian investors separate "loser" companies that are priced low but not worth much from undervalued "winner" companies that are selling at bargain prices. If you want to be a contrarian, look for:

▶ Companies with a stock price sitting within 10 percent of its 52-week low.

▶ Companies that might be an attractive acquisition to another company.

▶ Companies with a good cash flow in spite of current difficulties.

▶ Companies with a strong price-to-sales ratio, especially if they sell cyclical products or are experiencing temporary earnings shortfalls. Note the price-to-book-value ratio in a financial company.

Source:
Portfolio, a Smith Barney publication (August 1996)

Using price and earnings to spot good buys in growth stocks

You can predict a growth stock's future by looking at the company's price and earnings history. In most libraries, you'll find charts of prices and earnings, going back 10 to 35 years, published by the Securities Research Corporation.

The earnings line on the chart represents how well a company performs while the price line reflects Wall Street expectations for the stock. An earnings line on the chart that steadily rises signifies a growth company. Follow the price line and learn if the stock is overpriced or a bargain.

Here's how to use the chart:

Price line approaches the lower earnings line, or drops below it — it's a good time to buy the stock at a bargain price.

Price line remains above the earnings line most of the time — the company knows how to make money. The stock price is likely high but the future growth looks good.

Price line stays same but the earnings line keeps rising — the company is likely doing well.

Price line is close to the earnings line, sometimes drifting below it — the company is posed for slow growth. However, if the price line sharply drops below the earnings line, you should buy more stock.

You can plot your own charts, too. Contact the National Association of Investors Corporation at (810) 583–NAIC (6242) for graph paper with properly aligned price and earnings scales.

Source:
Worth (February 1996)

Overseas investments can be risky

Mazda. Nestlé. Sony. Mercedes. They're all familiar names in our day-to-day lives. But none of them trades on Wall Street.

If you want to own part of a foreign-based company, it's best to be an experienced, shrewd investor. Overseas trading is a good way for the uninitiated to lose a lot of money. You're not only betting on the firm's performance, you're betting against major currency fluctuations.

Getting an accurate quote for international stocks is tricky. Because of time differences, you may not be able to buy shares when you want. And if you're buying a big block, that could affect the price by hundreds or even thousands of dollars. Investment firms also find it nearly impossible to accurately track these businesses. In fact, most brokers will attempt to talk you out of buying abroad.

If you insist, however, they'll try to sell you an American Depository Receipt — or ADR. These are receipts for shares of international companies that entitle you to all the dividends and other perks a shareholder would receive. The chief difference is you pay in dollars, which means a fixed price per share. (When you pay in yen, lira, or any other foreign currency, the ever-changing exchange rates could increase the cost of your order almost instantly.)

ADRs are liquid, cheaper, and easier to trade than the overseas stocks they represent, but you still face much the same risks as overseas investors — changing currency values, tax hassles from overseas governments, and a lack of accurate company financial information.

If you really want to broaden your portfolio's horizons, buy mutual funds with international holdings or put your money in companies like Proctor & Gamble, Coca-Cola, Colgate, or McDonald's. All of these are based and traded in America, but do more than 50 percent of their business overseas. It's the best of both worlds.

Source:
Interview with Gary Alexander, broker, Interstate/Johnson Lane, Atlanta

Sunny day? Call your broker!

April showers bring more than May flowers. They also signal the beginning of the buying season on Wall Street.

The summer months are the favorites of investors. Sunny days and warm weather tend to drive up optimism, and ultimately stock prices. If it's cloudy, prices slump. And if the leaves on your trees are changing, hang onto your money. Shares tend not to perform well in autumn.

Sunny days make people feel better about life in general and more willing to spend money. Fall summons images of sending kids to school, which often means tuition payments.

One survey by Birinyi Associates shows July to be the best-performing month for playing the stock market, with a 1.56 percent average gain since 1915. August is second best, with 1.4 percent.

January is also strong (climbing 1.38 percent), but Mother Nature can't take credit for that. The new year surge comes as people buy back stocks they abandoned for tax purposes at the end of the previous year.

So what's the *worst* month on Wall Street? October, which has the dubious honor of claiming two major crashes — 1929 and 1987.

Sources:
Business Week (Feb. 14, 1994)
The Wall Street Journal (Sept. 27, 1993)

Initial public offering: Act early or forget it

Insider trading is, of course, illegal, but getting a leg up is crucial if you want to make money off an *initial public offering*. If you can't get an IPO at the offering price, it's probably not worth your while.

New stocks tend to peak after three months on the market. After a year or two, they begin to fizzle.

On the first day of trading alone, a company's stock will gain an average of 10.9 percent if you buy when the bell rings. If you purchase the IPO nearer to closing time of its first day, you'll only see a 3.3 percent increase at best — and that will take a full financial quarter. After a year, you actually begin losing money in most cases.

Source:
The Wall Street Journal (March 17, 1994)

Get money's worth with all or nothing orders

Place a large buy order with your broker and you may wind up with far fewer shares than you had anticipated. Sidestep this situation by asking for an *all or none* (AON) order. It will ensure that you get the number of shares you ordered.

Let's say you put in a buy order for 1,000 shares of XYZ Company at $25 per share but you don't specify all or none. You could wind up with 400 shares, 700 shares, or any combination of 100-share lots.

Or, you may wind up paying two commission fees on two 500-share orders made on two consecutive days.

The downside of an AON order: You run the risk of not getting the stock at all. Stock exchange rules dictate that restricted orders are held back until all shares in the order can be purchased. If you want only a few shares of a heavily traded stock, don't ask for an AON order.

Source:
The Individual Investor, Waterhouse Securities (August 1996)

Best stock picks for the 21st century

It's scary, but some people are willing to do it, like famed investment journalist Richard J. Maturi. He's willing to tell you which companies he believes will make big profits for you in the years ahead.

He has researched cash flow, market niches, management talent, insider ownership, and more to come up with a list of companies geared to perform well in the 21st century.

Among his recommendations are these top 16 industrial, consumer, and service company stocks:

Albertson's Inc. (Consumer: grocery store)
American Greeting Corp. (Consumer: greeting cards)
Automatic Data Processing Inc. (Service: computer and financial services)
Cincinnati Milacron Inc. (Industry: machine tools)
Giddings & Lewis Inc. (Industry: automated industrial systems)
McCormick & Company Inc. (Consumer: food processing/seasonings)
Pall Corp. (Industry: filtration products)
PepsiCo Inc. (Consumer: soft drinks)
R.R. Donnelley & Sons Co. (Service: commercial printing)
RPM Inc. (Industry: industrial coatings)
Rubbermaid Inc. (Consumer: household products)
Service Corporation International (Service: funeral services)
The Reynolds and Reynolds Co. (Industry: business forms)
The Home Depot Inc. (Service: building supplies)
Tootsie Roll Industries Inc. (Consumer: food processing/candy)
X-Rite Inc. (Industry: quality control instruments)

If you're ready to research companies to invest in, this list would be a good place to start. At least one investment expert believes that each company is a strong candidate for superior performance in the 21st century.

Source:
The 105 Best Investments for the 21st Century by Richard J. Maturi, McGraw-Hill, New York, 1995 (Richard Maturi offers a newsletter called 21st Century Investments, available by writing R. Maturi Inc., 1320 Curt Gowdy Drive, Cheyenne, WY 82009.)

The power of dollar cost averaging

Dollar cost averaging is the closest you can get to ideal investing. Why? Because it actually tilts the odds in an investor's favor. Yet many financial planning books fail to mention it.

Dollar cost averaging is simply a system for setting aside the same amount of money at regular intervals to buy stock or mutual fund shares. In other words, you invest in regular, set amounts instead of putting in big lumps of money at once.

Look at an example. Say you want to invest $1,100 into the mutual fund LookingUp. The price is $10 a share. After you buy into the fund, as your bad luck would have it, the fund price begins to drop. In four months, the price of each share is $9.375. You own 110 shares, and you have lost $68.75.

With dollar cost averaging, instead of investing a lump sum, you would divide your money up and put in a set amount each month, completely ignoring the ups and downs of the market. Here's what can happen:

Looking Up	First month $275	Second month $275	Third month $275	Fourth month $275
Mutual Fund Price/Share	$10	$6	$7.50	$9.375
Number of Shares Bought	27.5	45.83	36.67	29.33
Total Shares in Fund	27.5	73.33	110	139.33
Total Value	$275	$439.98	$825	$1,306.22

At the end of the fourth month, you own 139.33 shares, and you have made $206.22. Much better than the lump sum investment.

With dollar cost averaging, when the share price of a mutual fund drops, it is a window of opportunity to purchase more shares for the same amount of money. So, instead of looking at falling prices and thinking "The value of my fund is falling," you think, "Now I can pick up some shares at a bargain price." (Of course, if your fund price keeps plummeting, don't keep thinking "It's a bargain." If your fund is a dud, you may need to get out.)

Dollar cost averaging protects you from the wild swings of the stock market, and it keeps you from making common mistakes, such as putting a big lump of money into the stock market — right before it crashes!

Source:
The Wealthy Barber: Everyone's Common-Sense Guide to Becoming Financially Independent by David Chilton, Prima Publishing, Rocklin, Calif., 1996

How to pick a mutual fund

You've decided to jump on the mutual fund bandwagon. Pooling your money with other investors and letting a fund manager decide what stocks or bonds or other investments to buy sounds like a good idea to you. But how do you start?

The first part is easy: Decide you don't want to pay any sales charges or any commissions to brokers. Mutual funds that don't have a sales charge are called *no-load funds*, and, in the past, these funds have performed just as well as the more expensive funds.

At your library or bookstore, find the most recent copy of the *Handbook for No-Load Fund Investors*. You can use this book and some other publications at your library (*Morningstar Mutual Funds* and *Value Line Mutual Fund Survey*, for instance) to pick out a list of mutual funds you may be interested in.

Next, call the mutual funds using their toll-free numbers, and ask for a *prospectus* (a document that provides detailed info about a particular mutual fund or stock). Once your prospectuses start coming in, here's what you do:

Compare kinds of funds. You have three basic choices. A *money market fund* is very low risk. It makes high quality, short term investments. A *bond fund* (or *fixed income fund*) has higher risks but tends to pay a higher yield. A *stock fund* is the riskiest type, but it will usually make more money for you over the long term.

Compare performance. Beware of dazzling performance claims! Past performance and last year's yields aren't as important as you might think. Last year's top performer could be below average next year.

Instead, check the fund's *total return*. You will find this in the *financial highlights* section of the prospectus. Total return measures per-share increases and decreases in the value of your investment over time.

The financial highlights section will show you the yearly total return for the last 10 years. Look at each year, and look at the change in the total return from year to year. That will tell you how stable the fund's returns have been.

The fund will also show you the average total return for the entire 10 years. Many people only look at that number, and that's a mistake. An impressive 10-year return could be based on one outstanding year and nine so-so years.

Compare costs. Even no-load funds have some expenses, and you want to pay as little of these as possible. Expenses reduce your profits. Look out for these sneaky fees in the *fee table* in the prospectus:

Back-end loads (or *deferred loads* or *contingent deferred sales fees*). These are sales charges you pay when you sell your mutual fund shares. Most back-end loads start out at 5 or 6 percent of your shares' value, and get smaller each year you stay invested in the mutual fund. If you stay in the fund for six or seven years, you may not pay any back-end load.

12b-1 fees. No-load funds use this fee to pay for advertising and marketing. It usually runs from 0.25 percent to 1.25 percent. Since you pay this fee every year, it gets more important the longer you plan to stay in a fund. (If you plan to stay in a mutual fund for seven or more years, and you can't find a no-load fund with low 12b-1 fees, consider shopping for a fund with an upfront sales load. They usually have low 12b-1 fees.)

Reinvestment loads. These fees are taken out of the interest, dividends, and capital gains you chose to reinvest in your account.

Management fees. These fees pay the portfolio manager. They usually range from 0.5 percent to 1 percent of the fund's assets.

Exchange fees. Many mutual funds will let you exchange your shares for shares of another fund managed by the same person. Some funds will charge you for this service with an exchange fee.

Waived fees. The fee table may say that some of the fund's fees or expenses have been waived. That means your expenses may suddenly increase when the waiver ends. Keep reading in your prospectus to find out how much your expenses will increase.

Buying shares in a mutual fund isn't risk-free. But it can be safer than experimenting in the stock market. Professional money managers are handling your money. They are putting your money in a variety of investments, so your risk is spread out. And they are doing so much buying and selling at once, they usually pay lower costs than you would on your own.

Plus, mutual funds are easy to buy and sell. Just do a little homework, and you could be on your way to making your money work for you.

Source:
Invest Wisely: An Introduction to Mutual Funds, U.S. Securities and Exchange Commission, October 1994

Find your mutual fund style

What kind of mutual fund is right for you? It largely depends on how close you are to retirement, whether you want a steady income from your investment, and how much risk you can handle. Here's a chart of the major fund types so you can find those that match your own investment style and risk tolerance.

Source:
Standard & Poor's How to Invest: A Guide to Buying Stocks, Bonds, and Mutual Funds, The McGraw-Hill Companies, New York, 1996

How to track your mutual fund investment

When you send a check to a mutual fund company, you buy a certain number of *shares* in the fund. The fund will send you a confirmation letter telling you how many shares you own.

You can find out the value of your shares every day or every week by looking in the financial pages of a major newspaper.

Find your fund's name, then go to the column marked "NAV." The *Net Asset Value* is the value of one share in a fund. To find out what your investment is worth, multiply the NAV by the number of shares you own.

(Remember, if you've been reinvesting the dividends, interest, or capital gains you earn, you may own more shares than you think you do. You'll get reports from the fund at least twice a year, but you can call at any time and find out how many you own.)

Source:
Invest Wisely: An Introduction to Mutual Funds, U.S. Securities and Exchange Commission, October 1994

Index funds: staying in step with the market

You don't have to be fancy to win in the stock market. Index funds prove that. These mutual funds have a simple investment philosophy — they own (theoretically) all of the stocks followed in an index, such as Standard &

Fund Type	Capital Gains Potential	Income Potential	Total Return Potential	Risk Level
Stock Funds				
Aggressive growth	Very high	Low	Very high	Very high
Growth	High	Low	High	High
Income	Low	High	Moderate	Moderate
Growth/income	Moderate	Moderate	Moderate	Moderate
Industry specific	Varies	Varies	Varies	Varies
Precious metals	High	Low	Varies	High
Global	High	Moderate	High	High
International	Very high	Low	High	High
Fixed-income Funds				
High-grade corporate	Low	High	Moderate	Low
High-yield corporate	Very high	High	High	Very high
U.S. government	Low	Moderate	Moderate	Low
Municipal bonds*	Low	Moderate	Low	Low
Money market	Very low	Low	Low	Very low

* Income potential and attractiveness of municipal bonds partly depends on an investor's tax situation.

Poor's 500 index. Index funds don't try to beat the market average, just stay even with it, but that's all they have to do to beat the performance of most mutual funds. Index funds are perfect for investment beginners and people who lack the time or interest to play the stock market.

Institutional investors, such as pension funds, have long poured billions of dollars into low-cost index funds. Individual investors were first able to buy these funds in 1976 when the Vanguard Index 500 was set up. This fund duplicates stocks that make up Standard & Poor's 500 index. Index mutual funds can also be based on other indexes, such as:

Wilshire 5,000 — an index of the total stock market.

Standard & Poor's Mid Cap 400 — an index of middle capitalized stocks (midsize companies).

Russell 2,000 — an index of small capitalized stocks (small companies).

Good index funds perform about as well as the market average, of course. Most mutual funds don't. Over the last 10 years, for example, only one of four mutual funds achieved higher returns than the S&P 500 index. Most mutual fund managers fail to beat the market because trading fees, administration expenses, and other costs eat into their returns.

The advantages of index mutual funds include:

Minimal trading. Transaction costs tend to be low because stocks making up the index rarely change.

No portfolio managers. And that means no management fees.

Diversity. Investments that mimic a broad-based index are quite diversified.

If monitoring stocks is not for you, some experts suggest that you set up an all-stock mutual fund portfolio. Put 50 percent of your money into an S&P 500 index fund, 25 percent in a small cap index fund, and 25 percent in an international equity index fund.

As with any investment, you need to monitor your fund choices. At least once a year, review your fund portfolio to decide whether the reasons for choosing a fund continue to exist. If not, you might be better off getting out of that fund. Use this approach and you can be less concerned with day-to-day stock price fluctuations.

Sources:
A Commonsense Guide to Mutual Funds by Mary Rowland, Bloomberg Press, Princeton, N.J., 1996
Standard & Poor's How to Invest: A Guide to Buying Stocks, Bonds, and Mutual Funds, The McGraw-Hill Companies, New York, 1996

When never to buy a closed-end fund

Closed-end funds are usually poor performers. Avoid them.

When people talk about mutual funds, they're typically referring to open-end funds. Open-end funds trade every business day, constantly issuing new shares at or near *net asset value* and redeeming shares at net asset value.

The fund's net asset value is calculated by dividing the current value of the fund's investments by the number of shares investors own. You can find that figure in most newspapers.

Closed-end funds issue a fixed number of shares that are publicly traded like stocks on stock exchanges, usually on the New York Stock Exchange. The shares don't necessarily trade at their net asset value. Instead, since there's a fixed number of shares, the trading price can be affected by supply and demand as well as by perception of the fund's prospects.

Never, ever buy into a closed-end fund when it first comes on the market. You'll be paying a premium for the shares you buy. Later, the price will drop, and you can buy the shares at a discount. For instance, a closed-end fund can trade at a 5 percent discount — that means you can buy a dollar's worth of assets for 95 cents.

Only consider a closed-end fund when you can buy one with very low expenses at a hefty discount. In fact, the discount should be at least 10 times expenses.

Sources:
A Commonsense Guide to Mutual Funds by Mary Rowland, Bloomberg Press, Princeton, N.J., 1996
Standard & Poor's How to Invest: A Guide to Buying Stocks, Bonds, and Mutual Funds, The McGraw-Hill Companies, New York, 1996

Avoid funds with high turnover

Before parking your money in a mutual fund, check out the investment style of the fund managers. Some buy and sell investments frequently, trading every security once and sometimes twice a year. Other managers spend a lot of time visiting companies, talking to management, and evaluating their systems before buying 20 or 30 of the best companies they can find. Then, these managers hold on to the stocks for a while.

Funds with high portfolio turnovers yield lower returns. Every time a security is sold at a profit, you wind up paying capital gain tax as well as transaction charges. And, if the manager trades every stock in the fund every year, at least some gains will be short-term and therefore taxed at a higher rate.

Over a long period of time, such as 20 years, the loss of income caused by high turnover can be significant. You'll find the turnover rate in the fund's prospectus.

Source:
A Commonsense Guide to Mutual Funds by Mary Rowland, Bloomberg Press, Princeton, N.J., 1996

Avoiding money-robbing bond fund traps

Before you put your money in a bond fund, examine its holdings carefully. Check the fund's most recent annual or quarterly report or speak to a fund agent to learn if the fund contains any of these potential bond fund traps:

Derivative trap. Remember when Orange County, Calif., made headlines by losing millions because it was heavily invested in *derivatives*? Derivatives are basically a bet on the direction of interest rates. Many bond funds invest in derivatives as a hedge against share price fluctuations. That's fine if the derivatives work. While you can make a lot of money with derivatives, you can also lose your shirt. Avoid bond funds heavily invested in derivatives unless they are used to protect the U.S. dollar against bonds in foreign currencies.

Principal payout trap. Some bond funds use a part of your principal for your income payout when the fund generates less income. Say you put $100,000 in a bond fund that pays out 7 percent. You choose to receive $1,800 each quarter. Market conditions change and the fund is unable to generate sufficient interest. Most funds will decrease your periodic payout. Some funds, though, continue to pay you $1,800, withdrawing the difference from your principal. Avoid this problem by asking before you invest in any fund if your monthly payout would ever be taken from your principal.

High expenses trap. Stick with funds that have low expenses. Look for a fund with an expense ratio of less than 0.5 percent.

Also consider: You need to check the *average maturity date* of any bond fund you buy. To get higher returns, buy funds holding long-term bonds when interest rates are falling. If interest rates are rising, buy short-term bonds.

If you want to sell a bond fund before it matures, check interest rates first. If interest rates have risen since you bought the bond, its market price will probably be less than you paid.

If your bond fund holds foreign bonds, you also need to check the strength of the U.S. dollar before you sell. If your bond fund holds German bonds, for example, it will be worth more when the U.S. dollar drops against the German mark. Conversely, if the U.S. dollar rises against the German mark, the fund's value will be less.

Source:
Interview with Kenny Brandt, CFP, executive vice-president, WSB Advisors in Birmingham, Mich.

Cashing in old savings bonds

A $50 U.S. Series EE savings bond is a great high-school graduation present. It only costs half the face value — $25 — and you can redeem it any time, from six months to 30 years later. You pay taxes on the interest earned only when you redeem the bond.

Plus, if interest rates rise in the future, the yield your bond earns will also rise. That's because instead of having a fixed interest rate, U.S. savings bonds yield a rate equal to 85 percent of the 5-year Treasury rate over the time you own them.

In fact, the bonds make such good gifts, you probably have one or two stuffed in the bottom of a drawer or safe deposit box. And you could be one of the 7 million people who own bonds that have stopped earning interest. If so, it's time to cash in.

First, you'll need to find out the value of your old bond. That's easy. A teller at most any bank will have Treasury Department tables of savings bond redemption values.

Next, you need to find out what interest rate, if any, your bond is paying now. Bonds pay a guaranteed minimum interest rate until they mature, and Series EE savings bonds mature in 30 years.

You can get a chart showing the guaranteed interest rate that applies to your bond by writing to the Office of Public Affairs, U.S. Savings Bonds Division, Department of the Treasury, Washington, DC 20226. You can also try calling the Savings Bond Operations Office in Parkersburg, W.V., at (304) 480-6112, to talk to a live person. (The Treasury Department has a toll-free number, but the recorded message you get probably won't be helpful.)

You are going to have to pay taxes on your earnings when you cash your old bond in, but even so, you'll probably be better off putting your money somewhere that yields more interest.

Sources:
Everyone's Money Book by Jordan E. Goodman and Sonny Bloch, Dearborn Financial Publishing, Chicago, 1994
Money (25,4:53)
Q&A: The Savings Bonds Question & Answer Book, Department of the Treasury, U.S. Savings Bonds Division, Washington, D.C. 20226, 1994

The basic math you need to figure your investments' performance

Do you know what kind of return you made on your investments last year? You can't assume you made the returns published in the newspaper. You can go by the published returns only *if:*

1) You bought (or held over) all your shares at the start of a year, and
2) You reinvested all dividends and income, and
3) You never bought or sold shares in any other way throughout the year.

If you don't meet these criteria, then all you need is the year-end summary account statement from your brokerage firm or mutual-fund company and about 15 minutes for some basic math. (This method won't give you an exact answer, but it tells you what you need to know.)

A. On your year-end account statement, find the amount you added to or removed from your account during the year. Add up the money you put in, and subtract the money you took out. Remember to subtract any checks you received for dividends or interest. Divide this number by 2.
B. Add this new result to the beginning value of your account and subtract it from your year-end value.
C. Divide the new adjusted year-end value by the new adjusted beginning value.
D. To turn the number into a percentage, subtract 1 and multiply by 100.

Did you make more than you thought you did? Use this math once a year so you'll know how you're doing. You may need to fine-tune your investments. And, you won't be embarrassed when someone asks how your portfolio is performing.

Source:
The Wall Street Journal (Feb. 2, 1996, C1)

Are you tough enough?

How much risk can you stomach? Are you an aggressive investor who can handle short-term price swings for long-term potential gains, or would you rather forgo that potential in favor of a safe haven for your money?

Take this test provided by The Vanguard Group of Investment Companies to find out where you stand.

A. I have been investing in stock or bond mutual funds or in individual stocks or bonds for _____.
1. Less than one year.
2. One to two years.
3. Three to four years.
4. Five to nine years.
5. 10 years or more.

B. When it comes to investing in stocks, bonds, or mutual funds, I would describe myself as a/an _____.
1. Very inexperienced investor.
2. Somewhat inexperienced investor.
3. Somewhat experienced investor.
4. Experienced investor.
5. Very experienced investor.

C. I am comfortable with investments that may lose money from time to time — if they offer the potential for higher returns.
1. I strongly disagree.
2. I disagree.
3. I somewhat agree.
4. I agree.
5. I strongly agree.

D. I will still keep an investment even if it loses 10 percent of its value over the course of a year.
1. I strongly disagree.
2. I disagree.
3. I somewhat agree.
4. I agree.
5. I strongly agree.

E. In addition to my long-term savings program, I have an emergency savings fund equal to _____ months of my take-home pay.
1. Zero.
2. One.
3. Two.
4. Three.
5. Four or more.

F. I find it easy to pay my monthly bills from my current pay.
1. I strongly disagree.
2. I disagree.
3. I somewhat agree.
4. I agree.
5. I strongly agree.

G. Overall, my personal financial situation (that is, my job outlook and my ability to pay bills) is secure.
1. I strongly disagree.
2. I disagree.
3. I somewhat agree.
4. I agree.
5. I strongly agree.

Adding it up

The number of your answer is the number of points you get. If you picked Number 4 as your answer to a question, you get four points for that question.

Subtract five points from your total score if you answered Number 1 or Number 2 to Question C.

If you scored between	You are considered
0 and 26 points	Conservative
27 and 32 points	Moderate
33 and 35 points	Aggressive

Most people are too conservative. You don't want to take so much risk that you lie awake at night worrying. But unfortunately, many people are in investments so safe that inflation is growing faster than their money is. Even if your test scored "conservative," make sure a good percentage of your money is in individual stocks or stock mutual funds.
Source:
Moneywhys, Vanguard Marketing Corporation (Autumn 1995)

Investment clubs boost bottom line

Two heads are better than one. Ten or 20 brains are even better.

When it comes to putting your hard-earned cash into the market, investing as a group eases the ordeal of making some mighty hard decisions. And, when you join an investment club, you reap the benefits of other members' time and efforts. Instead of spending 15 to 20 hours a month studying stocks on your own, you divvy up this time-consuming task into monthly two- to three-hour segments.

That's not all. Just look at the now famous Beardstown Ladies, the group of farmer's wives, schoolteachers, and retired secretaries from Illinois. Here are 16 women whose 12-year-old investment club has enjoyed an annual return of 23.4 percent, beating professional money managers three to one.

Applying their "learn and earn" philosophy, your club's annual return can approach or exceed the 15 percent compounded annual rate of return earned by many clubs associated with the National Association of Investors Corporation (NAIC).

Investment club members combine their money, experience, and expertise to make good investment decisions. A nurse, for example, knows about health care and drug companies; a mechanic about cars and tool firms; a computer salesperson about high tech companies.

You learn how to pick stocks for your own portfolio as well. The same strategies used to evaluate a stock for your club can be applied to choosing your own investments.

How to get started. Few investment clubs invite new members to join because their existing members make long-term commitments. But don't let that stop you. You can start an investment club with as few as two people.

NAIC has a packet of information that explains how to organize a club. To get started, you first need to:

Talk to a few friends, family members, co-workers, or neighbors to assess their interest. If they want to form a club, ask them to talk to a few of their friends. Since this is a long-term venture, people should enjoy each other's company.

Invite everyone who is interested to a meeting in your home in about two to three weeks. Discuss your individual investment philosophies at this meeting to avoid disagreements in the future. Talk about your responsibilities to the club. Everyone should be willing to investigate and analyze stocks and make periodic reports. NAIC publishes manuals, forms, software, and videos and offers workshops that teach you how to do this.

Decide how much each member will contribute every month. Most clubs start with members investing $20 or $25 monthly. Some start with as little as $10 per month.

Elect officers, and decide on a club name.

Ask prospective members to recommend a stockbroker. Ideally, the broker should specialize in investment clubs, but that's not necessary to the success of your club.

Boosting your bottom line isn't the only investment club advantage. Socializing is involved, too. Meeting monthly, you establish friendships that can last a lifetime. Clubs gather in members' homes or in space provided by libraries and businesses. And, most clubs enjoy an annual meeting at a restaurant. Who would have thought that serious money decisions could be fun!

Source:
Interview with Barry Murphy, director of marketing, National Association of Investors Corporation (NAIC), Madison Heights, Mich.

Steer clear of investment scams

Con artists bilk people out of billions of dollars each year. The call, the letter, and nowadays, the e-mail message are used by "scammers" to rip you off.

No matter if it's stocks, real estate, commodities, or any other "sure thing," con artists generally use these similar tactics:

Guarantees. "You can't lose; it's money in the bank." Promises of big returns and fast payoffs should raise a red flag. Be leery, for example, if offered a risk-free investment paying 10 percent to 15 percent when certificates of deposit or treasury bills are only paying 5 percent. It's not even worth checking out this teaser.

Pressure. Never buy an investment on the spot, even if a friend or relative recommends it. Instead, ask for written information. That gives you time to do your research. And to cool off over the hot tip. Oftentimes, when asked for info, the swindler never sends it. If the call is from a credible and conscientious broker, you'll hear from him again.

The unfamiliar. Be very skeptical of someone pushing penny-ante stocks or stock in small, obscure, remote companies. If there are no analyst reports, company prospectuses, or company profiles from reputable rating services that can verify the stock promoter's claims, forget buying the touted investment.

Source:
Interview with Kenny Brandt, CFP, executive vice-president, WSB Advisors, Birmingham, Mich.

RETIRING RIGHT

Social Security savvy

When it comes to drawing Social Security benefits, married women who've worked outside the home have a choice. They can draw their own benefits, or they can draw 50 percent of the amount their husband draws.

At first, the choice seems clear. If your husband earned a good deal more than you, you probably believe you'll be better off drawing half your husband's Social Security benefits than you would the full amount of your own.

Actually, the answer is not that simple. As contradictory as it may sound, you'll probably be better off drawing your own.

Here's why: Social Security provides proportionally more benefits to lower paid workers, often women and minorities, than to higher paid workers. If you made $10,000 a year, you'd draw up to 70 percent of your income. If you made $50,000 or more a year, you'd probably receive less than 25 percent of your income.

If your husband made $50,000 a year and you made $23,000, you'll still be better off drawing off your own account because when it comes to Social Security lower pay equals more benefits.

Source:
Money and the Mature Woman: How to Hold On to Your Income, Keep Your Home, Plan Your Estate by Frances Leonard, Addison-Wesley, Publishing, Reading, Mass., 1993

Getting the facts on your Social Security account

Money has been paid regularly into your Social Security account throughout your entire working life. You've had the same Social Security number for over 40 years. And your Social Security account is in the hands of the U.S. government.

So, what could go wrong?

Unfortunately, plenty.

"Mistakes do happen with Social Security accounts," notes corporate attorney and employment law specialist James Zito. "Sometimes employers claim they are making payments but they've actually failed to, or they've made a mistake and not paid the money into the right account. Also, it's possible someone could have used your Social Security number — accidentally or fraudulently — and affected the balance in your account."

Don't wait until you need the money to check up on your Social Security account.

"Imagine getting set to retire, or becoming disabled, and desperately needing those monthly Social Security checks to start coming. Instead, you are faced with trying to straighten out your Social Security records," states attorney James Zito.

"To avoid that hassle, it's a good idea to periodically check your Social Security account and make sure the appropriate amount of tax dollars for the wages you've earned has been paid in and accurately recorded."

How do you get that information?

Simply call the Social Security Administration's toll-free number, 1-800-772-1213, and request a "Personal Earnings and Benefits Estimate Statement."

Source:
Interview with James V. Zito, attorney-at-law, Lipshutz, Greenblatt, and King, Atlanta

Social Security scams

Some scoundrels will even attempt to pull the wool over unwary eyes with a Social Security scam. Here are two to beware of.

Trash any mail you receive from The Social Security Protection Bureau. The Senate Select Committee on Aging itself has accused this phony group of fraud. For $7, the official-sounding organization will send you a gold-embossed Social Security card and a copy of your Social Security earnings record, plus providing you with representation in Washington, D.C.

The Social Security earnings record they send you (if you sign up) is nothing more than the government's own form, which you fill out, and they then mail to the Social Security Administration to request your record. You can request this record yourself for free by contacting the Social Security office at 1-800-772-1213. By requesting your own record, you won't have to worry about anyone else, especially a scam artist, having access to your private information.

In addition, the so-called benefits of your Washington representation are very unclear, says Senator David Pryer who is chairman of the Senate Committee on Aging. Beware of any similar mailings you receive from American Seniors, Inc.

Don't let anybody in who comes to your door and claims to be a Social Security agent. Recently, thieves have taken to passing themselves off as Social Security agents to gain access to senior citizens' homes. Once inside, they'll request access to checkbooks, steal checks, and ask that the victims sign certain forms. Later, they'll copy or forge signatures from these forms onto the stolen checks.

Save yourself the trouble. Never, ever let someone in you don't know. Be very careful about letting people in you know only casually.

Source:
How to Have a Great Retirement on a Limited Budget by Diane Warner, Writer's Digest Books, Cincinnati, 1992

Most common tax mistakes retirees make

Sometimes retirees find themselves in a bit of a capital crunch because they overestimated their nest egg or because they underestimated expenses. If you're in this situation, you certainly don't want to add to your woes by paying unnecessary taxes.

Even if your finances are fine, you don't want to waste any more of your hard-earned money on taxes than you have to. Here's what you need to know to avoid padding the pockets of the IRS unnecessarily:

▶ Remember to take advantage of the additional exemption available to you if you're 65 years or older.

▶ Don't think you have to report all Social Security benefits as income. Actually, only a portion of Social Security is taxable.

▶ Keep accurate records of your medical and dental expenses so you won't miss out on these deductions. Orthopedic shoes and hearing aids, as well as the batteries required to run the hearing aid, are also deductible. Wigs are deductible if they are essential to mental health.

In addition, if you drive yourself to the doctor, you can deduct your travel expenses, including parking and tollbooth fees. You can deduct nine cents per mile for mileage.

▶ Forget about listing interest income from municipal bonds. You don't have to because municipal bonds are tax exempt.

▶ Save yourself some cash by deducting a *capital loss* on stocks you own that lost money.

▶ Claim all the deductions you can if you run a small, home-based business. These include mileage or auto expenses, postage, a percentage of health insurance premiums and home costs (insurance, mortgage interest, taxes, utilities, etc.), and office equipment depreciation.

▶ Don't forget to deduct the cost of losses from accident, fire, or theft. You can also deduct the cost of any appraisal you had to have done to estimate your losses.

▶ Cash in on that one-time exemption of up to $125,000 of the profit made on a house sale. You have to be 55 years or older to take advantage of this deduction.

▶ Remember to deduct any penalties you had to pay for early withdrawal from a time savings account.

▶ Remind yourself to report all charitable contributions, including both cash and noncash contributions, such as clothing or other merchandise, on your tax return. You can also claim expenses you incur while working for a charity, such as uniforms, supplies, or your transportation costs to and from the organization. Just be sure to keep an accurate record of your bus fares or gas mileage. You can deduct 12 cents per mile for mileage costs.

▶ Don't forget to deduct the cost of investment or tax advice, which can include accountant or attorney fees, tax guides, and computer programs.

▶ Remember to deduct the fee for your safety deposit box if you use it to store investment documents.

Sources:
How to Have a Great Retirement on a Limited Budget by Diane Warner, Writer's Digest Books, Cincinnati, 1992
Retiring Right: Planning for Your Successful Retirement by Lawrence J. Kaplan, Avery Publishing Group, Garden City Park, N.Y., 1990
Taxes for Dummies, 1996 Edition by Eric Tyson, MBA, and David J. Silverman, EA, IDG Books Worldwide, Foster City, Calif., 1996
The Ernst & Young Tax Guide 1995, John Wiley & Sons, New York, 1994

The 9 most common retirement planning mistakes

1. Trust the government to take care of things. You overestimate how much money you'll receive from Social Security or your pension plan. According to the U.S. Department of Treasury, Social Security and pensions account for only 35 percent of the average retired person's income.

2. Put off planning. You wait until age 45 or after before you start planning.

3. Plan to keep working. You think you'll be able to work until the bitter end. Statistics show that very few people work beyond the age of 65.

4. Count on pulling your retirement nest eggs out of one basket. Too many people count on a single source of income, such as an expected inheritance, home equity, sale of a business, etc., as their retirement security. If this is your plan, you run the risk of finding out at the last minute that your nest egg wasn't as much as you expected it would be. To protect yourself, never count solely on one source for your retirement income.

5. Expect you'll have more money because taxes will magically disappear. Unfortunately, taxes do not always retire when you do. You may actually see a greater percentage of your income go toward taxes than when you were working. You can protect yourself with a portfolio that stresses investments that can withstand both taxes and inflation.

6. Too impatient with money growth. You don't give your investments and savings time to grow. Instead, you constantly move your money around, seeking higher returns and exposing yourself to greater loss.

   It may help to remember the Rule of 72, which will help you calculate exactly when your investment will double. Divide the interest rate of your savings or investment account into 72. The number you get will tell you how many years it will take for your money to double.

7. Neglect important personal decisions. You don't take time to consider questions such as what you'll do and where and with whom you'll live. If you want your retirement to be enjoyable, you need to have some purpose — something to look forward to.

8. Assume living expenses will drop. Like the old song said, "it ain't necessarily so." Depending on the retirement lifestyle you choose, you could have as many expenses as when you were working. You should assume that you will need at least 80 percent of your pre-retirement income if you plan on living like you did before you retired.

9. Think it will be just the two of you during those happy golden years. Lately, your chances of this have been quite slim. Since 1975, the number of adult children living with their parents has doubled. If it's not children, it's likely to be grandchildren. About 5.2 million children in the U.S. are being raised by grandparents.

Sources:
Feathering Your Nest by Lisa Berger, Workman Publishing, New York, 1993
Retirement Ready or Not: How to Get Financially Prepared in a Hurry by Lee Rosenberg, CFP, Career Press, Hawthorne, N.J., 1993

How to retire on someone else's money

Getting retirement money from your employer and keeping it from the government is not only legal, it's as easy as 1 ... 2 ... 3 ... 401k.

Here's how to take advantage of that miraculous savings plan known as the 401k and how to avoid the most common mistakes people make, according to one 401k plan manager:

First of all, join up early. Most people don't start thinking seriously about their 401k until they reach age 40 or so. Remember the advantage of compounded interest over a long period of time.

If you don't join up and your employer has a matching contribution, you're just allowing your employer not to pay you one of your benefits. When you join, max out what your employer will match.

Don't try to get out of your plan once you've joined. Once you join a plan, do not look at that money as money you are going to be able to use any time soon. People constantly ask their plan managers, "How can I get money out of my 401k to pay bills?" That's a big mistake.

When you take money out of a 401k plan, the only portion you're going to be able to get is the portion you've put in, and you're going to see at least 40 percent of that disappear.

First of all, you pay a penalty of 10 percent for withdrawing your money early. Then, you pay taxes. (No matter when you take your money out you will pay taxes. However, during your retirement years you'll be in a lower income bracket, so you'll pay a lot less.)

Keep contributing with every paycheck. Once you begin to participate in a plan, try to keep your standard of living to the point where you can afford to contribute with every paycheck. Most plans require that once you drop out, you have to stay out a year before you can rejoin.

Never take a payout when you switch jobs. When you switch jobs, you need to evaluate your new employer's plan to see if it will allow a 401k rollover. If it does, then it's as simple as requesting your former employer to roll over the funds into your new employer's plan.

You do not want to request that the distribution be mailed to you directly. The government will withhold 20 percent of whatever money you try to put your hands on. (The government's reasoning is that if you decide to spend your 401k money, you'll have to pay taxes on it next April. They figure they might as well go ahead and take some of that tax money now.)

If your new employer does not have a 401k plan or does not allow rollovers, then the best thing to do is to go to another financial institution, maybe a money market fund or a mutual fund, establish an IRA, and have the funds roll over into that IRA. Again, the checks from your previous employer should be mailed directly to the IRA rather than being taken by you.

Take some investment risk when you're young. Most 401k plans give you at least three investment choices. The Department of Labor requires that your employer educate you about your choices. Usually, there is one very risk-free choice (a money market fund or a low risk government security), a choice with moderate risk (bonds, stocks, and some money market funds), and a choice with high risk (all stock market investments).

The younger you are, the more risk you are able to take. A younger employee will want to be invested more heavily in the stocks. As you grow older, you can switch into the safer investments.

Most plans will allow you to switch once a year. Some plans are now allowing almost daily switching. Employees can call up an 800 number to find out what their balance is and to make switches between the investment choices.

Don't let life insurance salesmen convince you to buy life insurance before you are able to maximize the potential of your 401k plan. A 401k is the best way to save for retirement. Don't overlook insurance altogether, but look for term insurance that's available on a yearly basis. You may consider switching to whole life when you're close to retirement age.
Source:
Interview with Tim Anders, CPA and comptroller of direct mail firm, Peachtree City, Ga.

2 things you may not know about your 401k

1. You've always heard that you don't pay taxes on 401k contributions, but you actually do pay Social Security taxes at the point your contribution is withheld from your paycheck.

2. Does your employer match the money you contribute to your 401k? You may be misled if you think the company is matching your money immediately. Most employers do it based on their cash flow situation. The employer is only required to make the match by the time the tax return is filed for the plan. You are not necessarily earning interest on that money throughout the year.
Source:
Interview with Tim Anders, CPA and comptroller of direct mail firm, Peachtree City, Ga.

Diversifying your 401k plan

You'll come out ahead if you spread around the assets in your 401k plan. What happens when you don't diversify?

Take a conservative approach, putting all your money in bonds, and you'll miss out on soaring bull markets. Long term bonds have returned an average of 5.7 percent a year since 1926. Large company stocks have averaged 10.5 percent, and small company stocks have averaged 12.5 percent.

Take an aggressive approach, putting all your money in small company stocks or stock funds, and what happens during a sinking bear market? If you're human, you'll likely panic, sell those stocks, and take a loss.

Instead, cut your risk by diversifying, say the experts. Put your 401k assets in a mixture of cash investments, bond funds, and stock funds. If you're just starting to invest in the stock market, consider an index stock fund. An index fund tries to match the performance of an index, such as the Standard & Poor's 500 stock index. The S&P 500 index is a popular measurement of the stock market's performance based on prices of 500 common stocks.

So how should you allocate your 401k assets? If you're over 50, 20 to 40 percent should be in bonds or bond funds and in cash. Put the rest in stocks or stock funds. However, no more than 25 percent of these assets should be in your own company's stock.
Source:
U.S. News & World Report (10,23:80)

Retirement plan for the self-employed

When you work for yourself, you've got to fund your own retirement. Astute business owners can establish a qualified retirement plan called a Simplified Employee Pension (SEP) plan. The advantages:

Minimal paperwork. SEP plans are easy to set up. Simply call your financial planner, mutual fund manager, or stockbroker, and ask for the appropriate form. Fill out the form, select your investment, send in the money, and you've set up your SEP plan.

Tax-deferred contributions. If you are a sole proprietor, each year you can put up to 13.0435 percent of your net business income into your SEP. You don't have to pay taxes on that amount. You are not limited to the $2,000 per year contribution of an IRA.

Choice of investments. You can invest the money in your SEP anyway you choose. You are only limited by who holds your plan. For instance, if you establish an SEP plan with a broker, you can invest in stocks, bonds, or mutual funds. Set up a plan with a mutual fund manager and you can only invest in mutual funds.

Flexible contributions. The SEP contribution rule is flexible. You decide each year if you're going to contribute to your SEP account. Let's say you open an SEP account this year. Business is good, and you put in $8,000. Next year your income drops or your expenses rise, so you only contribute $1,500. Most other retirement plans don't offer this flexibility.

Flexible setup date. Unlike many other retirement plans, you do not have to establish an SEP by December 31 to take it off your taxes. Instead, you can set up and fund an SEP plan up to the date you submit your tax return or file an extension.

Marital benefit. If your spouse contributes to a 401k plan at work, you wouldn't be able to fully deduct an IRA for yourself. However, you can contribute tax-deferred money up to the legal maximum to an SEP.

Unlike some of the other retirement plans, you can't borrow from your SEP plan. Any money withdrawn prior to age 59 1/2 is subject to income taxes and a 10 percent penalty.

Source:
Interview with Dorothy E. Bossung, certified financial planner, president, Bossung Investments & Financial Planning, Bloomfield Hills, Mich.

Is an annuity right for you?

Centuries ago, when a man wanted his family to be financially secure after he retired or died, he deposited grain at the local granary. When he stopped working, the granary provided grain for him and his family for the rest of their lives. Those were the annuities of old.

Today, when you buy an annuity, you're buying a life insurance policy that pays you while you're still alive. Since annuities are underwritten by insurance companies, and insurance investments are protected from taxes, your money grows tax-free until you withdraw it. When you withdraw your money, it is taxed as ordinary income. Many annuities also provide a small death benefit for your beneficiaries. What's more, unlike other retirement plans, there's no limit on how much you can invest in an annuity.

Think an annuity is a good place to park your money for several years? You could be right if:

You won't need the money in the next 10 to 15 years. Annuities are for income after you retire. If you want the money to buy a dream cottage or finance your daughter's education, then certificates of deposit, mutual funds, or the stock market are better investments.

The IRS imposes a 10 percent penalty if you try to withdraw funds from your annuity before you reach age 59 1/2. And that's not all — remove your money too soon and you may also face *surrender fees* charged by the annuity company.

You need the tax deferment. If you are in the 28 percent or above tax bracket, sheltering some money from taxes in annuities could be appealing.

You expect to live a long time. Most annuities, like Ma Bell of old, provide a lifetime supply of income. The longer you live, the better deal they are.

You can buy annuities through insurance companies, certified financial planners, some stockbrokers, and even banks that handle insurance. But before you invest your hard-earned cash, do your research first.

Buy only from insurance companies rated A+ or better by *Best's Insurance Reports*, or those rated AA by either Standard & Poor's or Moody's Investor Service.

Call the state office that regulates insurance to find out if the company is licensed to sell annuities in your state.

Shop around for interest rates and payout schedules. Look at interest rates carefully, and remember the "if something looks too good to be true ..." rule. Insurance companies like to entice you with unusually high rates, then slash the rates later on.

Ask about commissions, back-load charges, and management fees. Let your agent know you are shopping around for the best terms.

Source:
Interview with Pamela J. Sarney, certified financial planner, Network Financial Management, Farmington Hills, Mich.

Insiders guide to annuity lingo

Thinking about buying an annuity? Now's the perfect time to bone up on these important terms:

Variable annuity — An annuity that works like a mutual fund. You buy a certain number of *accumulation units* just like you'd buy shares in a mutual fund. The insurance company invests your money in stocks, bonds, and other securities, and the size of the annuity payout depends upon the success of the investments. You do not receive a guaranteed rate of return but you are likely to receive higher payouts than with a fixed-dollar annuity.

Fixed-dollar annuity — An annuity that pays a set amount of interest, like a certificate of deposit. Your annuity payout will be the same every month. Each year, the rate of return is readjusted according to market rates.

Deferred annuity — An annuity you buy long before you need the income. Payouts are delayed until you need and request them.

Immediate annuity — An annuity you buy when you want to receive payouts within a year.

Single premium annuity —An annuity you buy all at once, with one lump sum of money.

Installment premium annuity — An annuity you buy over time by paying a premium at regular intervals.

Flexible premium annuity — Similar to an installment premium annuity except that each year, you can change the amount of your premium payment.

Issue date — The date your annuity becomes effective, usually when you pay the first premium.

Annuitization date — The date your annuity payout begins.

Mortality/expense fees — The yearly fees, usually 1.3 percent of the annuity's value, charged by many companies to manage your annuity. These fees also guarantee that your beneficiary receives all the money you invested should you die before the annuity is paid out.

Surrender fees — The penalty you may pay if you withdraw your money before a specified time.

Sources:
Interview with Pamela J. Sarney, certified financial planner, Network Financial Management, Farmington Hills, Mich.
The Best of America: Individual Deferred Variable Annuity Contracts Prospectus, Nationwide Life Insurance Company (May 1995)
Worth Magazine (July/August 1996)

The best annuity for you

Variable annuities are a little riskier than fixed annuities, but they give you a chance to keep up with inflation. The money you get from a fixed annuity is a sure thing, but a $750 check will likely be worth a lot less 20 years from now.

A variable annuity lets you put your money into a variety of investments that can grow, usually stock, bond, and money market mutual funds. These investments are called *subaccounts*, and many of them are run by mutual fund companies such as Fidelity, Dreyfus, and Janus.

You want to own several subaccounts so you can spread your risk around. If you have $50,000 to invest, you could split it into an international stock fund, a stock index fund, a bond fund, and a moderate-risk *total return* fund that invests in both stocks and bonds.

The fees on a variable annuity can be steep, so shop around. Some companies charge as much as 9 percent of your principal in surrender fees if you withdraw money early from a subaccount. Then, annual mortality/expense fees may run somewhere around 1.3 percent. And, don't forget that many mutual funds have their own management fees you pay annually.

When you buy a variable annuity instead of a fixed annuity, it's not as important to find a company with an A+ rating. The subaccounts you put your money in are separate from the insurance company's general operations. If the insurer fails, your funds are not frozen.

Source:
Interview with Pamela J. Sarney, certified financial planner, Network Financial Management, Farmington Hills, Mich.

Don't surrender to long surrender fees

When you buy an annuity, you rarely pay a fee upfront. Instead, like many mutual funds, you are charged a *back-load fee* (also called a *surrender fee*). The fee is typically 7 percent, and you only pay it if you withdraw your money. The longer your money is in the annuity, the lower the fee. It usually drops one percent point a year until, after seven years, the surrender fee hits zero.

Be forewarned, though — some annuities have surrender fees running as long as 35 years. That means if you took out a lump sum of money, you'd be paying a large chunk of it to the insurer. Ask about surrender fees before buying your annuity. And make sure that in your variable annuity, a surrender fee is not applied to each premium or contribution you make.

Some variable annuities are *no load*, which means they don't charge a surrender fee at all.
Source:
Interview with Pamela J. Sarney, certified financial planner, Network Financial Management, Farmington Hills, Mich.

Withdrawing money from your annuity

You retired two years ago and are currently receiving $150 a month from a $30,000 deferred annuity. Prices keep rising and you need another $50 a month to make ends meet. Take a look at your options:

Systematic withdrawals. Each year, you may withdraw up to 10 percent of the principal from your deferred annuity. Let's say your fixed annuity earns 6 percent a year. The $150 you currently receive is from the interest. For more income, you can tap into your principal for another $3,000 a year, or $250 a month, in addition to that $150.

Annuitizing. If you're looking for the highest monthly income, consider annuitizing. You convert your deferred annuity to an immediate annuity. One of the most popular immediate annuities is the *10-year certain and life*. You are guaranteed income until you die, and, if you die two years after buying this annuity, your beneficiaries receive payouts for another eight years.

The catch is once you buy an immediate annuity, you cannot withdraw the lump sum of your money or switch insurers. Deferred annuities are much more flexible.
Source:
Interview with Pamela J. Sarney, certified financial planner, Network Financial Management, Farmington Hills, Mich.

Annuity negatives

Don't park your money in an annuity before considering the negatives, particularly the added fees and minimal death benefits.

Variable annuities cost more than mutual funds. Put your money into a diversified mutual stock fund and you pay an annual fee averaging 1.4 percent. Put your money into a variable annuity and you pay an annual fee averaging 2 percent or more. The higher the annual fees, the lower your returns.

And that's just the beginning. Unless you're in desperate need of a tax shelter, annuities are probably a poor investment choice. Check out these negatives:

Surrender fees and tax penalties. Unless you hang on to your annuity for five to seven years, you face what's called a surrender fee. Moreover, if you withdraw money before you're 59 1/2, you'll also pay the government a 10 percent tax penalty.

Your federal tax liability. Capital gains on stocks in your annuity are taxed as ordinary income at rates as high as 39.6 percent. You lose the advantage of the lower capital gains tax (28 percent) on individually held stocks or mutual funds.

Your heirs' tax liability. Your beneficiaries will be socked with a big tax bill if your annuity is still funded when you die. Let's say you put $25,000 in an annuity. Over the years it swells to $75,000, and you don't withdraw any significant amount. Your heirs will owe income tax on the $50,000 appreciation, taxed as ordinary income, in addition to the estate taxes. Had that $25,000 been in stocks or a mutual fund that climbed by $50,000, your heirs would be able to take a *stepped-up cost basis* (value of stock at date of death), reducing the amount of taxes they'd have to pay.

The death benefit. Yes, annuities often provide a death benefit that ensure heirs receive at least the principal you put into the annuity, regardless of what the market does. The return of principal is not much of a reward for your life's savings.

Annuities in IRAs or pension plans. This is a definite no-no. If you put a tax-deferred annuity into a tax-sheltered retirement plan, such as your IRA, 401k, or pension plan, you may as well take a shower in your raincoat. You gain no tax benefit whatsoever because money in your retirement plan is already tax-deferred.

Annuity alternatives

If you choose not to put your money into annuities, what should you do with it? First determine your risk level for investments. If you're conservative and tempted by fixed annuities, consider U.S. Treasuries with staggered maturities or a no-load, triple tax-free municipal bond fund. Your after-tax return will be similar and you can cash out before you're 59 1/2 without a 10 percent tax penalty.

If, on the other hand, you are a more aggressive investor, one who would be tempted by variable annuities, look at a no-load growth fund.
Source:
Robert Preston, retirement consultant, Danbury, Conn.

How to take an early payout from your retirement plan: the 72-Q secret

So you want to take your money out of an annuity, IRA, 401k, or other qualified retirement plan before you reach 59 1/2. The law says you can't. Unless you're aware of a little-known rule the Internal Revenue Service calls 72-Q.

That's right. Under 72-Q, you can take a monthly check from your retirement plan before you reach age 59 1/2. The one catch is that the amount of the check cannot vary from month to month.

Say you invest $10,000 in an annuity when you're 45 years old. The law says you cannot touch it until age 59 1/2. When you're 52, you decide you'd like a monthly income of $75 from the annuity. Under the 72-Q rule, you can withdraw that amount every month until you turn 59 1/2.

Source:
Interview with Pamela J. Sarney, certified financial planner, Network Financial Management, Farmington Hills, Mich.

Why and how to choose a retirement investment planner

When it comes to choosing a financial planner to help you chart a course for your retirement, you probably can think of more reasons not to hire one than you can to hire one.

While it's true that you'll save money, prevent hassles, and protect your privacy by going it alone, you may also find that you'll benefit from a financial planner's special knowledge. Many people do. You may find a financial planner especially helpful if you're rapidly nearing retirement and haven't really made any preparations.

A good planner will help you avoid expensive mistakes, save you money in taxes, and help you choose the best investments for your situation. He'll help make sure you don't have any weak spots in your retirement plan that could later spring a leak and sink your retirement ship before you even see the red sunset.

There are no laws or regulations about who can and cannot label himself as a financial planner. So, financial planners come in all shapes and sizes, including investment brokers, investment advisers, accountants, certified financial planners, lawyers, insurance agents, and bank officers.

Here are some tips to help you choose a financial planner you can trust:

▶ Spend some time shopping around. Ask friends, family, and even your boss for recommendations. If you're having trouble getting any recommendations you can call the Institute of Certified Financial Planners at 1-800-282-7526 or the International Association of Financial Planners at 1-800-945-4237 for referrals of financial planners in your area. Make a list of names.

▶ Start to narrow down your choices. Call each planner you've listed, explain that you're shopping for a financial planner, and ask if he'll send you a background description and a list of services offered. This will take some time, but when you consider that the success of your retirement portfolio could depend on this person, it's time well spent. Once you begin to receive the information packets, you can begin the weeding-out process.

▶ Look for a planner with at least three years' experience in retirement planning. If a planner without this three years' experience tries to convince you to use his services because he's had experience relevant to retirement planning (such as working as a stock broker), keep looking. Don't compromise in this area.

▶ Seek a planner with experience in preparing plans for people similar to yourself in age, income, and profession. You may be able to find a planner who specializes in specific clients, such as teachers, for example. Avoid planners who use a one-size-fits-all plan.

▶ Choose a planner with a college degree in a related financial field, such as accounting, business, economics, or finance.

▶ Ask how the planner charges for his services. The most common types of payment are commissions, fees, or a combination of both, which is sometimes called *fee-based*. A good, ethical planner will explain clearly how he charges clients. Avoid any planner who's vague about fees or refuses to discuss charges until you have signed up for his services. Generally, your most cost-effective, efficient option is a planner who charges a fee plus commission.

▶ Pick a planner who participates in a professional financial organization, such as the International Association for Financial Planning, the Institute of Certified Financial Planners, the National Association of Personal Financial Advisors, or the Personal Financial Planning Division of the American Institute of Certified Public Accountants.

▶ Check out any planner you're seriously considering through the Securities and Exchange Commission (SEC) in Washington, D.C. Call the Office of Filings, Information, and Consumer Services at 1-202-942-8090 to find out if the financial advisor you are considering is a registered advisor and whether any violations have ever been filed against him. Keep in mind that an advisor with fewer than 15 clients is not required to register with the SEC.

For this reason, it's also a good idea to call your local Better Business Bureau to see if any complaints have been filed against a prospective planner. You should also check with your state attorney general and security commission to see if any criminal actions have been filed against an advisor.

▶ Talk to the top three or four candidates in person. Make notes, so you can accurately compare planners in the privacy of your home. Generally, these initial consultations should be free. If a highly recommended planner says he always charges for this session, you may want to agree to the fee but insist that it be applied toward the total cost of your financial plan if you decide to hire him.

▶ Request a résumé. Randomly verify various items, such as college degree or work experience.

▶ Ask potential planners what information they will need from you to prepare a plan, how long the plan preparation will take, and who is responsible for implementing the plan.

▶ Find out if you'll be working directly with the planner you're interviewing or with a less experienced associate. If the planner intends to have you work with an associate, either convince him that he'll have to do otherwise if he wants your business or drop him from your list of potential planners.

▶ Ask how often a planner thinks your retirement plan should be reviewed. If he says rarely or never, cross him off your list. You should review your plan at least once a year or whenever you have a major change in your life, such as marriage, divorce, or death. You should also review your plan if there is a big change in the tax law. A good planner will make himself available to address any concerns that come up during your regular review.

▶ Ask how he selects the financial investments he recommends. If he recommends limited partnerships, he should perform *due diligence*, or a thorough background check, on the company. If he's associated with any insurance companies, mutual fund groups, or securities firms, he should be very open and upfront about these business relationships.

▶ Inquire whether or not the planner regularly consults with other professionals, such as accountants or lawyers, for specialized information. A good planner will want to cover all possible bases for you.

▶ Ask if the planner offers alternative suggestions if you disagree with some recommendation he's made. Determine if he will be offended if you sometimes seek a second opinion. Don't work with any planner who doesn't want to give you the freedom to consult with other experts.

▶ Avoid any planner who wants complete control over your assets. Forget the planner who says he wants *investment discretion*, which means that he really wants the freedom to buy and sell investments for you without your permission. No matter which financial advisor you choose, you should always have the final say on any financial decision.

▶ Request permission to look at plans he's prepared for other clients. Try to determine from these plans what a particular planner emphasizes, such as reducing taxes or maximizing investments.

▶ Request three names of clients the planner has prepared plans for who had needs similar to yours. Ask if he does the majority of his work for companies or individuals. For your own personal retirement plan, you'll probably want a planner who has more individual than corporate clients.

▶ Find out if the prospective planner will put in writing the details that you agree upon, such as plan cost, who prepares the plan, how often the plan will be reviewed and who will do it, how the plan will be implemented, and any additional costs of implementation.

▶ Follow your instincts. If the planner refuses to explain complicated concepts in terms you could understand or acts condescending toward you, keep looking. In addition, you should avoid planners who seem more interested in your insurance coverage or total assets than your retirement goals.

If you can't put your finger on anything specific the planner did wrong, but you just don't feel comfortable or really respect the advisor, you should also keep looking. When everything finally feels right, you'll know you've found the right advisor for you.

Sources:
Feathering Your Nest by Lisa Berger, Workman Publishing, New York, 1993
Retirement Ready or Not: How to Get Financially Prepared in a Hurry by Lee Rosenberg, CFP, Career Press, Hawthorne, N.J., 1993

Financial fleecing

Stay away from any financial planner who gives you a bad feeling. In addition to trusting your intuition, here are some more obvious signs of an untrustworthy or unethical planner.

► Encourages you to make investments in which they own more than 5 percent interest.

► Asks that you give them money directly. Don't do this. Make your check out to the company that employs your advisor.

► Discourages you against getting a second opinion on specific investment advice.

► Charges timing fees in addition to normal switching fees for informing you of the best time to move money from one mutual fund to another. This is unethical behavior.

► Demands a power of attorney over your assets and investments. If you grant this power, your advisor will be able to buy, sell, and move your money around without your permission, and you are setting yourself up for fraud.

Source:
Feathering Your Nest by Lisa Berger, Workman Publishing, New York, 1993

Top places to retire if you're on a tight budget

1. Fayetteville, Ark.
2. Harrison, Ark.
3. Benton County, Ark.
4. Grand Lake, Okla.
5. Athens, Texas
6. Paris, Tenn.
7. Brownsville, Texas
8. Kerrville, Texas
9. Murray, Ky.

For more information on any of these locations, write to the chamber of commerce in the city of your choice.

Source:
Retirement Places Rated by David Savageau, Prentice Hall, New York, 1990

Starting a business after you retire

Don't let your bank decide whether or not you should start your own business. Getting a loan has little to do with your business success. If you have what it takes, you can make it. These 10 traits are typical of successful entrepreneurs.

1) I do things on my own. Nobody has to tell me to get started.

2) I'll take a chance, even if I'm unsure of success.

3) I like meeting new people, and I get along with almost everyone.

4) I can convince most people to go along when I start something new.
5) I like to be in charge and see projects through to the end.
6) I like to make plans. I'm usually the one who makes plans for my group.
7) I'm willing to work long and hard for something I want.
8) If I have to, I can make decisions quickly, and they usually turn out OK.
9) I mean what I say, and I deliver.
10) If I'm focused on a goal, nothing gets in my way.

If these 10 traits don't describe you perfectly, don't give up your goals yet. Rare is the person who possesses all the best traits for succeeding in self-employment. If your desire is strong enough, you can always improve.

Two good ways to start developing the know-how necessary for a successful business:

▶ Attend conferences on your area of interest.
▶ Constantly read articles on your field of interest and on operating a business in general.

Source:
Journal of the American Dietetic Association (95,1:21)

Free lunches and more under the Older Americans Act

Are you over 60? Services are available to you that could mean the difference between living on your own or moving into a nursing home.

Since the Older Americans Act was established in 1965, the federal government has funded local Area Agencies on Aging. These agencies run programs such as:

Meals-on-wheels
Senior cents
Hot lunch programs
Minor home repair
Transportation
Respite care
Telephone reassurances
Health screening

Access to these programs is only a phone call away. You can call the toll-free Eldercare Locator number — 1-800-677-1116 — and locate a local agency anywhere in the country that provides the service you need. For example, if your mother lives in Phoenix and you live in Cleveland, you can call the 800 number and find a Meals-on-wheels program in Phoenix that would deliver food to her.

Unfortunately, in some areas of the country, services are in limited supply and waiting lists are long. Some agencies will first assess your needs because they only provide services to the people who need them the most. Other agencies work on a first come, first serve basis.

Age is the only eligibility criteria. Your income is irrelevant. Most programs will ask for a minimal contribution if you can afford to make it.

Source:
Interview with James McGuire, director of planning and advocacy, Area Agency on Aging, Southfield, Mich.

ESTATE PLANNING

What about wills?

You may think making a will is sending an invitation to the Grim Reaper. That's morbid. Or you may think your property will automatically be distributed according to your wishes. That's pure dreaming.

If you're looking for peace of mind before you are laid to rest then you'd better have a will beforehand. A typical, well-crafted will divvies up assets according to your wishes. It ensures that the people you care most about are well provided for after your death. And it names guardians and/or trustees for your minor children or elderly parents.

When you die without a will, your estate assets are frozen while probate court handles your affairs, first paying off your debts and then dividing the remaining assets according to the rigid set of rules found in your state's intestacy (having no will) laws. The needs of your surviving family are not even considered. Nor are charitable donations, scholarship awards, or gifts for grandchildren. None of these beneficiaries is likely to see a dime if you don't have a will.

Source:
The Wealthy Barber: Everyone's Common-Sense Guide to Becoming Financially Independent by David Chilton, Prima Publishing, 1996

How to make sure your will is legal

No matter how simple your will is, you want to make sure it's legal.

In most states, you have to be 18 years old (19 in Wyoming) and of "sound mind" to write a will that's a legal document.

Wills can be formally prepared, handwritten (also called holographic), or oral.

A *formally prepared* will that is typed or printed is your best bet. Either hire a lawyer to create a formal will or use one of the many available books, prepared forms, or software programs to write your own. Your will must be signed, dated, and witnessed according to your state's laws. Usually, you must sign and date your will in front of three people who do not inherit anything.

A *handwritten* will, called *holographic*, is legal in 25 states. In those states, a holographic will does not have to be witnessed, but to be legal, it must be dated and signed by the person writing it.

An *oral* will, called *nuncupative*, is one made within hearing of two witnesses. It is valid in very few states and then only under the most unusual circumstances such as the impending death of a soldier in military combat.

A *videotape*, though useful evidence of competence, is not recognized by any state as a legal will.

Source:
Plan Your Estate by Denis Clifford & Cora Jordan, Nolo Press Self-Help Law, Berkeley, Calif., 1995

Should your spouse be the executor of your will?

It shows love, trust, and downright common sense to name your spouse as the executor of your will. Doesn't it?

Actually, not all spouses are good money managers. Moreover, after your death, a spouse will likely be emotionally drained and unable to deal with estate issues. The executor is responsible for:

▶ Providing a complete inventory of your assets
▶ Collecting money owed to you
▶ Paying off your debts
▶ Filing tax documents
▶ Distributing your estate assets

Do you really want to saddle your spouse with these duties after you die? A wiser move may be to name co-executors — perhaps your spouse and a businesswise friend or your spouse and a financial institution.

You don't want to pick your parents either. They are likely to die before you. The same goes for aunts, uncles, or grandparents.

Your best bet is an honest and reliable friend or relative. Make sure you pick an executor who lives nearby rather than across the country. Settling an estate is a drawn-out process. It can take several months or years, possibly involving many meetings with attorneys and family. Some states require your executor live in your state or require you to post a bond if the person lives out of state.

Finally, make sure you name a contingent executor in the event your first choice is unwilling or unable to act when the time comes.

Source:
The Wealthy Barber: Everyone's Common-Sense Guide to Becoming Financially Independent by David Chilton, Prima Publishing, 1996

What you can't give away in a will

You can leave most of what you own to your heirs in a will, except:

▶ Jointly held property (joint tenancy).
▶ Property listed in a living trust.
▶ Life insurance proceeds.
▶ Retirement plans, pensions, IRAs, Keoghs, etc.
▶ Pay-on-death-account proceeds (also known as an informal trust, bank trust account or Totten trust)
▶ Contract, partnership, or closely-held corporate assets.

Source:
Plan Your Estate by Denis Clifford & Cora Jordan, Nolo Press Self-Help Law, Berkeley, Calif., 1995

How to avoid probate

Why do you want to avoid probate court?

1) Probate is time-consuming and frustrating. Complicated paperwork can easily extend the process far beyond 12 months even if you have a simple estate and no one contests the will.

2) Probate is costly. It can wear away your estate's assets. In some states, for example, attorney fees are based on a percentage of the estate. The larger the estate, the larger the fees.

You can avoid probate court by using any of these legal tools to pass your property on to your survivors:

▶ **Joint ownership (joint tenancy)** — Joint tenancy, often written with "rights of survivorship," enables two or more people to own property together in equal amounts. You may own U.S. savings bonds in joint tenancy with your son, for example. When you die, the ownership of the bonds automatically transfers to him without going through probate. Your son only has to file notice with the government to retitle the bonds in his name.

▶ **Living trusts** — A living trust is an efficient way to transfer assets while you're alive into a legal contract between you and someone else (usually the trustee). Basically, the trust, like a will, states how you want your property handled after your death. A living trust, like joint tenancy, doesn't provide estate tax relief, but it is valuable for avoiding probate.

Living trusts are advisable if you and your spouse have more than $600,000 in assets and if you have minor children. In many states, you cannot leave more than $5,000 to a child in a will. If you have a living trust, no one will have to go to probate court for a *conservatorship* in order to oversee your child's finances.

A living trust also functions as a *durable power of attorney*. If you become incapacitated, the trustee you name in your trust agreement can act for you just like the power of attorney agent.

▶ **Life insurance policies** — Insurance proceeds, upon notification of your death, are paid directly to the beneficiaries named in your policies.

▶ **Retirement plans** — Money remaining in your retirement plan is usually payable to your spouse or other named beneficiaries upon your death.

▶ **Pay-on-death accounts** — Simply put, when you set up a bank account or retirement plan or when you buy a treasury bill or savings bond, you designate someone you want to receive the money when you die. In 16 states, you can also register a securities account, individual stock certificates, mutual funds, bonds, and other securities in a pay-on-death account with your broker.

Avoiding probate shouldn't be your only concern, however. You may leapfrog over probate but you'll still have to pay the piper. Especially if you put all your assets into a revocable living trust. Attorney fees, retitling assets, recording fees, and brokerage firm new account costs are just a few of the expenses you might incur.

That said, experts none the less agree that the costs of preparing a living trust are offset by the savings on probate expenses.

One last point to remember. If you don't transfer *all* of your property into your living trust, upon your death your heirs will have to go to probate court anyway.

Source:
Interview with Joel S. Golden, attorney specializing in estate planning and probate; Jaffe, Raitt, Heuer & Weiss, Detroit

How to disinherit your spouse

Unless your spouse willingly signs away inheritance rights to your estate, your family could be enmeshed in a messy, long-term legal battle. Get the dis-inheritance in writing, up front, without heavy-handed pressure.

Whether you live in a common law or community property state, your spouse, by law, is entitled to at least one-third, and oftentimes one-half, of your combined property and assets.

Source:
Plan Your Estate by Denis Clifford & Cora Jordan, Nolo Press Self-Help Law, Berkeley, Calif., 1995

Death and taxes: taking the sting out of at least one of them

If your parents have an estate that's worth more than $600,000 — and if they worked from the time they graduated from high school or college until retirement age and did any kind of investing, it's entirely possible that their estate is above that figure — you, your spouse, children, grandchildren, or other heirs could have to pay hefty estate taxes.

Richard Duff, an attorney, certified life underwriter, and author, advises some frank conversation to avoid inheriting a sizable tax bill along with Grandmother's silver tea set.

As much as it might seem maudlin or tacky to ask about your inheritance, it's important to plan for the future.

"Go to your parents," Duff says, "and say, 'Protect it for me. Put it in a trust and protect it for a lifetime. Don't just dump it out to me about the time I'm 35 or 40.'"

What's wrong with that, you might ask? Wouldn't everybody like to get a check with several zeros on it from an estate? Only if you like receiving a gift with a note attached that says, "Your Uncle Sam will be stopping by to pick up his half."

Putting money in a trust protects it from hefty estate taxes, marital distri-butions (a nice way of saying divorce settlements), and creditors.

To those with assets, Duff offers an admonition: Don't treat money with disdain, as if it's nothing worth paying attention to. Tax planning is as much about being trustworthy as it is about hanging on to what's yours.

"You're a steward of the assets," he explains. "You need to step up and realize you have an obligation to your fellow man, your community, and family. Recognize that money shouldn't control you because it's not really yours. It's not going to be here with your name on it forever. You need to control it."
Source:
Interview with Richard Duff, author of *Preserving Family Wealth Using Tax Magic*, Berkley Books, New York, 1995

Slash your estate taxes by 95 percent

If you plan it right, your family will pay only 5 to 10 percent of the estate taxes they otherwise would pay in full. The strategy: A *bypass trust*.

This plan is for any couple whose combined assets are more than $600,000. If you are worth less than $600,000, you're fine. Every American citizen gets a Unified Gift and Estate Tax Credit worth $192,800 that covers the first $600,000 of an estate.

Let's say you're worth $1 million and your spouse has $700,000 in her own assets. You set up a bypass trust and fund it with $600,000, the amount allowed for the federal estate tax exemption. When you die, the remaining $400,000 of your assets automatically goes to your spouse tax-free.

Under the marital deduction rule, your spouse pays no federal estate taxes on assets inherited from you. If you name your spouse *life beneficiary* in your trust, he or she can withdraw funds according to what you specify in the trust document.

When your spouse dies, $600,000 of his or her estate is also exempt from federal estate taxes. The $600,000 in your bypass trust, along with all accumulated interest and dividends, passes tax-free to your children, if named trust beneficiaries. Your children won't pay estate taxes on money in your bypass trust because your spouse as life beneficiary never legally owned trust assets.

So setting up the bypass trust protects $1.2 million (plus interest and dividends) from federal estate taxes. If you don't set up a bypass trust, only $600,000 of the $1.7 million your children inherit will be exempt from federal estate taxes. Your children will then have to pay federal estate taxes on $1.1 million instead of on $500,000. Quite a difference!

To further protect your heirs, purchase a life insurance policy that will cover your estate taxes — at least $500,000 on a $2 million estate — and put the policy in an irrevocable trust. The beneficiaries of this trust can use the policy's tax-free proceeds to pay your estate taxes.
Sources:
Interviews with Chris T. Christensen, president, Advanced Strategies Group, Southfield, Mich., and Robert Preston, retirement consultant, Danbury, Conn.

IRA's designated beneficiary wins big

It's a given. Fewer taxes means more money. So if you want your spouse, children, or friends to receive the largest possible payout from your individual retirement account (IRA) after you die, you must name one or more of them as designated beneficiary(ies) in the IRA.

According to Internal Revenue Service rules, your designated beneficiary(ies) must be specified in your IRA no later than April 1st of the year after you turn 70 1/2. (You can name your spouse as your beneficiary at any time.) If you don't identify a designated beneficiary, your heirs could be hit hard with taxes.

What's more, if your IRA has no designated beneficiary, the funds must be paid out within five years to your heirs. However, when you name designated beneficiaries, funds in your IRA are distributed over their lifetime.

Let's say you have $500,000 in an IRA when you die and your children are the designated beneficiaries. If properly invested, dividends and interest will accumulate tax-free over the life of your children. If your oldest child is 26, funds from your IRA could multiply tax-free 20 times to more than $10 million by the time this child is 65.

Source:
Interview with Robert Preston, retirement consultant, Danbury, Conn.

Why you need a durable power of attorney

Let's say you are traveling overseas and decide to extend your trip by a few weeks. While you're gone, though, your condominium fee and the home insurance payment comes due. You usually pay these bills with your monthly Social Security check. Fortunately, you had the forethought to plan ahead.

You've given your daughter *durable power of attorney* which enables her to endorse your Social Security check, deposit it, and write checks on your account. No one can question her capacity to do this because you've set out the limits of her power in a legal document.

When you set up a durable power of attorney, you appoint a trusted relative or friend to make business, property, asset, and financial decisions for you when you can't, usually because you become disabled or incompetent. You give that person the right to handle financial matters that include buying gifts, tending a garden, paying bills, making bank deposits, dealing with insurance, and selling a home or other property. Your agent also may use your funds to pay for your medical expenses that aren't covered by Medicare or health insurance. The more specific the instructions, the better your agent will handle your financial affairs.

What would happen if you had an accident, were unconscious for several weeks, and hadn't set up a durable power of attorney? Your financial affairs would still need managing, but no one would be authorized to write checks, sell stocks, or cash your Social Security checks.

Your spouse or another relative would have to go to probate court for a *conservatorship*, incurring court costs and attorney fees. A conservator appointed by the court has the same financial rights as a durable power of attorney's agent. But, unlike a durable power of attorney, a conservatorship gives you no say on how your finances are managed.

However, a conservator has to keep impeccable records of income and expenses. Every year, the conservator must file an accounting on your behalf with the court. This is expensive and time-consuming, but it does protect your financial position.

An alternative to the durable power of attorney is a *springing durable power of attorney*. The general durable power of attorney is effective as soon as you sign it, but the "springing" version only "springs" into effect when and under the conditions you specify. It lacks the flexibility of the general durable power of attorney. For instance, it can't be used to pay your bills when you're out of town.

You could specify in a springing durable power of attorney that it is only valid for three months following surgery. If your recuperation lasts six months, you're out of luck. Your agent will have trouble convincing the bank or other financial institutions that you are incapacitated. Your bills might go unpaid.

Rather than using the springing durable power of attorney, Joel S. Golden, an attorney specializing in estate planning and probate, believes you should name someone you trust durable power of attorney. If you are not comfortable giving that person that power, if you think the person will abuse that authority, then don't give him or her the power in the first place.

Source:
Interview with Joel S. Golden, attorney specializing in estate planning and probate; Jaffe, Raitt, Heuer & Weiss, Detroit

How to still have your say when you are disabled or incompetent

Imagine — you live far from home, your father suddenly dies, and now you're responsible for your mom who has Alzheimer's Disease. For the past several years, your dad has taken care of her, protected her, and made decisions about her medical care. Now, this responsibility is yours. The catch is you have no legal authority to make health care decisions for her because she never drew up a durable power of attorney for health care. What now?

Because most hospitals and physicians will not perform medical procedures on an incompetent or incapacitated person, you have to seek *guardianship* in probate court. That will give you the legal right to sign consent forms for her medical treatment. Without guardianship papers or a durable power of attorney for health care, critical care for her may be delayed or withheld.

Take the time to think about yourself. What would happen if you had a stroke or slipped into a coma following an accident? If you haven't set up a durable power of attorney for health care, your spouse or child(ren) will have to seek guardianship for you.

Seeking guardianship is costly. Court costs and attorney fees spiral as your family's lawyer presents evidence of your incompetency in probate court. Your family will have to testify in court. You yourself may have to appear, or a court-appointed agent may be sent to your home to check out your competency.

And that's not all. Every year, the court reviews the guardianship. A court-appointed agent visits your home to review your living conditions and medical condition. Any change in your guardian's authority requires another court hearing.

You can avoid the guardianship process entirely by planning ahead. Long before you are likely to need it, set up a durable power of attorney for health care (also called power of health care proxies). Unlike guardianship, you decide who will make medical decisions for you after you no longer are able. Your advocate carries out those directives.

For example, under what conditions do you want to be resuscitated if you have a heart attack? Do you want a feeding tube put in once you stop eating? Do you want the cord pulled if you're in a vegetative state? After how long?

Both guardianship and durable power of attorney for health care concern health care decisions. But the similarity ends there. You set up a durable power of attorney for health care and you ensure that you control medical decisions when you no longer can voice them. What's more, your family bypasses the red tape and high expense of probate court.
Source:
Interview with Joel S. Golden, attorney specializing in estate planning and probate; Jaffe, Raitt, Heuer & Weiss, Detroit

Protect your health-care rights with a living will

Thanks to a 1990 decision by the United States Supreme Court, you are entitled to direct your own medical care — not only while you're healthy but after you're incapacitated, too.

All but three states have a form containing specific language that you use to spell out the type of medical treatment you want to receive if you have a terminal illness or become comatose. It's called a *living will*, a *medical directive*, or a *directive to physicians*. Medical personnel must follow your instructions to the letter. Neither family wishes nor physician beliefs can override your directives in states that recognize them.

You simply fill out a preprinted form. The format of these forms varies from state to state, but for every form, you'll need to consider issues such as:

▶ If breathing is labored or ceases, do you want to be kept alive with a ventilator or respirator?

▶ If you are unable to eat, do you want a feeding tube inserted or an intravenous line, or do you want food and water withheld? What about other life-sustaining treatment?

▶ Do you want pain relievers, and if so, how often?

Your doctor should have a copy of your living will, and a copy should be in your medical record at the hospital you're likely to go to. In fact, if you are taken to the emergency room, you should be asked if you have an advanced directive before they start treating you.

Source:
Interview with Thomas V. Trainer, elder law attorney, Cooney, Trainer, and Wahl, Bloomfield Hills, Mich.

How to get more Medicaid money

You may be too rich to qualify for Medicaid. In the early days of Medicaid, if you had $1 million one day and gave all of it away the next, you would immediately be eligible for Medicaid benefits. Times change and so do rules. Since 1993, you can still give away that $1 million, but you no longer immediately qualify for Medicaid benefits.

Instead, we now have a "look back" period. The government looks back at the past 36 months (the past 60 months for a trust) to see how much money you gave away during that time. Then they figure out how many months that money would have kept you in a nursing home, and you don't get benefits for that period of time.

Here's how it works. Let's say you gave your children $35,000 during the past 36 months. Tomorrow you enter a nursing home and apply for Medicaid. Medicaid will not pay for your nursing home costs (right now, an average of $3,500 per month) for the next 10 months. Why? Because that $35,000 would have covered those costs for that period of time. So you or your family have to pick up the nursing home expenses.

So, what can you do to qualify?

Option one: Give your children the money long before you plan to apply for Medicaid. The government is only interested in money you give away during the current 36-month "look back" period. You don't have to tell Medicaid that you gave away $35,000 37 months ago.

It is unwise, though, to tell Medicaid that you plan to give away $35,000 today and apply for benefits 37 months from now. Keep it to yourself. Why? Because Medicaid penalizes for "early" disclosure and would likely deny you benefits for up to ten months.

Don't fail to report financial donations you've made during the 36-month "look back" period. If you do, you are committing perjury and probably a felony as well. The government runs background checks, looking into your 1099-DIV forms to check on the status of your investments. If fraud is suspected, criminal charges can be brought against you.

Better option: Use *excludable assets*. The government looks at your "accountable assets" (savings accounts, investments, and real estate) to determine your Medicaid eligibility. You can exclude many of your assets by converting cash and investments into:

Your home. The house you live in is your homestead, according to federal law. Therefore, it is not included as part of your accountable assets. You can live in a $150,000 home and qualify for Medicaid, but you don't qualify if you rent an apartment and have $150,000 in the bank.

Your automobile. You do not have to include your car in the accountable assets you report to Medicaid. (Some states may set a limit on the value of your car.)

Personal furnishings, jewelry, and household goods. Some states set limits on the value of the goods you can exclude. In other states, you don't have to include any of these personal items regardless of their worth.

Burial expenses. In most states, you can make yourself look poorer for Medicaid by paying for your funeral expenses ahead of time. You may set aside up to $8,500 for the cost of a funeral, putting the bulk of the money in an irrevocable funeral insurance policy. Your Medicaid exclusion also extends to burial plots and monuments bought ahead of time.

Annuities. Some states allow you to convert a fluid asset such as a certificate of deposit into an annuity. Annuities provide income to your spouse, but the government won't include them when determining your Medicaid eligibility.

Source:
Interview with Thomas V. Trainer, elder law attorney, Cooney, Trainer, and Wahl, Bloomfield Hills, Mich.

Giving the gift of life

Would you feel more successful in life if you could help the 46,000 Americans waiting for a transplanted organ?

If you decide organ donation is part of the legacy you want to leave behind when you die, you need to:

1. Hold a family discussion. Tell your spouse and children that when you die, you want to donate your organs (heart, liver, lungs, and kidneys) and/or tissues (skin, bone, heart valves, and corneas). It is also wise to tell your doctor.

2. Sign an organ donor card or sign up at your state's donor registry. You can obtain an organ donor card at state driver licensing bureaus. In fact, many states include organ donor information on the back of the driver's license, and some states lower the cost of getting a new driver's license if you agree to be an organ donor. Foundations such as the Mickey Mantle Foundation also supply organ donor cards. The card becomes a legal document once you and a witness sign it.

Most everyone from newborns to 75-year olds are potential organ and tissue donors. When you die, blood tests and sometimes X-rays and EKGs are done to determine whether or not your organs and/or tissues are suitable for transplant.

Currently, if you have active hepatitis, a very serious infection, or if you are HIV positive, it's unlikely you'll be able to donate.

If you have diabetes, your pancreas or kidneys may not be viable choices.

If you have cancer, you may be able to donate skin and bone, but not your organs.

If you have lymphoma or leukemia, you probably cannot donate your corneas.

However, each transplant center has its own set of criteria, and many select organ donors based on test results. What's more, technology constantly changes, and donors who are ineligible today may well be accepted tomorrow.

Source:
Interview with Penny Szeman, RN, BSN, CPTC, community education coordinator, Transplant Society of Michigan, Ann Arbor, Mich.

YOU AND THE LAW

Are finders really keepers?

You slide into the booth at your favorite coffee shop and discover you're sitting on something lumpy. You investigate. It's a thick envelope — stuffed with hundred dollar bills.

No one in the restaurant knows who owns the envelope. Do you get to keep your unexpected treasure?

Yes, but only if the rightful owner is given the opportunity to reclaim his money.

The right thing to do? Turn the windfall over to the police. They will hold it for a specific period, determined by state law. If, after that length of time, no one has claimed the money, you may be entitled to it.

Source:
The Court T.V. Cradle-to-Grave Legal Survival Guide: A Complete Resource for Any Question You May Have About the Law by American Lawyer Media; Little, Brown, and Company, 1995

When not to hire a lawyer

With attorney fees commonly starting at $200 per hour and rising rapidly, more and more people are choosing to represent themselves in court.

It's not as foolhardy as it might sound. It some cases a layperson representing himself actually gets more breaks than a lawyer would. The reason? The courts try to bend over backwards to show that they are fair to people who choose to represent themselves.

Best situations to represent yourself include small-claims disputes (lawyers often aren't even welcomed by the courts in these cases), contract disputes (unfulfilled contracts with people such as plumbers and builders), straightforward divorces (very little or no arguing involved), and simple personal injury claims.

If you're involved in a criminal case, a complex injury, or discrimination case, or one with lots of money at stake, better get a lawyer. She'll probably be worth every penny.

Source:
Business Week (Aug. 22, 1994)

How to represent yourself in court

▶ Decide if your complaint is worth taking to court. Talk to witnesses, collect bank reports, medical records, or insurance claim forms. Look through real estate and other public records to find out about your opponent. It may reassure you to know that lawyers don't have any greater access to witnesses and evidence than you do. If your opponent has very few assets, you may be better off dropping the claim.

▶ Consider a settlement before the trial if one can be worked out. There's nothing weak about taking this option, and it can save you a lot of time and money.

▶ Find out ahead of time about the judge who will hear your case. Try to determine what type of court style he has. This will help you determine how to present your case.

▶ Talk to the court clerk. Ask about court regulations. See if there is a booklet available that outlines the rules of the court.

▶ Rehearse opening and closing statements and direct and cross-examination questions with a trusted friend or relative before the actual trial begins.

▶ May sure any witnesses you plan to call will show up. If you have any doubt, subpoena them. Prepare your witnesses to testify.

▶ Make a list of common objections. Keep them handy.

▶ Consider legal coaching if you don't feel comfortable.

Go for it! Who knows? You may be the next Perry Mason.

Source:
Represent Yourself in Court by Sara Berman-Barrett and Paul Bergman, Nolo Press, Berkeley, Calif., 1990

3 reasons to take your case to small claims court

1. You can prepare and present your own case without having the hassle of paying a lawyer more than your claim was worth in the first place.
2. It's fairly simple. Technical law language and complicated forms are limited to the bare essentials.
3. Your case will be settled fast. Most cases come to court within a month or two after the complaint is filed. You'll get a decision a few days after the judge hears your case.

Keep in mind that most states restrict settlement in small claims court to cash awards of a set limit, which vary from state to state. This means that you can only receive cash for damages you suffered, not, for example, an exact replacement of your lawn mower. This avenue enables judges to process cases quickly.

Source:
Everybody's Guide to Small Claims Court by attorney Ralph Warner, Nolo Press, Berkeley, Calif., 1985

Small claims court: Do you have a case you can win?

Did you know that most cases are actually won or lost before they ever reach a courtroom?

Whether you're prosecuting or defending, the secret of setting yourself up for success is simple. It's the same as the Boy Scout motto: Be prepared.

Your first step is to decide if your case is worth taking to small claims court. You need to have an answer to the following four questions: 1) What happened? 2) Who did it? 3) Were they wrong? 4) How much did it cost?

If you can answer those questions and the cost of your claim doesn't exceed the amount set by your local small claims court, and your case doesn't involve an issue specifically excluded from small claims court, such as libel or slander, you're ready to prepare to answer the two questions that will either win or lose you the case:

1) **Can the loss you claim to have suffered be documented in court?**
You must be able to place a specific dollar amount on your loss and prove your loss. For example, you generally can't get money out of small claims court claiming only pain and suffering although they may enter in on the coattails of a case where you claim monetary loss. An example of a case well suited for small claims court would be one in which a landlord refused to return a tenant's security deposit for no good reason.

2) **Is the person you're suing legally responsible for your loss?**
To demonstrate that someone wronged you, you must be able to prove one of these three questions:
- ▶ Did the defendant act carelessly or irresponsibly?
- ▶ Did the defendant deliberately cause you harm?
- ▶ Did the defendant break a spoken promise or a written contract?

Coming up with answers to all these questions that will hold up legally in court is not easy. Consider checking out a recently published book from your local library that leads you step-by-step through the small claims court process.
Source:
Small Claims Court: Making Your Way Through the System: A Step-by-Step Guide by Theresa Meehan Rudy, Random House, New York, 1990

How to sniff out your local small claims court

Different states refer to their small claims courts differently. The easiest place to start tracking down a small claims court in your area is your local telephone directory.

If there isn't a small claims court listing in your local directory, try the following alternative listings:
- ▶ City
- ▶ Conciliation
- ▶ County
- ▶ District
- ▶ Justice
- ▶ Justice of the Peace
- ▶ Municipal

You'll often find small claims courts listed under one of these "parent" courts instead of under "small claims courts."

If you can't find a small claims court listing anywhere, try calling your local city courthouse. They'll be able to tell you exactly what you want to know.
Source:
Everybody's Guide to Small Claims Court by attorney Ralph Warner, Nolo Press, Berkeley, Calif., 1985

Top 10 ways to impress a judge

If you want to win your small claims court case, or any case for that matter, it helps to make a good impression on the judge.

Judges consider the impression you make on them *demeanor evidence*. They'll use this type of evidence when they have nothing else to go on but your word against your opponent's. That's why it's literally crucial to your case to make a good impression. Here's how:

1. Dress for success. In court, this means dressing conservatively, neatly, and appropriately in a dress or suit.
2. Stand when spoken to. Show respect to the judge and the court by standing when you talk to the judge, tell your story, or answer questions.
3. Remember that politeness pays. Always address judges as "Your Honor," and lawyers as "Sir" or "Ma'am." Never interrupt or argue with a judge.
4. Wait to begin until the judge is focused on your case. If the judge was distracted when your name or case was called or the basis for your case wasn't mentioned, briefly introduce yourself and describe your case.
5. Keep your statements as short and simple as possible. Let your evidence speak for itself.
6. Be organized and prepared. Have all your papers arranged so you can quickly find whatever you need. If you weren't able to locate or bring a crucial piece of evidence, be sure you can explain why.
7. Give your testimony in your own words. Don't read off a prepared statement. You'll appear unconvincing. If you're afraid you'll forget an important point, use notes or an outline.
8. Avoid legal jargon or any other language that may make the judge suspect you're trying to act like a lawyer. A judge will be more sympathetic and helpful to you if you avoid putting on airs of any type.
9. Listen between the lines. If a judge recommends that you try to settle your case out in the hall, heed his advice. He may be discreetly trying to tell you your case won't hold up in court, and you'll probably come out better with an outside settlement.
10. Ask for all additional costs to be reimbursed. At the end of your presentation, ask for any additional costs you incurred coming to court be added to any money you're awarded.

Source:
Small Claims Court: Making Your Way Through the System: A Step-by-Step Guide by Theresa Meehan Rudy, Random House, New York, 1990

Settling a dispute without a lawyer

As well as small claims court works, sometimes it still isn't your best bet for putting a problem to sleep. If you've got a consumer complaint that really can't be resolved with money or an ongoing issue with a neighbor's dog digging up all your flower beds, you're probably better off seeking an alternative solution. Here are some places to start:

Consumer Action Agency (CAA) — Many people turn to a CAA for assistance when they have a claim that's too big for small claims court, yet is not really worth a lawsuit. People also use consumer action agencies when they prefer replacement, new parts, or prompt repair instead of a cash settlement.

Consider contacting one of these agencies if you can't satisfactorily resolve a problem with a recently purchased major appliance, car, or contractor you hired to complete home improvements or repairs. A large company is more likely to cooperate with a CAA than respond to a small claims trial.

There are a number of different consumer action agencies you can contact, from government consumer action agencies to private consumer action agencies. For more information on government CAAs and the types of complaints they'll handle, write and request a free copy of the *Consumer's Resource Handbook*, Consumer Information Center, Pueblo, CO 81009.

The two most helpful business-oriented consumer action agencies are the Better Business Bureaus and Consumer Action Panels.

Better Business Bureaus — These nonprofit organizations are run by local and national businesses. If you provide a written complaint, they will contact the business on your behalf. They'll work with you until you're satisfied or until the company can convince them that you have an unjustified complaint.

Consumer Action Panels — Two major industries have consumer action panels to handle consumer complaints: automobile dealers (AUTOCAP) and makers of major home appliances (MACAP).

Once the panel receives your complaint, they will write a formal letter to the dealer or manufacturer requesting both an explanation of the problem and a solution which will satisfy the customer. If the problem isn't settled within a week to 10 days, a review board examines the situation and suggests a solution.

Although their recommendations aren't legally binding, many manufacturers are willing to comply with the board's ruling rather than face trade association sanctions. Usually, these boards have a high rate of success. A consumer does not have to agree to a solution if he is not happy with it.

Check your telephone book or contact your local telephone operator for assistance in locating these groups. If you aren't having any luck locating one of these consumer help groups, contact your local court system.

If they can't help you or recommend someone who can, try a national consumers' group such as Consumer Federation of America, 1424 16th St. N.W., Suite 604, Washington, DC 20036 1-202-387-6121 or the National Consumers League, 815 15th St. N.W., Suite 516, Washington, DC 20005 1-202-835-3323.

Licensing or regulatory boards — These agencies can help consumers handle complaints concerning professionals who must be legally licensed by the city, county, or state, such as doctors, lawyers, electricians, funeral directors, etc. These boards can bring disciplinary actions against professionals if they feel it necessary.

However, you can't always depend on licensing boards to satisfactorily resolve your disputes. Before you spend a lot of time working with them, talk with your local private consumer action agency or consumer affairs reporter to find out if the likely results will be worth your effort.

Media Programs — Call your local newspapers, radio stations, and television stations to see if they offer a consumer action service. If they do and they choose to address your complaint, you'll often have your problem satisfactorily resolved. Businesses spotlighted by the media for poor quality products or services usually respond quickly to avoid more bad publicity.

Arbitration — Arbitration is an attractive alternative for people who wish to settle disputes quickly and easily and don't want any decision made to be limited to monetary awards, which is typically the case in small claims court. Also, arbitration does not force responsibility for a problem onto one person's shoulders only. Both parties may be required to take action to resolve the argument.

In this procedure, the two parties in disagreement come together voluntarily before a neutral third party (the arbitrator — usually an expert on the problem under discussion) who listens to each side's argument, considers any available evidence, and tries to get the two parties to come to an agreement.

If he can't, then he will make a decision, usually within 10 days. Both parties agree before proceedings begin to accept the third party's decision, which is legally binding and can be enforced by the courts. Sometimes you can appeal a decision made during arbitration. It depends on the rules set before arbitration begins.

Arbitration is sponsored by both the Better Business Bureau (BBB) and the American Arbitration Association (AAA). The Better Business Bureau only offers arbitration for consumer complaints. It won't handle cases involving personal injury, property claims, fraud, or criminal charges. The BBB pays for arbitration that it sponsors. However, the BBB does not offer arbitration in all areas.

The AAA handles a much wider range of disputes than the BBB, including cases involving large amounts of money. However, their service is not free. Fees are charged on a sliding scale of 1 to 3 percent of the dollar amount involved.

Mediation — This dispute resolution service works best for people who plan to continue some sort of relationship after the dispute is settled, such as family members, neighbors, or local businesses and their customers. Mediation can also be used to resolve disputes involving larger sums of money than many small claims courts want to handle.

This process is voluntary and informal with no need to submit evidence or bring witnesses. Each side simply tells its story. The mediator involved, a neutral third party, uses a variety of skills, such as asking questions and suggesting compromises, to encourage the parties in dispute to reach a mutually agreeable solution.

Unlike judges or arbitrators, mediators do not make or impose a final decision. The decision has to be reached by the involved parties themselves. Once an agreement is reached, it must be put in writing and both parties must sign.

The signed agreement is binding and can be enforced by the courts. However, if you don't like an agreement, you don't have to sign.

To find a mediation service in your area, contact your local attorney general, small claims court, mayor's office, or look under "Mediation Services" in the yellow pages. You can also write for and request the Dispute Resolution Directory from the Standing Committee on Dispute Resolution; American Bar Association, 1800 M St. N.W., Washington, DC 20036.

Some small claims courts also sponsor arbitration or mediation programs. If one of these alternatives sounds more attractive than the hassle of court, call your local small claims court and ask if they provide either of these programs.

Source:
Small Claims Court — Making Your Way Through the System: A Step-by-Step Guide by Theresa Meehan Rudy, Random House, New York, 1990

Legal aid at your fingertips

When you need some quick and easy legal aid, try one of the new computer programs available. This new technology won't get lawyers out of your life entirely, but it will make dealing with them simpler and cheaper.

LegalPoint, a Windows program from Teneron Corp., provides legal assistance small businesses may find useful. It allows you to select from a menu of about 70 business-related forms, such as a bill of sale, an employment contract, and a partnership agreement.

When you pull up the type of document you need, an actual legal document appears on screen and you fill in the appropriate blanks. When you select a blank, the program offers suggestions for filling it in.

If you need additional advice, this program also provides a business law option that offers you more extensive guidance on the topic you're working on. Say, for example, you were working on a lease agreement. By using the business law option, you could pull up information on types of lease agreements, warranties, and the Fair Credit Reporting Act.

You can edit text or move a completed document to a word processing program to add your own logo or fine-tune the formatting. Once you're done, LegalPoint produces a professional-looking legal document.

If you're looking for a less expensive legal-aid program more geared for occasional or home use, consider It's Legal for Windows from Parsons Technology. With this program, you simply answer questions and It's Legal produces the legal document without you having to fill in any blanks. However, this program offers limited legal advice and you can't edit text or move your document to a word processing program.

For your own legal protection, you should still have any documents produced by a legal-aid computer program reviewed by a competent lawyer. So while these programs won't let you leave lawyers out completely, they can still spare you the money you'd have to spend for taking up the lawyer's time explaining what you wanted done as well as his legal fees for preparing the document.

Source:
Business Week (Sept. 19, 1994)

Free legal help for older people

Did you know that if you are over 60, you can get free legal help? In fact, the state you live in is required by law (the Older Americans Act) to give legal services to you.

All you have to do is call your local Area Agency on Aging. You don't have to be below a certain income level to qualify for services, but you may be considered a low priority if you have plenty of money to hire a lawyer.

Legal hot lines are another way to get free advice from a lawyer if you are over 60. The hot lines are staffed by lawyers who will give you advice, send pamphlets containing the information you need, or refer you to a special, low-cost group of lawyers or to a free legal services program.

Unfortunately, only some areas of the United States have legal hot lines in place, and some are only manned at certain times of the year (such as on Law Day, May 1).

To find out if a legal hot line is available to you, call your local bar association or Area Agency on Aging.

Source:
Finding Legal Help: An Older Person's Guide, Legal Counsel for the Elderly, 601 E Street, N.W., Washington, D.C. 20049, 1994

Hiring a lawyer for less

You need a lawyer. It's time to draw up your will or close on your new home or set up a trust for your children. But how do you make sure some "shark" doesn't take advantage of you?

Usually, for a simple transaction like a will or a health care power of attorney, a lawyer will charge you a flat fee — one price for the whole job. Here are some simple ways to ensure that price is right:

▶ Always comparison shop. Prices and work quality will vary. Call several attorneys to check on price.

▶ Call some smaller firms. They usually charge less than larger law offices.

▶ Attorneys who have recently graduated from law school will often work for less.

▶ A firm new to your area may charge less while they try to establish clients.

▶ Ask your lawyer how you can help. For instance, your lawyer may be able to give you a standard will that you can use as your guide to draw up your own. Then he can review the work you've done. Make sure you ask the lawyer how much he would charge if your work needs a major rewrite.

▶ Ask about fees *and* expenses. A lawyer's fee is for his time. Expenses can include charges for photocopying, typing, and filing.

▶ Always get the specifics of what the attorney will charge in writing.

▶ If you are on a very limited budget, ask about payment plans. You may not
have to make a lump sum payment.

Source:
Finding Legal Help: An Older Person's Guide, Legal Counsel for the Elderly, 601 E Street, N.W., Washington,
D.C. 20049, 1994

Finding the right lawyer for you

A lawyer needs to be someone you can trust. You don't want to shut your
eyes, jab your finger onto the "Lawyers" section of the yellow pages, and hope
for the best. You don't want to be swayed by attorneys who advertise or by
fake "referral services" funded by the lawyers themselves either.

Four better ways to find a lawyer are:

▶ Ask someone whose judgement you trust for a recommendation: your relatives, friends, clergy, social worker, or your doctor. Don't just ask them to
recommend a good attorney. You need to know the names of lawyers who
have provided similar legal services for them.

▶ Call your local bar association (found in the white pages or in the yellow
pages under "Lawyers"). They have a referral list. However, being on the
list is no guarantee that the lawyer is good. A better option may be to ask if
the bar association has any committees that do public service work for older
people. A lawyer who serves on one of these committees should have the
expertise you need.

▶ Check the lawyer directories at your local library. One of the best directories is the *Martindale-Hubbell Law Directory.* It lists lawyers by state and
by categories. The book gives a biography on over 600,000 lawyers and
even rates each lawyer.

▶ Get a referral from a community group, such as the Alzheimer's Association,
Children of Aging Parents, the Older Women's League, the state civil liber-
ties union, a local social services agency, or the local agency on aging. Make
sure you ask how they choose the attorneys they recommend.

Source:
Finding Legal Help: An Older Person's Guide, Legal Counsel for the Elderly, 601 E Street, N.W., Washington,
D.C. 20049, 1994

Fight back against bad lawyers

Heard any lawyer jokes lately? Odds are, you have. Making fun of — and
criticizing — the legal profession has become commonplace.

Most of the bad-mouthing is clearly unfair. There are thousands of ethical,
hard-working attorneys in America. But there are exceptions.

How do you file a complaint if a lawyer handles your case poorly, charges
you unfairly, or behaves in some other unethical manner?

Call the bar association office in your state, or the Clerk's Office of
your State Supreme Court. They can tell you how to contact your state's

disciplinary agency for the legal profession, says Ellen Rosen, assistant regulation counsel of the Chicago-based American Bar Association.

You'll be given a form that asks for specific information about the lawyer, yourself, any fee you paid, any lawsuit you're involved in, and what your gripe is with the attorney.

When the disciplinary agency investigates your complaint — unless they discover your charges are way off-base or the attorney can prove there's been a misunderstanding — your lawyer will be asked to respond. Then you'll be given an opportunity to reply to what the lawyer says.

What happens if the investigators determine you were right? According to Rosen, depending on the seriousness of the unethical behavior, an attorney guilty of misconduct faces disciplinary action ranging from private admonitions to suspension and disbarment.

Source:
Interview with Ellen Rosen, attorney-at-law, American Bar Association, Chicago

The pitfalls of 'legal romance'

You are going through a rough time and need legal help. Luckily, you find a lawyer you not only have confidence in, but also like. He's charming and movie-star handsome.

He asks you out on a date. Should you accept?

It's not a good idea. Here's why:

▶ In many states, state bar associations consider it improper for an attorney to have an intimate relationship with a client in a criminal or matrimonial case before the matter is resolved.

▶ If you are in an intimate relationship with your lawyer while engaged in a custody battle, it could hurt your chances of winning the case.

▶ Having a love affair with your lawyer could complicate your working relationship and make him less effective as your advocate.

▶ Normally, your attorney cannot disclose confidential information you've told him that can affect your case. But if you two are involved in a romance, communications between you may be considered simply part of your personal relationship — and therefore not protected from disclosure.

So if cupid strikes in the lawyer's office, it's best to wait until after your case is resolved before pursuing your romantic feelings.

Source:
The Court T.V. Cradle-to-Grave Legal Survival Guide: A Complete Resource for Any Question You May Have About the Law by American Lawyer Media; Little, Brown, and Company, 1995

How to beat a traffic ticket

You're in a huge hurry and the last thing you want to see in your rearview mirror are exactly what you see — the familiar flashing blue headlights. You're already late, and you don't want to add insult to injury by getting a traffic ticket.

Spare your feelings and save yourself some money by following the sensible advice of Mark D. Sutherland, Esq., a veteran traffic ticket attorney who's successfully defended over 1,000 traffic ticket cases.

▶ Remain calm. Considering that you're hurrying to get somewhere and you've just been pulled over by a police officer, you're probably feeling far from calm. Take a few deep breaths and fake calmness if you have to. Getting angry or exploding at the cop won't help you avoid a ticket.

▶ Place both hands on the steering wheel in plain sight. Right now, the cop is at least as afraid of you as you are of him and maybe more. He has no way of knowing whether he's pulled over some psycho or someone really nice like you.

▶ Stay still. Don't reach toward the glove compartment or under the seat or buckle or unbuckle your seat belt. Don't do anything to make him more suspicious or nervous than he already is.

▶ Be polite and courteous, however hard this may be. You're much less likely to get a ticket if you're friendly and polite than if you're hateful and abusive. It may be hard to believe but police officers are people, too. Really.

▶ Try to talk your way out of the ticket. Talk about the pressures and problems in your life. It's even better for you if you can get him to talk about his problems and pressures.
Whatever you do, don't discuss your driving, and don't admit that you're guilty of anything. If he issues you a ticket anyway (after you've gone out of your way to be nice and everything), you may want to fight the ticket in court. That's why you shouldn't discuss your driving or admit you could possibly be guilty.

▶ Keep your entire conversation with the cop quiet and low-key. Your aim is to be as forgettable as possible. This way, if he does give you a ticket, you'll have a good chance of successfully fighting it in traffic court. If he doesn't remember you, he will have a hard time defending his case against you.

▶ Realize that the cop will ask you all sorts of questions to try and get you to admit your guilt. Even though your instinct will be to answer, avoid saying anything that could suggest you're guilty. A typical question a cop will ask someone he's pulled over for speeding is "Do you know how fast you were going?" A good noncommittal answer to this question is "The speed limit, I believe."

▶ Know that once his pen touches his ticket pad, he has to write you a ticket. At this point, begin preparing your case for traffic court because that's the only way you're going to get out of the ticket now.

▶ Don't tell your side of the story. That's exactly what he wants, for you to slip up somehow and admit your guilt. Instead, get him to tell his. Where was he sitting when he saw you? Ask to see his radar. Question him about his car. Inquire about his day. Has it been tough? How long has he been on duty?

▶ Collect as many facts as you can, but don't argue or disagree with the cop. Don't attempt to try your case in the street by arguing it out with the police officer. You have absolutely no chance of winning. If you wait and argue in court, you do.

▶ Make notes of as many different details as possible. Write down as soon after you get the ticket as possible the following information: exactly where you were stopped (draw a detailed diagram of the area); the distance between where you committed the supposed violation and where you were stopped; the traffic around you; the weather; the clothes you were wearing, especially the color of your shirt; a distinctive feature of your car, such as wire wheels, fog lights, a dented door, etc; actions of the police officer, especially anything he did that appeared unusual.

In court, you can use details like these to establish "reasonable doubt" of the accuracy of the police officer's memory. If you haven't made yourself memorable, there's very little chance he will remember details like these, but you will (especially since you made notes), which helps make your testimony more believable than his.

▶ Check your ticket for accuracy, but don't point out any mistake to him. An uncorrected mistake will be more ammunition for you to use to attack the police officer's credibility in court. Don't give in to your instincts and rip the ticket to shreds. You may be able to use it as valuable evidence in your favor later on.

▶ Don't let the cop know you're planning on fighting the ticket in court. This will make you more memorable than you want to be if you plan to win.

▶ Drive around the block when he lets you go, then retrace the route where you got your ticket. Look for additional details to add to your notes, such as where the cop was sitting, any obstructions that could have interfered with his really having a good view of you, etc.

▶ Get ready for court. You'll have about a month to prepare. With a copy of Mark Sutherland's book *Traffic Ticket Defense* in hand and some good common sense, you have a good shot at being able to toss that traffic ticket in the trash without ever having to pay a dime.

Source:
Traffic Ticket Defense by Mark D. Sutherland, Esq. and Chris Sutherland, Bonus Books, Chicago, 1993

How to profit from class action lawsuits

Here's a quick brain teaser: Breast implants. Cigarettes. Airline tickets. What do these totally different subjects have in common?

Try *class action lawsuit*.

Women who had silicone breast implants that posed a possible threat to their health banded together and filed a class action suit against implant manufacturers. Other consumers, charging unfair prices, joined forces and went after the airlines. Both groups won. But an attempt at a class action suit that claimed cigarette manufacturers knowingly hooked consumers on nicotine was nixed before it started — the court ruled it didn't fit into the category "class action." Consumers will have to file individual suits for damages against the tobacco giants.

What is a class action? The name says it all. A group of people who are, in legalese, *similarly situated* (meaning they have the same problem) are designated as a class. They take action by filing a complaint on behalf of themselves.

"Although many states have their own rules allowing for class actions, for the most part federal law defines what a class is," notes attorney James Zito, a corporate law specialist. "It has to be more than a few people, and it also has to be a case involving some significant public interest — perhaps a health issue. Otherwise, the courts will not 'qualify' the class."

How do you join in? If a class of people is "qualified," all people in similar circumstances — those with cars that have faulty gas tanks, for example — are automatically members of that class unless they opt out (more about that possibility below).

"Oftentimes, if you are automatically part of a suit, you'll be given notice. You may be identified because of a record that you purchased a particular car or because of a warranty card you sent in," says attorney Zito.

Or you may see notices in the newspaper seeking people who qualify as members of a class. Remember ads asking breast implant recipients to call a toll-free number?

You may also have to do your own research. For example, a recent class action suit involved faulty water pipes installed in the 1970s and 1980s. People who read about the potentially expensive problem in the news and didn't know what kind of pipes they had asked builders or their subdivision developers, or they had their water mains inspected.

Money or morals? Winning a class action suit probably won't bring you big bucks. "Anytime there is a major incident that occurs where many people are affected, there's a rush by lawyers to find individuals who might be members of a class. The attorneys receive a percent of the settlement and that can mean big bucks — for the lawyers," says Zito. "But because the settlement is often divided among so many, for most people in the suit there is little money to be received."

However, as in the case of the faulty pipes, you may save yourself at least a portion of the expense of replacing your water lines thanks to a settlement.

But participation in a class action suit can have benefits that go beyond money. For example, attorney Zito points out, class action suits keep our judicial system from becoming overloaded: If you have 10,000 cases, all of which are identical except they involve different people in different places, a class action allows just one trial to take place in federal court to resolve all those cases.

"There's another public interest in allowing class action suits," he adds. "They cause changes in the behavior of manufacturers and suppliers of services who have been negligent or produced faulty merchandise."

When should you say no? "There's no harm in taking part in a class action suit," James Zito emphasizes. "Generally, there's no cost involved. But the real question is, are you better off suing individually? In most cases, if a class is 'qualified' by the federal court, you don't have a choice."

There are some exceptions, however — especially if your case is significantly different from others in the class action. Here's an example: A group of heart patients receives faulty pacemakers. They file a class action against the manufacturer. But one man's faulty pacemaker was also implanted incorrectly because of inaccurate information provided by the manufacturer's representative. That patient probably can opt out of the class action suit because he has an individual case against the pacemaker company.

You might also choose to opt out of a class action for personal reasons. "Say you have stock in an automobile company and yet you qualify as a member of a class that's suing the company over a problem with the model of car you own," attorney Zito states. "You can participate in the class action but you may have some moral objection to suing a company you have an interest in."

To opt out after you receive a public notice or a letter about a class action, simply write to the court and explain why you want to be excluded from the class.

Source:
Interview with James V. Zito, attorney-at-law, Lipshutz, Greenblatt, and King, Atlanta

How to legally change your name

There are plenty of reasons people want new names. Actors frequently change their given monikers for more movie star-sounding titles. Cary Grant, for example, started life as Archibald Leach. Other people just don't like the names their parents gave them. And a woman who's been known by the same last name for 50 years may balk at being stuck with a new last name after a brief, disastrous marriage.

Changing your name is easy. You definitely don't need a lawyer. Just go to the Clerk of the Court's Office and ask for the forms you need and instructions on how to file them.

You'll file a petition in your county court showing the reason you are changing your name — which can be as simple as the fact you don't like being called Bertha or Horatio.

Next, you'll request a hearing and advertise the fact you are changing your name in the official county publication. To find out which newspaper that is, call the Clerk of the Court's Office.

At the end of four weeks, you'll appear before a judge who will sign an order saying that henceforth your name is whatever you want it to be.

If you are a woman going through a divorce and you want your premarital last name back, simply have a request for the return of that name added to the divorce decree.

Remember to notify your local Social Security Office, your bank, and everybody else you do business with about your name change. To prove the newly named you is now the legal you, you'll need to provide certified copies of the court's order that changed your name.

The easiest way to take care of that? Simply go to the Clerk of the Court's Office after your name change hearing is over and request 10 or so certified copies.

A name change won't cost much although exact figures vary from state to state.

▶ Filing fee — $10 to $50
▶ Cost of publishing your notice in the official county publication — $40 to $50
▶ Certified copies of your name change — $1 to $2 per page

Source:
Interview with James V. Zito, attorney-at-law, Lipshutz, Greenblatt, and King, Atlanta

How to patent it yourself

Ever had a really brilliant idea for a new product, only to see it in a store several months later, making money for someone else? Maybe you didn't try to develop your idea because you thought it would just cost too much.

It can be expensive. Patent attorneys charge from $3,000 to $5,000, and the Federal Trade Commission says that most of the invention/promotion companies that advertise on late-night television are more likely to cost you money than make you money.

But, if you've got the time and the determination, you can get your own patent.

A recent book by patent attorney David Pressman walks you through the whole process, from researching whether your idea can be patented to evaluating potential profits and filing your patent application.

Pressman also shows you how to decide whether to manufacture and market your product yourself or try to sell your idea to an existing manufacturer. He even includes all necessary application forms.

What if you get halfway through the process and hit a snag?

You can always call a professional researcher, graphic artist, or patent attorney to help you over the rough spots — and pay them at their hourly rate. It will still cost a lot less than hiring an attorney to handle the whole process.

So if the next Hula-Hoop or Velcro fastener is burning a hole in your brain — go for it!

Source:
Patent It Yourself by David Pressman, Nolo Press, Berkeley, Calif., 1995

Write music? How to make sure no one steals your song

You've written a song, and it sounds pretty good. You may even dream of hearing it on the radio one day.

That could happen. But if it does, make sure you get the credit — and the money — you deserve for composing it.

"Your music is automatically copyrighted under the new federal copyright law," notes entertainment law specialist Bill Mohr. "It doesn't matter if you put a copyright notice — the circle with a 'C' inside — on it or not. The statutory copyright is immediate."

Unfortunately, an automatic copyright doesn't prove the song is your original composition. "It helps to share your composition with other people, so you'll have witnesses that you wrote it," attorney Mohr suggests.

But the safest route is to register your music with the United States Copyright Office in Washington, D.C. To obtain the copyright form, call 1-202-707-9100. The fee is $20 per composition.

"The preferable way to register is with sheet music. It can be a simple lead sheet, which is just a melody and lyrics, or a full score," Mohr explains. "However, you can also register sound recordings."

What if you hear music that sounds very much like the song you wrote?

"Unfortunately, that's a frequent problem," attorney Mohr says. "It comes up particularly when someone submits their composition to a publisher, a record company, or an artist and either they don't get a response or the song's rejected. But there was an opportunity for those people in the music industry to listen to the composition submitted to them. And sometimes they come out with a recording that sounds very similar to the work they rejected."

If that ever happens with music you wrote, consult an entertainment lawyer. He or she can look into the matter, see if there is a copyright infringement, and take legal remedies to get you the credit, and money, you deserve.

Source:
Interview with Bill Mohr, attorney-at-law, Atlanta

The 10 places in the U.S. where you're most likely to be sued

Legal suits these days range from serious to downright silly. Consider the case of restaurant owner David Pelzman and a no-show customer with a New Year's Eve reservation. Pelzman is suing for a breach of contract (not showing up for a reservation) and hopes to collect $440 in damages.

If you live long enough (and it may not have to be very long), you're likely to find yourself in the middle of a lawsuit. But to some extent it depends on where you live. Listed below are the top ten places in the United States where people are likely to be sued.

1. District of Columbia (Washington, D.C.)
2. Rhode Island
3. Massachusetts
4. New Mexico
5. Nevada

6. Delaware
7. Florida
8. New York
9. New Hampshire
10. Washington

People seem to be least tolerant in the Northeast. The most tolerant people (and the ones least likely to sue) live in the Rocky Mountains or Midwest.

The best states to live in if you want to avoid a legal hassle are Tennessee, Oregon, Idaho, Nebraska, Arkansas, South Dakota, Kansas, North Dakota, Indiana, and Utah, which is the best state of all to live if you want to stay out of court.

Just in case you're curious, the case of the no-show diner took place in Ohio, which ranks 26th among states in which you're most likely to be sued.
Sources:
Forbes (153,2:70)
Fortune (129,9:130)

How to access the government's secret files

Ever wonder what information the U.S. government has kept under wraps? While you can't peek at currently classified files, you can find out about all sorts of things the government has investigated in the past. The key? Knowing how to use the federal Freedom of Information Act (FOIA).

The FOIA allows citizens to request and obtain a variety of records compiled by federal agencies and departments — ranging from Air Force documents listing alleged UFO sightings to FBI files about criminal investigations.

The government doesn't have to honor all FOIA requests. For obvious reasons, you can't get information that could affect national security, trade secrets, facts that would place a criminal investigation in jeopardy, or files that would violate another citizen's right to personal privacy.

"You can get most of the information about yourself, but information about other people is restricted," explains FBI Public Information Officer Jay Spadafore. "Some information about yourself won't be disclosed if it identifies the person who gave the information and that person wanted confidentiality."

How to make a FOIA request. Since there are millions of records in government files, you must be able to reasonably identify what specific information you want — don't expect the government to do the searching for you.

Put your request in writing, along with your full name and birth date, and have your letter notarized. "That's to make sure we know that the person requesting the information is indeed who he says he is," notes the FBI's Spadafore. "We wouldn't want someone to be able to write in and get information on another person by saying he was that person."

Make sure you send your request to the agency most likely to have the records you're seeking. For example, says Spadafore, if you think the FBI has a file on you, remember there are 56 different FBI field offices. You must write to the specific office that conducted the investigation on you.

Not sure where to write? Spadafore suggests contacting each office in cities where you lived.

Has the FBI kept tabs on you? "I think there's a perception that the FBI does a lot more file keeping on people than we really do," says Spadafore. "We get a lot of requests from people who don't have any FBI files."

However, the FBI may have compiled information about you if you've ever been involved in a criminal case.

In addition, Spadafore points out, the FBI does background investigations for numerous federal agencies. So if you ever applied for a job with the U.S. government, you could well have an FBI file. You may want to use the FOIA to find out what information is in there, especially if you were denied employment.

Source:
Interview with Jay Spadafore, FBI, Atlanta

INSURANCE SECRETS

Will your insurance pay your claim?

The worst time to find out whether your insurance company will pay your claim is after you file. That's when you desperately need the money.

Find out now if your insurer has a good record of paying claims. Call your state Department of Insurance and ask for its list of insurance companies ranked by how well they pay claims.

If your insurance company isn't on the top third of the list, consider switching.

Source:
Buyer Beware: An Industry Insider Shows You How to Win the Insurance Game by Morey Stettner, Probus, Burrbridge, Ill., 1994

Is your insurance company healthy?

Insurance companies are rated financially by companies like A.M. Best, Standard & Poor's, Moody's, and Duff & Phelps. Make sure any company you buy life, health, or disability insurance from is rated A, A+, or AA. That tells you the company is financially sound and will be able to pay your claims. Don't settle for less. Your insurance agent should be able to show you this rating in writing. If he or she can't, there's something wrong with either the company or the agent. Keep shopping.

Source:
Interview with Donald Jay Korn, author of *Your Money or Your Life: How to Save Thousands on Your Health-Care Insurance*, Collier Books, New York, 1992

The best rates available

A smart and easy way to find cheaper insurance is to contact a company called Insurance Information Inc. at 1-800-472-5800. This company doesn't sell insurance. It finds the best quotes available for you through its database of 250 insurance companies around the country.

If you're not ready for a specific price quote, they'll just send you a packet of information. If you do want a quote, give them your credit card number, your age, and the amount of insurance coverage you want. For $50, the company will send you information on the five least expensive insurance policies available for you.

Insurance Information Inc. only sends information on companies rated A or better by A.M. Best, a firm that tracks the financial health of insurance companies.

You can take the information to your insurance agent, or you can call the insurance companies yourself.

Guarantee: If you already have an insurance policy, and Insurance Information Inc. can't save you more than $50, they will not charge you for the information they send.

Source:
The Tightwad Gazette, II by Amy Dacyczyn, Villard Books, New York, 1995

How to cash in your whole life insurance

Fred Caldwell is 68 years old and about to retire. He's built up a large cash value in his whole life policy over the years, and he no longer needs the coverage. Can he get his hands on that money?

All Caldwell has to do is ask his insurance agent to annuitize his cash value. The agent would invest the money in an immediate annuity that pays a monthly income. By purchasing a $60,000 immediate annuity, Caldwell could receive approximately $500 a month over the next 10 years.

You don't have to pay taxes on the part you've paid in over the years — the principal. You just pay taxes on the 45 percent or so that's interest income. Caldwell is in the 28 percent tax bracket, so he'd pay $63 in taxes every month. That's a pretty good deal.

Source:
Your Life Insurance Options by Alan Lavine, John Wiley & Sons, New York, 1993

The right life policy at the right price

Term insurance — whole life — variable annuity — what kind of insurance policy is right for you? It's no wonder most people don't shop around for insurance. It's difficult to decide what you're even looking for. But if you don't shop your insurance, you can end up paying twice as much as you have to for a policy.

Basically, you need to decide what you want from an insurance policy. If you just want a policy that will provide for your family after your death, you should buy *term insurance*. It's very low-cost, and it gives you a guaranteed death benefit.

For the best price on a term policy that you renew every year (the premiums will go up every year), call insurers who sell directly to you with no agents in between, such as USAA Life Insurance Co. Northwestern Mutual Life Insurance Co. also sells inexpensive policies through local agents.

If you're sure you won't need insurance after a certain point (when all your children are out of college, for instance), your best deal may be a *level premium* term policy. The premium stays at a fixed level for five, 10, 15, or 20 years.

With term insurance, you don't build up any cash value in your policy. That's OK if you're saving and investing money in other ways. If you need a forced savings plan that may not bring you spectacular returns but is very low risk, a cash-value plan may be the right one for you. Look into a whole life plan, a universal life contract, or an annuity that will pay you after you retire.

These plans are also right for you if you'll need insurance past age 70. Term insurance is extremely expensive for people over 70.

To save money on a cash-value policy, find coverage without paying an agent's commission. You can buy *low-load* (low commission) policies directly from insurance companies such as USAA Life Insurance Co. and Ameritas Life Insurance Corp.

Sources:
The Christian's Guide to Wise Investing by Gary D. Moore, former senior vice-president of investment at Paine Webber, Zondervan Books, Grand Rapids, Mich., 1994
The Wall Street Journal (Dec. 8, 1995, R17)
Your Life Insurance Options by Alan Lavine, John Wiley & Sons, New York, 1993

Don't buy too much life insurance

Nobody is pointing a finger at insurance agents here. Like anyone who sells anything, an agent is going to err on the side of overinsuring you rather than underinsuring. Don't trust an agent to tell you how much life insurance you need. Think about how much your family would really need if you weren't around.

As your dependents become less dependent, cut back on your life insurance. Cutting back is easy if you have a term life insurance policy. Cashing in a cash-value life insurance policy to buy term insurance or another cash-value policy is probably a bad idea. If an insurance agent wants you to cash in a policy, get a second opinion.

Source:
1001 Ways to Cut Your Expenses by Jonathan D. Pond, Dell Publishing, New York, 1992

Check guaranteed return rates on life insurance

In buying permanent life insurance, make sure the insurer bases future returns projections on historical data and not on unsubstantiated estimates. Insurance companies often inflate their expectations of future interest rates and minimize estimates of future company expenses. Compare guaranteed rates set by law and look at each company's past performance before you buy.

Source:
Real Life: The Ten Things Every Grown-Up Needs to Know by Tom Heymann, Fawcett Columbine, New York, 1994

Switching life insurance can be costly

Even if you're offered lower premiums, it usually doesn't pay to switch life insurance policies from one company to another. Administrative expenses and commissions are high on a new policy, dividends get larger as a policy ages, and cash values of whole life policies build up faster in later years. Plus the contestability and suicide provisions of a new policy usually require two-year waiting periods. At the very least, get a second opinion on the switch from the company or agent who sold you the first policy. And don't drop the old policy until you're sure the new one is in force.

Source:
The New York Times Personal Finance Handbook by Leonard Sloane, Times Books, New York, 1995

Save money on life insurance premiums

Don't throw money away! You can save by following this expert advice:

▶ Always pay premiums annually. The more frequently you pay, the higher the premium. Also, you are less likely to forget and have to pay a penalty or get another medical exam.

▶ Plan ahead so you don't buy new policies on a regular basis. It will cost less to buy one $50,000 policy than five $10,000 policies.

▶ Buy your policy within six months of your last birthday to lock in a lower premium — insurers often count your age from your nearest birthday.

▶ Avoid *reentry* term insurance. With this type of insurance, you will have to get a medical exam every one, five, or 10 years. If your health has declined, premiums will skyrocket.

Source:
Real Life: The Ten Things Every Grown-Up Needs to Know by Tom Heymann, Fawcett Columbine, New York, 1994

Improve your life insurance rating to get a lower premium

You'll have to pass a physical exam to get life insurance with a top-rated company, but even the best insurers cover some less than healthy people, taking moderate risks in return for higher premiums.

Insurance companies base their rates on standard risks — people with no significant health problems who have normal life expectancies. Some companies even offer discounted rates to individuals with above average health.

People with health problems are rated and pay premiums accordingly. Ratings start with Table 1 for slight problems like being a little overweight. As health problems increase, your rating goes up. With diabetes, for example, you would be on Table 2; uncontrolled hypertension, Table 4; liver problems, Table 8; an abnormal EKG, Table 12, and so forth. Some companies have 16 tables, so regardless of your health problems, you are likely to find a place somewhere on the tables unless you have advanced cancer or AIDS.

Expect to pay 25 percent above the standard price for each rating level. If you have a high rating, look for an insurance agent who is an expert on impaired-risk insurance. Because ratings vary from one insurer to another, you might get a better rating by applying to a certain company.

An agent who specializes in impaired risks can steer you toward the insurer who is most likely to give the lowest rating for your particular problem. For example, if you have hypertension, a certain company may be more lenient with that risk. Another may be best for those who have had bypass surgery.

You can also save money by waiting to buy life insurance until you've lost weight, stopped smoking, or addressed any other health problems that might make you a higher risk. The better condition you're in when you take the physical, the less you'll pay for your policy.

Source:
Interview with Andrew D. Westhem, author of *Protecting Your Assets*, Citadel Press, New York, 1996

Confused about life insurance? Hire an advisor

Purchasing life insurance can be a complex task. A fee-only consultant can help you sift among the many options and select what's best for you. Such consultants don't work on commission, so their advice is not apt to be as biased as that of an insurance agent. Ask your lawyer or other advisors for recommendations or look in the yellow pages under insurance consultants.

Here are a few things an insurance advisor can do:

▶ Provide a second opinion on policies you plan to buy.
▶ Tell you whether your existing insurance company is healthy.
▶ Evaluate whether an existing policy or annuity is appropriate.
▶ Help you choose policies, including riders and options.
▶ Negotiate lower commissions from your agent.

Source:
Interview with Kenneth M. Morris, author of *The Wall Street Journal Guide to Understanding Personal Finance*, Lightbulb Press, New York, 1992

Don't count on the government for health care coverage

Medicare kicks in when you reach age 65, but you can't count on it to take care of your medical costs. You still have to pay deductibles, coinsurance, and charges for services Medicare doesn't cover.

You have three choices to keep your health care costs under control:

▶ You can stay on your employer's health insurance plan after you retire.
▶ You can buy Medigap insurance to fill in Medicare holes.
▶ You can enroll in a health maintenance organization (HMO) that has a contract to serve people on Medicare.

Medicare has two parts. You're automatically enrolled in Part A at age 65, and you choose whether to purchase the inexpensive Part B. Here's what's covered and what's not under each section:

Part A

For the first 60 days you are in the hospital, you'll pay $696 (1994 figures). Medicare pays the rest. After the first 60 days, the longer you stay in, the less Medicare pays.

Medicare will pay for your first 20 days in a skilled nursing facility. Neither Medicare nor Medigap insurance will pay for most nursing home care.

Medicare will pay for home health care services and medical supplies you need at home, except for 20 percent of medical equipment costs. You have to pay that.

Medicare pays most of the costs of hospice care for terminally ill people.

You pay for the first three pints of blood you receive. Medicare pays for the rest.

Part B

For a doctor's services, medical and surgical services and supplies, physical and speech therapy, tests, and medical equipment — both in the hospital and out — Medicare pays 80 percent. You pay a $100 deductible plus the other 20 percent. (You pay half of the charges for mental health services.)

Medicare covers all the costs for blood or urine tests and other lab services.

As you can see, Medicare leaves plenty of gaps. Besides the $100 deductible and the 20 percent copayment, you pay for your own prescription drugs, for routine physicals, for dental care and hearing aids, for your first three pints of blood, for eye exams and eyeglasses, for full-time home nursing care, and for nursing home care. Also, Medicare only pays for a limited number of days in a hospital or skilled nursing facility.

If your retirement package didn't include health insurance and you don't want to join an HMO, you'll need to buy a Medigap policy. However, don't let a salesman pressure you into buying a policy before you're ready.

For a period of six months after you enroll in Medicare Part B, you have a guaranteed legal right to the Medigap policy of your choice regardless of your health conditions. During these six months, you can buy any Medigap policy sold by any insurer doing Medigap business in your state.

You also are entitled by law to a "free look" at any policy. That means that the insurance company must give you at least 30 days to review a Medigap policy. If you decide you don't want it, you can send it back and have all your money refunded.

Finally, it's against the law for any Medigap insurance salesman to sell you a policy that duplicates coverage you already have. If you think at any point you've been a victim of a dishonest insurance company, call the federal toll-free number for filing insurance complaints — 1-800-638-6833.

Source:
1994 Guide to Health Insurance for People with Medicare, U.S. Department of Health and Human Services, Health Care Financing Administration, 6325 Security Boulevard, Baltimore, MD 21207

How to choose Medigap insurance

All people over 65 and on Medicare need Medigap insurance. Medigap covers medical bills that government-provided health insurance doesn't pay. The federal government has set standards for 10 types of Medigap policies, called A through J. Insurance companies can sell the low-cost "core" A policy plus any or all of the others. Here are the main differences:

1) Policy A covers big hospital bills and pays the 20 percent copayment for medical expenses like doctor bills that Medicare requires you to pay.
2) Policy B adds coverage for the Medicare Part A deductible.
3) Policies C through J pay the above expenses plus additional benefits for skilled nursing home care, prescription drugs, and medical expenses incurred when traveling outside the United States.

Among policies C through J, look at two key components: How much you'll spend on prescription drugs and how the policy handles *balance billing* — a practice that leaves you responsible for the portion of the bill that Medicare and Medigap don't pay.

Medicare sets a limit on how much it will pay for certain medical procedures. It pays 80 percent of that amount and the Medigap policy picks up the remaining 20 percent. But if your doctor or hospital bills are more than the limit, which is called balance billing, you are responsible for paying the remainder.

Here are some pointers on choosing a policy:

▶ If you are in poor health, be sure to get the policy within six months of signing up for Medicare Part B. Those six months are considered an open enrollment period when any qualified person can buy a policy regardless of health.

▶ If you are likely to spend more than $3,000 a year on prescription drugs, buy J, which pays up to $3,000 worth of drugs a year.

▶ If your drug bill is likely to be less than $3,000 but more than $1,000, H or I may be your best bet. Choose I if you are concerned about balance billing; H if balance billing doesn't worry you.

▶ G is probably best if you don't need many prescription drugs but may run into a balance billing problem, because at-home recovery is included in this policy. Policy F may be good in this situation, as well, if it is a reasonable price.

▶ If neither heavy prescription drug use nor balance billing is a problem for you, choose the cheapest policy among C through J for good catastrophic protection.

▶ In comparing prices among policies, check the insurer's premium schedules, called *outlines of coverage*. Find out if the premiums will remain relatively stable or will rise each year as you age. You may be better off with a policy that costs more initially than one which has escalating premiums.

▶ Check for low-cost policies among social or professional organizations to which you belong or can join.

▶ Look for an insurer that offers electronic billing, which can save you money and aggravation. Also, some insurers provide *crossover billing* — that means your Medicare bills automatically go directly to the Medigap insurance company.

Source:
Protecting Your Assets by Andrew D. Westhem, Citadel Press, New York, 1996

When your insurer says your doctor charged too much

It happens all the time. You turn your doctor or hospital bill over to the insurance company, and you get rejected. The insurance company says your medical bill exceeds the "customary" or "usual" charge, and they refuse to pay the full amount of the bill.

Don't complain to the insurance company yet. Your doctor may be overcharging you. Insurance companies decide how much they will pay for a medical service by taking an average of fees charged by doctors and hospitals within your zip code.

First, ask your doctor why he charged more. He may tell you that he not only repaired your hemorrhoids, he also zapped some nearby fissures with his laser because he thought they would give you trouble later. You can take your doctor's answer back to the insurance company and possibly convince them to give you more money.

Don't visit a doctor in a nearby upscale neighborhood. If you live in a small town, don't go see a doctor in the big city unless you have a good reason to do so. Remember, the insurance reimbursement is based on an average fee in your zip code.

Fight the battle before you go to the doctor. Unless you have a medical emergency, find out before you see the doctor what he normally charges. Then call your insurance company and ask how much it will allow for that service. If your doctor's fees are too high, tell him so. He may be willing to lower his price. Or you may choose to visit another doctor.

Sources:
Fortis Benefits Insurance Company, St. Paul, Minn.
Money (24,13:107)

Health insurance: Making fee-for-service plans work for you

People who opt for a *fee-for-service* policy, the traditional indemnity health insurance plans we all grew up with, usually are buying the most expensive option but getting the greatest amount of flexibility. Under these plans, you choose your own doctor and are reimbursed by the insurance company after satisfying your deductible and copayment requirements. Here are ways to save money with such a plan:

▶ Find out whether your physicians' fees are considered "reasonable and customary" before you sign up for a fee-for-service plan. If your doctor charges $125 for a consultation and the insurance company considers $75 a reasonable fee, you'll be out the extra money in addition to your copayment or deductible and regardless of any *stop-loss* amount, your maximum out-of-pocket expense.

You can compare your doctor's fees with the norm by calling the Health Care Cost Hotline at 1-900-225-2500. For $2 to $4 per minute you'll learn the median fee and range of fees nationwide for more than 7,000 medical procedures.

▶ Buy high-deductible insurance — $1,000 or $2,500 per person. The insurance will probably cost thousands less so if you and your family are reasonably healthy you'll come out ahead. Plus you avoid the hassle of trying to get reimbursed for every visit.

▶ Shop around and negotiate fees with doctors, clinics, hospitals, and other providers in advance of scheduled visits and procedures.

▶ Make sure your plan has a stop-loss amount and a high benefits cap. For example, after you pay $5,000 in any year the insurance takes over and pays all your costs up to at least $1 million.

▶ Buy a plan with a 50 percent copayment to get lower premiums.

▶ For minor illnesses, make an appointment with a Nurse Practitioner (NP) or Physician's Assistant (PA). These professionals charge less than physicians and are trained to handle most routine medical functions such as colds, check-ups, X-rays, and other noncritical situations. If your doctor doesn't use an NP or PA, consider finding one who does.

Source:
Interview with Andrew D. Westhem, author of *Protecting Your Assets*, Citadel Press, New York, 1996

Making the most of your health insurance

Insurance companies regularly deny claims and refuse to pay for the full cost of treatment. Don't let it happen to you. Here's how to squeeze every penny possible from your health insurance company:

Read your full contract. Your employer or insurer probably gave you a summary of your health insurance when you signed up. Get a copy of the full contract from your insurer, and slowly read the entire policy. Take notes, and ask your insurance agent or benefits manager to explain anything you don't understand. Important exclusions are often listed in the fine print and footnotes.

Know the limitations. If you know your insurance won't cover an extra day in the hospital, plan to go home a day earlier if possible.

Check in advance whether you're covered for something. The insurance company certainly isn't going to let you know when you should have filed a claim. If you're covered for something but don't know it, you may as well not be covered.

Pay premiums on time, by check only. One of the chief reasons insurers cite for cancelling a policy or denying a claim is nonpayment of premiums. Send your payments directly to the insurer, not to your agent.

Get a doctor's prescription for every medical product or service you buy. Get prescriptions for wheelchairs, tests, and even for air purifiers and air conditioners, if possible.

Keep detailed records of all medical expenses. Write down doctor names, dates, and what was done. Even include the cost of mileage to and from the doctor's office. If your insurance doesn't cover it, you may still be able to take it off your taxes.

Record all contact with your insurance company. If you've called to ask whether an expense is covered and you're told that it is, try to get the person you spoke with to send you a response in writing. When you submit your claim, submit it to that person. Remind them of your conversation.

Photocopy everything. Never send a claim or any medical document to the insurer without photocopying it first.

Submit claims right away. Most policies have a 90-day deadline for submitting claims. (There's also a limit to how long the insurer can take to get back to you.)

Send in bills you know won't be covered. Some bills aren't covered, but do go toward your deductible. The insurer won't count them, though, if you don't send them in.

Use the "participating providers." Some plans give you a discount for using certain doctors and hospitals.

Ask your doctor for an itemized statement. Some medical care providers don't or can't give a second statement, so keep the original safely filed.

Find out if you need to file for major medical reimbursement, too. Don't just assume that one check is all you get. Sometimes you have to file separate claims for your basic plan and your major medical plan. You get reimbursed by your basic plan, then you file the balance under your major medical.

Submit to your primary carrier first. If you need to submit two claims (to two insurance companies or to a basic and a major medical plan), find out who to send your claim to first. If you send them in the wrong order, you may not get paid.

Use the toll-free number. Calls to your insurance company can be expensive if you don't use the 800 number. Ask when is the best time to call so you won't have to wait.

Take a filled-out insurance form to the doctor's office. If you're going to a new doctor, this will speed up their claims-filing process. A few days later, check to make sure the office filed your claim.

Bunch as much medical care into one calendar year as possible. That will help you meet your deductible.

Try to get reimbursed even for services that aren't covered. Call your insurer and ask if there are any circumstances under which the service would be covered. Sometimes a service is covered if you receive it at a hospital clinic instead of at your doctor's office.

Don't just accept it if your claim is denied or you think you're not paid enough. If you stick to it, you have a good chance of getting your claim approved or getting more money. Immediately submit a written request asking for information about the appeals process, the reason for the denial or decreased amount, and the kinds of information the insurer would require to reconsider your claim. Ask for a reply by a certain date.

Resubmit your claim. Include whatever medical information might counter their reason for denying your claim. Include copies of all previous correspondence, and tell them they can call your doctor or medical provider. Be sure to let your doctor know he may be contacted. Also state that you will call a specific person on a specific date if you haven't received a reply within four weeks.

If you are wrongly denied again, contact the state insurance department. Send them all of your correspondence with the insurance company, a copy of your policy (with the related parts highlighted), and ask them to schedule a hearing on your case. Small claims court is another option at this point.

Source:
Health Insurance: How to Get It, Keep It, or Improve What You've Got by Robert Enteen, Paragon House, New York, 1992

Join a group for health insurance deal

If you're not covered by an employee health insurance policy, find out if any professional associations you belong to offer group health policies. If not, look in a book called the Encyclopedia of Associations at your local library to find names of groups to join that might offer such policies. Such group plans don't generally require a medical exam. Avoid mail-order health insurance policies. Even though they are advertised as group insurance, frequently they are as expensive as individual policies.

Source:
Interview with Bob Hunter, insurance director, Consumer Federation of America, 1424 16th St. N.W., Suite 604, Washington, D.C. 20036

What about cancer insurance?

Cancer insurance is a rip-off, according to a congressional subcommittee that investigated it. Instead, buy a major medical policy with catastrophic coverage — that is, one with a high deductible of anywhere from $2,000 to $5,000. The premiums will be lower than a low-deductible policy, and you'll be covered for other illnesses besides cancer as well.

Sources:
Interview with Donald Jay Korn, author of *Your Money or Your Life: How to Save Thousands on Your Health-Care Insurance*, Collier Books, New York, 1992
Consumer Federation of America, 1424 16th St. N.W., Suite 604, Washington, D.C. 20036

Are you overexposed?

Your health insurance is covered by your employer so you feel safe. But that's no guarantee you won't be stripped of your assets in certain cases.

First, make sure you see your actual policy and check that the insurer is financially stable. Next, look for gaps in what's covered. Is there coverage for mental health conditions, including alcohol and drug abuse — such care costs thousands of dollars. What about care for your college-age children? Most family insurance policies cover kids only up to age 19. What about stepchildren? Check your policy to find out.

Look for a *stop-loss* amount. After you've spent a set amount on deductibles and copayment does your company step in to pay or hang you out to dry? A bill for intensive care treatment of a premature infant could leave you with a 20 percent copayment of more than $100,000 if there is no stop-loss amount in your policy. Keep in mind that your maximum out-of-pocket expense may be different for psychotherapy, dentistry, etc.

Note the cap on benefits. Example: Suppose your policy has a $500,000 *lifetime cap*. That leaves you responsible for any bills after that amount. Good policies will have at least a $1 million to 2 million cap.

If your policy covers you in all the above areas, hold onto it even if you're asked by your employer to pay more in premiums, deductibles, and copayments. If your employee plan comes up short, you have options:

▶ Pass up your employer's plan and buy a good plan yourself.

▶ If you get to choose your fringe benefits, opt for others such as life insurance, child care, tuition reimbursement, or disability, and pay for your own health care.

▶ Supplement the employee plan. You may be able to pay more for better coverage under the employer's policy. If not, consider a major medical plan with a large deductible to cover catastrophes.

Source:
Interview with Donald Jay Korn, author of *Your Money or Your Life: How to Save Thousands on Your Health-Care Insurance*, Collier Books, New York, 1992

How to select an employee health plan

If you work for a big company and don't already have several health plans to choose from, you probably will be offered some options soon. Having a choice of health plans is nice but can be confusing. Get started by asking co-workers what they think of coverage and services provided by their health plans.

Also ask your doctor or other health care providers which of the available health plans they recommend. If you want to keep seeing a particular provider, find out if one of the plans covers that provider's services.

Finally, use this checklist:

▶ Will you most often see a doctor, a nurse practitioner, or a physician's assistant?

▶ How easily can you change your primary-care doctor if you're unhappy?

▶ Can you see a doctor outside of the plan if you pay part of the cost?

▶ Are you likely to need any services listed as "exclusions" in the benefits description? What will this cost you?

▶ What is the procedure for getting second opinions?

▶ Is there a limit on your out-of-pocket copayments?

▶ Is there a lifetime cap on what the plan will pay for your health care?

▶ Are your current medicines covered? Are you restricted to certain pharmacies? Are they convenient? What are the drug copayments? Do they vary with the drug?

▶ What medical equipment is covered and under what circumstances?

▶ Does the plan provide health education and wellness programs that interest you?

▶ Are health facility hours and locations convenient? Are laboratory and other tests conducted in a convenient location? Is parking or public transportation available?

▶ How long does it take to schedule a routine checkup?

▶ Is the staff at the facility friendly, patient, and helpful?

▶ Which hospitals are affiliated with the plan? Are certain ones available only for a limited range of conditions or services?

▶ How is emergency care provided?

▶ What is the procedure if you need a specialist?

▶ How does the plan pick its doctors?

Sources:
Interview with Nancy Turnbull, Department of Health Policy and Management, Harvard University School of Public Health, Boston, Mass.
Get What You Pay for or Don't Pay Anything at All by Donna McCrohan, Crown Trade Paperbacks, New York, 1994
Health Care Choices for Today's Consumer, edited by Marc S. Miller, Living Planet Press, Washington, D.C., 1995

Choosing insurance plans when you both work

Can you and your spouse both get health insurance through your jobs? You need to choose one provider as your primary insurance. In deciding which plan to select, evaluate the following: 1) Which pays the most possible expenses; 2) Which has the highest benefits limit; and 3) Which has a stop-loss amount. If the plans are similar in those factors, compare deductibles and copayment requirements and choose the one that will cost less.

Also, find out if either employer offers a flexible benefits plan which allows you to choose from a menu of benefits. In these situations, one spouse might choose health insurance while the other gets needed coverage such as life or disability insurance.

Source:
Interview with Donald J. Korn, author of *Your Money or Your Life*, Collier Books, New York, 1992

How to keep your health insurance when you lose your job: Understand your COBRA rights

You have a lot of things to worry about when you lose your job. But thanks to the federal Consolidated Omnibus Budget Reconciliation Act (COBRA), losing your health insurance shouldn't be one of them — at least for a while.

With COBRA, any company that employs at least 20 people must allow you to remain on their group health insurance plan for up to 18 months. This applies to workers who quit or are fired — unless they were let go for gross negligence. The law doesn't apply if you work for some church-related organizations or the federal government.

The bad news is you have to pay the premiums and your former company can also charge you up to 2 percent extra as an administrative fee.

The good news is your premiums will still be at a group rate — far less expensive than the same coverage in an individual policy.

Some states, including Georgia, have extended COBRA coverage to 36 months. Check with your state insurance commissioner's office to find out if that's the case where you live.

Sources:
Interview with James Zito, attorney-at-law, Lipshutz, Greenblatt, and King, Atlanta
The Court T.V. Cradle-To-Grave Legal Survival Guide: A Complete Resource for Any Question You May Have About the Law by American Lawyer Media; Little, Brown, and Company, 1995

How to keep flex plan money when you are fired

You're fired or re-engineered out of your job. You may get severance pay and a future retirement benefit if you are vested. And of course, you'll get the *health flexible spending account* (HFSA) balance you've been paying into all year long.

Not necessarily!

Section 125 of the Internal Revenue Code says the flexible spending account is a "use it or lose it" proposition. You lose HFSA money not spent during the year even if you are fired or laid off.

Here are some tips on how to keep dollars you have paid into an HFSA from slipping through your fingers.

An HFSA lets you put aside pretax dollars for medical and dental expenses not covered by your health insurance. You decide at the beginning of the year how much you want to set aside, and your employer puts that amount in an account for you. For the rest of the year, pretax dollars are deducted from your paycheck to reimburse the account.

Your options if you are fired and haven't tapped the full amount in the account:

▶ Use it or lose it before your employment ends.

▶ Continue coverage by paying premiums through the end of the year with after-tax dollars. Because the flexible spending account is a type of health insurance, your right to keep paying into the account and continue coverage is protected by COBRA, the Consolidated Omnibus Budget Reconciliation Act. However, you no longer get to pay into the account with pretax dollars.

Neither of your options is very appealing. But Dennis Coleman, a national benefits consultant, notes that there is nothing to prevent you from electing continued coverage, using up the amount you've paid in, and then ceasing to pay premiums.

In fact, you can abuse the system. You are entitled to all of the money in the flexible spending account from day one, even though you haven't yet paid it all back. There is little a company can do if an employee spends all the money in the account and then chooses not to pay it back when he or she is no longer working for the company. The company may try to collect the money for the overspent account, but practically speaking, has little recourse.

Some employers may try to insist that if you want to continue coverage after you leave, you have to pay your premiums upfront. The money will be taken out of your last paycheck. You should protest. COBRA requires the same coverage for you as for other employees, and they aren't required to pay premiums upfront.

Why do employers continue to offer this benefit when a laid-off worker could abuse it? When you figure that you forfeit any flexible spending account money you don't use by the end of the year, you can see that the employer tends to come out ahead. The people who never use up their regular accounts more than offset the ex-employees who abuse the system.

Source:
Interview with Dennis Coleman, a principal at Kwasha Lipton (a benefits consulting firm in Fort Lee, N.J.) and a representative from the Internal Revenue Service

What you should know about workers' comp before you need it

Workers' compensation is something you hope you'll never need. No one wants to be sidelined with a job-related accident or illness.

But it's far better to learn about workers' comp when you're feeling fit and everything is fine — rather than hope you'll make the right financial and medical decisions when and if you are injured in your workplace.

What exactly is workers' comp? "Most states require employers who have more than two or three employees to purchase workers' compensation insurance to guarantee some medical insurance coverage for workers injured on the job," points out Atlanta-based attorney James V. Zito, who specializes in corporate and employment law. "This protects employees who may not otherwise be able to afford health care and cannot wait for a lawsuit to be settled before getting needed medical treatment.

"But the real protection is for the employer," Zito explains. A worker injured on the job could sue and bankrupt a company or factory. Workers' comp is a substitute for a lawsuit for damages.

Simply put, workers' comp is a type of no-fault insurance. It gives a guaranteed, specific payment to an employee injured in the workplace and unable to work permanently or temporarily — or to his family, if the worker died due to a work accident. In return, the worker (in most states) is not allowed to file a lawsuit against the employer.

To find out exactly what your state workers' comp laws are, contact your state Department of Labor. You'll find the number in the phone book.

What qualifies as an on-the-job injury? "To be eligible for workers' comp, your disability or injury must have taken place during your normal work hours, at the place where you work, and while you were performing your work," attorney Zito explains.

If you and a fellow worker toss a baseball around during your coffee break and you are accidentally "beaned," your concussion won't qualify as a work-related injury. Or if you come down with an illness, like appendicitis, that has nothing to do with your job, there's also no reason to file a workers' comp claim.

On the other hand, a workplace injury doesn't have to be as sudden and obvious as a steel worker injured by heavy equipment. It can be a disability slowly caused by a job requiring repetitive movements.

"In fact, carpal tunnel syndrome, a painful wrist and hand disorder, is now the primary injury among office workers," attorney Zito points out. Breathing toxic fumes or being exposed to chemicals can result in workers' comp claims, too.

How to file a claim

▶ **Contact your employer as soon as you are injured.** You should receive a claim form to fill out and instructions on submitting it to the insurance carrier and the workers' comp agency in your state.

▶ **Seek appropriate medical care.** Check with your employer to see if there are specific doctors you should see. In most states, an employee must post a list or "panel" of physicians covering many specialties that injured workers can consult. Unless it's an emergency, you need to see one of the listed panel physicians to make sure you're covered.

▶ **Consult an attorney.** That's not a necessity, but it could net you a quicker — and bigger — settlement in the long-run. "There are experts in every state in workers' comp, and they usually don't charge an upfront fee to the injured person. They are paid a percentage of any recovery. So it is to the attorney's benefit to maximize the settlement," says attorney James Zito.

▶ **Not happy with how your workers' comp claim has been handled?** Whether you have an attorney or are handling your claim yourself, in most states you can request a hearing before a workers' compensation judge.

Source:
Interview with James V. Zito, attorney-at-law, Lipshutz, Greenblatt, and King, Atlanta

Don't forget disability

You know life insurance is important to your family. You want them protected financially when you die. But what if you lose your income because you become disabled? Statistics show that your odds of becoming disabled during your working years are far greater than your odds of dying. You must protect your family against the loss of your income with disability insurance.

And don't fall into the trap of assuming you're covered by your employer. Take a close look at what disability insurance your company offers. Usually, an employer will cover about 60 percent of your salary, but you have to pay income tax on that money. So, you might end up with only 40 or 45 percent of your actual salary. You may want to look at some additional insurance.

The best plan is to be covered at work, but to pay the premiums yourself. You have to pull the money out of your own pocket, but you won't pay taxes on any money you receive when you're disabled. You only pay income tax when the money comes from your employer. When you don't pay taxes on the money, 60 percent of your income is almost equivalent to your salary.

How much you'll pay for disability insurance depends on your occupation. A carpenter will have higher premiums than a computer operator because he's got the more dangerous job. Many professional associations offer life and disability insurance to their members at good rates.

While you're shopping for price, shop for a stable insurance company, too. Insiders say companies selling disability insurance are leaving the market in droves. So many people are filing disability claims, the insurers are losing money. Check *Best's Insurance Reports* for A and A+ rated companies.
Source:
Interview with Todd Shapiro, agent, Lincoln Financial Group, Atlanta

What to look for in a disability policy

Whether you're deciding on an employee disability insurance plan or shopping for a private plan, keep the following points in mind:

▶ What is the policy's definition of disability? Some pay benefits if you can't do your regular job. Many others, however, pay only if you are unable to perform duties you are suited or trained for. Still others won't pay unless you can't handle any work at all.

▶ Does the policy cover both total and partial disability? Usually payments for partial disability must follow a period of total disability.

▶ When do benefits start? Most policies have a 90- or 120-day period before payments begin. Make sure you have enough savings to cover your expenses until then. The longer the waiting period, the lower the premiums will be.

▶ Find out what pre-existing conditions will make you ineligible for coverage.

▶ Is the policy noncancelable — that means it can't be canceled and the premiums and benefits are fixed as well — or is it guaranteed renewable, which means the policy's benefits won't change but premiums can go up?

▶ How long can you collect payment? It's smart to get a policy that covers you up to age 65, when retirement benefits kick in.

▶ Watch out for add-on features that add to premiums but don't really buy you anything substantial.

▶ Does the policy have a premium waiver once you're collecting benefits?

▶ Fill out your own health questionnaire. Insurance agents may be tempted to gloss over any health issues to make sure you get the policy, but you could later be denied coverage if the application misrepresented your condition.

▶ Expect to undergo blood and urine screening tests.

▶ Look for a clause that commits the insurer to pay for a rehabilitation program.

▶ If you're turned down, challenge the company's decision. It might have been made on faulty information.

Source:
Interview with Nancy Turnbull, Health Policy and Management Department, Harvard University School of Public Health, Boston

Paying for long-term care

Aging couples face a nursing-home nightmare if they don't plan in advance. One spouse (four times out of five, the husband) is admitted to a nursing home. Medicare doesn't cover any custodial care, so the couple begins spending savings to cover the $30,000 average yearly nursing-home bill.

Finally, the couple is broke and qualifies for Medicaid. Medicaid pays the nursing-home bills until the ailing spouse dies. The surviving spouse is left to spend the rest of her life in poverty.

You can keep this from happening to you by buying a long-term care insurance policy that will pay for custodial care in a licensed nursing home. Here's what to look for when you pick a policy:

▶ The policy should not duplicate Medicare coverage. Medicare will pay for medical equipment and supplies and for limited home visits from nurses, therapists, and medical social workers.

▶ The policy should supplement Medicare's respite service. The caregiver will need time for herself away from her duties. The policy should provide some respite service. The policy should also provide chore services such as household help, cooking, shopping, and patient personal hygiene.

▶ The policy should not exclude Alzheimer's disease or "mental or neurological" disorders. Also, policies should not require a hospital stay before nursing-home coverage begins.

▶ The policy should cover a four-year stay. Four years seems short, but not many people live longer than that in a nursing home. The policy may have a lifetime dollar limit instead of a time limit. To judge whether the dollar limit is enough, call four or five local nursing homes and ask for their annual rates for a semiprivate room.

▶ The policy should pay a percentage of the room rate, rather than a fixed dollar amount per day. Inflation could destroy the value of a policy that pays a fixed dollar amount, say $100, per day. You'll be safer with a policy that pays 80 percent of a semiprivate room.

A recent study showed that the average couple would be bankrupt after just 13 weeks of supporting one spouse in a nursing home. Get a good long-term care policy in your insurance portfolio immediately.

Source:
Money and the Mature Woman: How to Hold On to Your Income, Keep Your Home, Plan Your Estate by
Frances Leonard, Addison-Wesley Publishing, Reading, Mass., 1993

Hold down the cost of your long-term care policy

Long-term care insurance costs a bundle — but so does a nursing-home stay. Here are some ways you can save money on this expensive but sometimes essential policy:

▶ If possible, buy through your employer's group policy. Often these have better coverage than individual policies, and you can purchase them for your parents as well as yourself and your spouse.

▶ Buy young — a policy purchased at age 45 might cost about $375 per year compared with $1,700 per year if bought at age 70. Annual premiums won't go up unless they are raised for all local policyholders.

▶ Choose a 90-day waiting period before benefits kick in.

▶ Limit your benefit period to three or four years of care. This will give you enough time to transfer assets and qualify for Medicaid's assistance in paying the bills.

▶ Avoid home-care coverage. You're much more likely to need a long, expensive nursing-home stay than home health care. And this expensive coverage usually adds as much as 40 percent to your premium.

▶ Don't buy a policy that will provide increasing benefits to protect against inflation. Remember, you're paying in today's dollars for a benefit you may not even receive years in the future.

▶ Buy from a company that uses *front-end underwriting*, which means applicants' health histories are scanned diligently. Such companies tend to insure healthier people so they can hold down costs and save you money in premium increases.

Source:
Protecting Your Assets by Andrew D. Westhem, Citadel Press, New York, 1996

Cut the cost of homeowners insurance

You can save hundreds of dollars on your homeowners policy if you do your homework before you buy. Here are some smart shopping tips:

▶ Look for a policy through your employer, union, or professional organization. Some groups use their combined buying power to negotiate substantially lower rates.

▶ Get telephone numbers of insurance agents from your friends, the yellow pages, or from your state Department of Insurance. A few phone calls will give you an idea of price ranges and give you a feeling for what kind of service the companies offer. Consider both price and service in making your decision. Ask them what they would do to lower your costs. Don't forget to check the companies' financial ratings. When you've narrowed your list to three insurers, get exact price quotes.

▶ Choose a higher deductible. Deductibles typically start at $250. Increasing your deductible to $500 usually saves you up to 12 percent; $1,000, up to 24 percent; $2,500, up to 30 percent; and $5,000, up to 37 percent, depending on the insurance company.

▶ Buy home and auto policies from the same company to get a discount.

▶ Insure your house and possessions, not your land. It's not at risk for theft, fire, or weather damage.

▶ Invest in home security. Installing smoke detectors, dead-bolt locks, and unmonitored security devices can often result in at least a 5 percent discount. Some companies offer discounts of 15 to 20 percent if you install sprinkler systems and monitored fire and burglar alarms. Find out what systems your insurer recommends, what they would cost, and how they would affect your premiums.

▶ Investigate other discounts such as nonsmokers, reduced premiums on new or recently remodeled houses, or reduced premiums on homes insured for 90 or 100 percent of replacement cost.

Sources:
Interview with Kenneth M. Morris, author of *The Wall Street Journal Guide to Understanding Personal Finance*, Lightbulb Press, New York, 1992
Insurance Information Institute, New York
The New York Times Personal Finance Handbook by Leonard Sloane, Times Books, New York, 1995

Do you have enough home insurance?

The right measure of insurance on your house is its replacement value — the cost of rebuilding if disaster strikes. To figure that you may need help from a professional appraiser who will consider house size, average square-foot construction costs in your area, and other factors. Or ask a real estate agent or appraiser for average building costs in your area and multiply that by the house's square footage.

You can also get do-it-yourself worksheets from many insurance companies. These assign points to various house features, such as number of rooms and quality of construction. The estimated replacement value is the total of these points times a cost factor and your house size.

Insure at least 80 percent of your house's total replacement cost. Most insurers have a copayment or loss settlement clause that requires you to carry at least that much before they will pay you in full for a partial loss up to your policy limits. Your mortgage company may insist that you have full replacement coverage.

You may not be able to insure full replacement cost on older homes. Instead, you may have a modified replacement cost policy which pays for repairs using standard building techniques and materials used today rather than replacing outdated plaster walls and wooden floors.

Another factor to consider with an older home is the expense of rebuilding it to comply with modern building codes. Policies generally don't pay for this but you may be able to buy an endorsement for a specified amount toward these costs.

Personal property — your home's contents — is typically insured for up to 50 percent of the home's coverage. But there are limits on payback for valuables such as furs, jewelry, and silverware. Property benefits are computed on a cash value basis. That takes the age and condition of your possessions into consideration.

Homeowners policies also cover damage to other structures on your property such as a detached garage, shed, or gazebo. Typical coverage is 10 percent of the amount of insurance on your home.

To make sure your insurance coverage keeps up with inflation, improvements, and additions, review the policy every two to three years. In particularly inflationary times, review coverage every year or add an *inflation guard clause* to automatically keep pace with rising construction costs. Caution: Inflation-guard automatic increases can outpace actual inflation. The percentage insurers select may be too high or too low for your house. Check it against recent sales in your area.

Sources:
Interview with Sean Mooney, senior vice president, Insurance Information Institute, New York
Real Life: The Ten Things Every Grown-Up Needs to Know by Tom Heymann, Fawcett Columbine, New York, 1994

Is your house covered when you're away from home?

Be sure you know what's required by your insurer to protect your unoccupied house. Some companies require a certain level of attention, for example, a neighbor checking daily or turning off the water if you're away for an extended period. Others will refuse to pay any claims for damage from vandalism if you've been away for more than 30 days.

Source:
Get What You Pay For or Don't Pay at All by Donna McCrohan, Crown Trade Paperbacks, New York, 1994

Getting your money's worth on a property claim

Nearly everyone knows you should take a complete inventory of your personal property in case you need to make a claim on your homeowners or renters policy, but how many of us do? Make the task easier by obtaining an inventory worksheet from your insurance agent or get one from the Insurance Information Institute (1-800-331-9146).

Now, go from room to room and drawer to drawer documenting all your possessions — include furniture, electronic equipment, appliances, clothing, valuables, and anything that you would have to replace if it were destroyed. Locate receipts, and note price, date, and place of purchase, brand names, serial and model numbers. Take photos or videotape each large item and each wall of the house.

Copy all your records. Keep one set in a fireproof box at home and one set in a safe-deposit box. This list is invaluable in getting reimbursed so be sure to keep it updated.

Now that you know what you have, you can estimate your property's value at current prices and figure what it would take to replace it. That's how much insurance you should have on your home's contents. Check your policy or ask your agent to find out if you are insured for actual cash value or replacement cost. Replacement cost policies, which cost 10 to 15 percent more, pay the dollar amount needed to replace the damaged item. Actual cash value policies pay that amount minus depreciation.

You also need to know the limits your insurer will pay on certain items such as silverware, jewelry, and furs. For these items and others such as antiques, stamp or coin collections, musical instruments, camera equipment, art, oriental rugs, or other expensive or unusual merchandise, you may need to purchase special property *floater* or *endorsement* additions.

It may be wise to use a professional appraiser to verify your property's worth to avoid a dispute with your insurer in the event of loss. Sometimes you can get the service free from your bank or insurance company.

Sources:
Insurance Information Institute, New York
Real Life: The Ten Things Every Grown-Up Needs to Know by Tom Heymann, Fawcett Columbine, New York, 1994

If disaster strikes your home

You bought homeowners insurance in case of an emergency. To make sure you get the help you paid for after a fire, tornado, hurricane, or another catastrophe, take these precautions:

▶ If your home is badly damaged but can be repaired, do what you can to prevent further weather-related damage. Keep receipts for materials you buy. Note: Don't pay contractors a large sum for a temporary repair job. Insurance may not cover the cost completely. Temporary repairs will be included as part of the total settlement.

▶ Call your insurance company as soon as possible. Don't make permanent repairs until after a claims adjuster has assessed the damage.

▶ Avoid using electrical appliances until they have been checked by a technician.

▶ Most homeowners policies cover additional living expenses as well as repairs and personal property damage. Keep receipts for what you spend. Make sure any checks for these expenses are made out to you, not your mortgage lender.

▶ Provide information to the insurer about damaged possessions. Make a detailed list of items, dates of purchase, brand names, model numbers, and what it would cost to replace or repair the items. Take photographs of the damage.

▶ Don't throw out damaged furniture and other expensive items before the adjuster has a chance to see them.

▶ If your personal property was completely destroyed and you don't have an itemized list tucked away in a safe-deposit box, you'll have to work from memory. Start by picturing each room one by one and write a description of what was there.

► Make a list of all the structural damage to your home and other buildings such as swimming pools, garages, and toolsheds that you want to show the adjuster.

► Keep copies of the lists and any other documents you submit to the insurance company.

► Get written bids from reliable, licensed contractors for the repair work.

► Contact the adjustor again if you find additional damage or have additional information.

Source:
Interview with Sean Mooney, senior vice president, Insurance Information Institute, New York

Insurance rip-off

Never, never buy insurance from a lender to pay off a loan or mortgage in case you die. This type of insurance, called *credit life insurance*, costs way too much. You can buy a term policy to cover yourself if you think you need it.

Source:
1001 Ways To Cut Your Expenses by Jonathan D. Pond, Dell Publishing, New York, 1992

Challenge the home insurance inspector

Insurance agents will inspect your house regularly to check for any additions you've made. Study the agent's numbers carefully so that you won't be overcharged. His word isn't law. One common mistake to look for is including uncovered porch area in the square footage of the house.

Also, when the insurance company raises your premiums to account for inflation, make sure your rates are in line with the actual inflated value of your home.

Source:
SmartMoney, (5,11:118)

Who needs renters insurance?

Your landlord's policy doesn't cover your possessions. Unless you can afford to replace your furniture, clothing, electronic equipment, and other valuables, you need to have your own policy. Exception: College students under 26 living in a dormitory often have limited coverage through a parent's homeowners or renters policy.

Renters insurance protects you against loss from fire or smoke, lightning, theft, vandalism, explosion, windstorm, and water damage from plumbing. Policies also offer liability so that if someone is injured in your home or by any of your possessions, you are covered.

Here are some tips to help you get the coverage you need at the best price:

► Companies usually place a limit on the amount of coverage in a standard policy for jewelry, silverware, and computer equipment. You may need to buy a "floater" to cover the expense of replacing these items. Ask for a list of standard coverage limits.

► You can buy a policy to insure your possessions for either their cash or replacement value. Cash value is based on the age and condition of the items at the time of loss. Replacement value policies, which cost more, pay what it takes to purchase the items new.

► Low-deductible policies will cost more than those with a higher deductible.

► Frequently, you can get a discount by buying your renters and automobile policies from the same company. You might also save if your apartment or home has a security system, smoke detectors, or dead-bolt locks. In addition, your age and whether you smoke may affect your rates.

Sources:
Interview with Sean Mooney, senior vice president, Insurance Information Institute, New York
National Consumer's League, 815 15th Street, Washington, D.C., 20005

No day at the beach: Insuring your vacation home

Considering purchasing waterfront property? Be sure to find out what you're going to pay in homeowners insurance first. Insurance companies, especially in Florida, Hawaii, Texas, and Northeastern coastal areas are reducing availability of insurance so costs are going up. Factor in your insurance cost before placing a bid on a house. In many coastal areas mortgage companies may even require you to have homeowners insurance lined up in advance.

Prospective condominium buyers need to find a savvy insurance agent who can offer advice about how much owners can rely upon the condo association's policy and how much individual supplemental coverage to purchase.

You may be able to save money by purchasing perpetual insurance, sold by companies such as Mutual Assurance, Cincinnati Equitable, Baltimore Equitable, and Philadelphia Contributorship. With these policies you pay one large lump sum upfront. For example: If your annual premium is $500, you may make one payment of $5,000 to the insurer. Your premiums won't increase unless you want more coverage. If you sell your home or cancel your insurance, your deposit is refunded.

Source:
Interview with Andrew D. Westhem, author of *Protecting Your Assets*, Citadel Press, New York, 1996

Insuring your home business

Don't assume a homeowners policy covers your home business. It may, but it will probably only pay a maximum of $2,500 for business equipment in your home and $250 away from the premises. Many home businesses have more than that in a computer alone. You might also need extra liability coverage, depending on your type of business and whether customers come to your home.

You can buy a separate business owners policy or you may be able to add an endorsement to your homeowners policy that typically will add about $15,000 to your coverage — enough for most home businesses.

If you're in a high liability profession such as hair dressing or you are worried about lawsuits for defamation or libel, or if you have more than $15,000 in property, go with a business owners package policy that combines business and home insurance together.

Finally, if you use your car in your business, check that your auto insurance covers business as well as personal use. In some cases, depending on the type of business and the kind of vehicles you own, you may need a separate business auto insurance policy.

Source:
Interview with Sean Mooney, senior vice president, Insurance Information Institute, New York

How to slash your car insurance costs

Are you wasting hundreds of dollars every year on car insurance? If you think the price you pay for car insurance is outrageous, read on to find out what you may be doing wrong.

1) Shop around. Don't stick with that same old insurance company because it's the one you've always used. The exact same insurance coverage can cost hundreds more at one company than at another. Sit down with the yellow pages and make some calls. Ask agents with several companies what they could do to lower your costs. Make sure you check the financial ratings of the companies with your state Department of Insurance.

2) Go with a higher deductible. You can lower your collision and comprehensive costs by 15 to 30 percent just by increasing your deductible from $200 to $500. That means you'll pay $300 more yourself before you can make a claim, but it's almost always a wise move.

3) Don't overinsure old cars. Ask an auto dealer or your bank to tell you how much your car is worth. If it's under $1,000, you should probably drop your collision and/or comprehensive (fire and theft) coverages. Keeping these coverages is not cost-effective.

4) Buy a car with a "low profile." Some cars are expensive to repair or are favorite targets of thieves. These cars cost more to insure. Check insurance costs before you buy a car by writing to the Insurance Institute for Highway Safety, 1005 North Glebe Road, Arlington, VA 22201. Ask for the Highway Loss Data Chart.

5) Take advantage of discounts. Some discounts insurers commonly offer are:
   - ▶ Low annual mileage discounts. This discount is for drivers who don't put many miles on their cars.
   - ▶ Automatic seat belt or air bag discounts.
   - ▶ Anti-lock brake discounts. Some states require insurers to give discounts for cars with anti-lock brakes.
   - ▶ More than one car.
   - ▶ No accidents in three years.
   - ▶ Drivers over 50 years old.

▶ Driver training courses.

▶ Anti-theft devices.

▶ Good grades for students.

▶ No moving violations in three years.

▶ Auto and homeowners coverage with the same company.

▶ College students away from home without a car.

Source:
Nine Ways to Lower Your Auto Insurance Costs, Insurance Information Institute, New York

Car insurance you don't need

You may not know it, but when you buy an auto insurance policy, you're actually buying a package of several types of insurance. Some are required by law, others aren't. You probably should cancel some parts of the package when your car reaches a certain age and value. The six basic types of coverage are:

Collision. If you wreck your car (including running into your garage door) and it's your fault, collision insurance covers you. Consider cancelling this coverage if your car is worth $1,500 or less. Even if you total your car, that low amount is the most you'll receive from the insurance company. Coverage may not be worth it.

Comprehensive. Covers broken windshields, fires and other Acts of God, theft, vandalism, hitting an animal, etc. Chose the highest deductible you can afford.

Liability. Required by law. If you cause an accident, your liability insurance covers damage to property and covers the medical bills for passengers in your car and people in other cars. It's better to have too much liability coverage than too little. A good policy would pay up to $100,000 for a single injury, up to $300,000 for all injuries in any one accident, and up to $50,000 in property damage.

Uninsured motorists. Required in some states. Covers your costs if another car hits you but the driver doesn't have insurance.

Medical payments. You probably don't need medical payments coverage if you already have health and disability insurance.

Towing. An inexpensive towing coverage is included in most policies. Check to see if you already have towing coverage through an auto club or as part of your collision or comprehensive coverage.

Rental car warning: Most insurance policies transfer to rental cars. Check your policy for rental car collision and liability coverage before you go on a trip. Don't be suckered into buying rental car insurance.

Source:
Interview with J. Lee Lawson II, Allstate Insurance Company, Norcross, Ga.

Cash value or total replacement car insurance?

In some states you can get car insurance that covers the cost of repairing or replacing your car rather than basing payment on the car's book value. If car repairs cost more than the car's market value, the insurance company considers the car "totaled." With more complex car construction and with rising costs for labor and parts, more and more cars are being designated as totaled. If you have standard collision and comprehensive coverage, you get book value for your totaled car.

Typically, replacement value coverage costs about 10 percent more, but it may be worth it if you can't afford to replace your car. Example: Often a person's car loan is larger than the insurance settlement received. With standard insurance, you don't have enough to pay off the wrecked car, much less buy a new one.

Source:
The New York Times Personal Finance Handbook by Leonard Sloane, Times Books, New York, 1995

Questions you must ask before buying car insurance

Ask your agent these questions before you sign on the dotted line:

▶ Under what conditions can the company raise my premiums or cancel my policy?

▶ Do I make a claim through my agent or a central office?

▶ What is the average length of time before a claims adjustor contacts the insured once a claim is reported? How soon can all parties expect to be paid? How does this company compare with others in promptness of claims handling?

▶ What does the company require in terms of pre-inspections and qualified repair shops? Is there a good choice of approved shops close to my home?

▶ What information does the company require after an accident? Can I retain a copy of the company's accident form?

▶ Exactly what expenses that are the result of an accident are covered as part of the policy? What about child care costs, lost wages, and rental car costs?

▶ Is there a clause in the collision coverage that allows me to reject an unsatisfactory claim settlement?

Source:
Council of Better Business Bureaus, 4200 Wilson Blvd., Arlington, Va.

Get treated fairly after an accident

Follow these procedures to avoid costly, time-consuming mistakes on an auto insurance claim:

▶ Notify police immediately. Get the investigating officer's name and badge number as well as the address and phone number of the police station where the accident report will be filed. Ask the officer when the report will be filed and how you can get a copy.

▶ Take reasonable steps to protect your car from further damage by setting up flares, getting the car off the road, and calling a tow truck if necessary. Remember: When you call a tow truck, don't authorize repair work. Insurance companies usually want an adjuster to inspect the car to appraise damage first.

▶ Get names of other involved drivers, their addresses, and their work and home telephone numbers. Write down vehicle license plate states and numbers, drivers license numbers, insurance companies, names and telephone numbers of their insurance agents, and policy numbers, if possible.

▶ Obtain the names, addresses, and work and home telephone numbers of any passengers and witnesses.

▶ Make notes describing the accident, the vehicles involved, their approximate speeds, the setting, the weather, the traffic signs and signals, and the road conditions. Take photographs if possible or draw diagrams of the roads and the accident.

▶ Don't make any oral or written statements as to responsibility or blame.

▶ Don't tell others involved in the accident how much liability insurance you carry.

▶ Don't discuss specifics of the accident with others involved.

▶ Don't accept offers to settle on the spot without thinking about it carefully. You may later be held liable for the same damages.

▶ Notify your insurance company or agent of the accident as soon as possible even if the damage is minor and there appear to be no injuries. Call even if you're far from home or if someone else caused the accident. Ask your agent how to proceed. Commonly, insurers require a "proof of loss" form, as well as documents such as medical and auto repair bills and a copy of the police report.

▶ Don't deal with the other party's insurance company until you have discussed the matter with your own insurer or agent.

▶ Cooperate with your insurance company's investigations, settlement, or defense of any claim. Immediately turn over to the company copies of any legal papers you receive in connection with the accident. Your insurer will defend you in court if necessary so the faster they receive information and prepare their case, the better.

▶ Get an estimate from your mechanic or body shop — not the insurance company's — that will guarantee work performed. You don't want a shoddy repair job done by a shop that cuts corners to meet a fixed price. Your insurer may insist on more than one estimate.

▶ Keep records of your expenses for reimbursement. A no-fault insurer usually will pay medical and hospital expenses, and sometimes will pay other costs such as lost wages or perhaps part of the cost of a temporary housekeeper.

▶ Keep copies of all paperwork related to the accident in case you need to refer to it later

Source:
Council of Better Business Bureaus, Arlington, Va.

Protect yourself from a million-dollar lawsuit

Everyone's at risk of being sued these days, but you really need to protect yourself if you fit any of the following descriptions:

▶ You have substantial assets. The truth is, people are more likely to sue you if you have money. You need extra protection if your assets exceed the amount of your homeowners and auto liability protection.

▶ You rent out your home or hire housesitters. Someone could injure himself on your property, and you're liable.

▶ You run a business from your home. Again, extra visitors mean more possible injuries you're "responsible" for.

▶ You have unbonded or unlicensed hired help (cleaning women, gardeners, or baby sitters). If your gardener leaves a hoe where a passerby could step on it, you could be sued.

Fortunately, protecting yourself from a million-dollar lawsuit can cost less than $200 a year. If you fall into any of the above categories, you need what's known as an *umbrella policy*. Call your homeowner and auto insurance agents and find out how much it would cost to add $1 million in liability coverage to your current policy. An umbrella policy should be very inexpensive and definitely worth every penny.
Source:
Money (December 1994)

Avoid common insurance mistakes

Insurance is never hassle-free, but you can sidestep the most common insurance traps with this expert advice. Strategies:

▶ If you rent out your home, don't assume that everything is covered by your homeowners policy — check your policy or check with your agent to be sure.

▶ Tell the truth when you apply for any type of insurance. Misrepresentation could cost you a bundle in the long run if your claim is denied or you lose your coverage.

▶ If your coverage is cancelled and the insurer returns your premiums, don't cash the check — that indicates you agree with the company's decision. Better: Consult a lawyer, your insurance agent, or another advisor to find out your options.

▶ Choose an agent who has *draft authority* — that is, one who can authorize the settlement of small claims without an adjuster.

▶ Don't get life insurance if you don't have any dependents, and don't buy life insurance for your children.

▶ Buy health insurance when you're healthy. Many policies exclude coverage for any health conditions you had before you signed up.

▶ Check your health policy before you get pregnant. Many policies exclude this condition or pay only after you've had the policy for nine months or more.

▶ If part of your auto coverage is based on state no-fault laws, find out if it covers you when you drive in other states.

▶ Always call your insurance agent with claim information immediately — most policies have a deadline.

▶ Provide your beneficiaries with copies of your policies, including instructions and relevant phone numbers.

▶ Pass up accidental death benefits and mugging insurance — they cost too much and you get too little.

Sources:
Interview with Bob Hunter, insurance director, Consumer Federation of America, Washington, D.C.
Get What You Pay For or Don't Pay at All by Donna McCrohan, Crown Trade Paperbacks, New York, 1994
Health Care Choices for Today's Consumer, edited by Marc S. Miller, Living Planet Press, Washington, 1995

Trouble with a claim?

Having difficulty getting a fair settlement? Follow these steps:

1) Keep good records. Keep a file on your claim. Write down who said what and when they said it.

2) Contact your insurance company in writing and insist the company reply in writing to document the course of events. Send copies, not your original policy or any original policy materials.

3) Don't give up. If policy language is ambiguous, you will probably win in court. In such cases, judges will rule against the insurance company.

4) Contact your state Department of Insurance. While it won't necessarily take your side, the Department of Insurance can make sure the company is responsive to your problem. Send copies of all correspondence between you and the insurer with your complaint letter. Be sure to give the company's name and your policy number. Do not send your policy.

5) If results from the above steps aren't satisfactory, take your case to small claims court or to a lawyer. Small claims court, where you act as your own lawyer, is often useful for claims under $500. For major claims, it pays to use a lawyer. Again, keep good records.

6) Contact the Consumer Federation of America at the address below for help with a referral and to document patterns of insurance abuse.

Source:
Interview with Bob Hunter, insurance director, Consumer Federation of America, Washington, D.C.

Don't cash that claim check

You may be excited when you get that settlement check from the insurance company, but don't sign on the dotted line yet. That's just what the insurance company hopes you'll do. Once you endorse the check, you sign away your legal right to petition the insurer for more funds, even if you find another nick on your wrecked car later.

A cashed claim check is the same as signing a release form that says the insurance company is no longer responsible for any additional charges. And remember, an estimate is just an estimate. Even a claims adjuster may not have realized the full extent of the damage to your car until the repairs begin.

It's better to store the unsigned check safely away until all the repair work on your car is finished.

Source:
Interview with Roslyn Wade, banking industry expert, Exton, Pa.

Pick a preferred agent

You may be tempted to give your business to a small-time, struggling, brand-new insurance agent, but don't be a Mr. Nice Guy. You'll be better off buying the same policy through an agent driving a fancy car with a plaque on his wall that says something like "President's Club Member" or "Member of the Great Performers Club."

Insurance companies would never admit it, but buying through a *preferred agent* could really pay off for you. Preferred agents are the ones who generate the most business and have the best customers.

With their influence, they can sometimes get you a better price; they can stretch the rules on insurance policies; they can occasionally squeeze you into the preferred category instead of the standard, more expensive category; and they can lobby for you when you file a big claim.

They can even help keep you from being canceled if you do need to file a lot of claims. Go with the best and the biggest. You never know when you'll need a heavy hitter on your side.

Source:
SmartMoney (5,11:119)

Insurance frauds

Insurance bargains are out there, but if a deal sounds too good to be true, it probably is. Insurance fraud costs about 17 percent of your premium dollar, says Wayne Whitaker, spokesman for the Georgia Insurance Commissioner's Office.

Some fraud is committed by the consumer. A group of people will stage an accident, complete with wrecked cars and doctors' signatures. They'll claim soft-tissue injuries, which are impossible to prove. Everyone in on the deal gets a cut of the insurance payout.

Another popular fraud you could pull is getting an insurance policy in order to get a car tag, then canceling the insurance before you pay the premium. Don't try it. The insurance company is required to notify the Department of Public Safety when you cancel.

Fake proof of insurance cards are making the rounds these days among people who need a car tag, but you should resist the temptation of the low price. People convicted of insurance fraud can serve one to 20 years in prison and/or pay a fine up to $50,000.

Fraud works the other way, too. The Insurance Commissioner's Office is faced constantly with shady agents who claim to represent an insurance company. When you write a check for your premium, they pocket your money instead of sending it in. Make sure you are dealing with a reputable, licensed agent. If you have any doubts, call the Commissioner's Office in your state to check on the agent before you write a check.

On TV, you'll see well-known celebrities hawking insurance policies for older people. The policy only costs $6.95 a month and requires no health exam. These claims are so misleading that they are almost fraudulent. The $6.95 price is for every thousand dollars of insurance. Over 10 years, you'd end up paying nearly $21,000 for a $25,000 policy, and your cash value would be only $5,100. That's a bad deal.

Sources:
Interview with Wayne Whitaker, spokesman for the Georgia Insurance Commissioner's Office
Life Insurance for Older Adults, American Association of Retired Persons, 601 E Street, N.W., Washington, D.C. 20049, 1990

TAX STRATEGIES

What taxes do you owe on your garage sale profits?

Can you believe the Internal Revenue Service lets you off the hook on rummage sales? Most items you sell at a rummage sale will be priced far less than what you paid for them. Since you only pay taxes on a profit, you aren't breaking the law when you don't report the money you collect at your yard sale.
Source:
Interview with Neil Galanti, CPA, Atlanta

How to write off a wedding gift

When congratulations are in order for a business associate, your receipts should be in order, too. With good records, you can write off a wedding gift to a client or customer, up to $25. You have to show that the gift was made primarily for business reasons, such as to build goodwill, and not for social reasons. This would be easier to do if you could show that you just sent a gift, and didn't attend the wedding, or could document that you didn't do a lot of socializing with that client (via your calendar).
Source:
Interview with Daniel Breuning, a shareholder in charge of taxation with the public accounting firm of Madsen, Sapp, Mena, Rodriguez & Co., Plantation, Fla.

How to deduct more than the $25 limit for business gifts

Businesspeople can deduct the cost of Christmas gifts to their valuable clients and customers, but only up to $25 per person. You can't get around the $25 limit by giving separate gifts to your client's family members, or even by having your spouse give a separate gift to the client.

The only way to deduct more than $25 is to add in incidental costs, such as engraving, wrapping, or mailing. Items under $4 on which your name is imprinted are deductible, too.

So, you can deduct a grand total of $34 if you buy a $25 gift, wrap and mail it for $5, and send along a $4 pen with your company's name on it.
Source:
The Atlanta Journal/Constitution (Dec. 4, 1995, E6)

Company Christmas gifts

If your boss gives you a choice between a hefty ham or turkey and a $25 gift certificate, take the pork or poultry. You don't have to pay tax on these items of appreciation.

The IRS wants part of any gift certificate, cash, or item that can be exchanged easily for cash, no matter how small the amount. These gifts are considered part of your salary.

Source:
The Atlanta Journal/Constitution (Dec. 4, 1995, E6)

How to deduct a sympathy gift

Sending an expression of sympathy to the family of someone who dies is a time-honored tradition.

For your business tax return, flowers and other sympathy gifts are deductible only if there is a business connection. But, if you give a contribution to a charity in memory of someone, it's almost always deductible on your personal income taxes if you itemize. A charitable contribution should be more meaningful to the family, and it benefits a worthy cause.

You don't have to stop at memorials, either. You could make a charitable contribution in celebration of a graduation, a birthday, an anniversary, a wedding, a birth, a bar or bat mitzvah, or virtually any occasion that would warrant a gift.

In case you're feeling extraordinarily generous, remember that charitable contributions are subject to limitations — total contributions can't exceed 50 percent of your adjusted gross income — and you start losing the benefit of itemizing if your income goes above a certain level (about $160,000).

Source:
Interview with Daniel Breuning, a shareholder in charge of taxation with the public accounting firm of Madsen, Sapp, Mena, Rodriguez & Co., Plantation, Fla.

Let Uncle Sam get his own loans

Did you pop open a bottle of champagne when you saw how much your income tax refund would be?

Well, we hate to spoil the celebration, but all a big refund means is that you gave the government an interest-free loan for a year. Do you think the IRS would do the same for you if you owed *them* money for 12 months? Not likely.

Instead of shooting for a big refund, have less money withheld from your paycheck. You can claim an exemption for yourself and each dependent and claim another exemption for each $2,000 you have in itemized deductions, tax shelter losses, business exemptions, and Individual Retirement Account (IRA) contributions. People will try to tell you that you can't do it, but you can. Your employer has to report it to the IRS if you take more than 11 exemptions, but as long as you can justify it, you're fine.

"The IRS doesn't really want you to overwithhold," says Daniel Breuning, a shareholder in charge of taxation for the public accounting firm of Madsen, Sapp, Rodriguez & Co. in Plantation, Fla. "They just want you to withhold the right amount. They don't care how many exemptions you take as long as you don't have exemptions that are in excess of what you're legally allowed."

Just be sure your withholding is high enough to avoid penalties. It should be equal to the tax you paid last year or 90 percent of the tax you'll owe this year.
Source:
Interview with Daniel Breuning, shareholder in charge of taxation with the public accounting firm of Madsen, Sapp, Mena, Rodriguez & Co., Plantation, Fla.

Withholding penalty loopholes

Are you earning extra money this year — perhaps doing a little consulting on the side, working part time for a friend, or running a small home business? Are you making estimated quarterly payments on that money to the IRS? If you don't hand over tax money every three months, you could owe a big penalty come April.

But don't rush out for an estimated tax form yet. You can avoid making the quarterly payments and paying the penalty if you fit any of these descriptions:

▶ Taxes withheld from your pay will cover at least 90 percent of your total tax bill.

▶ You will owe less than $500 in taxes next April.

▶ Taxes withheld from your pay this year equal 100 percent of last year's tax bill (110 percent if your adjusted gross income is more than $150,000 or more than $75,000 if you're married and filing separately).

The third loophole is perfect for people whose income jumped this year. Since the minimum payment is based on last year's bill, you can enjoy your higher income without paying taxes until April. In the meantime, earn some interest on that money!

If you don't fit any of the above descriptions and you earn a paycheck, you can still avoid a penalty if you act soon enough. Simply increase the amount withheld from your paycheck by filing a new W-4 form with your employer. For some reason, the IRS considers money withheld from your pay to have been contributed evenly throughout the year.

That could mean a slim paycheck for the last few months of the year, but you'll be ahead of the game when April comes, and, most importantly, you won't owe a penalty.
Source:
IRS Publication 505 — Tax Withholding and Estimated Tax

Making claims without receipts

In 1930, the entertainer of "I'm a Yankee Doodle Dandy" fame, George M. Cohan, didn't have receipts for all his business expenses. He took his case against the IRS to court, which ruled that the IRS should allow reasonable expenses even when the records aren't complete.

Do your best to keep receipts and a journal of your expenses. But the IRS cannot tell you that a claim without a receipt is a false claim. If an auditor tries to dispute some of your deductions, mention the *Cohan rule*. When the agent realizes you know the law, he may immediately back down.

Warning: The Cohan rule doesn't apply to travel and entertainment expenses because they are so easily abused. Otherwise, you should be able to push an auditor to accept any reasonable expense that you can justify.

Source:
How to Beat the I.R.S. at Its Own Game: Strategies to Avoid — and Fight — an Audit by Amir D. Aczel, Four Walls Eight Windows, New York, 1995

How to turn your hobby into a tax deduction

You can't deny it. You've got seawater in your veins. You love the pungent tang of the salt spray, the roll of the deck beneath your feet, the chill damp of the wave-soaked wind as it rushes into your slicker. You're on the high seas every chance you get, and you've won or placed in every regatta you've entered.

And why not? You read all the sailing magazines, and you've put all the latest equipment on your boat. You've even gone to sailing school in the Caribbean. Why, you're the expert now, and the newcomers are asking you for advice.

Sounds like you're charting a course for a great tax deduction. All the costs of a pastime passion may be deductible as business expenses on your taxes by using the *safe harbor provision*.

Normally, to qualify your hobby as a business, you have to show a profit three out of five consecutive years. But if you follow some simple rules, you can deduct your expenses even if you never make a dime.

What you have to do is document that you really wanted to make money at your craft.

"Your intent was to make a profit, and to do that, you need to run it in a professional-like manner," says Professor Jim Dean at Nova Southeastern University in Ft. Lauderdale, Fla. "A lot of for-profit businesses have come out of hobbies anyway."

Here are some tips to help add credibility to your case that your hobby qualifies as a part-time business:

▶ Keep accurate records.

▶ Take courses or attend seminars to improve your skills or knowledge.

▶ Spend enough time at an activity to show you're serious about it. Sticking with our nautical example, you couldn't take friends out on your sailboat once a year and claim that you're teaching sailing. You'd need to be able to prove that you're giving lessons on a regular basis.

▶ Pay for advice when you need it.

▶ Make sure you are following the standards of the industry.

▶ Promote your services. That could mean having business cards or brochures printed, taking out an ad in a publication, joining an organization where you could do some business, or getting a booth at an event.

The first item on the list is the most important one. "Documentation is critical," Dean says. "If you show consistent losses, you increase your chance of an audit, so you have to have evidence to back up your claims."

Dean, who went through such an audit, was able to produce detailed records of his intent to make a profit. "When I drove somewhere, I logged it and claimed it," he said. "In my case, I had a lot of contact with people, so I had a calendar that showed all of my meetings. It showed I was regularly out there pursuing this as a business. Even phone calls — keep a log of the people you talk to. It just builds a weight of evidence. But you have to be diligent."

Otherwise, your tax deduction could go down with the ship.

Source:
Interview with Professor Jim Dean, Nova Southeastern University, Ft. Lauderdale, Fla. Professor Dean is a CPA, a personal finance consultant, and author of *Building for the Future*, Fleming H. Revell Publishing (a division of Baker Books), Ada, Mich., scheduled for late 1996 or early 1997 release.

Tax tips when you lose your job

If there's any benefit to losing your job to downsizing, it's that there's usually time to do some planning. If you've been working for the same company for several years or are at a high-level position, you're going to need it. Ask if your company will cover the cost of getting financial advice.

Most people who get early retirement or severance packages think they're going to take the money and start a new career, but retirement consultant Robert Preston's experience has been that 90 percent of them will just retire. Since that's so often the case, the severance package you receive becomes critical.

"The individual has a lot of negotiating power," Preston explains. "Usually the company feels very bad about letting you go, and you can use the guilt factor."

Ask for an extended payout. Depending on how the severance package is structured, the windfall could temporarily boost your tax bracket. Instead of a lump sum distribution, ask for an extended payout over two to three years.

Defer your salary. Your company may offer a *nonqualified deferred compensation*. Deferring a certain amount of your salary for a period of years or until retirement can help ease the tax bite.

Ask for incentive stock options. If you've gotten stock options as a benefit, you may have to exercise them within 90 days of when you leave. If that's the case, it makes a difference whether your stock option is *qualified* or *incentive*. If it's qualified, you'll be taxed when the option is exercised. If it's an incentive option, you won't pay taxes until you sell your stock and realize a capital gain.

Park any payouts in an IRA. Take the money from your company retirement plan and park it for a while in an IRA until you have a clear picture of your post-severance financial situation. "That's really the way to go," Preston says. "Usually there's so much pressure in those situations. Take those qualified plan benefits and put them in a separate IRA. ... You need to think about when your pension is going to start and your needs for cash."

Leave retirement money in place if possible. Your company might let you leave some money in the retirement plan and take out just enough to cover expenses until you get another job. You'll owe income tax on the amount you take out. If you're 51 or older when you're let go, you can avoid the 10 percent penalty on early withdrawal if you take equal payments over a period of time.

Make estimated payments. Unemployment compensation is taxable on the federal level and in some states, but taxes aren't usually taken out. So, you might want to consider making estimated payments. Or, if you file jointly with an employed spouse, have your spouse claim fewer exemptions.

Obviously, there's a lot to think about to make sure your family and your future are provided for. Take some time, get some help, and make your decisions based on your needs and aspirations.

"When you're downsized, squeeze everything you can out of that package because it will affect your quality of life," Preston says. "Once that money goes to Washington or the state capitol, it's gone."

Source:
Interview with Robert Preston, pension actuary, CPA and retirement consultant, Danbury, Conn.

Oh no, I owe! What to do when you can't pay your taxes

You owe the IRS, and you don't have the money to pay the bill. You have visions of being dragged off to prison, your home sold at auction, and your family out on the street, dressed in rags.

Relax. You've definitely got a problem, but not having the money to pay your taxes isn't illegal.

The IRS doesn't want to put you in jail. They're bill collectors, says Frederick W. Daily, a tax attorney in San Francisco. If you owe the IRS, Daily suggests you take these steps:

Don't ignore the bill! The federal government takes offense to such an attitude and will get increasingly cranky with each disregarded communication.

If you're in a desperate financial situation, you can ask the IRS to suspend collection action on your case. That means the IRS won't harass you, grab anything out of your bank account, or take your car. It doesn't stop the interest and penalties, but it gives you some breathing room, generally six months to a year.

Beyond suspension of collection, you've got three options — an offer in compromise, an installment agreement, or a remedy under the bankruptcy code.

Offer to settle. An offer in compromise is an offer to settle for less than the amount you owe. It's possible, but not easy. Generally, you can count on the IRS turning you down if you're employed, under 60, and in good health, but it's worth a shot.

Set up a monthly payment plan. If you owe less than $10,000, you can usually set your own payment schedule without negotiation. All you have to do is send in a Form 9465. A schedule to pay off your bill in under 36 months should be accepted without question, unless you have a history of defaulting on installments. It goes without saying that interest and penalties keep mounting, so make the term as short as possible.

If the bill is more than $10,000, you're required to make full financial disclosure, and the IRS gets to decide how much you should spend every month to feed, clothe, house, transport, entertain, and otherwise support your family and your lifestyle.

The bottom line is if you are spending more than acceptable amounts — and in high-cost-of-living areas, most people are — they'll give you 12 months to get rid of your high expenses, like that big car payment or house payment.

The last resort: File for bankruptcy. Chapter 7 is straight bankruptcy, which can wipe out taxes, but it is tricky because you can only use it if the debt is older than three years.

Chapter 13 offers an *individual reorganization plan*. You can't eliminate the tax debt, but you get up to five years to pay it. From the moment you file Chapter 13, penalties and interest stop. Another advantage: You may be able to completely wipe out some other types of debt so you can focus on paying off the IRS.

Source:
Interview with Frederick W. Daily, author of *Stand Up to the IRS*, Nolo Press, Berkeley, Calif., 1996

Protect your bank account from the IRS

If you have to make a partial payment on taxes you owe, and particularly if you anticipate having trouble keeping up with the payments, never send the IRS a personal check.

Why? Because your bank account number is on it, and the IRS will write it down. They have the authority to freeze that account to get the balance of taxes owed if you stop making payments. That would make your other outstanding checks bounce.

Instead, send them a cashier's check or attorney's trust fund check, with your last name, Social Security or employer ID number, type of tax (income or payroll), and the year of the tax in the lower left-hand corner.

And, as always, make a copy of whatever you send the IRS.

Source:
Stand Up to the IRS, Frederick W. Daily, Nolo Press, Berkeley, Calif., 1996

Don't write checks to IRS

Don't write checks to the "IRS." Write to the "Internal Revenue Service" instead. You're safer that way, say tax lawyers. Someone who steals your check can easily change the IRS to MRS., follow it with a name, and pocket your money.

Source:
The Wall Street Journal (May 25, 1994, A1)

How to build a low-tax dream home

You can see it now — your dream home. For some, it could be a stunning contemporary showplace, with soaring, open ceilings, tall windows, and curved walls. For others, it might be a country farmhouse with broad, wraparound porches; a stately brick-front manor; or a simple seaside cottage.

Whatever your idea of the perfect house, you can build it with an eye toward lowering the property taxes that will stay with you for years to come.

The single biggest tax-reducing strategy for building your dream home is to keep the design simple — as much like a cube or rectangle as possible. Angles and corners are key elements in tax assessment. A house with six or eight corners may not look any better than a cube-shaped house, but it will boost your assessment because it's more expensive to build.

Former tax assessor Steve Carlson found that it was impossible to assess a cube-shaped house at its true market value. The formulas he was required to use didn't allow for it. "I've assessed houses for $125,000 after they sold for $250,000," he writes. "I'm sure that the developers who built the houses saved big bucks with their cubical designs, but the savings weren't passed along to the home buyers. The developers didn't have to pass the savings along — cubical houses can be tasteful and beautiful. However, if you take charge of the construction project, *you* can pocket the savings."

The rule about simple design also applies to roof styles. Arched roofs or steep roofs with fancy dormers add to your assessment. They are expensive to build and maintain.

"People get the idea that the house they want must have certain features," Carlson says. "That's where you get houses with nice flat lawns with decks sticking out over them. What could you do on the deck that you couldn't do on the lawn? Sometimes expensive things get added without much thought."

Source:
Interview with former tax assessor Steve Carlson of Hinesburg, Vt. Steve Carlson interviewed assessors throughout the United States before he wrote *Your Low-Tax Dream House: A New Approach to Slashing the Costs of Home Ownership.* The book was later printed by Avon Books as *The Best Home for Less,* (New York, 1992). Available from Upper Access Publishing, Hinesburg, Vt., 1–800–356–9315.

Home improvements that won't raise your taxes

If you want to make a big difference on your property taxes, put your money into things that move. The rule is: If you can take it with you, it's not taxable, says property tax expert Steve Carlson. "Make your really nice things furniture instead of real estate," he suggests.

What does that mean in practical terms? Instead of doing built-in, floor-to-ceiling bookcases and big walk-in closets, opt for wall units and good quality armoires. In your kitchen, consider paring down the built-in cabinets and counter space, substituting a freestanding hutch for dishes and an island counter on wheels.

A moveable item goes into a certain tax category, even though a person buying your house may not care whether it's moveable or not. The assessors have to keep everything in categories. For instance, when you resell a house, if you've got a beautiful dyed concrete floor, the buyers can see it's a great floor. But the tax assessor has to rate it as a concrete floor, which is a basement floor.

Source:
Interview with Steve Carlson, former tax assessor and author of *The Best Home for Less*, Avon Books, New York, 1992. Available from Upper Access Publishing, Hinesburg, Vt., 1-800-356-9315

How to escape a whole year of property taxes

You can save a year's worth of property taxes by timing construction of your house to begin after your state's tax assessment day. It's a one-time savings, but it could keep several hundred dollars in your pocket.

Virtually all states have fixed dates for tax assessments. Let's say the tax assessment date for your state is April 1. A house that's built on March 31 will be taxed this year. A house built on April 2 won't be taxed until next year. It's a good idea to take a photo of how much construction was completed as of that date in case you're challenged later on.

Source:
Interview with Steve Carlson, former tax assessor and author of *The Best Home for Less*, Avon Books, New York, 1992. Available from Upper Access Publishing, Hinesburg, Vt., 1-800-356-9315.

Another way to sneak past the tax assessor

The most thorough assessment of your property occurs when the first major construction is finished. Instead of building a house with all the fancy extras, a smarter strategy is to build a bare-bones house that will get a low assessment. In most places, future assessments will mostly take place *from the outside*. That means that most interior improvements after the first inspection are unlikely to add to your assessment, unless the projects are large enough to require a building permit.

A good rule of thumb is to do the improvements that will inspire new assessments — exteriors and those that require permits — first. Then do the smaller interior improvements that will add to the value and comfort of your home.

Source:
Interview with Steve Carlson, former tax assessor and author of *The Best Home for Less*, Avon Books, New York, 1992. Available from Upper Access Publishing, Hinesburg, Vt., 1-800-356-9315.

Deal sweeteners may raise taxes

Have you ever been in negotiations for a house and had the seller offer to throw in some extras to sweeten the deal? Maybe the patio furniture or the riding lawnmower?

It may be a great deal, but don't put it in the purchase price of the house. That information is public record, and tax assessors look at it before assessing your property. Their goal is to try to assess your house as close to the fair market price as possible.

Try to work out a separate purchase for the personal property, even if it means paying more for the items.

Source:
Interview with Steve Carlson, former tax assessor and author of *The Best Home for Less*, Avon Books, New York, 1992. Available from Upper Access Publishing, Hinesburg, Vt., 1-800-356-9315.

Tax loophole for home-based employees

People used to get around the strict rules for taking home office deductions by leasing their offices to their companies, but Congress closed that avenue.

What is allowed is to have your company reimburse you for the expenses of maintaining your office at home.

To take the deduction, you must prove that you use the room exclusively for the convenience of your employer, says Professor Jim Dean of Nova Southeastern University in Ft. Lauderdale, Fla. A reimbursement may not be conclusive, but it would be a step in the right direction.

Most of the arguments that a home office is for the convenience of the employer are fairly common sense. A salesperson of a company with its home office in another city or state would probably be the most clear-cut example. The company is going to need some space for administrative matters or the storage of product or sales materials, and it certainly benefits the company not to have to rent space to store those items.

Sources:
Interview with Professor James Dean, Nova Southeastern University, Ft. Lauderdale, Fla.
How to Write Off Everything and Retire With Twice as Much Money by Robert Carlson, Agora Financial Publishing, Baltimore, 1996

How to ease the home office headache when you sell your house

Anyone who works out of his house has probably looked closely at the tax issues surrounding a home office. Some find that the benefits of having their business pay for a portion of household expenses are erased when it comes time to sell the house. That's when it gets tricky.

When you sell a personal residence, you don't have to pay taxes on the profits right away. You have two years to pay or buy a new house. Businesses can't do that. That means you have to pay taxes right away on any profit your business earns on the sale of your house. Your business owns the part of your house you've been claiming as a home office.

But there's a way around it. The feds specifically refer to "business use at the time of the sale," so some tax experts say you can disqualify your home office by adding a personal use, like moving a toy box, or even a cat box, to the office.

A safer strategy may be moving out of your home office altogether and renting space somewhere in the year before the sale.

There's nothing in the tax code that says how long the room must be no longer used for business, but you could have problems if you try to cut the angles too close, says tax expert Alan Weiner.

"If today you're using a room for business and you want to sell the house the day after tomorrow, and tomorrow you use the room for personal use, you might have a problem," says Weiner. If you know you'll be selling your house in the next year, go ahead and stop using the room for business."

Source:
Alan Weiner, CPA, JD, tax partner, Holtz Rubenstein and Co., LLP, Melville, N.Y.

Watch out for generous landlords

Did you scratch your head in amazement when your landlord said he'd write you a check to pay for new carpeting, paint, and lighting in your office? Do yourself — and your landlord — a favor and give him back the money.

If your landlord gives you money to make improvements, the IRS considers that taxable income. So let your landlord make the improvements. He'll be able to depreciate the remodeling on his taxes, and you'll save money on your tax bill as well.

"If the landlord amortizes the improvements and pays for them through rent, the landlord wins," says Ronald Schagrin, a commercial real estate expert in Ft. Lauderdale, Fla. "The tenant wins because he got the improvements, paid for them on an installment basis (through rent), and writes off the expense."

The downside is that the landlord may not get an equal return for his investment, and he'll probably increase your rent now that it's a nicer space.

Source:
Interview with Ronald Schagrin, associate/consultant, Industrial Properties, Lehrer & Company, Ft. Lauderdale, Fla.

Don't improve rental property — repair it

The IRS rules for home improvements hold true for your rental property, too. If you make improvements to your rental property, you have to add the cost of the improvements to the basis and depreciate it over a period of years. The cost of repairs, however, can be deducted immediately.

What's the difference? Repairs are done to maintain the current value of the property; improvements are done to increase the value.

Don't have one company do everything at the same time, or your friends at the IRS may consider it a major renovation. Spread out the work, and hire different contractors for various portions of the job.

Source:
Interview with Ronald Schagrin, associate/consultant, Industrial Properties, Lehrer & Company, Ft. Lauderdale, Fla.

Money-saving tip for a landlord

If you rent out property, make sure the lease doesn't say that a tenant's security deposit can be used as the last month's rent. Security deposits, as long as you plan to give the money back at the end of the lease, aren't taxable.

If you have it in writing that you'll take the deposit as the final rent payment, it becomes an advance rent payment and is taxable in the year you receive it, even if the lease doesn't expire for several years.

"It's the way it's written into the lease," says real estate consultant Ronald Schagrin. "If the landlord says, 'Give me first, last, and security,' the last month is taxable in the year the lease is established."

Source:
Interview with Ronald Schagrin, associate/consultant, Industrial Properties, Lehrer & Company, Ft. Lauderdale, Fla.

For the best tax scenario, get a lease on land

You can't depreciate land the way you do buildings, but if you're looking at commercial real estate as an investment, there's a way you may be able to get the same bang for your buck. Buy the building, and lease the land it's built on. Then you can depreciate the bricks and mortar and deduct the rent payments on the terra firma as an expense of doing business.

Leasing land is a tricky financing proposition, though.

"Banks aren't in the business of owning property," says Frederick F. Perry, vice president for private banking at NationsBank in south Florida. "They're in the business of loaning money."

It was a sentiment that several financial experts echoed.

"A more aggressive leasing company might get involved in it, but not a bank," says Robert Benson, a shareholder in the public accounting firm of Madsen, Sapp, Mena, Rodriguez & Co., in Plantation, Fla. "Banks are usually looking at getting you as liquid as possible. If you can get somebody to finance it, tax-wise the theory is correct."

Sources:
Interview with Robert Benson, a shareholder in the public accounting firm of Madsen, Sapp, Mena, Rodriguez & Co., Plantation, Fla.
Interview with Frederick F. Perry, vice president, private banking, NationsBank, Ft. Lauderdale, Fla.

How to shift income to your children

If you're careful, you can still lower your tax burden by shifting income to your child. The first $650 a child under age 14 earns on investments is tax-free. The next $650 is taxed in the child's low tax bracket.

Any investment income over $1,300 is taxed at your rate. It takes a big investment to earn over $1,300 in interest, so stashing away money in your child's name is a good tax-saving move.

Options still exist for parents who want to give even larger gifts to a child, too. Give the child property that will produce little or no income until they turn 14. Once children are 14, they are taxed at a low rate no matter how much they earn. Property that grows in value without producing income includes real estate, tax-exempt bonds, growth stocks, precious metals, collectibles, and annuities.

Variable annuities and life insurance are particularly useful tools because they're like a spigot — you can determine when you want the income and when you don't, says Chuck Tiedje, president of Wealth Development and Preservation in Ft. Lauderdale, Fla. These assets will not only accumulate on a tax-deferred basis, they'll also not be considered when your child applies for college financial aid. Neither annuities nor life insurance are considered to be available assets for college financial aid.

If you have income-producing real estate you'd like to hand over to your child (such as rental property), put it into a subchapter S corporation and give stock in the corporation to the child. The corporation can accumulate income until the child is 14, and then begin paying dividends that will be taxed at the child's rate. You can control the funds in a trust or a custodial account until the child is of legal age (with the custodial account) or a predetermined age (with the trust).

Sources:
Interview with Professor Jim Dean, Nova Southeastern University, Ft. Lauderdale, Fla., author of soon-to-be-released *Building Your Future*, Fleming Revel Publishing, Ada, Mich.
Interview with Chuck Tiedje, CFP, CLU, ChFC, president, Wealth Development and Preservation, Ft. Lauderdale, Fla.

Cash in life insurance without paying taxes

Many people are holding on to old life insurance policies that they could trade in for new ones with better benefits. Why? Because they're incorrectly assuming that they'll have to pay taxes on the proceeds when they cash in the old policy to buy a new one.

Section 1035 of the Tax Code says that as long as you use the proceeds to buy a new policy immediately, you can cash in an old policy and receive the proceeds tax-free.

The cleanest way to do it is to sign over the proceeds from the old policy to the new company. The IRS will consider this a simple *exchange of contract* as long as a competent agent does the documentation correctly. (The process can get tricky if you have a loan out against your original policy.)

Make sure you get signed documentation from the new insurance company guaranteeing that it won't be a taxable event for you. If they won't guarantee a tax-free switch, don't do business with them.

Sources:
Interview with Chuck Tiedje, CFP, CLU, ChFC, president, Wealth Development and Preservation, Ft. Lauderdale, Fla.
U.S. Tax Code

What to do with the house when you divorce

More often than not, a divorce proceeding includes the transfer of property, usually a house. You may transfer the house from joint ownership to one person's name, or you may sell the house.

If you transfer ownership from one spouse to another, tax liability isn't an issue. But if you plan to sell the house, you need to be careful in order to avoid major tax implications down the road.

If the couple is over age 55, they are eligible for a one-time, $125,000 tax exclusion. In that situation, it would be all right to sell the house before the divorce is final.

"But let's say he's 56 and she's 52," says Carol Ann Wilson, author of *The Financial Adviser's Guide to Divorce Settlements*. "If they sell the house before they get divorced, she loses her exemption. If they sell after the divorce, he takes his exemption, and she still has hers. Also, if they sell before the divorce, and she remarries, she's lost her exemption and her new husband loses his, too!"

Even if you are both over age 55, you may be able to save by changing the title of the house from joint ownership to tenants-in-common while you are still married, then waiting until after the divorce to sell. That way, each of you is eligible for a separate $125,000 capital gains exemption.

So, with a little bit of careful planning, there's an opportunity to avoid losing $250,000 in potential tax savings. Hiring a reputable financial adviser before you sell may be a wise move.

Source:
Carol Ann Wilson, certified financial planner, Denver, Colo. Wilson is also the founder of The Quantum School, an institute for financial planners to become certified divorce planners, and author of *The Financial Adviser's Guide to Divorce Settlements*, Irwin Professional Publishing, Chicago, 1996.

Moving out can mean losing more than a marriage

When a marriage breaks up, a normal first step is one spouse — typically the husband — moving out of the house. Then, eight or 10 months later, the couple decides to file for divorce. As that process drags on through the legal system, time is passing by, quietly but with great force. Suddenly, he realizes with some surprise that he's been living alone for quite some time.

The divorce finalizes, and as part of the settlement, they sell the house. But the market is soft, and it takes several months to sell. But at last, closing day comes, and he gets his check for his half of the profits.

"Finally!" he thinks. "All I have to do is buy a new home, and I'll avoid capital gains taxes."

Wrong.

The house hadn't been his primary residence for more than two years, which is the time limit on rolling forward the proceeds into a new house.

If you have moved out and you're going to sell the house, you'll need to keep a close eye on the calendar to avoid a hefty capital gains tax.

Source:
Interview with Carol Ann Wilson, certified financial planner, Denver, Colo. Wilson is also the founder of The Quantum School, an institute for financial planners to become certified divorce planners, and author of *The Financial Adviser's Guide to Divorce Settlements*, Irwin Professional Publishing, Chicago, 1996.

Taking the pain out of paying alimony

You can avoid paying taxes on alimony payments if you can get your ex to agree not to list them as a deduction on his or her income tax return.

How do you accomplish that little feat of magic? Sheinfeld offers at least one scenario where both parties will come out ahead.

Let's say the suggested alimony is $5,000 a month. If you're in the 28 percent tax bracket and you pay taxes on the alimony you receive, you'll net $3,600 a month. If your spouse has a large source of tax-free income or has so many other deductions that the alimony deduction will be of little value, he or she might offer to pay you $4,000 a month instead if neither of you reports it as a deduction or income. That would save him or her $12,000 a year and net you another $4,800 in support.

Source:
Interview with Alan Sheinfeld, certified public accountant with the firm of Duncanson and Sheinfeld, Hollywood, Fla., and co-author of *The Financial Maze: Divorce and Your Finances,* 1994

Deducting divorce expenses

The bad news is your spouse wants a divorce. The good news is, you may be able to deduct part of the expense on your taxes.

If you're going to receive alimony payments, the money you pay to an attorney or a CPA for tax planning can be deducted as a miscellaneous expense. (Remember, in order to deduct miscellaneous expenses, they must exceed 2 percent of your adjusted gross income.)

Make sure the attorney and other financial advisors provide you with an invoice that breaks down what portion of their services was related to tax planning and alimony payments. Tax planning is the key phrase.

Source:
Interview with Alan Sheinfeld, certified public accountant with the firm of Duncanson and Sheinfeld, Hollywood, Fla., and co-author of *The Financial Maze: Divorce and Your Finances,* 1994

Separated means separate returns

If you are separated and have a written order or agreement that requires you to pay alimony, those payments are deductible on your taxes, but only if you and your spouse are filing separate returns. Money that passes between spouses who are filing jointly isn't taxed and isn't deductible.

The order or agreement must be in writing, too.

Source:
Interview with Alan Sheinfeld, certified public accountant with the firm of Duncanson and Sheinfeld, Hollywood, Fla., and co-author of *The Financial Maze: Divorce and Your Finances,* 1994

The tax side of a two-house marriage

If you both owned a home before you were married, there's a tendency to sell one house and move into the other. Watch out! That could mean a big capital gains tax.

The IRS doesn't make you pay taxes on the sale of your home if you're buying another within two years, but that tax break doesn't apply to you.

About the only option that doesn't involve shelling out a lot of money to the IRS is to live in one house and rent out the other one. That way, there's no capital gains, and all or most of the rental income will be sheltered by rental deductions.

For couples over 55, there's a different issue to be considered because of the $125,000 tax exclusion that's available to a married couple only once. You could go ahead and use the exclusion, or, to avoid that, you could use the above-mentioned strategy, or one spouse could give the house to his or her children, either directly or through a trust. If you give the house away, you'll need to structure the gift carefully to avoid gift taxes.

Source:
Daniel Breuning, a shareholder in charge of taxation with the public accounting firm of Madsen, Sapp, Mena, Rodriguez & Co., Plantation, Fla.

How to prove you're an 'innocent spouse'

You just got married. She's been married before. She was young; he turned out to be a deadbeat who ran up a lot of credit card bills, cleaned out the bank account, and hit the road. In the divorce decree, the judge made him solely responsible for his debts. She hasn't seen him in a couple of years and would be happy to keep it that way.

The next thing you know, you've got a bill for several thousand dollars from the IRS. Seems the deadbeat not only walked out on his credit card debt while she was married to him, he also didn't pay all of his taxes. Both their signatures and Social Security numbers were on the tax return, and now that his ex-wife is remarried and has assets, Uncle Sam has come to collect.

"They want to make the new husband liable for the old husband's debt," says San Francisco tax attorney Frederick Daily, author of *Stand Up to the IRS*. "Talk about the shock of your life. It's a real test of your love."

But what about the judge's order?

"The IRS doesn't recognize a divorce decree and consider it binding," Daily says. "That's state law. We're talking about federal law."

Under the innocent spouse rule, you may be able to get out of paying off your ex's tax bill. Just be ready for a long, uphill battle. Here's what you'll have to prove:

▶ Your spouse substantially understated how much tax he owed.
▶ You didn't know about the understatement.

That part is usually easy, Daily says. "The typical case is the husband has a business, doesn't report all the income, or fudges on deductions," he says. "The wife sits at home, does the grocery shopping, and takes care of the kids. He says, 'Sign this,' and she doesn't look at it. Now, if the wife was involved in the business or was a CPA, she should have known."

Now the tough part:

▶ You didn't benefit from the underpayment of the tax. "Did they live the caviar lifestyle on a mechanic's income?" Daily asks. "That in and of itself should have put her on notice. You have to show the lifestyle didn't change for the claimed innocent spouse."

▶ It would be inequitable, or unfair, to hold you liable.

Also, to make the innocent spouse claim, the amount of tax owed has to be at least $500 and the adjusted gross income at least $20,000.

You can make the innocent spouse claim without the help of a tax attorney. With or without help, it can take months, even years, to resolve. If you try to file yourself, Daily advises you to follow the IRS's rules explicitly.

"The IRS is very rule-intensive and form-intensive," Daily says. "Many people fail because they want to do it their way, not the IRS way. They'll write a letter relating their tale of woe when the IRS has a form. To make it worse, the letter is usually hand-written and rambling. If you use the form that's made for the situation, they route it and you get some attention."

Source:
Interview with Frederick W. Daily, author of *Stand Up to the IRS*, Nolo Press, Berkeley, Calif., 1996

Keep more of your gambling winnings

Has Lady Luck smiled on you? Uncle Sam is going to want you to share the wealth with him. Any money you win from gambling is taxable income. Casinos or the lottery office will dutifully report to the IRS and give you a 1099 to do the same. Woe to you if their form shows up and yours doesn't.

But you can keep more of your winnings in your own pocket by keeping all the reminders of your streaks of bad luck, too.

So don't throw away those losing lottery tickets. They might be worth some money after all. Anything that shows losses to offset your winnings can be helpful in reducing the amount of taxes you'll owe the government.

But what if you flew to Vegas and incurred your losses at a casino? People don't usually ask for a receipt from the blackjack dealer, and he's not going to give you one anyway.

"It could be tough to prove," says Professor Jim Dean at Nova Southeastern University. "What you want is corroborating evidence to show you were at the location. Keep a log and receipts that show you went to Las Vegas or the Bahamas."

So hang on to your plane or cruise ship ticket and your hotel checkout receipt. Even a receipt from a casino restaurant could be helpful. Deductions taken for gambling losses, by the way, aren't subject to the 2 percent floor of your adjusted gross income normally required for miscellaneous deductions. It's also not subject to high-income phaseouts.

"Nobody likes to keep paperwork, but that's how you get deductions," Dean says. Most people try to claim the deduction without the proper receipts. That's dangerous, and unnecessary. Keep the receipts, and you'll keep more of your winnings — or, more likely, take some of the bite out of your losses.

Sources:
Interview with Bally's Casino, Las Vegas, Nev.
Interview with Professor Jim Dean, Nova Southeastern University, Ft. Lauderdale, Fla., author of soon-to-be-released *Building Your Future*, Fleming Revel Publishing, Ada, Mich.
Keys to Saving Money on Income Taxes by Warren Boroson, 2nd Ed., Barron's Educational Series, Hauppauge, N.Y., 1995
"With Taxes, It's Little Things That Count" by Joseph Anthony in *Investor's Business Daily* (Dec. 26, 1995)

Your free lunch from the IRS

Would you like to reach in your pocket and find money that Uncle Sam hasn't touched? Here are some examples of tax-free cash that you can use to boost your standard of living. You won't pay taxes on money from:

► Carpool passengers.

► Rebates, such as on the purchase of a new car.

► Payment from the rental of a property for 14 days or less.

► Life insurance proceeds.

► Child support payments.

► Gifts of cash or property.

► An inheritance (may be subject to state tax).

► Compensation from a lawsuit for physical injuries or illness.

► Mileage reimbursements.

► Money your insurance pays you for medical bills.

► Pre-tax dollars you put in a flexible spending account for medical expenses or dependent care.

► Scholarships, including ROTC and Fulbright scholarships, and grants used for educational purposes (for which no service, such as teaching, is required).

► Student loans.

► Contest prizes used for educational purposes.

Sources:
Interview with Chuck Tiedje, CFP, CLU, ChFC, president, Wealth Development and Preservation, Ft. Lauderdale, Fla.
Interview with Carol Ann Wilson, certified financial planner, Denver, Colo. Wilson is also the founder of The Quantum School, an institute for financial planners to become certified divorce planners, and author of *The Financial Adviser's Guide to Divorce Settlements*, Irwin Professional Publishing, Chicago, 1996.
How to Write Off Everything and Retire with Twice as Much Money by Robert Carlson, Agora Financial Publishing, Baltimore, 1995
Keys to Saving Money on Income Taxes by Warren Boroson, 2nd Ed., Barron's Educational Series, Hauppauge, N.Y., 1995
Tax-Wise Money by Robert Carlson, Agora Financial Publishing, Baltimore, 1996

Tax deductions under your Christmas tree

Was your income higher than usual this year? That means a bigger tax bite. Instead of spending all that extra cash on holiday gifts, give the gift that will give back to you in April. Make your January payment on your mortgage interest before January 1. That way, you get a one-time increase in your mortgage interest deduction.

The catch is that you have to do the same thing next year if you want 12 months of deductions. Happy holidays!

Source:
How to Write Off Everything and Retire with Twice as Much Money by Robert Carlson, Agora Financial Publishing, Baltimore, 1995

Your home could be your tax-free castle

For occupations that require you to live on the job, the value of your housing is tax-free income. Hotels often use this tax advantage for their managers who need to be on the property around-the-clock, but it can apply to other jobs as well. Farmers, forest and park rangers, caretakers, nannies, nurses, animal breeders, funeral home owners, and others might take advantage of the IRS rules.

If your job requires you to be on the premises full time, consider doing what one farmer did. He incorporated his business and contributed the whole farm, including his house, to the corporation. Then he signed an employment contract with a condition that he had to live on the farm. The corporation depreciated the house and deducted all the taxes, maintenance, and utilities, and the farmer didn't include the value of the housing as part of his taxable income.

Source:
How to Write Off Everything and Retire with Twice as Much Money by Robert Carlson, Agora Financial Publishing, Baltimore, 1995

Anyone for a therapeutic swim? How to deduct the cost of a swimming pool and more

Here are some of the more interesting items the IRS has allowed toward the medical deduction:

Swimming pools. A person with arthritis, polio, or other disorders might be able to deduct the cost of building a swimming pool for nonimpact exercise. Other modifications to your home to accommodate a permanent or temporary disability, such as putting in an elevator, air conditioning, or adding a ramp, can qualify as a medical deduction. (Check with a tax planner before you start. Improvements are deductible only to the extent that the cost exceeds the increase in value of your property.)

Eyeglasses. Glasses, no matter how stylish the frames, are deductible. So are wigs, if they're health-related.

Travel. If your doctor suggests a change of climate would benefit your health, say from New England to New Mexico, your travel expenses — but not your actual stay — can be deducted.

Rehab center. You can write off your plane tickets for a trip to a rehabilitation center for treatment of addiction.

Clarinet lessons. Even facelifts, hair transplants, prescription birth control, an Indian medicine man, and clarinet lessons (to alleviate dental malocclusion) have been ruled deductible, on a case-by-case basis.

Remember, the IRS says you can't itemize medical expenses until the costs reach 7.5 percent of your adjusted gross income for the year. Most financial planners suggest using the "bunching" method, saving up medical deductions for a year in which you think your income will be low and your expenses will add up.

Sources:
Interview with Alan Sheinfeld, certified public accountant with the firm of Duncanson and Sheinfeld, Hollywood, Fla., and co-author of *The Financial Maze: Divorce and Your Finances*, 1994
How to Write Off Everything and Retire with Twice as Much Money by Robert Carlson, Agora Financial Publishing, Baltimore, 1995
Keys to Saving Money on Income Taxes by Warren Boroson, Barron's Educational Series, Hauppauge, N.Y., 1995
Reed Abelson, writing in *The New York Times* (Feb. 26, 1996)
"With Taxes, It's Little Things That Count" by Joseph Anthony in *Investor's Business Daily* (Dec. 26, 1995)

When you help support your parents

Bob, Jane, Bill, and Mary are siblings. For years, their mother lived with their other sister, Betty. They all contributed to their mother's support, but agreed that Betty should take the tax deduction for their mother as her dependent since Mom was living with her.

Then Betty was killed in a car accident, and Mom decided to move to an assisted living facility.

Bob, Jane, Bill, and Mary agreed to split the cost of their mother's care. Who gets the tax deduction?

The law says you can claim another person as a dependent, even if they don't live with you, as long as you pay more than half that person's support for the year. (The person you're supporting can't file a joint return with a spouse and can't earn more than the personal exemption amount during the year.) The person doesn't even have to be related to you.

The payments have to be for actual living expenses, such as food, shelter, clothing, or medical care. They can go to a nursing home or to another person, like a nurse's aide who provides direct service.

But none of the hypothetical brothers and sisters in our example is providing more than 50 percent support. What they need to do is sign a multiple support agreement. The exemption can be assigned to anyone giving more than 10 percent of the year's support, and it can be rotated on a yearly basis.

Source:
Professor Jim Dean, Nova Southeastern University, Ft. Lauderdale, Fla. Professor Dean is a CPA, a personal finance consultant, and author of soon-to-be-released *Building for the Future*, Fleming H. Revell Publishing (a division of Baker Books), Ada, Mich.

$10,000 here, $10,000 there adds up to a tax break

If you wanted to leave $10,000 in your will — say, to a child, grandchild, sibling, or a valued and faithful employee — you'd have to leave $20,000 for them to have $10,000 after paying estate taxes.

Needless to say, that may place a serious restraint on your generosity. Leaving money through a will also deprives you of the joy of seeing your gift accepted and used to enrich a person's life.

For reasons unknown, the federal government, through its agent the Internal Revenue Service, looks favorably upon people who share their bounty with others while they are still among the living. You can give $10,000 in gifts every year to as many people as you want (for now anyway — tax laws are always in a state of flux, and legislation has been proposed to limit the number of gifts that can be made a year) without paying a gift tax.

What does this do for you, besides giving you a warm, fuzzy feeling? It reduces the size of your estate that will be taxable when you die. What does it do for the recipients of your generosity, beyond the obvious? They don't have to pay taxes on the gift.

Now *that's* a win-win situation!

Sources:
Interview with Dr. Judith Briles, author of *Financial Savvy for Women*, MasterMedia, New York, 1992. Dr. Briles is currently writing *The Money Maze*, the 1997 update of *Financial Savvy for Women*.
Interview with Steven C. Camp, financial consultant with a major brokerage firm, lecturer, and author of *Money: 127 Answers to Your Most-Asked Financial Questions*, Trunkey Publishing, Ft. Lauderdale, Fla., 1995
Interview with Richard Duff, author of *Preserving Family Wealth Using Tax Magic*, Berkley Books, New York, 1995

When is a taxable gift not a taxable gift?

A gift isn't taxable when it's a loan. Your adult children want to buy a business. You can give them advice about a good business opportunity, loan them the money at a fair rate of interest, and then send them prospects and opportunities. You've given them something of great value, but it won't cost you anything in gift taxes, and your children may be able to deduct the interest on the loan.

Source:
Interview with Richard Duff, author of *Preserving Family Wealth Using Tax Magic*, Berkley Books, New York, 1995

Sharing the wealth with your spouse's children

If you're married to a person supporting children from a previous marriage, you can give his or her children financial support without paying a gift tax. How? Give the money to your spouse since gifts to a spouse don't get hit with a gift tax.

Source:
Interview with Richard Duff, author of *Preserving Family Wealth Using Tax Magic*, Berkley Books, New York, 1995

Helping yourself while helping others

If you've saved more than $10,000 to help your grandchildren with their college educations, do yourself a favor. Don't write the child a check for the tuition. You may find yourself looking at a costly *gift tax event*. When you file next April, any gift over $10,000 ($20,000 for married couples) will be taxed.

Instead, write a check for the amount of the tuition directly to the school. You can't take a deduction for it, but you won't pay taxes on the money, either. It only works for tuition, though. Room and board aren't part of the equation.

You can use the same strategy to help a loved one with medical expenses. Instead of writing that person a check, write one directly to the doctor, hospital, nursing home, or other medical service provider.

Sources:
Interview with Steven C. Camp, financial consultant with a major brokerage firm, lecturer, and author of
Money: 127 Answers to Your Most-Asked Financial Questions, Trunkey Publishing, Ft. Lauderdale, Fla., 1995
Keys to Personal Financial Planning by D. Larry Crumbley, CPA, and L. Murphy Smith, CPA, Barron's
Educational Series, Hauppauge, N.Y., 1994

Turn your junk into a tax write-off

You can turn your old clothes, worn-out (but working) appliances, or the sofa you just replaced into several hundred dollars in tax refunds. Your junk may be a treasure to a charity like the Salvation Army or Goodwill. And you can make money without even going to the trouble of a yard sale. The IRS even lets you determine how much your old belongings are worth.

But how do you find out what an IRS auditor would consider a fair price for a '60s-style lamp?

Either check with stores that sell used items, such as thrift shops, or consult a booklet called *Cash for Your Used Clothing* by William Lewis, a Lincoln, Neb., certified public accountant. Lewis guarantees that the IRS will accept the values he has put on over 750 household items and clothes.

Some examples of his prices on items in good condition:

Men's long-sleeve dress shirt	$14.50
Adult's raincoat	$22
Maternity dress	$28
Women's casual shoes with laces	$15
Baby's snowsuit	$14.50
Washer and dryer	$600
Board games	$13
Old 8-piece golf set	$50
Telephone	$12

You can buy Lewis's booklet by calling 1-800-875-5927. It costs $25, so you might want to split the price with some charitable friends. (The booklet does carry a guarantee: If you don't save at least an additional $200 on your taxes by using the booklet, you can return it for a full refund.)

For very expensive items such as used computers, check the Yellow Pages for stores that sell them. Most places will give you a price estimate over the phone.

For an old car, check the *Blue Book* price guides at your bank or a used-car dealership. If you have a very old car almost ready for the junk heap, call a couple of local auto-parts yards. The Salvation Army, Goodwill, or a non-profit school should come pick the car up for you.

Remember, for noncash donations over $250, get a signed receipt from the charity. The receipt should briefly describe the items, for instance, "one box of clothes and one overcoat."

For cars worth over $5,000, an appraiser must complete Part III in Section B of Form 8283.

Source:
Cash for Your Used Clothing by William Lewis, Client Valuation Services, P.O. Box 22031, Lincoln, Neb., 68542–2031, 1995

How to make giving even more blessed

If you are a generous person who enjoys sharing what you have with others, there's a way to share the wealth with a charity without Uncle Sam putting his hand out as well.

Consider making a gift of an appreciable asset — stocks, bonds, or jewelry, for instance — instead of writing a check.

Here's how it works:

Let's say a person has $1,000 he wants to give to a church. He can write a check and deduct $1,000 at tax time.

Let's say the same person bought $100 worth of stock 10 years ago, and that stock has appreciated in value to $1,000. If he donates the stock certificates, the charity gets the current market value, the donor gets the $1,000 tax deduction, plus a bonus — the donor doesn't have to pay capital gains tax on the sale of the stock.

If the person kept the stock for himself instead of donating it, he'd have to pay about $280 to the IRS (capital gains tax is usually 28 percent).

Some things to watch out for:

▶ You must have held the asset for more than 12 months.

▶ The organization must be legitimate and have tax-exempt status. Unless he's a bona fide member of the clergy or executive director of a nonprofit agency, your brother-in-law is not a charity.

▶ If you're donating a tangible asset (a painting, for instance) instead of a financial asset (stocks or bonds), be cautious about establishing the appreciated value of the asset you're donating. If you paid $500 for a painting from an unknown artist 20 years ago and now you're donating it and claiming it's worth $500,000, expect to receive a nice note from your friends at the IRS. Abuses in the area of appreciated artwork have made such donations particularly suspect.

▶ Don't donate something you own if you would take a loss on it. You would be better off to sell it, take your tax loss, and then donate the cash from the sale. That earns you double points on your tax return: the loss and the contribution.

▶ If you're donating merchandise or property, get the charity to agree — in writing — to use the gift only for its exempt purpose. Artwork should go to museums, book collections to libraries, furniture to a homeless shelter, etc. If the charity uses the merchandise for other than its stated purpose, you can only deduct your purchase price of the item — not the appreciated price.

In fact, gifts of any kind of merchandise — paintings, furniture, jewelry, stamps, etc. — valued in excess of $500 will probably trigger an audit. Make sure you have a written statement from an appraiser to attest to the value of your possession.

Sources:
Interview with Steven C. Camp, financial consultant with a major brokerage firm, lecturer, and author of
Money: 127 Answers to Your Most-Asked Financial Questions, Trunkey Publishing, Ft. Lauderdale, Fla., 1995
Tax Wise Money Strategies: Protect Yourself from the Highest Taxes in History by Robert C. Carlson, Carroll
& Graf Publishers, New York, 1995

Deduct your charitable activities

You found out long ago that the value of your time isn't deductible. If you type the church's bulletin, work in a soup kitchen, or donate your professional services to a charity, you don't get to take that off your taxes.

But you can deduct any costs you incur while doing charitable work. If you use your car to transport items to the church yard sale, you can deduct either how much you spent on gas (keep up with your receipts) or you can deduct a certain amount for every mile you drove (12 cents a mile at the time of this writing).

Don't forget to deduct telephone costs, food, parking fees, and tolls. You can also deduct costs of paper and printing if you type a church bulletin or flyer at home.

If you spend more than $250 on a charity's activities, you'll need an acknowledgment from the charity saying that you did incur those costs and you weren't reimbursed.

Plus, if you attend a theater production where the tickets are priced extra high for the benefit of a charity, you can deduct the "extra" you paid for the ticket. If you buy the ticket then decide you can't make it to the event, be glad. You can now deduct the whole cost of the ticket.

Sources:
William E. Donoghue's Lifetime Financial Planner, William E. Donoghue with Dana Shilling, Harper & Row,
New York, 1987
Year-End Tax Planning for 1995, Grant-Thornton LLP, 1995

How to keep earning money on a charitable donation

You can actually donate money to a charity, receive an immediate tax deduction for it, and continue to live off the interest for the rest of your life. There are three little-known ways to accomplish this amazing feat.

The first method is simple: It's called a *pooled income fund*, and it's a mutual fund operated by a church or a charity. The mutual fund is invested in things that produce income, like government bonds. All you do is send a check to the charity's headquarters, and the fund manager sends you a regular check just like a mutual fund would.

You get a safe, steady income for life; you don't have to make investment decisions; and, since the money is given to the charity at your or your spouse's death, you get to take an income tax deduction now. You also avoid probate problems with this plan.

You can also donate stocks that have gone up in value to a pooled income fund. You may need money from your stocks, but you don't want to sell them because you don't want to pay taxes on your profits.

Through a pooled income fund, a charity can sell the stocks and invest all the money they earned for you. The charity can then send you regular checks from that invested money. You don't have to pay taxes on the gains; you get a larger income than you had before; and you avoid any stock market drops in the future.

The second method is very similar to the first. It's called a *charitable gift annuity*, and it involves an insurance company instead of a mutual fund. You send your money or stocks to an insurance company connected with a charity, and you get a tax deduction and an income for life.

The advantage to this method is that you are guaranteed an income that won't change from month to month. Your income from a mutual fund could vary depending on interest rates.

The third method is called a *charitable remainder trust*. It's for people who want to manage their own money. You'll need an attorney to help you set up the trust. You deposit money, stocks, or property into the trust. The trust pays you while you live and distributes any remaining money to your charity when you or your spouse dies.

You get an immediate tax deduction when you set up the trust or deposit anything into it. You can put stocks or real estate that has gone up in value into the trust and then sell it without having to pay taxes on the profit.

Some churches or charities even have lawyers available who will help you set up a trust for a low fee or for no fee at all.

Your financial planner may not be familiar with these powerful financial tools, but don't let that stop you from taking advantage of them. You can get information from your church, favorite charity, or from one of these sources:

American Baptist Foundation
P.O. Box 851
Valley Forge, PA 19482–0851

Christian Church Foundation
222 South Downey Avenue
P.O. Box 1986
Indianapolis, IN 46206

Presbyterian Church Foundation
200 East Twelfth Street
Jeffersonville, IN 47130

Reformed Church in America
Office of Gift Planning
1790 Grand Boulevard
Schenectady, NY 12309

The Episcopal Church
815 Second Avenue
New York, NY 10017

United Church of Christ
Planned Giving Program
475 Riverside Drive
New York, NY 10115

Source:
The Christian's Guide to Wise Investing by Gary D. Moore, former senior vice-president of investment at Paine Webber, Zondervan Books, Grand Rapids, Mich., 1994

Can I put a banner on that Port-a-Potty?

Understanding that little things can make the difference between a happy and an unpleasant experience, a company once underwrote the expense of providing portable toilets at a civic event. Being humble community servants, they declined the organizers' grateful offer of public recognition for their gift.

This may have been one of the rare exceptions to the rule that companies should always provide sponsorships and receive public recognition instead of making an outright donation to a charity.

A business can only deduct 5 percent of its income as charitable gifts. But there are no limits on reasonable advertising and promotional expenses. So, if you have your own business and you'd like to make a donation, then give to your heart's content, but put your company's name on it somewhere.

Here are tips for increasing your company's exposure as a sponsor and for bolstering your claim that your expenditure was for advertising and promotion:

▶ Ask the charity to recognize your sponsorship in a newsletter or in promotional materials. For newsletter articles, always ask to have your company's name and phone number included.

▶ For an event, make sure there's a place to hang a banner, exhibit your logo, put up a display, or set out some brochures.

▶ Ask to be included in the information provided to the media, and obtain a copy of the releases that were sent out in which your sponsorship was mentioned.

▶ If your sponsorship is mentioned in a newspaper article or shows up in any press photos, keep copies of those for your records. Ask for the newspaper's circulation figures, or for Arbitron or Nielson ratings for radio or television stations. These are the same figures used to establish advertising rates.

▶ Ask the charity for a report on the number of people who attended the event, and/or received the newsletter in which your sponsorship was mentioned.

Any charity worth its salt will be happy to accommodate you because the organizers want to be able to come back to you in the future for support.

Sources:
How to Write Off Everything and Retire with Twice as Much Money by Robert Carlson, Agora Financial
Publishing, Baltimore, 1995
Pat Curry, media consultant and past chairman, board of directors, Habitat for Humanity of Broward, Ft.
Lauderdale, Fla.

Make sure your savings bond is really tax-free

Like millions of other Americans, you may have bought a Series E or EE
U.S. Savings Bond in order to build a tax-free college fund for your child. You
need to make sure you really qualify for that tax break. If you don't, you could
be storing your money in an investment that doesn't pay the best interest rate
for no good reason.

You never have to pay state or local income taxes on savings bond interest earnings. To make sure you don't pay federal income tax, follow these
important rules:

Never put the bond in your child's name. This is the most common
error. The bond must be registered in the name of an adult who is 24 or older,
so put the bond in your name. Your child may be listed as a beneficiary, but
only your spouse can be a co-owner.

Redeem the bond in the correct year. Bonds must be redeemed in the
same calendar year that you pay tuition and fees. And the bond money can
only be used to pay tuition and fees, not books, room, or board.

Make sure your income isn't too high. For the bond to be tax-free, you
can't make over $45,500 as a single taxpayer or over $68,250 as a married tax-
payer. Married couples must file jointly. If you make over these amounts, the
tax break starts to phase out until it completely disappears at $60,500 for sin-
gle taxpayers and $98,250 for married taxpayers. (These numbers are for tax
year 1993.)

For more details, request "Questions and Answers about Savings Bonds
for Education," from the Office of Public Affairs, U.S. Savings Bonds
Division, Washington, DC, 20226.

Source:
Q&A: The Savings Bonds Question & Answer Book, Department of the Treasury, U.S. Savings Bonds
Division, Washington, D.C. 20226, 1994

Should you buy tax-free bonds?

Is it smart to buy a tax-exempt bond to build savings for college or retirement? It depends. You need to compare the amount you'd earn on a tax-free
bond to the amount you'd earn on an investment after paying taxes. The tax
bracket you're in is important.

Here's how to do the math:

1) Subtract your federal tax bracket from 100. That gives you the *reciprocal
   of your tax bracket*. For example, if you're in the 28 percent tax bracket, the
   reciprocal of your tax bracket is 72.

2) Divide the interest you'd earn on the tax-free bond (also called the *yield*) by the reciprocal of your tax bracket. Move the decimal point two places to the right, and you've got the equivalent yield for a taxable investment.

Using this formula, you can see that earning 8 percent interest tax-free is equivalent to earning 11.1 percent interest and paying taxes on your profit (if you're in the 28 percent tax bracket.) If you can find an investment that yields more than 11.1 percent in interest, you'd be better off even though you'll have to pay taxes on your earnings.

By the way, if you know the interest you'd earn on the taxable investment, you can apply this formula backward. For instance, a taxable corporate bond that yields 10 percent in interest is equivalent to a 7.2 percent interest rate that's tax-free. Multiply 10 by the reciprocal of your tax bracket (72), move the decimal point over two places, and you've got 7.2.

Source:
The Touche Ross Personal Financial Management and Investment Workbook by John R. Connell, Paul R. Gordon, W. Thomas Porter, and Robert E. Zobel, Prentice Hall, New York, 1989

Mutual fund tax trap

Every mutual fund investor can get stuck in a tax trap when it's time to sell shares. But you can avoid it by keeping one simple handwritten record on a piece of paper in your mutual fund file.

Here's the trap: When you cash in your shares, you have to tell the IRS how much profit you've made. Like most investors, you probably reinvest your dividends. Every time you reinvest, you buy shares. Those shares are never the same price twice. If you've held a bond fund for five years, it could have more than 60 reinvestments and 60 prices.

Figuring out how much money you've made over the years can be a weeks-long nightmare. And some funds are better than others at helping you come up with old records. Congress is considering passing a law that will require mutual fund companies to give you the information you need when you sell.

In the meantime, put a piece of paper in the front of the file folder you keep for each mutual fund you own. At the top, write down the number of shares you originally bought and the price you paid for each share. Then, every time you get a notice from the mutual fund company saying it has reinvested your dividends, write down the number of shares bought and the price paid.

You'll love yourself for keeping this simple record when it's time to sell your shares.

Source:
Forbes (Aug. 29, 1994)

Mutual fund tax magic

There's more than one way to report the sale of mutual fund shares to the IRS. And the way you choose determines how much tax you'll pay on your investment. Don't pay more than you have to.

Example: You've held a mutual fund for a couple of years and bought shares at various prices — 250 shares at $10 on 2/1/94, 20 shares at $13 on 1/3/95, 200 shares at $14 on 4/12/95, and 200 shares at $12 on 7/28/95. You now hold 670 shares and you're ready to sell 200 of them. It's December 1995, and the current price is $11 per share. How you do your accounting makes a huge difference in the amount of taxes you'll owe on the sale:

Method one: Average cost-single category. You calculate your gain or loss based on the average price you paid for all your shares. In the above example, you'd show a **loss of $176. Tax savings!**

Method two: Average cost-double category. You separate your shares into long-term and short-term holdings and come up with a separate average cost for each. The IRS lets you specify which group you're selling. In the above example, if you say you're selling short-term shares, you could show a **loss of $400. Bigger tax savings!**

Method three: First in, first out. With this method, the first shares you sell are the first ones you bought. You show a **gain of $200. You owe IRS!**

Method four: Specific shares. You identify exactly which shares you are selling. You show a **loss of $600. Biggest tax savings!**

Plus, don't forget to subtract any sales charges and fees you may have paid over the years.

Source:
Calculating Your Gains and Losses, Fidelity Investments, Fidelity Distributors Corp., Boston

Working with a tax preparer

Congratulations to all those gutsy people who prepare their own tax returns. You're saving the cost of hiring a CPA, but are you sure you aren't paying more in taxes than you should be?

If you have had a big change in your life recently or if you have several deductions to itemize, income from stocks and bonds, and a pension distribution, you may need a tax preparer's help. But don't hire someone who's only available during income-tax season. Find someone who will meet with you in October or November for a tax-planning session.

For instance, one recently divorced woman was having trouble supporting two children and making ends meet. A CPA showed her how to keep better track of contributions to charity, gave her advice on child-care deductions, and helped her reduce expenses so she could start an individual retirement account. She saved so much on her tax bill that the CPA's fee was well worth it.

Besides being too busy to meet with you for tax planning, here are other traits to avoid in a CPA:

▶ Steer clear of any pompous CPA who quotes the Internal Revenue code while talking to you.

▶ Beware of CPAs who say they've never had a client get audited.

▶ Never use a CPA who promises a refund from the IRS. Also, avoid any CPA who asks for a fee based on a percentage of the refund.

Source:
Keys to Choosing a Financial Specialist by Raymond J. Lipay, Barron's Educational Series, Hauppauge, N.Y., 1992

Hiring a CPA for less

You can lower your CPA's fee by doing some of the work for him: Keep organized records.

▶ Label plain manila folders with specific financial categories — travel expenses, medical expenses, charitable contributions, etc.

▶ Arrange canceled checks and bank-deposit slips in monthly order along with the related bank statements.

▶ Keep an up-to-date checkbook.

Source:
Keys to Choosing a Financial Specialist by Raymond J. Lipay, Barron's Educational Series, Hauppauge, N.Y., 1992

Is an audit in your future?

It might come as a surprise to you that since 1988, less than 1 percent of all taxpayers have endured the traditional face-to-face audit. Even so, your chance of getting audited largely depends on where you live and how much money you make.

You'd better sharpen your pencils and recheck your math if you live in these cities: Anchorage, Alaska.; Las Vegas, Nev.; Cheyenne, Wyo.; San Francisco, Los Angeles, and Laguna Niguel, Calif.; Boise, Idaho; and Atlanta, Ga. Reviewing eight years of records, the General Accounting Office found that audits were most common in these areas.

The districts with the lowest rate for audits were: Albany, N.Y.; Milwaukee, Wis.; Boston, Mass.; Newark, N.J., Detroit, Mich.; Philadelphia, Pa.; Cincinnati, Ohio; and Baltimore, Md.

If your annual income is over $100,000, your chance of being audited has gone down dramatically since 1988, from 11.4 percent to 3.4 percent in 1995. If you're making less than $25,000 and filing a short form, though, the rate of audits has actually doubled for you, from 1 to 2 percent.

Very small businesses are a new target, too. Those with less than $25,000 worth of business have seen the audit rate shoot up from just over 2 percent to nearly 6 percent.

Source:
Report issued by Transactional Records Access Clearinghouse, Syracuse University, Syracuse, N.Y., April 13, 1996. Internet address: http://trac.syr.edu/tracirs/home/html

Top audit triggers

The IRS made a mistake in 1991. They sent an auditor to make life miserable for Amir Aczel, a professor of statistics in Massachusetts. Not only did the IRS end up owing Professor Aczel money, but Amir decided to declare war on the government.

After studying thousands of tax returns, Aczel broke the secret code the IRS uses to select taxpayers to audit. Here are four minor audit triggers he discovered:

Nice, whole numbers. Numbers such as $2,987.93 are more believable to the IRS than numbers such as $3,000.

Inconsistencies from year to year. If your daughter changes her name, write an explanation to the IRS so they don't think she's a fake dependent.

Lack of agreement between your state tax return and your federal form. Big shifts in income and/or expenses from year to year.

Even after you've rid your return of all these audit triggers, the IRS computers are certain to tag you for an audit if you fall into this important category: Your total itemized deductions on Schedule A divided by your adjusted gross income on form 1040 is 0.44 or higher.

For example, if your adjusted gross income is $60,000 and your total itemized deductions are $15,000, you're safe ($15,000 divided by $60,000 equals 0.25).

If your itemized deductions divided by your adjusted gross income is 0.35 or higher, you're entering the Caution Zone for an audit. Once you hit the 0.44 mark, you're a sitting duck for an audit. You need to hire an accountant and start doing everything in your power to convince the IRS you're clean.

If you want more of this mathematical approach to figuring your chance for an audit, buy Professor Amir Aczel's book, and, as your high school teacher would say, put on your thinking cap!
Source:
How to Beat the I.R.S. at Its Own Game: Strategies to Avoid — and Fight — an Audit by Amir D. Aczel, Four Walls Eight Windows, New York, 1995

Mind games to play with IRS agents

It's an IRS agent's job to make you feel uncomfortable, intimidated, and strained to the limit. He wants you to buckle under the pressure and admit you made unreasonable claims and deductions. If you don't buckle, he figures you're probably honest.

Fortunately, agents are human, too, so you can play mind games as well.

► Agents are typically overworked. Try to figure out if your auditor is very busy. Is his calendar full? Does he check his watch often? If so, delay. It's against the law to lie to the IRS, but it's no crime to say, "I'll get back to you on that." The agent may give up on you.

► Do the agent's homework for him. Clearing up a small issue perfectly may make the agent willing to close your case without searching for further errors. Suppose you cashed in an IRA account early without paying the penalty. Admit your mistake and make the correction in perfect accounting form. You've saved face for the auditor and given a small gain to the government. That may be enough.

▶ Ask a lot of questions. "Why do you need this?" "What should I do with these?" You may throw off the auditor or at least tire him out.

▶ Let him believe he is "educating" you. Some idealistic agents, particularly young ones, have a mission to teach you about the tax system so you'll file correctly in the future. Ask questions like, "How can I learn from this experience so that I won't be audited again?" Catering to an agent's "call" to educate can take you a long way.

Source:
How to Beat the I.R.S. at Its Own Game: Strategies to Avoid — and Fight — an Audit by Amir D. Aczel, Four Walls Eight Windows, New York, 1995

The top 10 places to live to avoid criminal charges from the IRS

The data is in, and it's clear that taxpayers get away with a lot more in certain parts of the country than in others.

In an analysis of internal government records, the Transactional Records Access Clearinghouse at Syracuse University found that taxpayers in certain federal judicial districts were 10 times more likely to face criminal charges from the IRS than those in other parts of the country.

The unfortunate folk were most likely to live in Charleston and Wheeling, W.Va; Tulsa and Oklahoma City, Okla.; Louisville, Ky.; the Manhattan and Bronx boroughs as well as some northern suburbs of New York City; Indianapolis, Ind.; Miami, Fla.; and Pittsburgh, Pa.

The places where the IRS was most likely to leave you alone? Madison and Milwaukee, Wis.; Montgomery, Ala.; Topeka, Kan.; Detroit, Mich.; Boston, Mass.; St. Louis, Mo.; Philadelphia, Pa.; Houston, Texas; and Des Moines, Iowa.

When you look at the disparities and see what goes on, it's amazing, TRAC program administrator Randi Mahoney says.

The clearinghouse has a host of information about the IRS (and other federal agencies) that it makes available to the public. You can check out their IRS web site at http://trac.syr.edu/tracirs/home.html.

Source:
Interview with Randi Mahoney, program administrator, Transactional Records Access Clearinghouse, Syracuse University, Syracuse, N.Y.

Will the IRS send you to jail?

There is a universal fear that failure to pay your taxes will land you in jail. Maybe the federal government would like you to believe that, but in the real world, the chances of being prosecuted are only slightly higher than one in a million.

The number is 17 per million, to be exact. In fact, the FBI says you're five times more likely to be murdered than to have the IRS recommend filing criminal charges against you. (This is supposed to make us feel better.)

In 1994, the latest year with complete information, the IRS recommended that the Justice Department file criminal charges in 4,542 instances. The Justice Department accepted the recommendation in just about half those cases. Nearly all of those prosecutions netted convictions, and slightly under 1,000 people actually spent time in prison.

Criminal prosecutions are a last resort for the IRS, mainly because they take up a great deal of staff time — more than a year and a half for a conviction. You'll probably only be prosecuted if the IRS believes it can prove you knowingly violated the law.

The top 10 charges referred by the IRS for criminal prosecution were:

1. money laundering
2. tax evasion
3. fraud and false statements
4. evading currency regulations
5. willful failure to file a return
6. conspiracy to defraud the U.S.
7. drugs — control and enforcement
8. false claims against the U.S.
9. mail fraud
10. bribery of a federal witness

Source:
Report issued by Transactional Records Access Clearinghouse, Syracuse University, Syracuse, N.Y., April 13, 1996. Internet address: http://trac.syr.edu/tracirs/home/html

Free tax information

You can find the answer to just about any tax question you have in a free pamphlet from the IRS. Every year, the IRS updates over 100 publications to help you fill out your return and answer your questions. You can order any publication at no charge by calling the IRS at 1–800–829–3676. A few of the most helpful publications are:

▶ Your Federal Income Tax (for Individuals) — Publication 17
▶ Tax Guide for Small Business — Publication 334
▶ Travel, Entertainment, and Gift Expenses — Publication 463
▶ Medical and Dental Expenses — Publication 502
▶ Child and Dependent Care Expenses — Publication 503
▶ Moving Expenses — Publication 521
▶ Selling Your Home — Publication 523
▶ Charitable Contributions — Publication 526
▶ Miscellaneous Deductions — Publication 529
▶ Investment Income and Expenses — Publication 550
▶ Tax Information for Older Americans — Publication 554
▶ Survivors, Executors, and Administrators — Publication 559
▶ Mutual Fund Distributions — Publication 564
▶ Pension and Annuity Income — Publication 575

- ► Nonbusiness Disaster, Casualty, and Theft Loss Workbook — Publication 584
- ► Individual Retirement Arrangements (IRAs) — Publication 590
- ► Earned Income Credit — Publication 596
- ► Tax Highlights for Persons with Disabilities — Publication 907
- ► Business Use of a Car — Publication 917
- ► How to Depreciate Property — Publication 946

Source:
IRS Publication 910 — Guide to Free Tax Services For Tax Year 1995

Tax records: How long should you keep them?

We've all got them — boxes of records that are older than our children. We hang on to them because we think we'll need them if we ever get audited. But sooner or later, the need for space overtakes you. How long do you need to hang on to that stuff?

When it comes to your house, the answer is as long as you own it. Receipts for any improvements you make should go in a file to apply against capital gains if and when you sell or for your estate after you're gone. What's an improvement? Anything that adds value to the house. Things that are done to maintain the value of the house — like painting, roof repairs, or replacing a toilet — are considered repairs.

Other records, like those pertaining to your business, including your yearly organizer, should be kept for seven years. For some kinds of investigations, the IRS can come back six years later.

"Of course, sometimes you're better off not having the records," points out CPA Alan Weiner.

Any really important documents, like insurance policies, savings bonds, stock certificates, etc., should be kept in a secure place out of the house, like in a safe-deposit box. Also, make backups of important files stored on your computer's hard drive, put them on disk, and put them in the safe-deposit box, too.

Source:
Alan Weiner, CPA, JD, tax partner, Holtz Rubenstein and Co., LLP, Melville, N.Y.

MONEY AND THE PEOPLE YOU LOVE

Flower power

Wondering whether to send that bouquet of flowers to your honey at her home or place of work? Well, wonder no more.

According to a recent survey by 1-800-Flowers, you'll get a lot more mileage for your money if you send the flowers to work. Eighty-five percent of 862 women interviewed preferred to receive their flowers there.

The reason is simple — many more admirers to share their special moment.
Source:
The Wall Street Journal (Feb. 14, 1995, A1)

5 easy ways to win the marital money wars

The only way to win a money battle with your spouse is to head it off at the pass.

A minister in a large Southern church requires every happy couple, young and old, to come to one counseling session with him before he'll lead them to the altar. He spends five minutes talking about honoring one another and the rest of the hour talking about money. "Money will be at the root of 90 percent of the arguments you'll have once you're married," he states.

To avoid major money conflicts after you're married, you must talk about money issues before the honeymoon. If you're already married, plan a "honeymoonish" evening to talk about money. Leave your kids with a baby sitter and go out to dinner at a nice restaurant. Take a pen and a pad of paper so you can record all the decisions you make while the two of you are in a harmonious mood.

The calm, preferably prehoneymoon conversation should include:

▶ How each of you handles money. Many couples get married without knowing if their spouse is in debt, how many credit cards the significant other owns, and whether he/she can balance a checkbook. You must find out these details. One easy way is to exchange credit reports. If your spouse-to-be is overly reluctant to reveal his/her finances to you, let that be a sign!

▶ Who will be the family's chief financial officer. Naming one person to be in charge of paying the bills works best. Then you'll avoid those, "I thought *you* were paying the light bill" arguments. Just make sure the other spouse reviews the budget every month. Both spouses should know where the money is going.

▶ Whether you will have joint or separate bank accounts. One advantage of joint accounts: They force you to talk often about money, usually several times a week, instead of waiting for a big blowup or a once-a-month reckoning. Separate accounts may make you more suspicious about where your spouse's money is going. Joint accounts are also a good idea if one spouse makes a lot more money than the other.

▶ How you'll deal with emergencies. Plan to set aside three to four months worth of expenses in a savings account. This emergency account is extremely important. Whether you save the money shouldn't be up for discussion — just discuss how you'll do it. You'll also need to write a will and buy disability insurance.

▶ What your financial goals are. Do you want to save for retirement (of course!), a yearly vacation, a college education, a new car? Create a budget that includes money for savings.

Money talks may not be the most fun you've ever had, but they sure beat money battles. Don't let money turn your happy honeymoon into an ugly divorce.
Source:
Fear of Finance by Ann Diamond, HarperBusiness, New York, 1994

What to find out from your spouse before it's too late

When an active middle-aged man suddenly died on his favorite golf course, it was a tragedy in more ways than one. He had always handled the family funds. His wife, in fact, bragged that she knew nothing about their finances, not even where the safety deposit box was. After he died, she spent nearly a year looking for his assets.

Do you want to put your spouse through a similar agonizing experience? Meet each other's stockbroker, banker, insurance agent, and attorney now. It's not too soon to create a net worth statement listing bank accounts, stocks, bonds, mutual funds, annuities, pensions, real estate, and other assets. Each of you should keep a copy of that statement. Each of you should also know where those assets are kept as well as the location of your safety deposit boxes.
Source:
Thy Will Be Done: A Guide to Wills, Taxation and Estate Planning for Older People by Eugene J. Daly, Prometheus Books, Buffalo, N.Y., 1990

Divorce and credit: Don't get burned

Sally and Brad were recently divorced. Their court-approved divorce decree stated that Brad would pay the balances on their three joint credit cards. Months later, Brad had neglected to pay off the balances, and all three credit card companies contacted Sally for payment. She insisted that, according to her divorce decree, she was not responsible for the accounts. Unfortunately, Sally was wrong.

No matter what your divorce decree says, you are legally responsible for any joint accounts in both your and your spouse's name. Any accounts that aren't paid off or are paid late will show up on your personal credit report.

If you are getting a divorce, protect yourself:

▶ Look closely at accounts held jointly, including mortgage, home equity loans, and credit cards.

▶ Ask creditors to convert any joint accounts to individual accounts. Or, if you can't convert them, close the accounts and try to reopen them as individual accounts. Remember to close or convert any individual credit accounts in which you authorized your spouse to be a user.

▶ If your spouse has agreed to pay off a debt, have the account converted to his or her name instead of yours.

▶ Don't depend on a divorce decree to force your spouse to pay off joint debts. Be responsible for the accounts yourself.

Source:
Facts for Consumers, Credit and Divorce, Bureau of Consumer Protection, Federal Trade Commission, Sixth and Pennsylvania Ave. N.W., Washington, D.C. 20580, 1993

How to write off your family's medical expenses

If you help a child or your parents pay their medical bills, you may be able to take it as a tax write off — even if you don't claim them as dependents on your tax form.

You can deduct all medical expenses that your insurance doesn't cover (all expenses that add up to over 7.5 percent of your income, that is). You can deduct medical expenses for you, your spouse, your dependents, and anyone else you support.

Let's say your daughter moved back home after college, went to the dentist for a root canal (you paid for it), and finally got a job. If she made more than $2,500 in one year, you can't claim her as a dependent on your tax form. But you can still deduct the $1,000 dentist bill you covered.

Also, you probably can't claim your parents as dependents, but if you help support them, you can deduct their medical expenses.

Divorced or separated parents may benefit from this tip, too. If you pay a child's medical expenses but don't claim the child as a dependent, you can probably deduct those expenses. You have to meet three easy conditions:

1) You and your spouse must be legally separated or divorced, or have been living apart for the last six months of the year.

2) You and your ex together must have provided more than half of the child's support.

3) Either you or your ex had to have custody of the child for more than half the year.

The more people you help support, the easier it is to exceed the magic number: 7.5 percent of your income. Another way to make the most of this deduction is to bunch as many medical expenses into one year as possible.

If your budget is tight at the end of the year, you can use a credit card to pay for the medical service or product. You get to deduct the expense in

the year it was charged even though you don't actually pay the bill until the next year.
Source:
SmartMoney (5,11:123)

The cost of kids

You can't put a price on your child's precious smile or his first step, but there's no getting around the fact that kids aren't cheap.

The Family Economics Group of the United States Department of Agriculture estimates that a child born in 1992 to a family making more than $52,000 a year will cost Mom and Dad $180,692 before he or she turns 18. (Factor in a 6 percent annual inflation rate and the cost jumps to $314,550.)

And those costs are only for second children. Firstborns cost roughly 3 percent more. (And these figures don't cover college, prenatal, or childbirth costs.)

If you're only planning on one child, the costs go even higher. Expect to spend $380,605 (including inflation) for bluejeans, haircuts, bicycles, and birthday parties. If you live in the Northeast, add another 2.5 percent.
Source:
The Wall Street Journal (Sept. 10, 1993)

Cheap and easy ways to entertain a child

Whether you're at your wits' end with what to do with your own children or you just entertain one or two now and then, here are some novel toys you can whip up from everyday items around the house. It's guaranteed cheap and simple fun for every kid.

▶ Intrigue them with invisible ink. Kids delight in writing and sending secret messages written with invisible ink. Let kids dip cotton swabs in lemon juice and write their messages on paper. Once the "ink" is dry, have kids hold the paper close (but not too close!) to a hot light bulb. The ink will turn brown, and the secret message will magically appear. Make sure an adult supervises this activity. If you don't have any lemon juice, you can also make invisible ink by dissolving 1 teaspoon of baking soda into 2 teaspoons of water.

▶ Surprise Dr. Seuss fans with a special breakfast of green eggs and ham. Simply add some blue food coloring to eggs before scrambling.

▶ Let 'em go nutty with silly putty. Combine two parts of liquid white glue with one part of liquid starch. Mix well. Keep away from clothes and carpet.

▶ Stage a puppet show. Old socks make great playtime puppets. Use glue or thread to attach old buttons for the eyes and nose, and use yarn for the hair and mouth.

▶ Entice them with easy embroidery. Draw a simple design on a paper plate. Punch holes at regular intervals in the design. Thread a blunt needle with yarn or embroidery thread and let kids sew along the lines.

► Whip up play dough in a pinch. Combine 1/2 cup salt, 1 cup flour, 2 tablespoons of vegetable oil, and 1/2 cup of water. Add food coloring to get the color you desire. For extra fun, sprinkle on some glitter.

► Have fun with finger-paint. Shaving cream makes great finger-paint. Good painting surfaces include a cookie sheet or a vinyl tablecloth. A drop of food coloring adds color.

► Delight them with a different kind of puzzle — a sponge puzzle. Take an old sponge and cut it up into different shapes. Let them try to put it together again.

► Entertain them with edible monsters. Let them design their own edible creations. Give them toothpicks and chunks of cheese or pieces of fruit and let them indulge their imaginations and their appetites.

► Make stack-a-sack forts and castles. Lay large paper bags flat, fold the top over and crease. Fill with crumpled newspapers. Fold the bag on the crease line and securely tape or staple it closed. Stack away!

► Let them make music. Show them how to create their own kazoo from a cardboard toilet paper tube. Punch a small hole one inch from one end and cover the other end with wax paper. Use a rubber band to secure the wax paper. Make music by blowing or humming into the open end.

Source:
Don't Throw That Out!: A Pennywise Guide to Creative Uses for Over 200 Household Items by Vicki Lansky,
The Book Peddlers, Deephaven, Minn., 1994

Choosing a good day-care center

Working parents, don't feel guilty about putting your child in day care. Experts agree that some form of communal day care is good for children. It sharpens social skills and helps the child learn to associate with others.

Selecting good day care is a matter of asking the right questions:

► What are the hiring requirements for the teachers and staff? Ideally, all caregivers should have some background in early child development.

► What is the child/teacher ratio? For infants up to age 3, the best ratio is three children per one adult. For ages 2 to 3, four children per adult. For ages 3 to 6, eight children per adult.

► How are illnesses handled? There should be a clear policy about sick children.

► What is a typical day like? It's a good idea to visit the school unannounced and just watch for a while.

► What are the goals of the school? Is it to teach new skills, mold behavior, or baby-sit?

► Are the children supervised at all times, even during naps?

► Is there plenty of play equipment, and is it appropriate to the children's ages?

Source:
Caring for Your Baby and Young Child by Dr. Steven P. Shelov, Bantam Books, New York, 1991

Teaching toddlers to save

If you don't want your kids to be impulse buyers when they grow up, start young. To teach toddlers to wait for satisfaction, play hiding and finding games. Hide a present in a room and give clues to where it is. That makes not getting the prize right away a fun experience.

Later, start offering choices: "Would you like one cookie now or two cookies after you finish playing with Sally?" Don't make your child wait more than an hour or so for the prize at first.

Warning: Don't play these games with money. You don't want your kids to think money is something to hide and search for.

Source:
A Penny Saved: Using Money to Teach Your Child the Way the World Works by Neale S. Godfrey, Simon & Schuster, New York, 1995

New money messages for your teens

When your teen begs for new clothes or a compact disc player, the words that jump to mind are usually the ones you heard from your parents: "Money doesn't grow on trees!" or "What do you think I'm made of, money?"

Next time your teen says she "needs" a new pair of tennis shoes, ask, "What do you plan to do to get them?" With this question, you are at least presenting your child with real world economics, and, maybe, you'll get to work with your child to figure out how she can earn extra money instead of listening to all the usual whining.

Source:
No More Frogs to Kiss: 99 Ways to Give Economic Power to Girls by Joline Godfrey, HarperCollins Publishers, New York, 1995

Investing in your daughter

Teaching your daughter about money takes time, but it's time well-spent. Here are three fun (and usually *pretend*) shopping trips that will help girls build a financial foundation. (These trips can work for boys, too.)

▶ Next time you or someone you know is going to buy a new car, ask them to take along your daughter so she can watch a negotiation in action. Many women never learn to negotiate, and end up paying more than they should for cars, houses, and services. Before she goes, discuss what to listen for and what the goal is.

▶ Take your teen on a pretend shopping expedition for a CD player or a piece of computer equipment. Start by looking through newspaper ads or catalogs. She should make a list of the features she wants and how much she wants to spend. (At this point, you might mention that she could see 10 or so movies for the price of the CD player. Which would she rather do?) Have her get prices from three stores. Ask her to discuss the product benefits and differences with a store employee.

► Invite three to seven of your daughter's friends for this half-day mall game. The girls should play in pairs. Print a form for each team that includes the budget for the day, the required items to purchase, and a time limit. The girls should discuss a spending/buying strategy, then visit various mall shops to find the items on their list. When they make a "purchase," they should write down the price of the item and get a salesperson to initial the sheet. The team that gets the most for its money wins.

For many more ideas on giving economic power to girls, look for Joline Godfrey's book *No More Frogs to Kiss* (HarperCollins, 1995).

Source:
No More Frogs to Kiss: 99 Ways to Give Economic Power to Girls by Joline Godfrey, HarperCollins Publishers, New York, 1995

How to erase your children's debts

Your 13-year-old daughter loves to visit the mall. You thought she was just hanging out with friends and window shopping. But you discover she's bought some expensive jewelry. She signed a contract saying she has six months to pay for it.

Your daughter has no income other than her allowance. That won't cover the diamond necklace. And you certainly don't want to buy it.

Are you stuck with the bill?

No. Unless a law spells out specific exceptions, any consumer contract entered into by an underage child is not enforceable. That lets you — and your child — off the hook. The merchant can repossess the jewelry, but you won't be held liable for any money owed on it.

What to watch out for:

Your teen-ager could end up legally forced to pay for a purchase if she was 17 when she signed a contract to buy something — if she made payments and kept the goods until she turned 18.

Why? Because the law says she is no longer a minor and, by making payments, she's ratified the contract.

However, if she stopped making payments before she turned 18, in all likelihood your youngster would not be held liable for the debt.

Source:
The Consumer's Guide to Understanding and Using the Law by Daniel Johnson, Betterway Books, Cincinnati, 1994

Employing your children

Many people who start a business dream of someday bringing their children into the company, with an eye toward passing it on to them in the future.

Putting your children to work in the family business doesn't have to wait until they're out of college, though. It can start as young as age 6, the tax courts have said. Kids can earn up to $3,000 a year without paying any taxes. Wages above that amount are subject to withholding tax, but at a much lower rate. Children under 18 can work for their parents, and their wages aren't subject to Social Security, Medicare, or federal unemployment taxes. If you pay your kids for working around the house, that payment isn't subject to Social Security or Medicare taxes until they reach the age of 21.

You just have to be careful that the children are being paid a reasonable amount for work that's appropriate for their abilities. Obviously, you won't have your elementary school student answering the phones and taking important messages, or your middle schooler doing the company books. But simple filing, opening the mail, or cleaning up would fit the abilities of even the youngest school-age children.

"As long as you don't violate the child labor laws, it's a great idea," says certified public accountant William Adair with the firm of Adair, Fuller, Witcher, and Malcom, PA, in Ft. Lauderdale, Fla.

Bill Fern, a wage and hour analyst with the Child Labor Team at the Wage and Hour Division, says that as long as you're the sole owner of the business and the children aren't working in a field that's designated hazardous (like mining, roofing, or handling dynamite), there shouldn't be a problem.

"If you meet the parental exemption, there's no limit on the number of hours that can be worked," Fern said. "Of course, state and local laws can have restrictions. We had a case of two kids, ages 9 and 11, helping their dad do a little bit of office work on the weekend that turned into a bad situation because he wasn't the sole owner of the business and somebody didn't like it."

As most farm kids could tell you, they can do any work their parents deem fit, including running machinery and driving vehicles.

It seems bizarre, but if you're in the business of harvesting evergreens and making wreaths from the cedar, pine, or holly, you are exempt from some aspects of the child labor laws. There's a loophole for everyone!

Sources:
Interview with William Adair, CPA with the public accounting firm of Adair, Fuller, Witcher, and Malcom, Ft. Lauderdale, Fla.
Interview with Bill Fern, wage and hour analyst, U.S. Department of Labor, Employment Standards Administration, Wage and Hour Division
"Child Labor Requirements in Nonagricultural Occupations Under the Fair Labor Standards Act," Circular E, Employer's Tax Guide, Department of the Treasury, Internal Revenue Service, 1996

Free books for last-minute book reports

Your child has a book report due in a week. The last copy of the book he or she needs has been checked out of the library, and the bookstore has sold out. What do you do?

If there's a computer handy, hop on-line. Odds are you can find what you're looking for in no time. There are a number of classic books in the public domain, meaning no one can copyright them. With just a few keystrokes, you can download a copy and print it out on your home printer.

The biggest site is called Project Gutenberg, which adds another four titles each month. Others are the Online Book Initiative and Internet Wiretap. All are easily accessible through the World Wide Web.

You may not be able to grab the latest John Grisham thriller, but you will be able to page through works such as *The Scarlet Letter*, *Wuthering Heights*, *Dracula*, and *The Adventures of Tom Sawyer*. At last count, more than 75 works of great literature were available on the Internet.
Source:
Online Books Frequently Asked Questions, http://www.cs.indiana.edu/metastuff/bookfaq.html

Financial advice for single parents

Everyone admits that the ideal situation is a happy two-parent home, but the ideal isn't always possible. More and more families are headed by one parent.

Benefits are that the children and parent tend to be closer, you can raise your child by your own beliefs without having to compromise with a mate, and children tend to be more independent and mature because they have to shoulder more responsibility than other children.

On the other hand, finances can be difficult. The child may lack a same-sex role model. Plus, parenting in general is stressful, doubly so when there's no one else to shoulder the problems.

Single parents should keep these ideas in mind:

▶ Take advantage of all the resources available to you. Some church groups provide low-cost child care. Public health facilities ease the burden of health care. There are also clinics which offer counseling on an ability-to-pay basis.

▶ Take care of yourself. If you don't feel well or don't get enough sleep, you can't be the type of parent you want to be. Set up a regular time for yourself and get out of the house. Don't forget, you're entitled to a life, too.

▶ Set firm limits for your child and enforce them.

▶ Create a large support network of friends and family.

▶ Don't put a guilt trip on yourself. Your child is doing just fine with one parent. You don't need to go to extreme measures, or buy expensive gifts, to make it up to your child.
Source:
Caring for Your Baby and Young Child by Dr. Steven P. Shelov, Bantam Books, New York, 1991

Wedding bells and bank notes

After a college education, footing the bill for a wedding can be the single biggest expense parents face. Each family's finances will determine who pays for what, but traditionally, here's how you and your future in-laws would split the costs.

The bride and her family pay for:

▶ Invitations and announcements

▶ Wedding dress, veil, and accessories

▶ Bouquets or corsages for honor attendant, bridesmaids, and flower girl

- ► Flowers for ceremony and reception sites
- ► Wedding and reception photographs
- ► Rental fee for church or wedding site
- ► Fees for music, such as organist at church
- ► Transportation to and from church, such as limousine
- ► All reception costs — food, drink, music, decorations, gratuities
- ► Groom's ring

The groom and his family pay for:
- ► Bride's engagement and wedding rings
- ► Marriage license
- ► Ceremony official's fee
- ► Bride's flowers
- ► Honeymoon
- ► Rehearsal dinner

Source:
The New Bride's Book of Etiquette by the editors of *Bride's Magazine*, Grosset & Dunlap, New York, 1981

How to save money on a wedding

If wedding bells are ringing in your future, hold on to your wallet, because the jingle you hear may be money leaving your pocket. Planning a wedding can be a huge expense and a tiring affair. But, with time and a little legwork, a wedding does not have to break your bank account.

To save money, you must be open to creative ideas and be willing to shop around. The more time you have to plan, the more money you can save.

Here are just a few money-saving ideas:

- ► Want a limo to transport the bride and groom to and from the reception? Call a funeral home. Some funeral homes will rent their limousines and almost always offer lower prices.
- ► Instead of having a traditional wedding cake, decorate a Styrofoam cake for the pictures and serve sheet cake. Sheet cakes are much less expensive, and your guests will never know. Just wheel the "wedding cake" back into the kitchen to be cut. You can include an actual layer of cake in the Styrofoam cake to cut in front of your guests. But make sure you remember which layer is the real one or you could be facing a very embarrassing moment.
- ► Lower the cost of the ring-bearer pillow by making your own. This isn't a complicated project; it's a snap for a crafty family member or friend who wants to help.
- ► Determine the number of guests you want to invite and stick to that number. Every time you add a guest, the cost of your wedding increases.
- ► Don't use a florist who charges a consultation fee. A florist shouldn't charge extra for advice on decorations, and most don't.
- ► Get all the details in writing when dealing with businesses like florists and photographers. You need written proof of what you agreed to, especially when planning many months in advance.

▶ Always pay wedding deposits and purchases with a credit card. That protects you in case the business closes or doesn't fulfill written agreements.

▶ Check on each prospective business through the Better Business Bureau. This can potentially save money and prevent frustration.

▶ To save money on gifts for bridesmaids and groomsmen, ask your photographer to make a picture of each wedding party member and his or her guest. Then frame the photo yourself. Or, for an even less expensive option, get copies of a group wedding picture made for each attendant.

▶ When deciding whether or not to serve alcoholic beverages, remember that some states have liability laws that hold the host of the party jointly liable if an accident occurs. Check with your caterer and insurance agent to find out what type of protection you need.

One area usually worth the extra money is good photographs. Make sure you meet with your photographer beforehand to discuss his style of photography and what role you want him to have in your wedding.

Most of all, remember this is your wedding and you can spend as much or as little as you want. With a little thought and a lot of planning, you can have enough money left over to enjoy a special honeymoon.

Sources:
Interview with Dicki Arn, owner of Dicki Arn Photography, Birmingham, Ala.
Interview with Alan Field, co-author of *Bridal Bargains: Secrets to Throwing a Fantastic Wedding on a Realistic Budget* , Windsor Peak Press, Boulder, Colo., 1996
Easy Wedding Planning by Elizabeth and Alex Lluch, Wedding Solutions, San Diego, 1995

Custom-designed civil ceremony

You don't have to have a big church wedding if that's not your style. A civil ceremony is an option many couples are choosing. A judge may perform a civil ceremony in his office, or you can marry in the registrar's office. Other officials like a justice of the peace, mayor, governor and yes, a ship's captain, can perform a marriage. Two witnesses are required.

Source:
You and Your Wedding by Winifred Gray, Bantam Books, New York, 1984

At-home wedding hazards

Many couples these days want to get married in their homes, especially if it's not a first marriage. At first glance, having a wedding at home seems a lot easier and less expensive than dealing with a hotel or a country club. However, be sure you consider the following:

▶ Where will guests put their coats and purses?

▶ Will there be enough bathrooms? Who will ensure that the bathroom is stocked with all the necessities during the reception?

▶ Does your homeowner's insurance cover any damages to or loss of property and lawn?

▶ Where will the ceremony and reception take place in bad weather?

▶ Do you need to rent a tent and a dance floor?

▶ Will you need to hire waitresses, bartenders? How many? Who will clean up?

▶ Where will the guests park? Should you hire valet parking attendants? Will it be necessary to hire police to direct traffic?

Source:
The Complete Jewish Wedding Planner by Wendy Chernak Hefter, Harper & Row, San Francisco, 1988

Picking a nursing home for someone with Alzheimer's disease

Providing care for a spouse or parent with Alzheimer's disease takes its toll. The stress is overwhelming, affecting your work, your health, and your relationship with other family members. Community care is practically nonexistent. Therefore, at some point you may need to consider a long-term care facility.

Ideally, your search for an adult foster care home, home for the aged, or nursing home should begin long before you need one. Allow yourself plenty of time to locate a facility that provides the best possible care. Remember, the finest facilities usually have long waiting lists.

Begin your search by getting a list of long-term care facilities from friends and doctors. Visit each place. Make an appointment for your first visit, and if you like the facility, return without an appointment. Ask questions. Compare one facility to another using these criteria:

Cost. Long-term care facilities are expensive and often not covered by Medicaid or other types of insurance. Monthly rates run from $1,000 and up. Beware of facilities that charge considerably more for what they call "dementia" units. The cost of these units should equal or be competitive with traditional care units.

Extra charges. Be wary of charges added to the daily rate; they quickly mount up. Ask for a list of extra fees. Are they reasonable? Are they necessary?

Medicaid. If you're looking at nursing homes, ask whether the home has beds approved by Medicaid. If your spouse or parent qualifies for Medicaid, he or she must be in a Medicaid-approved bed to obtain coverage.

Resident rights. Observe the staff. Residents should be treated with dignity, respect, and affection. They should not be bullied or ignored.

Environment. Don't be fooled by an attractive decor. A bright, cheerful, homey atmosphere, one where staff and residents smile and talk to each other, is more important than matching drapes and wallpaper. Hallways and rooms should be odor-free. There should be an activity room for residents. Notice if there are pictures, symbols, or signs around to help residents find bathrooms, bedrooms, and other important areas.

Rooms. Look in the rooms. Are residents surrounded by their own furniture and personal belongings? What about privacy? How are roommates selected and can they be changed?

Food. Visit the facility during mealtime. Meals should not only be nutritiously balanced but appetizing as well. Notice if staff members are feeding residents who need assistance. Are nourishing snacks available for residents when they want them?

Staff. What are the staff's qualifications? Are they sensitive to the special needs of people with dementia? Do they have a positive attitude? How many nurses and aides cover days and afternoons? How many on nights? You don't want your parent or spouse sedated because the facility is short-staffed.

Staff training. Find out how often in-house training sessions are held and which topics are covered. Observe nurses and aides. Do they seem to know what they're doing?

Medical care. Is there a doctor, especially one specializing in caring for older people, on staff or on call? What about pharmacists, mental health professionals, and dentists? How closely do doctors monitor medications? Many people with dementia get even more confused when ill or over-medicated.

You can never ask too many questions when trying to find suitable long-term care for your spouse or parent. People with dementia are very sensitive to their environment, especially to nonverbal messages of affection, respect, and approval.

Source:
Selecting Dementia Care Programs in Long-Term Care Facilities, jointly published by Citizens for Better Care and the Alzheimer's Association, Michigan, 1991

Better funerals: Save money and buy peace

The average funeral bill totals $4,500, with a burial typically costing $3,500 more. These outrageous prices are possible because people are easy to take advantage of in times of grief.

After their son died in a car accident, his parents drove his body from the hospital to a crematorium and held a simple church service for close friends and family. They spent $200, and they gained extra peace because they were able to be personally involved in all the arrangements.

Because grieving consumers are so vulnerable, the Federal Trade Commission has passed some regulations to protect you. Now, you have six ways to save money:

Call funeral homes for prices. Funeral providers must give you price information over the phone. You do not have to go to the funeral home in person.

Choose direct cremation or immediate burial instead of embalming. Funeral providers can't tell you that embalming is required by law. It isn't.

Buy an inexpensive alternative container for the cremation. Any container you buy will be destroyed during cremation, so some people buy alternative containers made out of pressboard, cardboard, or canvas. A funeral director can't tell you that you must have a casket for direct cremations. And they must make an unfinished wood box or an alternative container available to you.

Don't let the funeral director arrange for items such as flowers, obituary notices, and pall bearers if he charges a service fee. He must tell you if he adds a service fee to the price of these items. You can choose to make these arrangements yourself.

Don't pay top price for a casket thinking it will preserve your loved one's body. Funeral providers can't tell you that any casket or vault will keep out water, dirt, or other substances forever.

Plan your own funeral. You can make sure your family gives you a simple and inexpensive funeral by writing down your preferences beforehand. Tell relatives what you have decided.

You can plan an extremely low-cost funeral by choosing to donate your body to science. Many medical and dental schools will pay for transportation of your body and for cremation. Most schools will return the ashes if your family requests them. You do have to make these arrangements yourself — many schools won't except a body donation from relatives once you're dead.

For more information on funeral planning, contact the Conference of Funeral Service Examining Boards, 15 Northeast 3rd Street, P.O. Box 497, Washington, IN 47501. The Conference provides information on laws in various states. It also accepts and responds to consumer questions and complaints about funeral providers.

Sources:
Funerals: A Consumer Guide, Federal Trade Commission, Bureau of Consumer Protection, Washington, D.C. 20580
The Wall Street Journal (Dec. 8, 1995, R19)

HOME FINANCING

Building a home? How to keep costs down, quality up

You're ready to build your dream home. You've shopped spec houses and tramped through dozens of models. You've chosen a builder and looked at plans, and you're all ready to sign that contract, right?

Wrong, says Kay Cantrell, who's been building houses in all price ranges for 20 years. That's how you end up paying much more for your house than you bargained on.

Most buyers don't look at the details of a house plan. They think they can always make changes as the house is being built. But the price of your home is based on a *spec list* of materials that's outlined in the original plans. The spec list includes things like woodwork, flooring, carpeting, tile, countertops, lighting fixtures, and appliances.

Unless you request special materials upfront, the builder will price the house using standard materials for that price range. If you continue to make changes in the plans and upgrade materials during construction, you could end up with a much more expensive house than you ever dreamed possible.

Here are a few tips to make it easier to work with a builder — and to end up with a house you like and can afford.

- ▶ Ask the builder for references before you sign a contract. Don't be embarrassed to call them and ask tough questions.
- ▶ When you're doing your tour of spec and model homes, take a notebook and write down all the special features and materials you'd like to include in your new house.
- ▶ When you go over the plans and materials list with your builder, show him the items on your list and ask how much they would add to the cost of the house.
- ▶ Be sure you meet the builder's deadline for choosing materials, fixtures, and appliances. Otherwise, you may be charged extra for rush orders, and your house still won't be finished on time.
- ▶ Keep a diary of each change you ask for, with the date and the cost. Even better, some builders keep a running change-order list on a computer. If yours does, ask for a new copy with each change.
- ▶ Schedule your walk-through 10 days to two weeks before you plan to close so the builder will have time to correct any problems or to finish all installations.
- ▶ Unless you're a construction expert, hire an independent building inspector to do the walk-through with you. This will cost you $150 to $250, but it's good insurance against serious problems later on.

▶ If you can, set your move-in date 10 days to two weeks after the builder says the house will be ready. Bad weather, delays in delivering materials, and labor scheduling problems are things even the most well-meaning builder can't control.

Source:
Interview with Kay Cantrell, president of the Greater Atlanta Home Builders' Association, Atlanta

Seasons equal savings when buying a house

A little patience can save you thousands of dollars when you're house hunting — even in a seller's market. Real estate listings boom in March, April, and May, but owners get a little antsy if they haven't had an offer by mid-July. The longer a house is on the market, the more willing the seller is to accept a lower bid.

Winter is also a good time to look for a place to live. The distraction of the holidays shrinks the number of potential buyers. Also, few people like to house hunt in cold weather, which puts the hearty few who do in a position of power. There's typically a small rush in December, but prices stay comparatively low.

Unless you find your dream house at an affordable price, never place a bid in the early days of a listing. Nor is it a good idea to make an offer in late August. The beginning of the school year is a busy season for realtors, since people want to find homes and move in before the kids start classes.

Source:
Interview with Lucy Morrisroe, realtor, Harry Norman Realtors, Atlanta

How to slash closing costs

Closing costs add a significant piece of pocket change to the total cost of a house. You have to pay for the loan application, the appraisal, the credit check, the lender's attorney, title insurance, the survey, homeowner's insurance, recording the deed, tax service, state transfer, points, and your attorney.

These charges can range from $2,500 to $7,000 or more for a $100,000 loan on a $125,000 home. And there can be other fees: termite or radon inspections and upfront escrow payments to cover homeowner's insurance and taxes, to name a few.

A little advance planning in the home-buying process can help you reduce those expenses.

▶ The first and best advice is: Don't accept closing costs as written in stone. Try to negotiate all charges. Even the application fee, which frequently is a set and nonrefundable fee charged by banks, may be negotiable by some lenders. If you don't ask, the answer is an automatic no.
There is no such thing as a fixed real estate broker fee, as some realtors would have you believe. You have wiggle room here. Ask them to lower their take on the deal. It never hurts to ask. If they are anxious to close the deal, they will bite.

▶ Secondly, try to get the most out of the fees you do pay. Most of the time, you have to hire an attorney. Hire one at the beginning of the project, not after you have negotiated price and terms and signed a binder. A good portion of the hard work is done by that point.

Your attorney can help negotiate the best price and find ways to lower closing costs. Depending on how the agreement is set up, attorney's fees don't have to be higher because you signed him or her on early. But even if it does cost more, it could be worth it.

Some attorneys charge a fee based on a percentage of the price of the house (.5 percent to 3 percent). Others charge a flat or an hourly fee. Check around for the best deal. Remember, plenty of attorneys are out there, waiting to serve you.

Don't ask the seller's real estate broker to recommend a lawyer. Remember, he or she is not on your team. Ask local officials, your own broker, or a bar association.

▶ Widen your search for mortgage money. Banks don't always offer the best deal. Lenders are eager to have your business so *negotiate*. Sometimes mortgage brokers charge fewer points and/or shave a small percentage off the interest rate.

Mortgage money can come from relatives or individuals who want to invest in home loans. Credit unions also can be a good source of reasonable financing.

▶ Ask the seller if he would be willing to provide a low-cost mortgage on the house. It does happen. A homeowner eager to sell may be willing to arrange terms with you. The seller can always repossess the house by foreclosure if you don't meet payments and terms.

▶ Get a free copy of your credit report from TRW (by calling 1-800-392-1122) before you begin loan pre-qualification. Make sure the information is correct. Take steps to correct any errors to ensure a smooth qualification process.

▶ Check to see when the current homeowner bought the house. If the owner purchased it in the last couple of years, you might be able to cut the $500 to $600 survey cost by seeking an amended survey rather than paying for a completely new survey.

▶ Wait until you have saved enough to make a traditional down payment. If you can't put down 20 percent, you will pay extra in high interest private mortgage insurance, required by the lender.

▶ You'll have the upper hand at the bargaining table if you'll seriously consider two or three houses before you zero in on one. If the broker, seller, and other parties are not willing to work with you in negotiating price or fees, back off and try one of the other choices.

▶ Want to keep on saving after closing? Consider prepaying some of the principal on your loan. A mere $25 per month can knock $23,000 in interest off a $100,000 30-year loan at 8 percent.

Source:
Interview with Marc Eisenson, author of *The Banker's Secret*, Good Advice Press, Elizaville, N.Y., 1991. *The Banker's Secret* describes how to save money by prepaying your mortgage.

Money tips for home buyers

Paying points upfront to get a lower interest rate is usually not a good idea. You'd probably be a lot better off if you took that extra money and put it in a mutual fund, especially if you plan on moving after five years or so.

Even if you got a 20-year loan and stayed in your home for the full 20 years, you'd only save about $6,000 by paying an extra 2 points ($2,000) up front. If you put the $2,000 in a mutual fund yielding 10 percent interest, you'd have $14,800 after 20 years.

Source:
Home Mechanix (December 1995/January 1996)

Home buyer's snooping kit

Your realtor has found several homes that meet your strict criteria, and now you're ready to visit them. You don't want to be fooled by clean rooms, fresh flowers, or smells of baking cookies wafting from the kitchen. You want to be ready to snoop in basements and sniff out problems with the house. Carry a big bag filled with the following items:

► Binoculars. To inspect the roof and the chimney exterior where it joins the roof.

► Camera, paper, pens, and checklist. To help you remember the details of each house. Look at five or so houses in one day, and you'll be surprised at how they run together.

► Flashlight. Good for basement snooping, especially for examining the basement ceiling for sturdiness.

► Marble. Drop one on the kitchen or bathroom floor. A rapidly rolling marble means the floor is sagging.

► Pocket knife. Perfect for discovering dry rot. Poke your knife into a joist in the basement or attic, then let go. If the knife stays in place, the wood is firm. If it falls out easily or if a dry, wood-colored powder is on the knife and the floor, the house probably has dry rot.

► Socket tester. Find out if the house has a good electrical system by testing sockets all over the house.

► Tape measure. Discover how big those rooms really are. You'll be glad to have measurements later.

Check the water pressure while you're snooping, too. Try turning the faucet or shower on full blast and flushing the toilet. If the sink's water blast slows down, you may have plumbing problems.

Source:
Financial Freedom: A Wealth Manual for the Middle Class by R. Bryan Stoker, Lifestyle Publishing, Maryland, 1994

Buying a house for less

Buying a home will probably be the biggest investment of your life, but why pay more than you have to?

To avoid an overpriced house, study recent sales in the neighborhood. Read real estate ads and compare prices. Go to city hall and look at the deed on the house.

It never hurts to ask the previous owner what he or she paid. (Double-check their response against city records.)

Even if your lender doesn't require you to have the house appraised, it's a good idea. This will tell you the "fair market value" of the house — the worth of the lot plus the cost of rebuilding the house at current rates. The result is adjusted in accordance with the prices of comparable homes in the area.

Source:
How to Avoid the 10 Biggest Home-Buying Traps by A.M. Watkins, The Building Institute, Piermont, N.Y., 1984

Try before you buy

Can't afford a mortgage and not even sure you want one? Or do you want to buy a new home but haven't yet sold your old one? Consider renting with an option to buy.

Ken and Daria Dolan, authors of the monthly newsletter *Straight Talk on Your Money*, call this real estate strategy one of the smartest money moves they've ever made.

Generally, with this arrangement, a part of your rent payment goes toward a down payment if you decide to buy the house or condominium at an agreed-on price within a certain time period, like a year. You don't get any refunds if you decide not to buy the home, but you would have been paying rent anyway, so you've lost nothing.

The Dolans didn't end up buying the first condo they rented with this strategy. In fact, while living there, a faulty city water pipe in front of the condo caused more than $25,000 worth of damage. When the year lease was up, the Dolans moved to a house, again renting with an option to buy. They bought the house after six trouble-free months.

A homeowner very motivated to sell should be more than willing to discuss this option with you. It certainly doesn't hurt to ask.

Sources:
Ken and Darian Dolan, authors of *Straight Talk on Your Money* and co-hosts of a daily national personal finance call-in show on the WOR Radio Network, quoted in *Money* (24,12:41)
Successful Real Estate Investing in the '90s by Peter G. Miller, HarperPerennial, New York, 1994

Adjustable rate mortgage trap

When you shop for an adjustable rate loan, ask about the limits on negative amortization. Here's why:

Suppose you signed an adjustable rate mortgage for $50,000 in 1978. Your interest rate was 9.15 percent. By 1981, interest rates had doubled to 17.39 percent. If your monthly payments had kept pace with the interest rates, they would have risen from $408 to $722. But, you were smart — you got a payment cap. Your payments stayed at $408.

Sounds great. But by 1981, your mortgage had swelled from $50,000 to $58,350. You paid out $20,000, but you were $8,000 more in debt than you were three years earlier.

Your monthly payment is too low, so you're losing value, or equity, instead of gaining it. That's called negative amortization. You will end up paying the full interest costs later through larger payments or more payments, and you'll pay interest on that interest. You've lost ground.

Source:
The Mortgage Money Guide, Federal Trade Commission, Washington, D.C.

Cut housing costs

Housing costs should be no more than 28 percent of your annual gross income. That means:

If you make	You can spend on housing
$20,000	$467
$30,000	$700
$40,000	$933
$50,000	$1,167
$60,000	$1,400

If you're living in a house beyond your means, check out these four ways to reduce costs.

Move. You may be able to find a nicer home in a less expensive location.

Cut property insurance costs. Have you checked lately to make sure you're paying the lowest premiums possible? Try raising your deductible, installing smoke detectors, or installing a burglar alarm system.

Lower your property taxes. First, check to see if you qualify for any personal exemptions such as being a veteran or a senior citizen or having a particular illness. Next, make sure your property assessment is in line with other properties in your town. If it isn't, file a complaint.

Refinance. If you can lower the interest rate on a 30-year mortgage by 2 percent, you can save almost $100 a month on a $60,000 mortgage. You may have heard that you have to pay refinancing charges to get a new loan, but that's not necessarily true. You can get a loan that lets you spread out the refinancing charges over many months, or you can get a deal that lets you pay a slightly higher interest rate in return for paying no refinancing charges.

Source:
Ninety Days to Financial Fitness by Joan German-Grapes, Macmillan Publishing, New York, 1993

2 overlooked ways to lower monthly mortgage costs

You may be sending your mortgage company more money than necessary every month. If your down payment was under 20 percent and you've lived in your house for more than a few years, try taking these steps to reduce the extra charges you pay along with your mortgage:

Stop paying private mortgage insurance. Almost everyone who makes a down payment of less than 20 percent is forced to buy private mortgage insurance. But what the lender doesn't tell you is that when you build up your equity to more than 20 percent of the value of your house, you can drop the mortgage insurance. (You build equity both by making regular payments and by the value of your house rising.)

You may have to get an appraisal if property values have shifted in your area, and that can cost around $250. You'll still save lots of money, though. The Mortgage Bankers Association says private mortgage insurance fees on a $67,500 loan range from $338 to $675 a year.

Get rid of lender's escrow accounts. If you made a down payment of under 20 percent, the lender probably required you to put money for property taxes and homeowner's insurance into an escrow account. Some states require lenders to pay you any interest that escrow account earns. Other states don't. Even if the lender sends you the interest money, you could probably find a better interest rate yourself if you set up your own escrow account.

Your lender would never tell you so, but you may be able to do just that. Call your mortgage company and ask if you have enough equity to set up your own escrow account or if you can arrange other ways besides an escrow account to pay property taxes and insurance.

By paying into your own escrow account, you can collect your own interest. Monthly payments of $250 at 4 percent interest would yield $65.73 a year.

If you are searching for a mortgage loan, make sure you ask lenders when you can drop the private mortgage insurance and when you can begin paying property taxes and homeowner's insurance yourself.

Sources:
Mark Eisenson, writing in *The Banker's Secret Bulletin.* Get a sample issue of this newsletter for $1. Send money to *The Banker's Secret,* Box 78, Elizaville, NY 12523
The Tightwad Gazette, II by Amy Dacyczyn, Villard Books, New York, 1995

Invest in your home to earn financial freedom

No broker is going to tell you that prepaying your mortgage is a good idea. That's not the way they make money. A broker would rather you put the money in stocks or bonds, where he or she earns a commission.

But if safety is important to you, nothing beats the certainty of paying down debt. Paying off your mortgage early is one of the smartest, no-risk ways to accumulate wealth, according to financial wizard R. Bryan Stoker, author of *Financial Freedom: A Wealth Manual for the Middle Class.*

You shouldn't prepay your mortgage if you have a fixed mortgage rate around six percent or less and you can put your extra money in a low-risk investment earning 10 percent or more. Otherwise, consider earning money safely by investing in your home.

Example: On a 30-year $100,000 mortgage with an interest rate of 10 percent, you save $9,000 by paying an extra $5 a month. By paying an extra $200 a month, you save almost $125,000 and you completely own your home in just 15 years.

If you'd like to pay off the mortgage in 10 years, you'd need to add $438 to each monthly payment. (If you have an interest rate of 8 percent, it would only take an extra $327 a month to pay off this mortgage in 10 years.)

Warning: Read the fine print in your contract and make sure your loan carries no prepayment penalties. If there are penalties, you may want to refinance. You may pay less in penalties if you save for a while and make a large payment every six months or so.

Source:
Financial Freedom: A Wealth Manual for the Middle Class by R. Bryan Stoker, Lifestyle Publishing, Maryland, 1994

The costs of refinancing

The biggest cost of refinancing may be a prepayment penalty on your present mortgage. To find out if your loan has a prepayment penalty, check your mortgage documents. Prepayment penalties are against the law on FHA and VA loans and loans from federally chartered credit unions.

Other refinancing costs may vary widely from area to area and lender to lender, but count on paying from 3 to 6 percent of the amount you have left on your loan.

Closing costs	
Application Fee	$ 75 to $300
Appraisal Fee	$150 to $400
Survey Costs	$125 to $300
Homeowner's Hazard Insurance	$300 to $600
Lender's Attorney's Review Fees	$ 75 to $200
Title Search and Title Insurance	$450 to $600
Home Inspection Fees	$175 to $350
Loan Origination Fees	1 percent of loan
Mortgage Insurance	0.5 percent to 1 percent
Points	1 percent to 3 percent

Try to get the lender who holds your current mortgage to waive some of these fees. The lender may be willing, especially if your fees for the title search, surveys, inspections, etc. are still current.

Source:
A Consumer Guide to Mortgage Refinancing, The Federal Reserve Board and the Office of Thrift Supervision, Washington, D.C.

The decision to refinance

When interest rates drop, you have to make the decision to refinance your mortgage or keep the one you have. Base your decision on some simple math:

Step One. Find out what your mortgage payment will be after you refinance. Subtract that from your present monthly mortgage payment.

Step Two. Contact several lenders and find out how much it will cost you to refinance, including all closing costs, fees, and prepayment penalties.

Step Three. Divide your total refinancing cost by the number you came up with in Step One. That's the number of months you need to stay in your home to break even after refinancing.

You should only refinance if you plan to stay in your home for at least several months after the break-even point.

Source:
Everyone's Money Book by Jordan E. Goodman and Sonny Bloch, Dearborn Financial Publishing, Chicago, 1994

The real truth about reverse mortgages

If you're concerned that your retirement nest egg may not make a big enough omelet to support you for very long and you're desperately searching for other sources of sustenance, you may have considered a *reverse mortgage*.

A reverse mortgage, also called a *home-equity conversion mortgage*, is a loan against your home. Retirees who need cash but don't want to move often resort to reverse mortgages. You're only eligible for one of these mortgages if you own your home outright.

You can receive money from this loan in several ways such as a single lump sum of cash, a monthly cash payment, a type of credit line that lets you decide when and how much cash to get, or some combination of these methods.

You don't have to make monthly repayments on a reverse mortgage. However, when the loan period is up, you have to repay all the cash advances you've received over the years as well as whatever interest you owe on those cash advances.

Typically, you don't have to repay a reverse mortgage until you sell your home, move away, or die. If you die, the bank who granted you the reverse mortgage loan will sell the house to get their repayment.

A reverse mortgage may seem like the solution to all your troubles. However, you should consider the pros and cons very carefully before you enter into a reverse mortgage contract. A reverse mortgage can be a very expensive way of financing your retirement. You can end up paying fees up to a third or even up to half of what your home is worth.

You'll get the best deal on a reverse mortgage the older you are, the more equity you have in your home, and the cheaper your loan costs are. Generally, reverse mortgages work best for people in their 70s. For example, the payout for a 60-year old with a reverse mortgage will be considerably smaller than the payout for a 70-year old with this type of mortgage.

There are some safety features built into reverse mortgages. For example, you can never owe more than what your home is worth when you must repay the loan. In addition, reverse mortgage loans are nonrecourse loans, which means that the lender can't go after any of your other assets to pay off the loan or seek repayment from your heirs.

However, if you aren't planning to stay in your home for a long, long time, a reverse mortgage loan can be a very expensive way of financing your retirement. In addition, sometimes the terms of a loan like this may require that a homeowner move once the loan period is up. This can be a very traumatic experience, especially if you have a great attachment to your home or are not in any physical condition to move.

Because of the possibly serious consequences of a reverse mortgage, make this a last-ditch retirement option after you're sure you've exhausted all other sources of income.

If you decide that a reverse mortgage is the right route for you, read *Your New Retirement Nest Egg: A Consumer's Guide to the New Reverse Mortgage* by Ken Scholen (NCHEC Press, 1995). This book offers helpful advice to consumers who are shopping for a reverse mortgage.

Source:
Your New Retirement Nest Egg: A Consumer's Guide to the New Reverse Mortgages by Ken Scholen, NCHEC Press, Apple Valley, Minn., 1995

Planning home improvements? Think twice

Every homeowner has dreamed of sprucing up the place he or she lives, usually after watching one too many episodes of "This Old House." Major changes can boost the value of your home, but be sure the changes you make are ones that will give you a good return on your investment.

Renovating the kitchen is not always an easy job, but it's the one project that virtually guarantees a higher property value. Appliances and styles become outdated quickly, which makes this room ripe for change. If you're happy with the kitchen, focus on the bathroom in your master suite. Maybe add a walk-in closet or a Jacuzzi tub.

One of the quickest ways to lose money is to build a pool. It's a lot of fun in the summer, but you'll only get a portion of your money back. (On the other hand, if you buy a house with a pool already installed, you probably won't lose anything, since you've avoided the hefty installation costs.) It's also a bad idea to convert one of the traditional rooms in a house (like a dining room or a living room) into something else. You may love the new library, but the next owners will wonder where to put their dining room table. Along the same line, don't make the garage the new family room. It will only come back to haunt you when you put out the "For Sale" sign.

Source:
Interview with Lucy Morrisroe, realtor, Harry Norman Realtors, Atlanta

Selling your home? Little-known secrets that will get you the best price

Don't make this common mistake! The best time to ready your house for selling is *before* the "For Sale" sign goes up in the front yard.

According to Realtor Billie Selman of Remax Executives in Atlanta, working on repairs and sprucing up your home while trying to sell it is a bad idea. "You'll have so much to explain that potential buyers will become overwhelmed," she says.

Maximize curb appeal. Ask several real estate agents for their advice. "Most will be happy to talk to you for free. You'll meet them and can have an agent in mind if you decide to list your house," says Selman.

She advises looking critically at your front yard — make sure it's neat with shrubs trimmed. Pay close attention to your front entrance: "It's the main thing potential buyers see. Without spending much money, you can make it delightful."

For example, place potted flowers by the door (in the winter, use ivy or holly). Paint the door a stylish color. For ideas, consult a current decorating magazine. Inexpensive flower-filled window boxes and shutters will add charm to the front of your home.

Putting your house on the market in spring or summer? Here's a creative, colorful solution for a bare yard: Selman suggests planting flowers that attract butterflies or hummingbirds. Local garden suppliers sell combinations of flower seed, mulch, and fertilizer — mixed together for easy planting — that will coax flowers out of average soil.

"Put out a bird feeder and a birdbath," Selman states. "Make the yard feel inviting to everyone — including nature."

Get rid of clutter. Start packing as soon as you decide to sell. "Basements, attics, and garages should be cleaned out. Donate what you don't want," Selman advises. "Remember: An organized closet looks larger than a disorganized one."

Depersonalize your home. "That may sound odd, but if you have an exciting seashell collection or a beautiful doll collection on display, potential buyers won't remember the house, they'll remember the things," she explains. "Pack it up."

Clean, clean, *clean*. "You won't get a second chance to make a first impression," emphasizes Selman. If the carpet needs a professional cleaning, get it done now. "People are going to peek inside your refrigerator and stove. So clean them, too." Pay for a deep cleaning of your whole house if you can't do it yourself.

Eliminate mildew, smoke, and pet odors. "Real estate agents say, 'If I can smell it, I can't sell it,'" Selman says.

Fix the little things. "A leaky faucet or a burned-out light bulb cost almost nothing to fix," Selman explains. "But if ignored, they'll be serious plumbing or electrical problems in the mind of buyers."

Touch up peeling outside trim. Otherwise, you may lose a sale to someone who assumes the whole house needs painting.

Ugly carpeting? "Toss it," Selman insists. "Reveal the hardwood floors underneath. Or recarpet in a neutral color. Never get white. It's hard to keep spotless and turns off buyers."

Stuck with a dated kitchen? "If the cabinets are cheap and unattractive, paint them white," advises Selman.

"If you have a 1950s kitchen, play up the retro theme. Nostalgic looks are in," she adds.

To create a more spacious look, clear kitchen counters. Put away everything you don't use daily. Display fresh flowers and a colorful bowl of fruit.

Organize bathrooms. Place vanity clutter in a basket. "Having only one color of towels out looks best," Selman reveals.

Make small bedrooms seem larger. "Remove everything extra from the bedroom," Selman says. "Putting things in corners — chairs, plants — makes a room appear smaller."

Selling the house yourself? Make a simple fact sheet (including annual utility costs) to give prospects.

Let people look around without much interruption. "If you follow them, do it discreetly. If they've missed anything, mention it as they're leaving," Selman insists. "Just like you need to try on an outfit before buying it, people need to try on a house and be allowed to think about it."

Source:
Interview with Billie Selman, realtor, Remax Executives, Atlanta

When should you try to sell your own house?

Selling your own home is a do-it-yourself job only when you're prepared to do the same work a realtor would do. This includes:

▶ Taking an objective, critical look at your property — what negatives would a buyer see? Clean, paint, polish, and prune until the pickiest buyer couldn't nit-pick.

▶ Do a survey of what other houses like yours, preferably in your immediate neighborhood, have sold for in the last six months. Better yet, hire a professional appraiser. Keep his report handy for buyers to look at.

▶ Make up a flyer using a great picture of your house. Provide all the important information, including taxes, schools, and a survey of the property.

▶ Plan to be available to show your house at short notice, especially on weekends.

▶ Get a disclosure form at an office supply store. Fill it out honestly and completely, describing any problems you've had with the house, stating when and how they were repaired.

▶ Plan your advertising strategy. Write your ads to sell the best features of your house in as few words as possible.

▶ Talk to several local bankers and keep current on their rates, so you can refer buyers if they need financing.

▶ Be prepared to answer questions about schools, churches, hospitals, shopping, transportation, and any other important facilities in your town.

▶ When you price your house, leave enough of a "cushion" so that if you do eventually list with a realtor, you can list at your price and still pay the realtor's commission.

Selling a house is hard work and will occupy much of your time and energy. It will also cost you $50 to $150 per week for newspaper advertising. If your house is fairly priced, in a desirable area, and in a part of the country where properties "for sale by owner" are common, you have a better chance of marketing your own house successfully.
Source:
Interview with Gwen Skrine, realtor, Dora Jane Smith Realtors, Griffin, Ga.

Your lease and your rights

"There are probably more people who never read their leases than those who do," says real estate law specialist Randall Lipshutz. "They just don't want to be bothered."

But if you want to know your rights when you rent a house, apartment, or condo, you've got to read your lease. The lease spells out whether pets are allowed, how many people can live in your apartment, if and how you can break your lease, and the procedure to get your security deposit back.

One thing a lease can't legally state, thanks to the Federal Fair Housing Act, is that only adults can live in a specific housing complex. "Landlords can no longer restrict children," Lipshutz points out. "The only exceptions are communities specifically designed for the elderly."

How to legally get out of a lease. Some leases give you the right to cancel if you give a certain amount of notice, usually at least 30 days. That gives the landlord adequate time to try and rent the property. Generally, you'll have to pay a penalty, usually the equivalent of a month or two's rent.

Getting back your security deposit. In some states, like Georgia, you and your landlord must go through the property and write up an inspection checklist together when you move in. You do the same thing when you move out.

What recourse do you have if your landlord refuses to return your security deposit? What if your landlord simply lies about the condition you left the property in?

Once again, your lease should outline your rights. It may provide for arbitration, or it will tell you where to go to court to recover your money.
Source:
Interview with Randall M. Lipshutz, attorney-at-law, Lipshutz, Greenblatt, and King, Atlanta

Homeowners' Money Secrets

Brand-new houses need care, too

If you've just bought a brand-new house and think you don't have to worry about maintenance for a few years, read on. ...

An experienced builder tells us that younger trees, full of moisture, are now being cut for construction and used almost immediately.

When the moisture in the wood evaporates, the wood shrinks, causing movement in the house. Moldings may separate, baseboards may pull away from walls, and windows and roofs may leak.

This movement is especially noticeable if you move in during the winter and turn on the heat, which speeds up the shrinking process. To limit the shrinking and stabilize the house, use flexible caulking in the areas of shrinkage as they occur.

Take care of any leaks immediately. Water damage is one of the most serious threats to the structure of a house.

Also, you should know that modern, lead-free paint doesn't have the same sealing power that the old-fashioned leaded paints had. It's a good idea, says our expert, to repaint a wood-shingled house within three years of purchase.

Source:
Interview with Kay Cantrell, president of the Greater Atlanta Home Builders' Association, Atlanta

How to cash in on your historic neighborhood

Your neighborhood doesn't have to be filled with restored, million-dollar, 18th-century homes — like Washington, D.C.'s Georgetown — to be historic.

Whether the local houses are tiny bungalows, 1950s ranch houses, or Civil War Era mansions, your neighborhood may contain architecture or be the site of historic events that make its character special — and worth preserving. And if your neighborhood is officially declared a "historic district" by the government, you could cash in on tax breaks, grant money, and rising property values.

Is your neighborhood already on the National Register of Historic Places? Find out, or find out how to get it included, by calling your local State Historic Preservation Office. Every state has a historic office listed in the phone book.

Your neighborhood may not be on the National Register but it could be designated a historic district under a local ordinance. Ask your county planning and zoning department.

How can living in a historic district save you money? When people find out they live in a historic neighborhood, they usually begin fixing up their property, notes Richard Cloues, Deputy Georgia State Historic Preservation Officer. That will increase your property values.

But, best of all, higher property values doesn't mean your property taxes will automatically soar. Many states have tax relief programs for homeowners in historic districts.

In Georgia, for example, if you fix up property according to preservation standards (your State Preservation Office can give you guidelines), your tax assessment will be frozen for eight years.

"There are also federal tax credits available if you own a rental, office, commercial, or industrial space in a historic district," Cloues adds.

In addition, grant money is available for fixing up buildings in historic neighborhoods that could help the public. For example, is there an old library or courthouse not being used that would make a great community recreation hall?

Contact your state Historic Preservation Office and find out how your neighborhood can get grant money to pay for renovations.

Are there disadvantages to living in a historic area? That depends on what you consider disadvantages.

Just because you live in an area listed on the Historic Register doesn't mean you have to do — or not do — anything to your home. You can paint it purple and green polka dots and tear down a 200-year-old porch if you want to.

On the other hand, if you live in a district that has been given historic status by your local city or county government, your renovations may be restricted. These rules can keep you from tearing down that Victorian gazebo you consider a ramshackle eyesore. But these rules can also keep high-rise apartments, office buildings, and gas stations from popping up in your backyard.

Most regulations aren't petty. And sometimes you can even get free help when you live in an officially designated historic area. In Atlanta's historic Druid Hills neighborhood, for example, homeowners planning renovations can get no-cost professional advice from architects and landscapers serving on their local preservation commission.

Sources:
Interview with Richard Cloues, The Georgia State Historic Preservation Office, Atlanta
The Druid Hills News (10,2)

Wise ways to save money on your water bill

Install a $5 low-flow faucet aerator. One of these devices will reduce water flow by 50 percent, but your water pressure will seem stronger because air is mixed with water as it leaves the tap. A family of four typically saves 3,300 gallons of water a year. You can find low-flow faucets at your local hardware store.

Caution: Don't install a low-flow faucet aerator on your kitchen faucet if you have a portable dishwasher because the reduced flow will affect the dishwasher's performance.

Test your shower with a watch and a bucket. Turn on the shower the same as you usually do. Hold the bucket directly under the shower head and see how many seconds it takes for the water to reach the one gallon mark. If it takes less than 20 seconds, you'd benefit from a low-flow shower head.

For a family of four who normally takes five-minute showers, a low-flow shower head will save at least 14,000 gallons of water a year. Before you buy a new shower head, check with your local utility company. Some offer low-flow shower heads for free. If yours doesn't, most hardware stores carry these water-saving shower heads.

Use a plastic bottle to flush less water. If you don't already have a low-flush toilet, consider installing a displacement device in your toilet tank. This nifty gadget saves one to two gallons of water per flush by reducing the amount of water your tank will hold. With a small plastic bottle, such as a juice or laundry soap bottle, you can make your own displacement device. Here's how:

First, remove the bottle's label. Then, put a few stones in the bottom of the bottle for weight and fill with water. Place the bottle in your toilet tank, being careful that it doesn't interfere with the flushing mechanism. You may have to experiment a little to see what size bottle your tank will hold and still have enough water to flush effectively.

Test for leaks with dye. One tiny faucet drip can waste 50 gallons of water a day. A leaky toilet will waste 46,000 gallons of water in six months. To tell if you have a leak in your toilet, add some dye to the tank. If you don't flush and the dye shows up in the bowl anyway, you have a leak.

Put a trigger nozzle on your hose. It will save at least 20 gallons of water when you wash your car.

Use a broom instead of a hose to clean your steps and driveway. You'll save hundreds of gallons of water. An added bonus — you burn more calories sweeping than squirting.

Water your yard in the morning. Don't waste water on grass beginning to turn brown.

Don't leave the water running while you're brushing your teeth, shaving, washing the dishes, or washing your car. Either turn the water on and off as you need it, or in the case of shaving or washing dishes, put enough water in the basin to get the job done and leave the water turned off. When washing your car, use a sponge and a bucket of water. Every minute you leave a faucet running wastes three to five gallons of water.

Source:
50 Simple Things You Can Do to Save the Earth, Earthworks Press, Berkeley, Calif., 1989

Easy ways to make your house more energy efficient

Keep your fireplace damper closed. If you leave it open, 8 percent of your heat will escape through the chimney.

Keep light bulbs clean. Dirt absorbs light and requires more energy. You'll also save money on lighting by using fluorescent light bulbs instead of incandescent.

Turn your heat thermostat down. For every degree lower you go, you save 2 percent on your heating bill.

Add insulation, caulking, and weather stripping. In most homes, nearly half the energy spent to heat or cool a house literally goes out the window, out the attic, etc.

Contact your utilities company about having an energy audit done to help you find any energy leaks in your house. Many utility companies offer this service for free. If yours doesn't, they'll still often provide guidebooks to help you do your own.

Turn your water heater down to 130 degrees. If you have a dishwasher and no backup heater, you may have to leave your heater's temperature at 140 degrees.

Wrap your water heater in a special heater blanket, which you can find at most hardware stores. When wrapping gas heaters, be sure not to block off any air vents. Energy savings: 7 to 8 percent, especially if your heater was located in a typically chilly area, such as a basement.

Drain about two quarts of water from the valve faucet at the bottom of your water heater every two months. This helps prevent sediment buildup, lengthening your heater's life and improving its efficiency.

Install a low-flow shower head. You can cut water heating costs by as much as 50 percent.

Wash only full loads of clothes. Don't use hot water unless it's really necessary. Always rinse in cold. A cold rinse won't affect the cleanness of your clothes. Clean the lint trap on your dryer after every load.

Clean or replace air-conditioning filters once a month. A dirty filter makes your air-conditioning fan work harder and use more energy than a clean one. Don't turn your air-conditioning thermostat down lower than normal when you first turn it on, thinking it will cool the house faster. It won't, but it will waste energy.

Don't keep your refrigerator or freezer too cold. Even 10 degrees colder than you need will increase energy costs 25 percent. Your refrigerator's temperature should be between 38 and 42 degrees, your freezer, 0 to 5 degrees.

Clean your refrigerator coils once a year. It will improve the refrigerator's efficiency. The coils are usually on the back or bottom of most refrigerators. You can either vacuum them, or buy brushes made especially for cleaning coils.

Source:
50 Simple Things You Can Do to Save the Earth, Earthworks Press, Berkeley, Calif., 1989

Keep your electricity on: how to get help paying the bill

Tragically, each year brings reports of people — especially older folks — who have suffered and even died when their power was turned off.

That doesn't have to happen. There are financial assistance programs available to help you keep your electricity on.

Do you or someone you know need help paying electric bills? Here are some options (check with your local power company to see which ones are available in your area):

Preferred billing. This spreads your total annual electric bill over 12 months with approximately equal monthly payments. You are billed only for the predetermined budgeted amount. So you don't have to worry about paying extra large electricity bills during parts of the year when you use more energy.

Extended payment arrangements. If paying a total bill on time is a hardship, don't just assume there's nothing you can do. Don't wait for the power to be turned off. Contact your local power company to work out an individualized payment arrangement.

Emergency help. In some states, there are partnerships between charitable groups and power companies to help when customers can't pay their utility bills. In Georgia, for example, customers can contact their local Salvation Army office for information on Project Share. Funded by voluntary contributions among Georgia Power customers who add one to five dollars to their monthly bills, plus matching funds provided by Georgia Power, Project Share helps needy Georgians with emergency food, shelter, clothing — and utility bills.

Social Service Agencies. If customers can't pay their bills, power company employees can refer them to agencies that may be able to provide financial assistance. Call your power company for information.

Source:
Interview with Rick Kimbell, spokesperson, Georgia Power Company, Atlanta

Proven ways to lower the cost of air conditioning

Remember the days when air conditioning was considered a luxury? Not anymore. In fact, if you live in a hot climate — or have certain health conditions, like asthma — it's a downright necessity.

However, paying more money than you have to in order to keep your home cool is not a necessity. Here are energy-saving tips that will lower your air conditioning bill:

▶ Keep leaves, grass, and shrubs cut back from outdoor air-conditioning units. Your units will work more efficiently.

▶ Don't forget to clean or change your air-conditioner filter once a month. Dirty filters restrict air flow and make air conditioners work harder.

▶ Can you learn to be comfortable at a slightly higher temperature? You use 3 to 5 percent more electricity for every degree you set your thermostat below 78. So try sticking with 78 degrees or higher. Set your thermostat even higher while you're at work or on long outings — and save more money.

▶ Keep your draperies or blinds closed during the hottest part of the day to reduce the extra heat produced by direct sunlight.

▶ Find out if your home has adequate insulation. That's the most important factor in controlling the amount of energy it takes to keep your home at a comfortable temperature. Experts recommend you have a R-value — a measure of resistance to heat flow — of at least R-30 in ceiling areas.

▶ Don't forget about fans just because you have air conditioning! Ceiling fans installed in the rooms you use most can keep you cool and lower air-conditioner use.

Source:
Interview with Rick Kimbell, spokesperson, Georgia Power Company, Atlanta

Do's and don'ts when your power goes out

Losing power can be frightening, especially if you're alone, or the weather is bad. Be prepared. Put blankets, candles, and extra batteries for flashlights and transistor radios in an easy-to-find location.

▶ Make sure you know where to locate a first-aid kit.

▶ Keep a manual can opener handy. If you only have an electric opener, you won't be able to eat canned goods during a power outage!

▶ Do you have a home emergency generator? Learn how it works before you need it. Remember: Improper operation could send the generator's electricity backward over your regular power lines and electrocute power workers.

▶ Use food in your refrigerator first. But try to open the refrigerator as little as possible. That will keep food cooler and slow spoilage.

▶ If it's cold weather, wear layered clothing, such as several sweaters, to keep warm. And don't forget: A cap helps hold in body heat.

▶ Close off as many rooms as you can and gather your family in the warmest location. A room with a fireplace is best.

▶ Has a storm knocked down power wires? Don't try to figure out if they are "live" or not. Assume all fallen wires are dangerous! Call your local power office immediately.

▶ What should you do if you're in a car or truck and a wire falls on you? If you aren't in immediate danger, stay put. Help will come eventually. If you try to get out, the vehicle will ground your body, and there's a good chance you could be electrocuted.

Source:
Interview with Rick Kimbell, spokesperson, Georgia Power Company, Atlanta

How to spend less time cleaning your house

There's no known way to make cleaning the house fun, but the right short-cuts will give you a sparkling home and more time to do what you want.

▶ Clean only what needs to be cleaned. If there's a stain on the carpet or rug, spot clean it. Don't shampoo the whole thing. Doing so wastes time and ultimately hurts the rug.

▶ Throw stuff away. If you don't like something, toss it or donate it to charity.

▶ Keep cleaning supplies convenient. If a broom is easy to reach, you're more likely to use it. Have sponges handy under every sink.

▶ Carry supplies on a cart or in a wagon rather than trudging back and forth to pick them up.

▶ Be patient. Let dirty dishes soak. Allow bathroom cleaners to penetrate soap scum and mold. If you start scrubbing too soon, you simply waste energy.

▶ Start at the top. Dust and dirt will fall as you clean. If you start from the bottom, you're going to have to clean some areas twice.

▶ Get hydro-help. A bowl of soapy water will cleanse a number of trinkets and you can use the shower to wash off venetian blinds. Try using a car-wash brush attachment to clean patio furniture.

▶ Sweat the small stuff. Before something gets out of hand, deal with it. If one room is starting to look messy, straighten it up.

▶ Make it a social event. Buy a portable or speaker phone and chat with your friends as you clean. Or, if you're a particularly good salesperson, talk your friends into coming over and helping. (Though you'll probably have to repay the favor.)

▶ Surrender without shame. Start with a reasonable goal in mind and don't try to exceed it.

Top time-wasting chores

Laundry. Towels don't have to be thrown in a washing machine after one use. After all, they're only wet. It's also rather pointless to wash yard and work clothes after a single wearing. They'll only be filthy again the next time you putter in your garden. If you don't have a full load, don't do the laundry. You're wasting time, electricity, and water.

Vacuuming. With today's new age/stain resistant carpets, vacuuming is overdone. Rooms that get a lot of use may need to be vacuumed every day or so, but low-traffic areas (like a bedroom) only need to be cleaned once a week. A good doormat will also cut down on excess dirt.

Windows and bathrooms. These are frequently overcleaned. Glass, even when dirty, is still transparent. Wash your windows only when they become offensive to you. And in your bathroom, the hard surfaces repel dirt. Who cares about hard water buildups?

Floors. If your hardwood floor is properly sealed, leave it alone. Too much wax will give it a dull finish. Just sweep it once in a while. And good carpets can go at least two or three years between shampooings.

Polishing. Bringing the shine back to blackened items, like a grill, is a waste of time. Polishing silver and other shining metals will only delay tarnishing.

Dishes. Forget about cleaning those dishes in the china closet or upper cabinet. Wait until you have to use them. And never hand-dry dishes. That's what dish drainers were built for.

Sources:
How Do I Clean The Moosehead? by Don Aslett, New American Library, New York, 1989
Mary Ellen's Clean House! by Mary Ellen Pinkham and Dale Burg, Crown Publishers, New York, 1993

Quickie cleaning

Uh-oh! You told your guests to call before they came over, but you expected to have at least a few hours notice — not a few *minutes*!

Getting the place spotless may be impossible, but you can make it more than presentable in just a few seconds, if you use a few tricks from professional cleaners.

▶ First, turn up the lights. Light houses are friendly. Dark houses have shadows and make cobwebs and dust seem more ominous.

▶ Next, spruce yourself up. Shave, put on makeup, change clothes. Do anything to divert the attention to yourself.

▶ Only clean where the guests will be sitting. If it's a nice day, shuffle them onto the porch or deck. If you must be inside, close the doors that expose the really messy rooms.

▶ Clean your walkway, too. If there's junk all over the place, it will give a miserable first impression. Get rid of dog bones, baseballs, dirty doormats, etc.

▶ Remove the clutter and litter from the room and put things in order. Be sure to leave reading materials or half-finished projects, though. They reflect well on you and distract from other messes.

▶ Put the dog or cat in another room or outside. (Animals suggest typical pet messes.)

▶ Vacuum if you can.

▶ Shine those mirrors and glass furniture tops. If they're sparkling, the room looks better. If streaked, though, you've done more harm than good.

It's not a bad idea to leave the vacuum or a bottle of furniture polish out for the guests to see. That way, you can comment that you were in the middle of cleaning the house when they called.

Source:
How Do I Clean the Moosehead? by Don Aslett, New American Library, New York, 1989

Better weeding

If you see more dandelions and wild onions than blades of grass when you look out the window, it might be a good time to visit the local garden center and pick out a quality herbicide.

While you can manually dig out a few scattered weeds, an out-and-out infestation is best fought chemically.

Mow your yard and give it a thorough watering a few days before applying the herbicide. This will encourage weed growth, making weeds more susceptible to the poison.

When spraying, keep the nozzle close to the ground, hitting the weeds directly. Keep children and pets away until the chemicals dry.

Don't water the yard for several days. Once the weeds dry up, rake them and throw them away. New grass now has room to grow.

Source:
The Time-Life Gardener's Guide: Lawn and Ground Covers, Time-Life Books, Alexandria, Va., 1989

Keeping your grass green and healthy

If your grass has taken on a bluish-gray color, it's probably thirsty. Most grasses need an inch of water a week to keep their luster.

When Mother Nature fails to produce rain, you'll have to take out the hose and sprinklers if you want to keep the neighbors jealous.

Allow your sprinklers to run for an hour or so. It's best to give your yard its soaking all at once rather than a little at a time (it helps encourage root growth).

If there has been sufficient rain, *do not* water your yard. Doing so will only result in extra weeds and possible grass fungi.

If you live in an area that imposes water restrictions during drought periods, let your grass grow a little higher than normal to retain moisture. Stop fertilizing the yard, too, since this will only encourage growth and the need for water. Get rid of any weeds, which steal water from the grass.

Source:
The Time-Life Gardener's Guide: Lawn and Ground Covers, Time-Life Books, Alexandria, Va., 1989

Cheaper pest control

Don't be pestered into spending money on insects. A sparkling clean house discourages most pests, and for the persistent ones, try home remedies.

Peppermint turns away mice. They don't like the smell.

Cloves or red pepper keeps ants away.

Salt water makes fleas flee.

Fresh bay leaves in your cupboards will keep pests away for up to a year.

Beer knocks out garden slugs and snails. Sink a pie pan or lid of a jar into the ground and fill it with beer.

Plain boric acid is the main ingredient in roach-control products.

Source:
How to Pinch a Penny 'Til It Screams by Rochelle LaMotte McDonald, Avery Publishing Group, Garden City Park, N.Y., 1994

Keeping your junkyard dog out of the garbage

Place a paper or plastic bag inside the garbage pail. Make a paste of alum powder and water and spread it around the edge of the bag. Don't put it on food. A commercial product that will achieve the same results is Bitter Apple.

Tabasco sauce, Chinese mustard, and vinegar mixed together makes for a bitter taste. If the dog gets even a lick of this combination, it will serve as an immediate correction.

Another way to make the garbage can less appealing is to blow up balloons and pop them close to the dog's face so it startles him. Then tape one or more balloons near the garbage pail at night. The dog should stay away.

Make sure your dog isn't going after the garbage because he's hungry!
Source:
When Good Dogs Do Bad Things by Mordecai Siegal and Matthew Margolis, Little, Brown, and Company, Boston, 1986

Quick fix for a furniture scratch

Nicks and scratches may give a piece of furniture character, but they can also be just plain ugly. Lemon oil or alcohol rubbed in gently with a bit of very fine steel wool will often take care of the problem.

To hide a deep scratch, you'll need to change the color of the scratch to the color of the wood. Some felt-tipped pens will blend with oak, walnut, or mahogany. Brown crayons often work to fill in a hole. So does shoe polish. You could even buy a "touch-up stick" from your local hardware store, but a crayon will be just as effective.
Source:
The Weekend Refinisher by Bruce Johnson, Ballantine Books, New York, 1989

Protect furniture fabric forever

When you buy a nice piece of furniture, invest a few more dollars in one or two cans of spray-on fabric protector. That way, you don't have to ban food, drink, shoes, and children from your nice furniture. The fabric will look nice for years in spite of accidental spills.
Source:
1001 Ways To Cut Your Expenses by Jonathan D. Pond, Dell Publishing, New York, 1992

How to buy the right amount of paint

A good tape measure and a calculator can save you a bundle at the paint store. Buying too much paint can be incredibly expensive. If you don't get enough, you may end up with a different shade than the one you started with.

Measure the length of the room and either the width (if you're painting the floor or ceiling) or height (if you're painting the walls). Multiply the two figures together. The result is the total square feet.

If you're painting the outside of the house, measure the perimeter and height from the foundation to the roof line. Once again, multiply the two figures. (If your house has a triangular-shaped gable end, add two feet to the overall height of the house.)

If you're painting a mason surface, you'll need more paint than for wood. And if you're changing the color of a room or your house's exterior, you'll need two coats. Touch up jobs of the same color should only require one coat.

Take your numbers and surface conditions to your paint dealer. He or she can then determine exactly how much you'll need.

Source:
How to Paint Anything by Hubbard H. Cobb, The Macmillian Co., New York, 1972

Picking the right paint for your house exterior

Can't tell the difference between oil and latex (water-based) paints? Don't worry, you're not alone.

Oil-based paints have a high gloss when they dry. They're wonderful for touch-up work, such as covering small cracks and dents. Unfortunately, oil paints have to be thinned and cleaned with mineral spirits, benzene, or turpentine. And cleaning brushes is a nightmare.

People sometimes assume that latex paints, because they are water-based, will wash off with the first heavy rain. In fact, they're just as durable as oil paints and you can use them on most of the same surfaces. The chief difference is that you'll spend a lot less time cleaning up afterward.

Source:
Outdoor Home Repairs Made Easy by Peter Jones, Butterick Publishing, New York, 1980

Hiring a painter

Hiring a contractor to work on your house can be a frightening experience. Many painters, plumbers, and roofers are one-man shows, and many are unreliable.

Before you hire someone to paint your house, take these steps to protect yourself:

► Call your insurance agent and find out how much liability coverage you have. You are responsible if someone gets hurt while painting your house. A worker falling off a ladder could wipe you out financially.

You can ask the painter to show you insurance papers before you hire him, but realize that the papers could easily be fake. Or, (and this happens quite often) the painter may tell you that the person who was hurt wasn't his employee and isn't covered by his insurance. He was an independent contractor he hired to help get the job done.

► Before the painters open a can of paint, make sure the paint store has been paid. In many states, if a painter doesn't pay the store, you are responsible for the payment. The paint store could place a lien against your home until you pay.

Paint is fairly cheap, so you wouldn't be out too much money if this happened to you. But this step gets very important if you are having a hardwood floor put in, or anything done with expensive materials.

When you hire a contractor, you assume that they will be reliable and pay for the materials they use and pay any subcontractors they hire. But you'd be smart to protect yourself by asking for proof.

You need to get a document from the contractor called a *lien release* or *waiver*. Ask all material suppliers and subcontractors who work on your home to sign this document. They will be signing away their right to come after you for payment.

▶ Don't give the painter a large amount of money before he starts. If he says he's short of cash and needs the money to buy the paint, buy the paint yourself.

Your best bet is to pay half the money when half the job is done, 40 percent when the job is completed, and the other 10 percent when you feel sure that the job is finished satisfactorily. Holding back some money at the end will protect you against any problems that show up after the painters have left.

▶ Never just show a painter the color you want and depend on them to get it right. You need to specify the brand name and the order number of the paint.

▶ Your best bet is to paint a small patch of your house yourself to check the color before you hire a painter. Paint never looks the same on your wall as it did on the small chip you picked out.

Sources:
Clark Howard's radio show, WSB radio, Atlanta, 1995, and *Clark Howard's Consumer Survival Kit* by Clark Howard and Mark Meltzer, Longstreet Press, Marietta, Ga., 1993

How to get out of an ironclad contract

Ever make a decision you instantly regret? There's a little-known law made just for you: You are allowed three business days to completely change your mind after you sign a contract that could put the security of your home at risk.

For instance, your home needs a major face lift, repairs, or an addition. You don't have the money to pay upfront, so you decide to finance the job and use your home as security. You sign a contract.

Over the next three days, no contractor may start work on your home, and no lender may pay you or the contractor until the three days are up. That gives you the chance to cancel. If you decide to cancel, you must simply notify the creditor in writing. The creditor must return to you any fees you may have already paid. You are home-free.

Source:
Consumer Handbook to Credit Protection Laws, Board of Governors of the Federal Reserve System, Washington, D.C.

Homeowners' associations: What to watch out for

Imagine moving into a new subdivision and giving your home an expensive paint job, then learning you have to completely repaint your house. Why? Because the dark blue you chose wasn't exactly the blue "approved" by your homeowners' association.

Or, imagine wanting to work out of your home and discovering you legally can't.

To avoid problems like the scenario above, attorney Randall Lipshutz advises owners of condominiums and houses who belong to homeowners' associations to make sure they read and understand their association's covenants and rules. And never buy a home without asking about homeowners' association membership and rules. Realtors trying to sell you a home have been known to forget to mention the neighborhood governing body.

Homeowners' associations (also known as neighborhood associations) are growing in number. Sometimes the membership is voluntary, but often it is mandatory — especially in condominiums and new subdivisions.

"Very few new developments are going in that don't have a mandatory neighborhood association," declares Lipshutz, who specializes in working with homeowners' and condominium associations as well as housing developers.

"They make sense because the membership fees provide a structure to pay for amenities, like a pool, tennis courts, and clubhouse."

"The association can also protect property values by assuring that certain standards of maintenance will be upheld."

What kind of rules can homeowners' associations enact? The exact do's and don'ts vary from state to state and neighborhood to neighborhood. "But one restriction a neighborhood association cannot legally impose is any covenant that discriminates on the basis of race, color, religion, or national origin," Lipshutz points out.

The kinds of rules you are most likely to encounter are restrictions on the use of your home (you may not be able to rent it or run a business out of it), the color of your house, how your front yard should be maintained, and whether or not you can have pets.

What to watch out for. "You need to pay attention to the fact that covenants can generally be amended," attorney Lipshutz emphasizes. "Just because when you moved in pets were permitted doesn't mean that rule won't ever be changed."

What can you do to make sure Fido will always be welcome?

Lipshutz advises residents to become active in their neighborhood associations. "Go to the meetings — not just to vote on board memberships but to hear reports on what they are doing and what they're planning for the future. Have input. The key is to be involved."

You also need to make sure you pay your association fees on time. "Some people don't think that's too important," attorney Lipshutz says. "But if you don't pay, there can be serious consequences. You can be sued for the assessment. A judgment against you can result in a lien against your property. Your wages can even be garnished."

Do residents ever sue their associations? "Yes," Lipshutz says. "Associations can be wrong. They cannot make rules that are different for one person as opposed to another. If they do, they can be held liable and stopped."

Source:
Interview with Randall M. Lipshutz, attorney-at-law, Lipshutz, Greenblatt, and King, Atlanta

BUYING, SELLING, AND CARING FOR CARS

How to avoid legal hassles when you sell your car

It seems simple enough. You place an ad; someone comes over, looks at your car, pays you for it, and drives off into the sunset.

However, if you haven't taken certain precautions, that sale could come back to haunt you with legal problems.

"A car can cause death and injuries," attorney James Zito points out. "Until both the right to ownership and the motor vehicle's title are properly transferred to the new owner, you may still be considered the car's owner, and you could be held at least partially liable for any accidents it's in."

Fortunately, there are ways to protect yourself from that scenario as well as from other post-sale headaches — if you take these precautions.

When you write the bill of sale:

▶ Identify your car by the motor vehicle I.D. number.

▶ State that your car has been sold to the person who is buying it. Know who that person is. (Ask for a full name, address, and driver's license number.)

▶ Date the bill of sale accurately. Never use a future date.

▶ State the mileage, whether it is accurate, and whether the odometer has been tampered with.

▶ Indicate if the car is free of any liens. "If you do owe money on it, that's OK," attorney Zito adds, "as long as it is indicated on the certificate of title."

▶ Make sure the bill of sale states you are selling the vehicle "as is," with no warranty. "During discussions with the prospective buyer, be careful describing the car's condition. If the car drives fine, it's all right to say so, but you should add that you aren't a mechanic. If you say the vehicle is perfect and it breaks down in a week, you could find yourself with legal woes," attorney Zito explains.

▶ Note that your car's title has been transferred to the new owner and that he has adequate liability insurance in his name.

▶ State that the new owner has paid you, received the car, and now owns the vehicle. Have him initial the statement.

▶ Make two copies of the bill of sale, one for you to keep and one to give to the buyer. Each of you should sign the other's copy.

Don't be stuck with a title to a car you've sold. When you sell your car, you're required to sign the back of the certificate of title and hand it to the new owner. Then he is supposed to take the document to the State Department of Motor Vehicles and have the title officially transferred into his name.

"If the new owner doesn't do that, your state's records will show you are the car's current owner," says Zito. "So if the vehicle is involved in a robbery or a hit-and-run accident and is traced to you, you'll have some explaining to do."

That doesn't mean you'll be held responsible for the crime or accident, but you will have to convince the police you don't own the car.

"To avoid this kind of mix-up, make sure you keep a copy of the bill of sale and a copy of the certificate of title showing you signed it over to the new owner," advises James Zito.

It's also a good idea to send a letter to your State Department of Motor Vehicles saying you no longer own the car, along with a copy of the transferred title. And let your insurance company know you've sold your car — send them copies of the bill of sale and the transferred certificate of title, too.
Source:
Interview with James Zito, attorney-at-law, Lipshutz, Greenblatt, and King, Atlanta

Lemon losers

Knowing what not to buy is just as important as knowing what you want when you go car shopping. Jim Mateja, national automotive expert, recommends you steer clear of these vehicles when you begin looking for new wheels:

▶ Any turbo-charged car (Turbo simply means the engine isn't powerful on its own.)

▶ Any GM car with the 350 cubic inch V-8 diesel engine (Lousy resale value.)

▶ Any used Vega (A born lemon.)

▶ Any 1974 model car (This was the year before the catalytic converter appeared. That means lousy mileage and frequent stalls.)

▶ The 1981 Cadillac Eldorado, DeVille, Seville, and Fleetwood (The engine in these models was only made for one year.)

▶ The 1982 Chevrolet Cavalier and Pontiac J2000 (No power.)

▶ Any 1985 Buick Electra, Olds 98, Cadillac DeVille (Numerous transmission problems.)

▶ Any 1975 to 1979 Honda Civic or Accord (Tend to rust.)

▶ Any 1980 or 1981 Honda Prelude (More rust.)

▶ Any 1976 or 1977 Dodge Aspen or Plymouth Volare (Rust, poor mileage, minimal performance.)

▶ Any American Motors Corporation (AMC) Alliance or Encore (Distress merchandise, even when new.)

▶ Any Renault LeCar, 18i sedan or wagon, or Fuego (The French aren't known for their automotive industry. There's a reason.)

▶ The Dodge Omni or Plymouth Horizon (If the car has either a 1.7 or 1.6 liter engine, walk away. You'll never find replacement parts.)

- ▶ Any Chrysler powered by a 2.6 liter four-cylinder engine supplied by Mitsubishi (Temporary engines mean repair nightmares.)
- ▶ Any 1980 Chevy Citation, Buick Skylark, Oldsmobile Omega or Pontiac Phoenix (Poor assembly.)
- ▶ Any Ford Pinto (There are lingering concerns of explosion in rear-end collisions.)
- ▶ Any Fiat (Tend to break down frequently.)
- ▶ Any 1980 Jaguar (Even the company president says these are bad cars.)
- ▶ Any Audi (Expensive to fix, service, and maintain. Is image worth that much?)
- ▶ The 1986 Yugo (Not only a bad car, but nearly impossible to find parts for.)
- ▶ Any 1972 to 1979 Ford and Mercury rear drive cars (Possible transmission problems.)
- ▶ Any 1974 to 1978 Ford Mustang (Poor mileage and an embarrassment to the prestigious line.)
- ▶ Any 1981 to 1983 Chrysler Imperial (Simply a renamed Cordoba, with the price increased by several thousand dollars.)
- ▶ The 1982 to 1985 Ford EXP or Mercury LN-7 (Just plain ugly.)
- ▶ Isuzu I-Mark (No resale value at all.)
- ▶ Any GM car powered by the 3-liter carbureted V-6 engine (Second only to the diesel as GM's worst engine.)
- ▶ Any Chevrolet Chevette built since 1976 (Small, cramped, and sluggish.)

Source:
Best Buys in Used Cars by Jim Mateja, Bonus Books, Chicago, 1995

6 things you must know before buying a used car

- ▶ Dealers have a much higher profit margin on used cars. That means there's more room for you to negotiate.

- ▶ Always try to have your mechanic inspect a car before you buy. If the dealer refuses to allow an inspection, insist on a warranty. Don't be suckered into paying for this warranty, either.

- ▶ Know when to walk away. If you can't get what you want, leave. If the dealer really wants to sell you the car, he'll stop you before you leave.

- ▶ Don't discuss financing until you're certain you've received the best deal. Once you start talking about paying for the car, the price won't drop any further.

- ▶ Don't trade in your car. The dealer is going to try to resell your vehicle to someone else for a higher price. Why shouldn't you pocket that money? Sell it yourself. A little hassle can mean a lot of extra cash.

- ▶ If you're buying a car that's four to seven years old, insist on a discount of 30 to 35 percent off the National Automobile Dealers Association retail asking price. If it's older than eight years, try for 40 to 50 percent off.

Source:
A Car Dealer's Secrets Revealed by S.M. Quarles, D.C., Austin, Texas, 1993
What Car Dealers Don't Want You to Know by Mark Eskeldson, Technews Publishing, Fair Oaks, Calif., 1995

How to buy a car by computer

If you're tired of dickering with dealers and driving all over trying to make a deal, consider buying a car by computer.

If you have a modem and a connection to an on-line service that gives you access to the World Wide Web, you're all set. All you have to do is dial up DealerNet by typing in http://www.dealernet.com/.

Browse around until you find a car that interests you. You can even compare the car of your choice with other models to see how it fares in terms of trunk space and mileage.

To check prices, type in http://www.enews.com/magazines/edmunds. You'll find out how much a dealer has to pay for a car as well as how much they're likely to charge you. All this information will help you dicker a better deal out of your dealer.

Of course, if you're really tired of driving from dealer to dealer to find the best deal, you can always order right on-line. Just type in http://www.autoby-tel.com/ to call up Auto-By-Tel, a free on-line buying service. In a few days, you'll get a call from a nearby dealer, who will deliver your new car for a fixed price above invoice.

Source:
Fortune (133,4:168)

Save thousands on the car you want, without haggling

If you've got a good idea of the kind of car you want, but not enough time to visit all the showrooms in town, you might want to consider hiring an auto buying service. Brokers at these companies can save you hours of aggravation and thousands of dollars when it comes time to pay.

Normally, car dealers charge 10 to 15 percent above the invoice, or wholesale, price. Brokers only ask 1 or 2 percent. Why the big difference? Overhead. A dealer has to keep hundreds of cars on the lot and pay a hefty rent for the showroom. Brokers usually do business out of small offices.

It works like this. You decide you want a new Jeep Wrangler, but don't have time to comparison shop. A broker will call dealers in surrounding cities and states and get the best fleet price they can. (That means the car is sold roughly at invoice.) Once the Jeep is found, the broker calls you back, describes the vehicle to you and asks if this was what you were looking for. If so, you're ready to roll. If not, the search continues.

The process takes anywhere from one day to several weeks. It all depends on how picky you are and how high the demand is for your chosen vehicle. Still, when you have the choice of paying a $300 to $400 commission as opposed to several thousand dollars, isn't it worth the wait?

Source:
Interview with Helene Belisario, owner of Atlanta Buying Consultants, Atlanta

Got money to burn? Lease a car

The ads make it sound great. "Lease a brand-new car for as little as $200 per month! Take your friends and family for a ride in your new luxury vehicle." In truth, you're the one being taken for a ride — by the dealer.

Confusing contracts and poor disclosure laws make leasing one of the best ways for the auto industry to get your money. Dealers like to say, "You're only paying for the time you use the car," but they often neglect to mention that those payments don't build any equity. So, after one to five years of monthly payments, you're no better off than you were to begin with.

Negotiating for a leased car is harder than haggling for one you buy. Currently, dealers are reluctant to tell you the interest rate or sales-price figures they use to determine your monthly payments.

Fortunately, that could be about to change. The Federal Reserve is on the verge of revising the regulation that governs car and truck leasing. The new rules would require the dealer to itemize what you will have to pay. The dealer will have to list the cost of the vehicle, your monthly bill (including insurance and taxes), the residual value of the car when the lease expires, and any extra charges you might face at the end of the contract.

The base price of a leased car is just as flexible as the price of a car you buy, but most dealers won't tell you this. Never agree to pay the sticker price. Learn what the car is worth before you sign any agreements.

If you do decide to lease, look for a deal that's manufacturer-subsidized. A manufacturer may subsidize a lease if they think the car is going to hold its value particularly well. If the car will hold its value and be worth a lot of money when the lease is up, your monthly payments should be pretty low. In other words, a high "residual value" should equal low monthly payments.

With all the difficulties of negotiating a lease, why is it so popular? Credit smart advertising. With catch phrases like "no money down" and "low monthly payments," who could resist checking it out?

Leasing does occasionally make sense. There are some tax benefits (though experts say they're not worth the money you'll pay). Or if you're in a position where you want to present a successful image via a late-model luxury car, leasing may be a good short-term option.

People who love and can't live without late-model cars are good candidates for a lease. If you're planning to buy a new vehicle every three or four years, then you lose little by leasing. Financial experts, though, say the best way to get your money's worth is to buy a car and drive it until it dies. You can get eight to ten years out of a good car, and half of those years are payment-free.

Sources:
A Car Dealer's Secrets Revealed by S.M. Quarles, D.C. Austin, Texas, 1993
Kiplinger's Personal Finance Magazine (50,4:89)
Money Magazine (March 1995)
What Car Dealers Don't Want You to Know by Mark Eskeldson, Technews Publishing, Fair Oaks, Calif., 1995

How to outwit odometer fraud

Odometer fraud is a common way to cheat buyers of used cars. Since car values normally go down as miles driven go up, a dishonest seller will roll back or disconnect the odometer, the dashboard instrument that indicates how many miles a vehicle has been driven. Consumers have overpaid $2,000 and up on cars with rolled-back odometers.

Federal law requires that a used car seller provide accurate odometer information on the car title. If the mileage isn't noted, the title must state why, such as odometer has turned over or odometer has been broken and repaired. The car should also have a sticker attached to the left door frame that provides the date of odometer repair and what actual car mileage was before repairs.

Here are some ways you can identify odometer tampering:

▶ Cars that are only a few years old are the most likely to have rolled-back odometers. Ask about the former owner's profession. You can expect a salesman's car to have many miles.

▶ Be especially wary of leased vehicles with low mileage. On average, a leased car is driven 30,000 miles a year. A high percentage of leased cars have had their odometers rolled back before they are put up for sale.

▶ Check the car for signs of tampering, such as marks on the odometer cable or unevenly aligned mileage numbers. Interpreting uneven numbers can be a bit of a trick because an odometer's numbers normally look uneven when they roll over. The trained eye can tell, however. Get someone who's very familiar with cars to help you make this judgment call.

▶ If a car really has low mileage, most, if not all, of the equipment should be original. Check car parts that wear out, such as tires and water pumps. One sign that a water pump has been replaced is that it is a different color from the engine.

Also check for an old-looking brake pedal and accelerator, driver's door, and rubber door molding (does it look scrubby?), and the driver's side seat, carpet, and armrest. Compare how worn the driver's side of car looks in relation to the rest of the car.

If you suspect tampering:

▶ Ask to see mileage numbers on oil stickers, inspection stickers, and tire warranty cards. However, a very careful con artist will have changed the numbers on these items as well.

▶ Check the mileage reading on previous titles. You can pull information on previous titles at the Department of Motor Vehicles.

▶ Get in touch with the car's former owners. The Department of Motor Vehicles will be able to help you track down their names and addresses.

If you wish to report suspected odometer fraud, contact your state attorney general.

Sources:
Interview with Jerry Estes, antique car collector with 44 years experience buying cars
U.S. Department of Transportation, National Highway Traffic Safety Administration, 400 7th Street S.W., Washington, D.C. 20590, 1994

Getting your money out of anti-lock brakes

These days, almost all cars come with the option for anti-lock brakes if they aren't already included in the standard package. Since anti-lock brakes prevent wheel lock-up and skidding when you have to slam on your brakes in a hurry, they're a great safety innovation. However, they won't do you much good if you don't use them properly. Here's what you need to know:

1) Forget what you've learned about "pumping" the brakes when you need to slow down in a hurry. There's also no need to steer into a skid. With anti-lock brakes, it's best to slam on the brakes and simply aim your car in the direction you want to go.

   If you pump the brakes in a car equipped with an anti-lock brake system, the system won't be able to work the way it was designed to, and its effectiveness as a safety feature will be reduced.

2) Push down on the brake pedal hard. Don't worry if you feel the pedal pulsating or vibrating. That's natural since the anti-lock brake system is pumping the brakes faster than any human could.

3) Don't overcorrect by turning your wheel. With anti-lock brakes, you only need to turn the wheel enough to avoid hitting something. The car will automatically travel in exactly the direction the wheel is turned.

4) Try out these new braking techniques before you need to call on them in a emergency situation. It's best to practice in a large empty parking lot where you have plenty of room to stop and swerve without hitting another car. Visit such a place on a rainy day and practice slamming on your brakes. This way you can also get the feel for not overturning into skids.

Source:
U.S. Department of Transportation, National Highway Traffic Safety Administration, 400 7th Street S.W., Washington, D.C. 20590, 1994

When your car needs repair: Where to go for what

When your car needs work, should you go to a dealer's service department or an independent shop? It all depends on what type of problem you need fixed.

Sal Fariello, who's worked in the auto repair business for over 20 years as everything from a mechanic to a manager, offers a few suggestions about where to go for different types of car maintenance and repair.

Oil changes. Independent shops often do just as good a job as dealers, and they're often cheaper. Shop around. Quick service specialty shops such as Jiffy Lube do quality work for reasonable prices. Goodyear and Firestone also offer oil changes at good prices.

Exhaust system work. If your car needs a new muffler or other exhaust system repairs, you can't beat large discount muffler chains such as Meineke or Midas. They're fast, inexpensive, and knowledgeable. Steer clear of dealers for this type of work.

Tune-ups. Your best bet is probably an independent repair shop. Use your owner's manual for guidance as to what type of tune-up your car needs.

Brake jobs. A bad brake job can be a mistake you pay for with your life. That's why it's best not to look for bargain in this area. You should stick with a reputable car dealer's service department or a large franchised service center operated by a tire company. Their prices will probably be similar. Only work with a reputable, highly skilled mechanic and be sure he's using high-quality parts.

Wheel alignment. Your best bet for a wheel alignment is the service department of a reputable tire store such as Goodyear or Firestone. Car dealers don't do a lot of this type of work and often neglect the equipment. Tire dealers, on the other hand, take tire alignments seriously so the tires they sell to their customers will last longer, and they'll have repeat business.

Automatic transmission repairs. For good transmission work done quickly, go with a transmission specialty shop such as AAMCO or Lee Myles. These shops stock several rebuilt transmission units as well as a wide assortment of replacement parts that enable them to fix your car quickly.

AAMCO, in particular, does a very thorough transmission job, replacing clutches and seals as well as thrust bearings and bushings. Many car dealers with service shops sublet any transmission work they need done out to one of these specialty shops.

Manual transmission repairs. You'll probably be better off going to a new car dealer's service department for manual transmission problems. That's because manual transmission problems can be much harder to fix than automatic transmission problems. A dealer will have the special tools required to fix manual transmissions, but an independent shop may not.

The factory forces car dealers to buy these tools, so they're guaranteed to have the equipment to fix your car. Since independent shops generally don't have a high volume of manual transmission repairs, they often don't bother to buy the special factory equipment.

Whatever shop you choose, be sure to ask about the brand name of any part going into your car. Call a few auto parts stores and check the reputation of that brand. If it gets a bad rap, request that the mechanic use a better brand. Otherwise, you'll likely have to have the part replaced again, probably right after the warranty has expired.

Also, keep in mind that even the best-known shops sometimes get busted for ripping off an unwary consumer. Your best protection is knowledge about your car and a second opinion if someone quotes you an unusually high price, suggests repairs you don't think you need, or otherwise arouses your suspicions.

In addition, it's generally a good idea to check out any car shop you plan to use with your local Better Business Bureau before you take your car in for maintenance work or repairs.

Sources:
How to Avoid Getting Mugged by Mr. Badwrench by Sal Fariello, SFT Publishing, Bay Shore, N.Y., 1988
What Auto Mechanics Don't Want You to Know by Mark Eskeldson, Technews Publishing, Fair Oaks, Calif., 1994

Avoid auto repair rip-offs

According to the U.S. Department of Transportation, almost 40 percent of the money Americans spend on car repair is wasted. Part of the waste is due to fraud. The other part is due to mechanics' misdiagnosis and incompetence.

You have to know what kind of service your car needs and how it can be done most economically. Here are just a few of the ways consumers unwittingly waste money on car repair.

Oil changes and lubrication. Don't waste your money having your oil changed every three months or 3,000 miles. This is totally unnecessary unless you've been towing a trailer or driving under extremely harsh conditions such as in a dust storm.

Frequent oil changes were important 20 years ago when neither cars nor motor oils were as good as they are today. Those old rules simply don't apply anymore. Follow your car manufacturer's recommendation about how often you should have your oil changed. You can safely go to the limit of that recommendation.

Here are some things you'll want to watch for. Make sure the motor oil you get has the correct viscosity and API service classification your car manufacturer recommends. Also, make sure you get a name brand oil filter. Some off-brands are as low in performance as they are in price.

If your oil change includes lubrication, make sure your power steering fluid, automatic transmission fluid, brake fluid, coolant, and windshield washer fluid are properly checked and topped off if necessary. Your suspension and steerage linkage fitting should also be greased as well as your door and trunk hinges and latches, shift linkages, and parking brake cables.

If a mechanic suggests you need additives in your oil, say goodbye. Regular oil contains all the additives your engine needs unless your car's engine is clunking and burning oil like crazy. In that case, pouring oil thickener in the crankcase may quiet the clunking and slow down the oil burning.

Tuneups. Tuneups are the one area of auto repair most ripe for rip-offs. The more you know about what type of tuneup your particular vehicle needs, the better off you'll be. Here are some general guidelines your mechanic should follow:

Cars with ignition points, usually those built in 1974 or earlier — Tune up every 10,000 to 15,000 miles. Replace condenser, points, and sparks plugs every time. Check the distributor cap; replace if necessary. The PCV valve should also be cleaned during every tuneup. (A regularly cleaned PCV valve will usually not have to be replaced.) Replace the fuel filter and rotor every other time. You'll probably also need a new air filter and breather element every other time.

Cars with electronic ignition, but no computer controls, 1975-1979 General Motors models, 1975-1983 other models — Tune up every 17,000 to 22,000 miles. Replace fuel filter, rotor, and spark plugs. Clean PCV valve;

replace if it hasn't been cleaned regularly. Check air filter, breather element, and distributor cap; replace if necessary. You should also check the air filter and breather element between tuneups and replace when necessary.

Cars with computer controls, 1980 and after on General Motors models, 1983 and after on other models — Tune up every 25,000 to 30,000 miles. Replace fuel filter, rotor, and spark plugs. Clean PCV valve during each tune-up; replace if it hasn't been cleaned regularly. Check air filter, breather element, and distributor cap; replace if necessary. You should also check the air filter and breather element between tuneups and replace when necessary.

All tuned-up cars should be tested on an analyzer to make sure no other problems exist and to make any necessary adjustments, such as air/fuel ratio, idle speed, and timing.

Automatic transmission repairs. Sometimes, during a routine fluid and filter change, a mechanic will show you the transmission oil pan he had to remove to get to the filter. He'll point out metal particles accumulated at the bottom of the pan and tell you those particles mean you have serious internal damage that must be fixed right away.

This is nothing but a scam. If you fall for it, you'll end up paying for an expensive transmission overhaul that won't do your car a bit of good. Actually, all automatic transmissions accumulate some metal particles in the pan. It's perfectly normal, so there's no need to be concerned. Just have them put your transmission back together, drive away, and don't look back.

Engine service. Two common rip-offs in this area are the bogus valve adjustment and the phony cooling system flush. Some cars, especially imported models, require routine valve adjustment. The problem is, many mechanics never do the valve adjustments customers request. Sometimes, they don't even remove the valve cover, a step they have to do if they intend to adjust the valves.

If you're suspicious of your mechanic, here's an easy way to tell if he's working for you or working you over. Dab a bit of paint or colored nail polish to one of the nuts that fastens the valve cover to the cylinder head. Pick an inconspicuous spot and place the paint so that it touches part of both the nut and the valve cover. You'll know no work was done if you get your car back and your paint is undisturbed. If this is the case, go back to the shop and get your money back and don't do business with those bad guys again.

Every car's cooling system needs to be drained every couple of years. Antifreeze left in a car for too long won't do its job properly and can lead to more serious problems down the road.

A proper cooling system flush will flush out the radiator, the engine block, the heater core, the cooling system hoses, and the coolant system reservoir. Then, the mechanic should add a new 50-50 mixture of antifreeze and water. However, many repair shops only flush the radiator and add new antifreeze. This won't help your car and can hurt it.

To protect yourself and your car, ask the mechanic about his normal procedure for flushing your cooling system. If he's only planning on draining the radiator, take your car somewhere else or make it perfectly clear to him that you want the engine block flushed too and the entire system back flushed. Back flushing means that clean water is used to pump all the coolant out of your cooling system. This process should continue until the water being flushed through the cooling system comes out clear.

Don't let a mechanic give you a run around about how hard it is to back flush a cooling system. Remind him that it's simple enough for the average Joe to do at home with a back-flush kit from an auto supply shop.

Sources:
How to Avoid Getting Mugged by Mr. Badwrench by Sal Fariello, SFT Publishing, Bay Shore, N.Y., 1988
What Auto Mechanics Don't Want You to Know by Mark Eskeldson, Technews Publishing, Fair Oaks, Calif., 1994

How to find a mechanic you can trust

The good news is 80 percent of mechanics are basically honest. The bad news is many of these mechanics are basically incompetent. They prefer to tinker with a vehicle for hours, working by the hit-or-miss method — replacing parts until they find the problem. Not only is this totally inefficient, it's also costly.

However, you can find an honest mechanic who knows what he's doing. All it takes is some shopping around and a little know-how.

First, stay away from shops which regularly offer free inspections or advertise extremely low prices. Chances are slim that you'll find top-notch mechanics there, and your chances of getting ripped off are very good. Most shops offer these specials solely to lure in customers so they can sell them extra repairs.

Such shops often employ poorly qualified mechanics and pay them a small salary. Then, the shop owners pay the mechanics a commission of 10 to 25 percent for every additional part they sell. A mechanic who wants to make enough money to live on will have to sell $50 to $100 of extra repairs to every customer who comes in the shop.

"Flat rate shops" tend to be more trustworthy. Instead of paying mechanics an hourly wage, a flat rate shop pays its mechanics by the number of repairs completed. For example, the mechanic may receive 40 percent of the labor fees charged for a particular repair.

This system encourages mechanics to work fast. The mechanics won't try to sell you additional repairs you don't need, but you may end up with shoddy repair work because the mechanic works too fast. Trust your intuition here. You can find qualified mechanics working in these shops.

If you suspect a shop pays its mechanics at least partially by commission, ask a mechanic or the shop owner. Although most will provide this information willingly, you should definitely search for another shop if they won't.

You can save yourself time by calling and requesting auto shop referrals from your local American Automobile Association (AAA) office. This office will give you the names of AAA approved shops in your area. These shops meet AAA's standards for qualified mechanics, customer service and satisfaction, proper tools and equipment, appearance, and insurance.

Unfortunately, this AAA program is currently available in only 30 states. If you don't have access to a local AAA who provides this service, ask for auto shop and mechanic referrals at a local auto parts store, such as NAPA, which caters specifically to professional mechanics. Of course, you should also check out any shop you're considering with the Better Business Bureau.

Most mechanics trying to keep up with technology take two to three classes a year. Ask to see any licenses or certificates that show the mechanic has completed course work.

One certificate you're likely to see is the Automotive Service Excellence (ASE) certificate. It indicates that a mechanic has passed a written test covering some aspect of automotive repair.

Don't assume that just because a shop displays the ASE symbol, all mechanics there are ASE-certified. Only one mechanic in the shop needs to be certified for a shop to display the ASE symbol. Request an ASE-certified mechanic for any work done on your car other than a lube and oil change.

Don't settle for a mechanic who stresses his years of experience and prides himself on not needing continuing education courses. Years of experience gained working on cars in the 60s and 70s won't be much help to the owner of a computer-controlled 80s or 90s car.

Finally, expect to pay decently for a mechanic with good diagnostic and repair skills. The extra cost will be worth it.

Expect a good shop to charge for diagnostic testing whether it does the repairs or not. Beware of any shop that doesn't. Many professional mechanics will refuse to work on any car until a diagnostic test has clearly indicated a problem which needs repair.

As always, your best protection is a healthy dose of common sense. Don't work with a shop or mechanic who won't explain any necessary repairs in language you can understand. Get a written estimate before the work is started. Let the mechanic know he needs to call you before he makes any repairs other than the ones you've discussed. If a mechanic suggests your car needs major repairs, get a second or even a third opinion before you authorize any work.

Source:
What Auto Mechanics Don't Want You to Know by Mark Eskeldson, Technews Publishing, Fair Oaks, Calif., 1994

How to save $200 a year on gas mileage

► Have tuneups done as often as your owner's manual recommends. Although many new cars no longer require traditional tuneups, a well-tuned older car uses 9 percent less gasoline than a poorly tuned car.

▶ Keep tires properly inflated. This will extend the life of the tires and conserve gas. You should also have your tires balanced and rotated every 6,000–8,000 miles.

▶ Choose radial, steel-belted tires over other types. They'll improve your gas mileage.

If you'd like to do the world a good turn while you're saving money on your car, consider buying your tires from tire companies that recycle.

▶ Keep your car's fuel filters clean. Clogged filters waste gas.

▶ Avoid letting your car idle unnecessarily. Idling becomes inefficient after about a minute. You'll save more gas by turning off your engine, then cranking the car again when you're ready to go.

▶ Lighten up. Don't haul around any more heavy things in your car than you really need. An extra 100 pounds piled into your car will decrease your fuel efficiency by over 1 percent.

▶ Track your gas mileage. With an up-to-date gas log, you'll quickly notice a loss of gas mileage and be able to get it fixed promptly.

Source:
50 Simple Things You Can Do to Save the Earth, Earthworks Press, Berkeley, Calif., 1989

How to diagnose and handle the most common car problems

Car problems are never convenient, but you'll have more control if you can tell your mechanic what you think is wrong with the car instead of putting yourself at his mercy by having him tell you.

Here are some of the most common symptoms of a sick car and the most probable cause of the problem:

Engine will barely turn over or won't start at all. *Problem:* Run-down battery or its connecting wires are loose, broken, or corroded.

Solution 1: Check battery terminal posts and battery cables for corrosion. Carefully scrape off any corrosion with something sharp, such as a pocketknife, then reconnect cables. Caution: Make sure you connect cables back to their proper posts. Afterwards, you can spray the battery posts with lacquer to protect the connections from moisture and slow future corrosion.

Solution 2: If your battery has run down because of a short in your electrical system or because you left your lights on all day, you can usually charge up the battery, and it will work as well as ever. Be sure to get any shorts fixed so your battery won't run down again. If you don't have a short or haven't left your lights on, you probably need a new battery.

Caution: If you jump-start your car, be sure to connect positive post to positive post and negative post to negative post. Otherwise, you can seriously damage your electrical system or cause the battery to explode. Batteries emit hydrogen gas when they're being charged, so be very careful about letting sparks or flame near the battery If they do, they may also cause an explosion.

For your protection, wear safety goggles (regular glasses will help if you have nothing else) when working with batteries.

Solution 3: If your dome light is still bright when you turn the key, then your problem is probably a solenoid switch or a faulty starter. See a mechanic.

Hissing noise. Steam coming from underneath hood. *Problem:* Your motor has overheated, or you have a leak in your cooling system. *Solution:* For an overheated engine, turn on the heater. If you can't stand the heat, put car in neutral and race the engine a little. If you think you can make it to a gas station without hurting your engine, do so. Otherwise, pull over at the first safe stopping place and let your car cool down. If you can get to a gas station and obtain access to a hose, running cold water over the radiator may cool it down.

Never remove a radiator cap when a car is hot unless you have plenty of experience working with cars. Even then, you run the risk of burning yourself severely.

If you see water or steam escaping from a leaky hose, wrap the leaky hose with electrical tape until you can get it replaced.

Burning smell. *Problem:* Electrical wires may be burning through their plastic coverings. You may have left your hand brake on, or your car tires may be badly out of alignment. *Solution:* Check to make sure hand brake is not on. If it is not, stop and try to locate the source of the smell. Have any hot wires replaced immediately.

Smell or see smoke. *Problem:* Your engine may be smoking due to excessive oil consumption. This is not dangerous. If smoke is coming from the engine compartment, you may have a gas, oil, or electrical fire. *Solution:* Stop the car, get out immediately, and move at least 50 feet away. Don't go anywhere near the car again unless you're sure that any fire is completely out. If your engine is only burning excessive oil, you'll either have to have your engine rebuilt or buy a new car. If you continue to run the car the way it is, it will eventually break down.

Thumping noises. Car bumps up and down. *Problem:* Flat or blown-out tire. *Solution:* Slowly ease the car onto a flat spot off the road where the tire can be easily changed. For safety, place blocks of wood or large rocks under the front and back of the tire diagonally across from the flat. Don't continue to drive on a flat tire. You'll ruin your tire and may damage your wheel rim. If you don't have a flat, a wheel may be out of balance. Have your tires balanced. It will halt the thumping and bumping and add significantly to your tires' lives.

Shrieking or whining sound. *Problem:* You may have a fan belt slipping. *Solution:* See a mechanic unless you know how to fix slipping belts yourself.

Growling or bubbling sound. *Problem:* You may be low on power steering fluid. *Solution:* Check levels and add extra fluid if necessary.

Grinding noise occurs when gears are shifted. *Problem:* Your transmission is probably dying. *Solution:* If you can drive your car without it making a really awful noise, put it in second gear and drive to your repair shop.

Grinding noises. Steering wheel shakes slightly, especially when you brake. *Problem:* You may have problems with your ball bearings. *Solution:* Discuss your suspicions with a mechanic.

Clutch clatters when you start off. *Problem:* Unless your clutch is actually slipping, you don't have a problem. *Solution:* Get a slipping clutch repaired immediately. It makes a car dangerous to drive.

Break pedal slides slowly to the floor when you press it. *Problem:* It's probably a defective master cylinder in your brake system. New cars have dual master cylinders so that if your brakes give out, they'll only go out in the front or the back, and you probably won't lose all your braking power like you can in a older car. *Solution:* Get the faulty cylinder fixed as soon as possible because it's dangerous to drive with defective brakes. If you're in a pinch and you have to drive somewhere, make sure the car is full of brake fluid. Pump the pedal to brake. Downshift to slow down.

Brakes don't work at all. *Problem:* A bad leak has probably caused your hydraulic brake system to fail completely. *Solution:* Shift into the lowest possible gear to slow the car down. Use the emergency brake, but be aware that it may cause you to jerk or swerve. If you show no signs of stopping, run into a hedge or up onto a curb. Just somehow stop before you hurt yourself or someone else. Get your car fixed as soon as you get it stopped.

Car hesitates when you put it in gear. *Problem:* Automatic transmission fluid may be low. *Solution:* Check automatic transmission fluid levels and add extra if needed. If that doesn't solve the problem, have transmission fluid and filter changed. If that doesn't work, you may need a new transmission.

Car pulls to left or right. *Problem:* Tires are out of alignment. *Solution:* Have wheels aligned as soon as possible. If car pulls hard when you put on brakes, have brakes checked immediately. You may have a worn brake pad, shoe, drum, or disc. Have brakes checked immediately. This is a dangerous situation.

Clunking sound when you shift from reverse to forward in a rear wheel drive vehicle. *Problem:* You could have a worn universal joint. *Solution:* See a mechanic immediately. If your universal joint breaks, your drive shaft can fall down, stopping you flat in the road. Rarely, a drive shaft that drops off suddenly can cause a moving car to flip.

Sources:
Interview with Jerry Estes, antique car collector with 44 years experience repairing cars
Living Cheaply With Style by Ernest Callenbach, Ronin Publishing, Berkeley, Calif., 1993

Car maintenance timetable

A well-maintained car is a reliable car. Follow the maintenance timetable below to keep your car running well and save yourself the time and trouble of an unexpected car breakdown.

Every week:

▶ Check fluid levels of your oil, brakes, power steering, transmission, windshield washer fluid, and battery water if you have a battery that requires regular maintenance. If your battery is maintenance-free, simply check the battery electrolyte indicator.

▶ Check tire pressure of all tires, including your spare.

▶ Test headlights, back-up lights, taillights, and turn signals to make sure no bulbs need replacing.

Once a month:

▶ Test brakes by taking your car out for a drive. Accelerate to 25 miles per hour, then apply brakes. Note if car pulls to one side or the other. Listen for unusual noises.

▶ Inspect tire treads. If tread-wear indicator bars are visible or tread depth is 1/16th of an inch or less, replace the tire.

▶ Check battery connection terminals for corrosion. If corrosion is evident, use a sharp object, such as a screwdriver or pocketknife, to scrape connections clean. Spray battery posts with lacquer to help prevent future corrosion. Also, check battery cables for corrosion or cracks and to make sure you have a tight connection.

▶ Check shocks by pushing down on the front bumper, then the back bumper. If the car bounces more than twice when you push down, it's time to have your shock absorbers replaced.

▶ Examine your exhaust system, including the tail pipe, for holes or rust.

▶ Look at hoses to make sure no hose has leaks or shows signs of excessive wear. Make sure hose connections are tight. Replace broken or cracked hoses.

▶ Inspect belts and replace any that are frayed, loose, or very shiny. Make sure belts are tightened to the proper tension.

Every six months:

▶ Have tires rotated.

▶ Replace windshield wipers.

Once a year:

▶ Replace air filter.

▶ Take your car in for a tuneup if you've driven your car enough miles to warrant one. Check your owner's manual for details.

▶ Get your tires' alignment and balance checked.

▶ Have steering checked and adjusted if necessary.

▶ Take your brakes in for a complete examination.

▶ Get your alternator, voltage regulator, and battery tested to be sure they are all working properly.

▶ Have your catalytic converter, exhaust pipes, and muffler checked for corrosion and loose connections.

▶ Get chassis examined for bent, cracked, or loose parts.

Once every two years:

▶ If your radiator coolant looks discolored, have your system flushed, and the discolored coolant replaced with new.

Source:
Your Quick and Easy Car Care and Safe Driving Handbook by Laura Flynn McCarthy, Doubleday, New York, 1988

Car engine health hazard

During snowy or icy weather, be sure you remove any ice or snow packed around or in your exhaust pipe before you start your car engine. Otherwise, you may risk carbon monoxide poisoning, which can be fatal.

Recently, the *Morbidity and Mortality Weekly Record* reported 24 cases of carbon monoxide poisoning, two of which were fatal. People who were injured or died had turned on the engine and sat in the car waiting for it to warm up without bothering to remove snow from around the exhaust pipe.

A similar situation may occur if you back your car into a mound of dirt and plug your exhaust pipe with soil. If for any reason you suspect that your exhaust pipe may be clogged, check to be sure it's clear before you start the engine.

Source:
British Medical Journal (312,7032:718)

Cheap and easy car cleaning

Is your car starting to show its age? Before you dash off to the auto supply store to pick up the latest in cleaning supplies, try a few materials you probably have lying around the house.

▶ Rub your dingy blackwall tires with a thin coat of brake fluid. When wiped dry, they'll look as good as new.

▶ Foaming bathroom cleaner, oven cleaner or Shout laundry stain remover will clean whitewalls. Just leave the cleaners on for 15 seconds, then hose off.

▶ You can use household detergent to wash the car itself. If it's a sunny day, rinse each section immediately to avoid streaking.

▶ Take care of fly spots with ammonia and water.

▶ Tar vanishes with a dab of WD-40.

▶ A mixture of soapy water and kerosene will get rid of salt.

▶ Cola makes grease on windows and windshields disappear.

▶ An empty spray bottle filled with alcohol will save you a lot of time scrubbing ice off of your windshield in the winter. (Alcohol breaks up the frost, but doesn't freeze, making it easy to wipe off.)

▶ And if you've been collecting dead insects on your windshield or radiator, a quart of water mixed with 1/2 cup of baking soda will clean it up in a hurry.

Source:
Mary Ellen's Clean House! by Mary Ellen Pinkham and Dale Burg, Crown Publishers, New York, 1993

Are you responsible for what your kid does behind the wheel?

Already a nervous wreck every time your teen takes the car out on a date?

Well, here's something else to add to your worry list: You are legally responsible for what your kid does while driving.

Few parents realize it, but they can be stuck with lawsuits if their teens back over mailboxes or injure someone in a wreck.

"Virtually every state has what is known as the family car doctrine," says attorney Edward Greenblatt. "It says that if your child is a minor living at home and he or she drives down the street, with or without a license, in your car, you are liable for automobile-related injuries and damages to property."

Source:
Interview with Edward Greenblatt, attorney-at-law, Lipshutz, Greenblatt, and King, Atlanta

INSIDERS GUIDE TO HIGHER EDUCATION

Why attend college

Is there any reason to go to college? Does it ensure financial security? What about plumbers who make $100 an hour?

Only about one-fifth of all American families are headed by college graduates but those families earn one-third of all U.S. income and half of the disposable income. Disposable income is the money left over after paying basic expenses.

Source:
Real Life, Real Answers by Dana Shilling with the staff of John Hancock Financial Services, Arbor House William Morrow, New York, 1988

Biggest mistakes parents make in financing college

The biggest mistake parents make is being swayed by the whims of government financial aid. A family I talked to recently had quit claiming their child on their income tax three years ago. Based on government financial aid rules, they thought their daughter could get independent status and receive a block of financial aid.

The year before the daughter enrolled in college, the feds changed all the rules, making it very difficult for a 17-year old living at home to be declared independent. That family lost everything — the benefit of claiming an income deduction for three years and the benefit of financial aid.

Government financial aid rules change annually. It depends on who has control of Congress at a given time. To make decisions on government whims is like playing the stock market based on tips. Long-range financial planning will outweigh playing whims like that any day.

The second mistake families make is not saving a penny. You ought to save for your kids' education even if you think they will get scholarships.

The third biggest mistake is letting your child be overburdened while he's in school. I see kids now who think they have to juggle three jobs and go to school. Their grades suffer, and even more than that, they are already under the stress of being in the work force.

College work-study jobs are a good idea, but kids who try to handle both regular work and school are usually overburdened.

Source:
Interview with Dennis Matthews, associate dean of enrollment, Oglethorpe University, Atlanta

How to earn a free education for your kids

You can add a nice, fat bonus to your paycheck by working for a university. Your kids get to go to college for free.

And they don't have to go to the school you work for. A tuition exchange program gives your children a list of schools they can attend without paying tuition.

You don't have to be a college professor to work for a university, either. Colleges employ many administrative assistants, just like large corporations.

You may not make as much money working for a school as you do working for a big company, but sending your kids to college tuition-free is a big benefit. With today's tuition rates, that could be worth $20 or $30 thousand a year, per child.

Questions to ask in a job interview:

Which schools besides this one can my child attend tuition-free?

How long do I need to work here before I am eligible for that benefit? (Five years is fairly common.)

Source:
Interview with Dennis Matthews, associate dean of enrollment, Oglethorpe University, Atlanta

One lousy way to save for college

Overheard at busy Atlanta lunch counter: "We'll be using our 401k money to send our child to college. We're saving for retirement in other ways."

Don't make the mistake this Georgia businesswoman is making. First of all, if she pulls her money out of her 401k before she reaches retirement, she'll suffer severe withdrawal symptoms. She'll lose around 40 percent of what she's invested. Plus, she won't even see the portion her employer has been matching over the years.

The only reason to look at your 401k when you need to send your child to college is to take out a loan against it. And that's not a good idea either.

▶ Only about 50 percent of 401k plans even allow you to take out a loan against your money.

▶ You must pay back the loan within five years.

▶ You do pay interest on the loan.

▶ If you leave your job, you will probably have to pay back your loan in full immediately. Taking out a loan when your job situation isn't extremely stable is a very bad idea.

Source:
Interview with Tim Anders, CPA, comptroller, and 401k plan manager, direct marketing firm, Peachtree City, Ga.

When you can't pay full tuition

If that full four-year scholarship just didn't come through, you do have some money-saving alternatives to attending a four-year college full-time.

▶ Attend a local community college for two years and then transfer to a university. A community college costs less, and you can live at home.

- ▶ Get a full-time day job (best, one that provides employee educational assistance) and go to school at night.
- ▶ Get a part-time job and attend school. Some jobs might lead to career opportunities after graduation.
- ▶ Attend a nearby four-year state university and live at home.

Source:
Lifetime Financial Planner: Straight Talk About Your Money Decisions by William E. Donoghue with Dana Shilling, Harper & Row, New York, 1987

Student loans aren't free money

The costs of borrowing to earn your diploma can add up quickly. It's not unusual to get a $50,000 bill with your degree these days. And if you don't have a job lined up after school, that can make your postgraduate years a lot more stressful than those midterms.

If your loans came from several different institutions, consolidation is always an option, but shouldn't be your first choice. While you will only have to write one check per month, you'll also extend the payment time. Stretching a loan is almost always a bad idea, since you'll only pay more in interest.

Not all consolidation is bad. If you're having trouble making ends meet or if you're about to borrow money at a higher interest rate, consolidation is worth thinking about. Also, if the bank's rate for a consolidated loan is better than what you pay on your credit card, it's not a bad idea to move that debt over.

If your student loans are subsidized by the government, the news is mixed. On the plus side, the interest rates on these are often lower than what most commercial banks charge — sometimes by as much as 3 percent. However, if you're forced to file for bankruptcy, government-backed loans generally cannot be erased. Other loans can be.

Source:
Life After Debt by Bob Hammond, Career Press, Franklin Lakes, N.J., 1995

5 steps to choosing the right college

- ▶ Find a good match for you. You'll find plenty of college guidebooks that tell you to look for colleges with money or with great book series or with writing programs or with graduate placement programs ... but these things may not be important to you.
- ▶ Sit down and come up with a list of what's important to you. If a school isn't a good match, you're going to transfer ... and that will be unpleasant. You hate to see people go to a school because it's the place their Mom, Dad, or high school counselor wants them to go. If the school is a reach for you academically, for instance, you'll probably become unhappy.
- ▶ Take everything in print you get from a college with a grain of salt. Print materials are advertisements. It's a very competitive market for colleges and universities. If you are in charge of marketing an institution, you're going to put all your positives up front.

▶ Visit the campus on a nonvisitation day. On visitation days, the campus looks as good as possible. Instead, make an appointment 10 days ahead for a regular school day. Stay in the dorm overnight, go to classes, see the campus when the garbage cans aren't empty and everything isn't specially painted and swept. You want to be able to base your decision on what life is really like at the college.

▶ Use college fairs when you're a freshman or a sophomore in high school, not when you're a senior. College fairs are meant to introduce you to a list of colleges you can then begin to investigate.

Don't go to a college you've never visited, particularly if you're going to make a $20 thousand investment. There's nothing fun about being unhappy your first semester at a school. There are enough pressures already.

Source:
Interview with Dennis Matthews, associate dean of enrollment, Oglethorpe University, Atlanta

Going back to school

Going to college when you are older than most of the other students can be intimidating. But it doesn't have to be.

If you're planning on taking classes for the first time in a long time, talk to other people who have gone through the experience. You will be surprised to find out how many people finished college later in life. Their experiences and wisdom will be very helpful.

The biggest obstacle you will probably face in returning to school is the balancing act it requires. Because you have more responsibilities, like working and family, than the traditional college student, you will have to manage your time more wisely. Make sure the school you choose offers classes at times convenient for you.

If you are concerned about feeling out of place, attend a university with a high average student age. These universities are more willing to work with older students and may even offer programs to help older students adjust.

Source:
Interview with Robert Beard, assistant director of admissions, Georgia State University, Atlanta

The safest and most dangerous college towns

College admission counselors are required to tell you the campus crime statistics if you ask for them. The problem is, those numbers don't mean much unless you plan on spending your next four years locked behind the campus walls.

To know how much danger you'll really face when you go to a college, you need to know how safe the area surrounding the school is. Two college security experts have come up with a list of safe and dangerous college towns using the FBI's Crime by County Report. The crimes include murder, rape, robbery, aggravated assault, burglary, larceny, and motor vehicle theft.

New York City, however, reports only one crime figure for all five city boroughs. Some neighborhoods in New York are very safe compared with other crime-ridden neighborhoods.

If you'd like to go to a school in a big city, the experts advise you to call the police precinct nearest the school and ask an officer about the safety of the surrounding neighborhoods. Your college could be in a safe part of a high-crime town.

Schools in 10 safest college towns
University of Northern Iowa (Cedar Falls)
James Madison University (Harrisonburg, Va.)
University of Iowa (Iowa City)
Northwest Missouri State University (Maryville)
Indiana University of Pennsylvania (Indiana, Penn.)
University of Tennessee: Martin
Nicholls State University (Thibodaux, Louisiana)
Michigan Technological University (Houghton)
SUNY College at Oneonta (New York)
Slippery Rock University of Pennsylvania

Schools in 10 most dangerous towns
Saint Louis University (Missouri)
Southeastern Louisiana University (Hammond)
Georgia Institute of Technology (Atlanta)
Georgia State University (Atlanta)
University of South Alabama (Mobile)
Louisiana State University and Agricultural & Mechanical College (Baton Rouge)
Southern University and Agricultural & Mechanical College (Baton Rouge, La.)
University of Baltimore (Maryland)
Johns Hopkins University (Baltimore, Md.)
Loyola College (Baltimore, Md.)

The University of Iowa reports a campus crime rate of 0.61 but is in a college town with a crime rate of 1.65. Compare those numbers with Georgia State University, which reports a campus crime rate of 0.09 but is in a college town with a crime rate of 13.37. Look beyond the numbers and interview the local police for the true picture of crime and police protection at your school.

Source:
Crime at College: The Student Guide to Personal Safety by Curtis Ostrander and Joseph Schwartz, New Strategist Publications, Ithaca, N.Y., 1994

How to prepare for law school

To succeed in law school, you'll need to build the mind of a lawyer. Here's the best way to do it:

▶ Learn to read critically (literature courses will help).
▶ Take courses which teach you to write and speak clearly and forcefully.

▶ Become a creative thinker who can bring original solutions to problems of law.

▶ Boost your brain power with logic and mathematics courses.

▶ Acquire a general understanding of economics, ethics, and social sciences. Courses in cultural studies will help you understand human institutions and values on which our law is built.

Source:
Beyond the Ivy Wall: 10 Essential Steps to Graduate School Admission by Howard Greene and Robert Minton, Little, Brown, and Company, Boston, 1989

Scoring points with your professor

Professors, believe it or not, are human. Whether a professor likes you or not can make a difference at grade time. To get on a teacher's good side:

▶ Show up for class — on time.

▶ Appear interested in the subject. Ask an occasional question.

▶ Don't yawn, read the newspaper, write letters to friends, or laugh during class, unless the professor makes a joke, of course.

Source:
Peterson's College 101: Making the Most of Your Freshman Year by Ronald T. Farrar, Peterson's Guides, Princeton, N.J., 1988

Taking good lecture notes

Attending class is a waste of your time and money if you don't learn anything from your professor's lecture. A sure way to improve how much you absorb and remember from a lecture is to take good notes. Here's how:

▶ Do the assigned reading ahead of time. That way you'll have a basic idea of the subject, and your notes will make more sense.

▶ Get to class on time. A professor usually outlines the lecture — or tells you what the class will be about — in the beginning of the class. The teacher may ask whether there were any questions from the reading at the start of class, too.

▶ The professor may sum up at the end of the class. Perk up your wandering attention.

▶ Listen for organizational clues. For instance, the professor may say, "And, a third consequence of this action was ...." Write that down!

▶ Don't write too much. Listen well and write what is important.

▶ Understand the terminology. Each subject has its own jargon. If you don't understand a word, write it down and ask about it after class. Chances are that word will come up again.

▶ Review the notes after class when they're fresh in your memory. If your writing is hard to read, now is the time to make it more legible.

Source:
Peterson's College 101: Making the Most of Your Freshman Year by Ronald T. Farrar, Peterson's Guides, Princeton, N. J., 1988

COMPUTER KNOW-HOW

Buying computer software

Before purchasing the newest upgrade for a program on your computer, watch and wait a few months. Let other eager beavers ferret out any bugs in the program. What they find will give you some idea of whether or not you want the new version or just prefer to stick with your old one.

Source:
The Wall Street Journal (Feb. 1, 1996, B1)

Computer buys

Small computer dealers will tell you secretly that they can't beat the prices of the big, discount office supply stores or computer superstores. In a pinch, small dealers will even shop retail at the discount stores.

Source:
Interview with small computer dealer, Peachtree City, Ga.

Put your money in the monitor

When you're buying a computer to run Windows, your best bet is to put your money in the monitor.

Of course, you need a good computer to go with your monitor so you must first decide what speed computer you want. Make sure it has at least eight megabytes of memory and at least a 340-megabyte hard drive. Shop around to find the best deal.

Now, put the rest of your effort and money into selecting the best monitor you can afford. The reason is simple. There isn't a lot of difference among computers, but there can be a big difference in monitors. And since you're going to spend most of your time at the computer staring at the monitor, select one that will be comfortable to use.

If your computer runs a graphic-user interface such as Windows, it will adjust how much data it can display on the screen according to the size of your monitor. With a big-screen monitor, you can see your entire spreadsheet simultaneously, instead of having to scroll back and forth between sections. You can also open two programs at once and work in them side by side. Common computer screen sizes these days range from 14 to 17 inches.

When choosing your new monitor, trust your eyes to tell you how well a monitor will work for you instead of relying on such specifications as "dot-pitch size" or "scan rate."

Be sure you shop around at several different stores and look at as many monitors as possible. Look for a sharp image and a low- or no-glare screen.

Just keep in mind that any monitor that looks less than perfect in a store's ideal conditions will look even worse when you get it home.

Unless you plan to be producing a lot of artwork on your computer, you can save some money by avoiding luxury features such as precise color calibration. Generally, a mid-priced unit that is easy on your eyes is your best bet.

Once you get your new monitor home, be sure you configure it properly for maximum performance. If you have an Apple system and you bought a Macintosh monitor, you're home-free. Macs automatically configure themselves.

But if you're running Windows on an IBM-compatible computer, you're going to have to match the pixels (the thousands of tiny dots that make up the images on your computer screen) to your monitor size. If you don't set up your display correctly, you'll only get bigger, grainier images.

Generally 640 pixels high by 480 pixels wide works well for a 14-inch monitor; 800-by-600 pixels for a 15-inch monitor and 1024-by-768 pixels for a 17-inch screen. However, the settings will also depend on your eyes and how far away from the monitor you sit.

Source:
Business Week (Oct. 10, 1994)

Making sense of modems

In order to experience any of the on-line world's wonders, from e-mail to Internet, you're going to need a modem.

Modems offer many other conveniences as well. You can access your e-mail at work from the comfort of your easy chair at home; you can transfer files from one computer location to another; you can even use a modem to print a document out at another location.

In addition, most of the modems available today can send and receive faxes. Plus, using a modem to talk to friends and family who live far away can slash soaring phone bills.

A modem makes all this marvelous stuff possible by translating computer data (MOdulating and DEModulating it into a series of high and low tones which accounts for the screech you hear when your modem connects to another modem) into information that can be transmitted over ordinary telephone lines, a system originally designed to carry only voices.

If you recently bought a computer, it probably came with a modem. If you have an older computer model and wish to add a modem, arm yourself with a few facts and decide what you want before you start shopping.

External or internal?

First, decide if you want an external or internal modem. External modems simply sit next to your computer and work outside it. Internal modems work from inside your computer. Both types have advantages and disadvantages.

External pros:
▶ Easy to hook up and troubleshoot.

▶ Has visible indicator lights to tell you when you've connected and to let you know how a transmission is proceeding.

▶ Portable.

▶ Easy to resell.

External cons:

▶ Takes up desk space.

▶ Requires an extra electrical outlet.

▶ Must be connected to one of the serial port connectors on the back of your computer.

Internal pros:

▶ Usually cheaper and faster than external models.

▶ Doesn't take up any desk space.

▶ Doesn't require an extra electrical outlet since it draws its power from the computer itself.

▶ Doesn't use any of the serial port connectors on the back of your computer.

Internal cons:

▶ Can be difficult to install if you aren't familiar with computers.

▶ No visible indicator lights to tell what's going on with the modem.

▶ Usually only available for DOS/Windows machines.

Speeds and standards

Once you've decided external or internal, it's time to consider speed. What concerns you when it comes to speed is how fast the modem will send and receive data. Nowadays, modem speed is measured in *bits per second* (bps). Baud and bps used to be the same, but rapid changes in technology continue to widen the gap between these two terms. Just know that they are not the same, and that bps is what matters to you.

Generally, buy the fastest modem you can afford. Make sure that whatever modem you choose meets industry standards and is compatible with your computer setup. Be sure that the modem you buy says that it is "Hayes AT Command Set" compatible.

Modems that meet standard requirements generally carry a "V" label. A 14.4 bps speed modem should carry the V.32bis designation if the modem meets industry standards. A 28.8 modem that meets industry standards should have the V.34 designation.

In addition, any modem you purchase should have a V.42 error correction and a V.42 bis data compression standards. A modem with a V.42 bis data compression standard will let you transfer data at up to four times its normal word rate. For example, if you had a 28,800 bps modem with V.42 bis data compression standard, you could actually transfer data at a rate of 115,200 bps.

Don't let anyone talk you into buying a modem designed as V.FC or V.Fast. These speed standards are not the same as regular industry standards. V.FC and V.Fast were standards set by manufacturers who were in a hurry to get their products to market before other regular industry standards were approved.

Consider buying a modem that supports upgradable software or ROM (read only memory) chips. When upgrades (such as faster speeds or other improvements) become available, you can simply buy a new ROM chip to replace your old one or download updated software on-line instead of having to buy a completely new modem.

Basically brand names make little difference as long as the modem meets industry standards and comes with a fairly good guarantee. However, the Internet Support Staff at Woods County Telephone in Wisconsin has found that some brands seem to cause significantly fewer problems than other brands. Their recommendations: Hayes, Motorola, or U.S. Robotics.

Be sure to unplug your modem during a lightning storm. They seem to be especially susceptible to damage. However, any type of power surge can damage your modem. If you buy an expensive modem, consider investing in a surge protector that includes two RJ-11 jacks. These protectors are usually called ISOFAX or FAX line protectors.

Sources:
Internet Support Staff, Wood County Telephone, Wisconsin Rapids, Wis.
The Wall Street Journal (Sept. 29, 1994, B1)
University of Chicago Campus Computer Stores, Internet Address: http/www-ccs.uchicago.edu/technotes/Modems.html#glossary

Protect your data

By their nature, computers make information more accessible. Therefore, you have to be doubly careful when dealing with confidential material in electronic form. Keep these security tips in mind whenever you are working with valuable documents.

▶ Don't share your computer password, and don't ask others to share. Choose a password that is at least six characters long. A program designed to crack computer codes can guess a three-letter password in 15 minutes or so. A six-letter password will take a computer-cracking program an average of two years.

Don't choose passwords linked to some aspect of your life, such as family names or birthdays or pets' names. To protect your computer from viruses, don't use a common system password. For example, everyone in the office shouldn't use the same password, such as *secret* or even the word *password*. Some viruses are programmed to try commonly used passwords to break into a computer system.

Change your password once a month. This will reduce the risk of someone guessing your password. Just make sure you remember what you've changed it to!

Don't keep a written copy of your password in your office. If you have to keep a copy there, at least don't keep it near the computer.

▶ Guard important dial-in numbers as carefully as you do your password.

▶ Be careful when selecting names for sensitive files. If you don't want anyone to look at your budget report, it's best to avoid naming this file anything that relates to money or budgeting.

▶ Don't store confidential data on your hard drive. Keep this information on disk instead. Make an extra copy of this information to store on a back-up disk if necessary. If you have huge amounts of confidential information you need to store, consider purchasing a removable hard drive. At the end of the day, you can simply remove the hard drive and lock it away safely, which makes it impossible for anyone to access your important data. However, you must be consistent about removing the hard disk and locking it up. Otherwise, this security feature is not worth the money.

▶ Be very careful about storing sensitive information on a laptop or note-book computer. Theft of these types of computers is on the rise. Since a laptop or notebook is often linked to a company's mainframe computer, someone could use one of these computers to download vital information. Don't leave your laptop alone and visible, such as in a hotel room or on an airplane. Either store the laptop in another locked bag or carry it with you at all times.

▶ Log off your terminal when you leave the office for any length of time. Leaving your computer unattended is like leaving the ignition keys in your car.

▶ Lock your office door whenever you leave. This will eliminate temptation.

▶ Back up your data frequently. Save information weekly or even daily.

▶ Keep your diskettes locked up and carry the key with you.

▶ Stay with the printer while printing. Destroy all bad copies of confidential printouts.

▶ Don't bring your own software to work. You might transmit a virus to your company's system. You should also be very careful about installing soft-ware on your computer that you have downloaded from a network.

Consider installing a virus detection program on your computer. This spe-cialized software will help you detect a virus before it has time to do any harm. You can also help prevent a virus by using a special utility program which designates .EXE and .COM files on your computer as "read only." This will prevent unauthorized access to them.

Source:
Records Quarterly Management (29,1:14)

How to upgrade a computer system safely

If you've got a lot riding on your computer system, such as an entire busi-ness, follow the three-step-upgrade system of Peter Rothschild, who learned the hard way. While upgrading from a vacuum tube IMB to a more modern minicomputer, his IBM died and his new computer informed half his cus-tomers they owed nothing when they really did. That upgrade almost bank-rupted Rothschild.

Now, when Rothschild upgrades, he makes sure he follows three simple rules to protect himself and his business.

1) Upgrade a little at a time. Use your old system to back up your new com-puter until you're sure the new system is bug-free.

2) Only use a programmer who is willing to insure you against loss.

3) Use off-the-shelf software instead of custom-designed. With mass-produced software, you can always call on the manufacturer for help. With custom-designed software, if the designer disappears, you're out of luck.

Source:
Inc (16,10:132)

An overview of on-line services

If you're tired of hearing people talking about on-line this and on-line that while you continue to feel like an on-line outsider, read on to find out how on-line access can save you both time and money.

Basically, being on-line means that one computer in one location is connected to another computer in another location. All you need to achieve special on-line status is a computer, a telephone line, and a modem.

It makes modems simpler if you think of them as a special telephone for the computer. A modem allows one computer to dial up another computer and "talk." (For more tips on modems, see "Making sense of modems" earlier in this chapter.)

On-line services are worth looking into because they offer easy access to information you might not otherwise have handy. Say you wanted to read up on the latest bill Congress was considering. Before on-line services, you would probably have had to drive to your local library to find this information. With an on-line service, however, you can turn on your computer and modem, access your on-line account, type in Congress, and have a large list of information on Congress appear right at your fingertips, including the latest bills under consideration.

You can even find the most up-to-date financial information on stocks, bonds, and mutual funds, as well as full explanations of each of these investment types.

The e-mail (see "The essentials of e-mail" later in this chapter for more information) offered by on-line services also makes it easier to talk to friends and family halfway around the world. Plus, you pay only a fraction of the cost you'd pay for a regular phone call.

At this time, there are five big companies offering on-line services. If you're just itching to get on-line, your best bet is to call and request an information pack from each company. Also, be sure to ask if the company will let you try out their services on a free trial basis. Many will let you use the service for free for at least a couple of hours, which should be enough to help you decide which service you prefer.

Compare services and prices offered, then choose the company that seems to suit you best. Don't forget to cancel any unwanted on-line services you may have signed up with on a free trial basis. Otherwise, once your free hours expire, you may be billed. Below are the names and phone numbers of the five biggest on-line service providers:

▶ America Online — 1-800-827-6364

- ▶ CompuServe — 1-800-848-8199
- ▶ Delphi — 1-800-695-4005
- ▶ GEnie — 1-800-638-9636
- ▶ Prodigy — 1-800-776-3449

Here are a few of the highlights each service has to offer:

America Online offers fun and easy on-line access, but not necessarily great depth. Some of their most popular attractions include countrywide chat forums and transcontinental computer games.

CompuServe probably offers the most in-depth variety of databases, files, forums, and services. *PC Magazine* gave CompuServe its "Editors' Choice" award for business use.

Delphi offers inexpensive access to Internet. (For more information on Internet, see "Insiders' guide to Internet" later in this chapter.) It also lets members create their own forums on whatever subjects they choose. However, Delphi is not as easy to use as some of the other services.

GEnie provides access to a well-rounded selection of business services, including the Dow Jones News/Retrieval Service. It also includes a wide variety of family and hobby forums.

Prodigy provides the best access to sports coverage and bulletin boards. If shopping is your bag, then Prodigy, with its extensive electronic mall, should definitely be part of your game plan. This service is a good choice for people who are new to personal computers.

Sources:
PC Magazine (14,4)
The Practical Guide to Practically Everything, Peter Bernstein and Christopher Ma, editors, Random House, New York, 1995

Insiders' guide to Internet

Although everyone's raving about Internet, you may find it hard to pin down details as to exactly what Internet is and how you can benefit from it. In a nutshell, here's what you need to know.

All about Internet

The Internet is a huge network of computers that links about 20 million people in over 50 countries around the world. Internet started out as a Defense Department project in 1969 to protect valuable information in case of a bomb attack. It has gradually evolved from there. No one person or organization runs the Internet. It is basically run by volunteers. It is not a commercial service like CompuServe or America Online.

You can find information on any topic imaginable on the Internet. Information resources include discussion groups, research databases, electronic mail (e-mail), and software for your computer.

Internet contains more information than you could ever need or use. Unfortunately, information on the Net is not always easy to access because it is not organized according to any master plan. Information resources come and go.

One day an information source may be as close as your fingertips. The next day it may be as scarce as daffodils in a desert because the people who provided that information took a leave of absence.

However, because so many resources are available on Internet and because newer and better search methods become available to Net users every day, Internet is a service well worth exploring.

How to get connected

You need four things to access information on Internet: a computer, a communications software package, a modem, and a telephone line.

You'll find surfing the Internet a much more satisfactory experience if you buy the most powerful computer you can afford.

A very basic communications software package usually comes with your computer. You can download one more suited to your needs once you get on-line and find another software package you prefer. Some of this software is free (freeware) or available for a small fee (shareware).

Your best bet when it comes to buying modems is to buy the fastest one you can afford that is compatible with your computer system. See "Making sense of modems" earlier in this chapter for more suggestions on purchasing a modem.

If you already have a telephone connection, you're all set. There's no need to pay for another line unless you want to talk on the phone at the same time you're on-line. In any case, it would be wise to wait on ordering another line until you've surfed the Net a few times and determined what you really want.

Once you have all those essentials in place, you're ready to search out a service that gives you access to Internet. You can hook up through commercial on-line service providers, such as CompuServe or America Online. This is a good option for on-line beginners.

However, if you have a little on-line experience and you're not interested in the other services commercial on-line providers offer, you'll probably be better off going with an Internet service provider (ISP). You can get a list of Internet service providers and other helpful startup information by calling the InterNIC at 1-800-862-0677.

Sources:
Beginners' Guide to Legal Information on the Internet by Valerie Footz, Librarian, Access to Justice Network, Edmonton, Alberta
Business Week (March 28, 1994)
ET's Help Desk. Internet address: http://www.televar.com/~straalsu/helpdesk.html
Internet Starter Kit: Everything You Need to Get On the Internet by Adam C. Engst, Hayden Books, Indianapolis, 1993
The Whole Internet User's Guide and Catalog by Ed Krol, O'Reilly & Associates, Sebastopol, Calif., 1992

The essentials of e-mail

Electronic mail (e-mail) combines the convenience of a quick phone call with the cost savings of sending a letter. In fact, e-mail is often cheaper than regular mail.

Besides banishing the frustrating game of phone tag by letting you send and respond to messages at your convenience, e-mail will also allow you to quickly send large amounts of information to people all over the world, saving yourself the time and expense of tons of phone calls.

Best of all, you don't have to be a technowizard to enjoy the advantages of e-mail. All you need to get started is a computer, a modem and a communications program to run your modem, a phone line, and an e-mail program. Some modem communications software and e-mail programs are combined.

One of the most popular e-mail programs today is *Eudora*, a freeware program (which means you can download it from on-line for free). It can be used with either a Macintosh computer or an IBM-compatible computer.

E-mail addresses provide all the information computers need to send information from one user to another user anywhere in the world. An e-mail address consists of two basic parts: your log-in name (whatever name you use on-line) and your domain (the location of your computer or your Internet service provider or your commercial provider).

The two sections are connected by the @ symbol. An example would be sroe@mindspring.com. The first part, sroe, is the person's log-in name. The part following the @ symbol is the domain, or location, of the person.

Using most e-mail programs is easy. When you're ready to send a message, you'll need to fill in the following information.

To: Place the e-mail address of the person you are sending mail to here.

From: Place your e-mail address here. Many e-mail programs fill this in for you automatically.

Subject: Briefly describe what your e-mail message concerns. To be polite and politically correct, you should always provide this information. It helps e-mail recipients prioritize their mail.

Cc: In this field, put any e-mail addresses of people to whom you would like to send copies of your message. Cc stands for carbon copy.

Bcc: Use this field when you'd like to send a copy of your message to someone, but you don't want the other recipients to know about it. Bcc stands for blind carbon copy.

Attachments: List any documents here that you want to send along with your message. Then choose the Attach Document command in your e-mail program.

Now you're ready to type your message in the big blank box below all this stuff. Once you're finished, just hit the Send button and your e-mail is on its way.

Sources:
The AIM Lab, e-mail address: aimlab@uiuc.edu
User's Documentation, MindSpring Enterprises, Atlanta

E-mail etiquette

▶ Remember that e-mail is not as private as a regular letter. If you're dealing in top-secret stuff, you may want to use some other medium besides e-mail to deliver your message.

▶ Make the subject clear. If you're responding to a previous e-mail, indicate this briefly in the subject field with a RE: at the beginning of your subject message. Example: RE: The meeting yesterday.

▶ Express yourself clearly. The person who reads your e-mail is not going to have the benefit of seeing your expression as you wrote. This makes it somewhat sticky to try and transmit humor and sarcasm on-line. It can easily be interpreted incorrectly. Check your letter for clarity and correct spelling and grammar before you send it.

▶ Be careful about sending emotionally charged e-mail. Once you send an angry or hateful letter to someone, it's too late to retrieve it.

▶ Don't type in all CAPS. It's considered rude because most on-line users interpret all CAPS as shouting.

▶ Keep paragraphs short and limit lines of text to 70 characters or less. If you let your lines run longer, they may appear as gibberish to the e-mail recipient.

Sources:
The AIM Lab, e-mail address: aimlab@uiuc.edu
User's Documentation, MindSpring Enterprises, Atlanta

Con artists on-line

While opportunities abound for you to enrich your life through Internet and other on-line services, you have to keep an eye out for cyberspace scam artists who hope to somehow separate you and your money.

Although many on-line providers take steps to ensure that you'll be protected from on-line scams, there are times when criminals are able to outsmart them. However, you can easily protect yourself if you learn how to recognize and respond to on-line risks.

In general, you should be wary of an on-line user who:

▶ Lists an anonymous-looking address. You should be suspicious if you see an address like this: 1234@amon.penet.fi.

▶ Has difficult-to-check references, such as "seen on the Oprah Winfrey show." If you can't verify that he actually was on the Oprah Winfrey show and that he is who he claims he is, avoid him.

▶ Talks too much about money.

▶ Wants you to part with your money or your personal password.

▶ Says, "This is not a scam."

▶ Asks lots of questions (so many you become suspicious).

▶ Uses lots of capital letters.

To protect yourself:

▶ Remember that everything you read on-line is not necessarily true.

▶ Be suspicious of offers that seem too good to be true. They probably are. Watch for catch phrases like "quick and easy," "make money fast in your spare time," "high returns and low risk," "easy cash," "big bucks," and "hot."

▶ Be wary of exaggerated profit claims or claims of inside information. Profits claims are often overstated and supposed inside information is usually worthless.

If you have any doubt, or even if you don't, check out any individual or service you don't personally know before you part with any of your money.

Some common scams of cyberschemers

▶ The "chain letter" scam: Just like their traditional, "chain mail" counterparts, the sender of the letter promises fame, fortune, and the fulfillment of dreams if only you'll send along a small amount of money. In cyberspace, the con artist may post a bulletin board message with the same promises. Certainly you won't miss the money — cons usually ask for no more than $10 — but if you do respond, your name and address will be added to a list that marks you as a potentially easy target for other schemers.

▶ The "good advice" scam: The con artist using this scam poses as a financial wizard. Victims are lured by messages that promise stock options and investment opportunities. Just keep in mind that although a company or individual seems legitimate, you get no guarantees in cyberspace.

If you are attracted by the "good" financial advice offered by a fellow Internet user, get the person to give you the name, address, and phone number for the firm he works for, then check him out before following any suggestions he offers. Keep in mind that sometimes people who are really pushing a certain stock are being paid to do so.

▶ The "cheap stock" scam: The con artist posts a message that promotes a low-priced, infrequently traded stock. Don't fall for promises that this stock will offer a high yield for little money up front. Usually, this offer is completely bogus, but is worded in such a way that you may be tempted to make an investment.

If several users do purchase the stock, however, the value is increased. It is then that the con artists will quickly sell all of their previously purchased shares, making a tidy profit. By moving quickly, the con artist makes money before the price of the generally worthless stock falls.

To find out if a seller is a licensed security dealer or whether a stock or security is registered for sale in your state, call the North American Securities Administrators Association at 1-202-737-0900 to get the number of your state's securities agency.

If you do spot what looks like an on-line scam, ignore that tempting offer and report it to your on-line provider or a local chapter of the Better Business Bureau.

Sources:
DollarSense (Jan. 1, 1996)
Newsbytes News Network, (Feb. 21, 1996)
Your Money (16,4:63)

How to cope with a computer crisis

According to the law of averages, if you own a computer, sooner or later it's going to suffer from some sort of complications. Coping with a computer crisis can cause the less technically inclined to develop mental and physical complications of their own. However, a contrary computer doesn't have to cause a health crisis. If you know what to look for, some seemingly unrepairable computer problems are quite easy to fix.

First, make sure the computer is plugged in. This may sound ridiculous, but it's surprising how many electrical cords wriggle themselves right out of their outlets.

If everything appears to be plugged in, unplug everything anyway and plug it in again. The problem could have been that you just weren't getting a good connection. Also, if you use a power strip, make you haven't accidentally turned off the switch with your foot.

Once you've determined that a simple plug-in is not the problem, you should check to see if you have power in the outlet you plug your computer into. Unplug a working lamp from an outlet you know works and plug it into the outlet you use for your computer. If the lamp doesn't work, your problem is probably a blown fuse in the outlet.

If the lamp does work, it's time to check the cable connections between your computer, monitor, printer, and modem. Push on each end of each connection to make sure it's pushed in as far as it can go.

If you still haven't discovered the solution, it's time to get a little wild and actually take the cover off your computer and peek inside. If you're careful, this isn't as crazy as it might sound.

Before you begin, make sure you've unplugged your computer. Now, remove the four or six screws that hold the cover on and set them safely aside. Don't put them where they can fall inside the computer's guts. It can be a real nightmare getting them out.

Once, you've got the top off, look inside for the disk drive (the slot that you pop disks in and out of). Make sure any cables running to the disk drive are plugged firmly in place.

Next, look for green circuit boards. Depending on your style of computer, they will either be lying flat or standing on edge. Gently, push down on the top edge of each board to make sure it's in its proper spot.

Replace the cover and screws. Try your computer. With a little luck, it will work. If today is not your lucky day, pull out your computer warranty or call a local computer repair person. At this point, your computer probably needs professional assistance.

Source:
Fortune (133,7:195)

INSIDE THE WORKPLACE

What you don't know about falls can kill you

Most of us think of construction workers as big, strong, and tough as nails. But the truth is, construction workers are anything but invincible. In fact, although it's not widely talked about, construction work is downright dangerous.

If you work in the construction industry — or know someone who does — here's a frightening but true statistic.

According to the U.S. Occupational Safety and Health Act office, falls are the leading cause of U.S. construction worker fatalities. And falls cause more than 100,000 on-the-job injuries each year.

Want to learn how construction site deaths and accidents can be prevented? Contact your nearest OSHA office through the Department of Labor and request a copy of "Fall Protection in Construction." The 30-page book is free for the asking.

Source:
Workers' Compensation Cost Control (4,7)

Working too many hours? The hidden dangers

It's been a hard eight-hour shift. The thought of going home and putting your feet up in front of the television seems awfully inviting.

Then the bad news comes: Someone has called in sick. Your boss wants you to work a second shift. You grit your teeth and say OK. After all, you could use the overtime pay.

But you may not be doing yourself— or your boss — a favor.

Here's why:

▶ Fatigued workers are more likely to injure themselves on the job.

▶ Research shows that more than three-quarters of all workers are sharpest from 7 a.m. to 9 p.m. So employers who insist on round-the-clock shifts may be paying hefty overtime to workers who can't give their jobs their best shot.

▶ Scientists have discovered that when you're tired— even when you're fighting to keep awake — you can still fall into "microsleep." It may last for just a moment or two, but you can be completely unaware of your surrounding for those few seconds. That spells danger if you are operating machinery or driving a truck.

▶ If a company pushes you to work too hard when you are tired and you have an accident, your boss may be held legally responsible. Likewise, if your employer lets you drive home when you are exhausted and you have a wreck, he could be liable.

What to do when you have to work long hours. Longer than normal hours on the job may sometimes be necessary — but a little planning can make heavy workloads safer:

► If you are working with someone else, divide up tasks. Less monotony will help keep you alert.

► Normally work alone? Scientists have found that isolated workers have more potentially dangerous *microsleep*. So ask your supervisor if you can work near others.

► Does your boss need a good source of temporary fill-in workers? Remind him that retired employees may fill the bill.

► You wouldn't drive drunk. Don't drive exhausted! If you need a nap before hitting the road, find a safe place at work to catch a few winks. It could save your life — or someone else's.

Source:
You and the Law, the National Institute of Business Management (25,2)

Guaranteeing yourself a raise

Simply needing more money will never get you a raise. You've got to plan for it. Work for it. And prepare for it. A little luck doesn't hurt, either.

Before approaching your boss, take a critical look at your own performance for the past year. Have you been doing a fair, good, or exemplary job? If it's not the latter, you need to do some polishing before you make your request. Go overboard with your workload. Do more than asked and volunteer for more. Forget about coffee breaks and be willing to put in some overtime. It's rough work, but if you focus on the reward, it gets easier.

At the same time, try to have more meetings with your supervisor. If you normally get reviewed only once a year, ask his opinion of your performance every month or two. That way, you can correct criticisms and make mental notes of his praises. When it comes time to negotiate, be sure to remind him of the compliments.

Get to know your company's budget process, too. Generally, businesses only give out raises at certain times of the year. If you submit your request too late, all your efforts will have been wasted.

When you finally do sit down with your boss and ask for the raise, come prepared. Be ready to cite examples of how you have saved the company money. If you've launched any successful projects, learn what it would have cost to bring in a consultant to do the same thing. Now is also the time to mention that overtime you've been logging.

Never threaten your boss when negotiating a new salary. If he or she calls your bluff, you could be left unemployed. At the same time, don't walk away empty-handed. If you can't earn more cash, try to negotiate other benefits, like extra vacation or having the company pay any membership fees for professional organizations to which you belong.

Remember, it's not need that gets more money; it's performance.

Sources:
Interview with Len Contardo, assistant director, Alumni Career Services, Georgia Institute of Technology, Atlanta
Interview with John Youngblood, associate director, Emory University Career Center, Atlanta

Keeping home life out of the home office

The biggest distraction when you work at home isn't the television or the refrigerator. It's your family. You may have chosen to "telecommute" to be close to them, but too many interruptions can be professionally fatal.

Draw a line between your professional and home life. Remind your children and spouse that even though you work out of the spare bedroom, you're still working. Set hours for yourself and insist that your family respect them. Also, your office should be called that, not "my desk" or "my work area." Downplaying its importance only opens the door for more interruptions.

If you've got pesky neighbors constantly knocking on your door, answer with a portable phone on your ear. They'll get the hint.

Finally, dress for work. It's hard to think of someone in a sweatshirt and shorts as a businessperson. Just as professional clothes send a message to clients, they send a message to your family — and maybe yourself.

Source:
The Virtual Office Survival Handbook by Alice Bredin, John Wiley & Sons, New York, 1996

Failed business dreams may make yours come true

The failure rate of small businesses is staggering. Unfortunately, many of those failed firms are unable to repay their small business loans, which results in the repossession of their offices, equipment, and furniture.

If you're planning to start your own firm, buying those items at auction can save you hundreds, or even thousands, of dollars — money that will come in handy down the road.

It works like this: Banks repossess the items and put them up for bids. The Small Business Administration (SBA) is standing by and will repurchase the items for either the fair market value or the remaining balance on the loan, whichever is lower. An auction firm, contracted by the SBA, will then resell the items to the highest bidder.

Ads usually run in the Sunday paper. You can also contact the SBA directly and ask to be put on the mailing list. The SBA will alert you to upcoming auctions and give you an idea of what will be available.

SBA auctions are the most frequent of government auctions, held as often as six times per month.

Source:
Interview with John Jones, assistant director for economic development, Small Business Administration, Atlanta District Office, Atlanta

A sure sign you should change jobs

Got the Monday morning blues on a Thursday afternoon? It might be time to think about switching jobs.

Nobody likes his job all the time, but if the little things are getting to you more and more, you're probably burning out. Don't ignore the subtle signals. When your work begins to suffer, your chances of being fired increase.

If you're feeling trapped, avoiding your boss more than usual, or simply going on "autopilot" when discussing important issues, your career is probably at a dead end.

Don't mistake short-term blahs for job dissatisfaction. Everyone has rough spots. But if you're constantly searching for ways to leave early — or worse, nobody notices when you do — it might be best to start looking for a new job before your employer gives you no choice.

Source:
The Wall Street Journal (March, 23, 1994)

When to put off a job switch

Before you quit your job, check the vesting schedule on your 401k. Hanging in there for another couple of months could make a huge difference in your retirement savings.

Just because your employer is matching some of the money you contribute to your 401k doesn't mean you can get all that money when you quit your job. How many years you've been with the company may determine how much you get.

At some companies, you are *fully vested* from day one. That means you can leave your job at any time and get all the money your employer has contributed to your 401k.

Other companies have a *vesting schedule*. Here's an example:

After you work three years, you may be 20 percent vested — you get 20 percent of what your employer has contributed as of your third-year anniversary. After you work four years, you get 40 percent, and after six years, you get 80 percent. At all companies, once you've worked seven years, you are fully vested.

The vesting schedule of your company could make a difference when you want to leave your job. Staying a little longer could be worth your while if it means getting that extra money as a contribution from your employer.

Source:
Interview with Tim Anders, CPA, controller, and 401k plan manager at a direct marketing firm, Peachtree City, Ga.

Dramatic way to get a job interview

It's vitally important to keep your name in a potential employer's mind. But how do you do it? Follow-up calls can be annoying after a point and follow-up letters can easily be set aside and forgotten.

Consider sending a telegram.

No question it's a risky move. You certainly don't want to send a singing telegram, for instance. But a carefully worded telegram listing two or three of your accomplishments or qualifications will capture a manager's attention.

If your credentials aren't impeccable, don't try this. And if the job is in a low-key environment, this probably isn't the best idea. But if the company is looking for a dynamic, aggressive personality, a telegram might clinch the position for you.

Source:
The Complete Job Interview Handbook by John J. Marcus, Harper Perennial, New York, 1985

How to answer the $100,000 questions in an interview

Going up for a big job? Don't sweat it! While every interviewer and every company is different, some questions are simply standard. You should always be prepared to answer the common questions.

Most interviews start on a personal level, as your potential boss gets to know you as an individual. Don't let things get too intimate. Keep your responses tailored to the position.

The meaning of success? "Success" should mean more to you than a house and family although these are important. Mention your career goals as well.

Hobbies? If asked about your hobbies, try to establish common ground with the interviewer. Glance around the office to get an idea of what the person enjoys, taking note of pictures and personal objects. But don't bluff. If your interviewer is a golf enthusiast and you don't know Jack Nicklaus from Jack Nicholson, avoid the subject.

Tell me about yourself. Be on the lookout for open-ended questions, such as "tell me about yourself." They can be a stumbling block if you've only prepared for more detailed questions. This is your best chance to toot your own horn.

Work experience? When the questions begin to focus on your work experience, you begin to tread on dangerous ground. If you've been out of work for a while, be ready to explain it. And never — NEVER — discuss arguments or falling outs with your boss.

If you were fired, be honest. It speaks well of your integrity. Turn the situation around. Mention what you've learned from the incident.

Strengths? When asked about your professional strengths, hone in on those that will matter the most in the position for which you're applying.

Go to an interview loaded with examples of your capability. Stories that show how you were able to foresee difficulties or work under deadline will back up your claims.

Be sure to emphasize any (successful) new systems or procedures you have instituted. It shows your potential as a leader. Make sure you don't take credit for your boss's work, though.

Controversial issues. Stay away from controversial topics. While it is illegal for interviewers to ask how you would feel working for someone of the opposite sex or a homosexual, the questions do arise. Stress that such things don't matter to you. You're only interested in a person's capabilities.

Goals? Have well-defined and realistic goals in mind. At some point, you're bound to be asked where you want to be in five or 10 years. If you stumble, it could hurt your chances. If you only plan to stay a short time at the company, keep it to yourself.

Travel/relocation? If asked how you feel about travel and relocation, be open unless you have personal responsibilities that forbid either option. The interviewer could be gauging your commitment. Later on, you'll have the chance to learn how much travel is involved and how likely it is that you will be moved.

Weaknesses? You will face questions about your weaknesses. Admit to them. Otherwise you come off looking immature and egocentric.

At the same time, don't rattle off a list of your problems. Mentioning just one will usually suffice. And NEVER mention a failing that might affect your ability to do the job.

Some weaknesses can be viewed as strengths, such as working too hard, letting work interfere with your personal life, and impatience at delays.

Mention what you're doing to compensate for your problem. If you show steps you are taking to improve yourself, it makes the failing seem less important.

Source:
The Complete Job Interview Handbook by John J. Marcus, Harper Perennial, New York, 1985

Résumés that work

One of the things people forget about résumés is they're not meant to get you a job. They're meant to get you an interview. That's why it's important that yours stand out from the crowd.

Make sure your résumé is easy to scan. It will only get a few seconds in front of a manager's eyes, so long-winded descriptions of duties will do you no good. Instead, highlight your increasing responsibilities from job to job. Show that you know how to learn quickly. Stress your interpersonal skills, too. How you work with others and help build a team is important, no matter what kind of work you do.

Take a sniper, rather than a shotgun, approach when sending out résumés. Pursue positions that fit your skills. Applying for anything that opens up is a waste of time. Tailor your résumé to the specific job opening.

Use action words. Instead of simply saying you were employed some-where, say you worked there. Other good words are "control" and "handle." These give the impression that you contributed to your last job, as opposed to just drawing a paycheck.

Keep the print legible. The type size should either be 10 or 12 points. You can make adjustments on your computer. The "Times New Roman" font is most preferable, since it looks the most professional.

Print your résumé on heavy stock paper (usually about 24 pound). A watermark is a good idea, but make sure it's right side up when held up to the light. The paper itself should be a neutral color such as bright white or light gray. Splashy colors are only acceptable when applying for an advertising or artistic job.

In today's electronic age, it's a good idea to include your e-mail address, too. It's an easy way for your potential employer to communicate with you that makes you both feel in control of the situation. More conventional methods, like phone tag, always catch somebody off guard.
Source:
Interview with Len Contardo, assistant director of Alumni Career Services, Georgia Institute of Technology, Atlanta

Better résumés for recent grads

Emphasize extracurricular activities. Don't worry if your grade point average in college or high school was not the best. Extracurricular activities are often considered more important. But try to have at least one leadership role instead of just being a member of many different organizations.
Source:
Interview with Chris Rudolph, human resources administrator, Flowers Bakery, Villa Rica, Ga.

Better résumés for liberal arts graduates only

Getting a job when you've majored in English instead of accounting is a challenge. But don't make it any harder than it already is. Here are four red flags that warn off one newsletter publisher when he receives résumés from the "liberal" crowd:

Your college's literary magazine. If you worked on it, don't mention it. As a general rule, employees who love to write poetry and short stories don't understand the pressures and realities of the business world. And, as many disgruntled employers have discovered, smart, talented poetry lovers are often just not interested in their jobs. You are probably an exception to this stereotype, but if you talk too much about your literary loves, you may never get a chance to prove yourself.

The letter's salutation. Never, never write the sexist "Dear Sir" or "Gentlemen." Don't choose the stilted "To Whom It May Concern" or "Dear Sir or Madam," either. When you're replying to a blind ad, you'll appear more sophisticated if you either leave the salutation off or write some variation of "Dear Publisher," "Dear Personnel Manager," etc.

European studies or travels. Downplay or don't include these fabulous experiences. An employer may believe that, having seen Rome, you won't stay in a humdrum job for long.

Lifeless, formal cover letters. Remember, your writing skills are expected to be better than average. Instead of saying "I am presently employed by ..." say "I now work in ..." Watch out for cover letter clichés such as "I am confident that my background and skills fit your needs ..." or "I would appreciate the opportunity for an interview" or saying that you are seeking a challenge and your prospective employer gives you an opportunity to meet that challenge. Instead, make every effort to say in plain language who you are and why you want to work for the company.

Source:
"From the Publisher's Desk ... How to Study a Resumé," *The Working Communicator*, Chicago

Learning to love your work ... again

Job burnout doesn't always mean you need a change in careers. You may just need a change in your work environment and your lifestyle. If a bad attitude is dragging you down at work, these tips can be real lifesavers:

Add color, light, and music to your workspace. Your work environment is probably designed for the left side of your brain — that means it's geared toward accomplishing your work tasks in a logical, practical way. Just as important is the creativity that springs from the right half of your brain Energize your workspace to enhance your enjoyment and to inspire you to be more creative while you're working.

Identify your best skills by thinking back to the activities you like most of all. Your favorite projects are probably those where you completely lose track of time, even though the work is hard. Once you've established which skills you prefer to use, the trick is to find at least one opportunity at work to exercise these skills.

Visualize your success — athletes do it, and you can, too! The first step is to identify a challenge in your life. Next, make yourself relax, then picture yourself successfully meeting the challenge. The more detailed the picture, the more powerful the image will be when you do confront the challenge.

Practice self-affirmation. Your thoughts really do affect your attitude and your actions. And who's more likely to get promoted, the person with a positive outlook or the guy with the really nasty attitude? If you find yourself thinking too many negatives during the day, emphasize the positive. Write down something good about yourself, like, "I am a dependable, easy-going person who is good at coming up with creative solutions to problems."

Treat yourself well. As important as it is to take good care of other people, it's just as vital to nurture yourself. Make time in your schedule for friends, exercise, and relaxation — you'll feel healthier and you'll perform better at work as a result.

Forget the lists every once in a while. To-do lists and schedules are useful tools for managing a busy life, but you need to be able to throw them out the window occasionally. Take a spontaneous break — an unplanned walk in the park will relieve the tedium of routine and provide a window of opportunity for joy.

You can't control all aspects of your job, but these simple techniques will help you focus on what you can do in response to your environment. Try these tips for six months. If you still can't manage the stress, consider making a job change — the choice is yours.

Source:
Journal of the American Dietetic Association (93,12:1384)

Don't panic over a pink slip

If you haven't gotten the dreaded pink slip yet, chances are you will someday.

Labor Secretary Robert Reich says that Americans are going to have to get used to the idea of changing jobs as many as four to six times during their working life. But, the news isn't all bad.

Most people who lost professional and managerial jobs in the 1980s have found new employment with comparable pay. When the big firms laid off workers, other companies hired them.

Many companies that are restructuring and laying off workers are hiring other people with different skills.

If you do get a pink slip, find out if your present company offers outplacement counseling. They may help you identify new leads and polish your résumé and interviewing skills. After that, you're still not all alone in your job search. Try these resources:

▶ Use your network of personal and professional contacts. About 70 percent of successful job hunters find work through someone they know. Your contacts may not know of a job opening, but they may be able to give you another name to call.

▶ Your contacts can also tell you what another company is like and what its future plans are. That will help you tailor your résumé and cover letter to the specific needs of the company.

▶ Once you've learned about a company, consider showing up in person to apply for a job opening.

▶ If you are discouraged about the process of finding a new job, join a support group of people in the same boat. The cost is low, and the potential for raising your spirits is high.

▶ About 20 percent of job seekers find their next company through an executive recruiting firm. If you choose this route, stick with a contingency search firm that collects a fee from the hiring company only when you are employed.

▶ Read trade publications and the want ads. Ten percent of job seekers find jobs this way.

▶ Consider paying a small fee to have your résumé included in an electronic database that is scanned by employers and recruiting firms. A more expensive option is paying a specialized company to send a mass mailing of your résumé and cover letter to the heads of firms across the nation.

Before you invest any money in one of these alternatives, check to make sure they are reputable and successful for some clients.

▶ If you have been fired, be aware that many of the costs of your job search are tax deductible. Keep track of all your expenses: résumés, placement agency fees, postage, telephone calls, transportation to interviews, and any periodicals you purchase for the purpose of finding a new job.

Unfortunately, the more money you made at your last job, the longer it can take to find the next one. According to experts, the formula is one month of interviewing for every $10,000 of pay at your last position.

Since potential employers may consider the way you have spent these months out of work, stay busy while you're looking for employment. Take classes to upgrade your skills; learn a foreign language; do volunteer work.

And when you do get an interview for the job of your dreams, show them that you are willing to do what they need. Your next paycheck could be right around the corner.

Sources:
Money (March 1994)
The Wall Street Journal (May 11, 1993 and April 15, 1994)

YOUR JOB AND THE LAW

When your office makes you sick

Everyone has a cold or feels a little out of sorts on occasion. It eventually passes.

But what if you and your fellow co-workers start feeling bad with symptoms — like headaches, fatigue, infections, and nausea — that don't go away? And your doctor can't pinpoint a cause?

That's happening more and more these days. In fact, the National Institute for Occupational Safety and Health receives hundreds of requests a year to investigate work-related mystery illnesses.

The culprit frequently turns out to be the office itself. Chemicals from carpeting, ventilation systems that recirculate stale air, and numerous other factors all lead to an illness called *sick building syndrome*.

If you think your job is literally making you sick, talk to your supervisor. NIOSH can give advice on probing the quality of the atmosphere in your workplace.

Source:
You and the Law, the National Institute of Business Management (21,11)

How to take time off and keep your job

Need to take time off because of an illness? Or to help out a family member who's sick?

Exactly when workers can take leave without being penalized — and how much they can take — has been redefined recently by Department of Labor regulations interpreting the Family and Medical Leave Act.

The FMLA lets workers take time off without the fear of losing their job when they, or their immediate family members (husbands, wives, parents, or children), are seriously ill.

The problem is, there are now new, strict definitions of what "seriously ill" means.

When is time off OK?

In the past, only conditions that caused workers to miss work three days in a row were considered serious illnesses that met FMLA leave rules.

Now, some chronic conditions that come and go, but don't necessarily knock you totally out of commission, can qualify you for time off. If you have asthma, epilepsy, or diabetes, for example, you can use FMLA leave to care for the condition at home when necessary.

Also, you'll qualify for FMLA leave — up to 12 weeks off in a 12-month period — if you or a family member has a long-term illness that requires ongoing medical treatment. That includes chemotherapy for cancer, dialysis for kidney disease, and physical therapy for arthritis.

When can you be penalized for missing work?

You may be so sick from a stomach virus that you can hardly get out of bed. But you probably can't take FMLA leave. Here's a list of other common ailments that don't qualify for FMLA time off — unless there are complications that require extensive medical care:

▶ flu
▶ common colds
▶ routine dental procedures
▶ earaches
▶ headaches (migraines can be an exception)
▶ stress
▶ allergies
▶ nausea
▶ minor ulcers
▶ plastic surgery and other cosmetic conditions (like acne)

Sources:
Personnel Law Update (20,3)
You and the Law, the National Institute of Business Management (25,4)

Parents who adopt get time off, too

Parents who adopt need time to bond with their new babies, too, and the federal government finally realized that. If you are adopting a child, don't overlook your right to time off.

Under the Federal Family and Medical Leave Act, you are entitled to take unpaid leave time when you adopt.

The FMLA is fairly new, and it hasn't been added to some employee handbooks yet. So if you're a soon-to-be adoptive parent, ask your supervisor for details about taking time off when the new addition to your family arrives.

Source:
You and the Law, the National Institute of Business Management (25,2)

Why drug testing can jeopardize your job — even if you're drug-free

More employers these days are just saying "no" to employees who use drugs.

"Obviously, you don't want to have employees who are stoned performing dangerous functions," says corporate law and employment specialist James Zito. "In addition, in some states like Georgia, employers can receive a

5 percent discount each year on their workers' compensation premiums if they maintain a drug-free workplace."

Five percent of a million dollar workers' comp premium for 1,500 employees, for example, adds up to $50,000 — a strong financial incentive for making sure employees aren't using drugs.

One way to find out if workers are under the influence is sophisticated drug testing.

Who must take drug tests? Under the Federal Drug-Free Workplace Act, any employers who receive federal grants or contracts have to prove that they have a drug-free work place. States have also initiated drug-free acts — so if you are on any government payroll, chances are you may be required to take a drug test.

In many states, it is legal to require new employees to be drug tested prior to beginning work. And any time an incident occurs that results in property damage or a workers' comp claim, it's perfectly legitimate for the employer to require all the people involved to be tested to see if drugs contributed in any way to the accident.

How are employees tested for drugs? Usually, with a urine test. A sample is divided. One half is put away and stored. The other is tested to find traces of broken-down drugs, including a variety of narcotics, amphetamines, hallucinogens, cocaine, or marijuana.

If the preliminary test is positive, then a more detailed test is run on the balance of the urine sample. If that also comes back positive, your employer will be notified.

Can a positive drug test be wrong? "Drug testing labs are very thorough. They don't want to make mistakes and have people lose their jobs unnecessarily. If you test positive, you have more than a trace of drug metabolites in your system. You aren't going to test positive if you walked by someone smoking marijuana and accidentally inhaled some pot smoke, for instance."

That doesn't mean you can't get a false positive, however — for something as simple as eating poppy seed bagels. "Opiates are made from poppies and the molecules in poppy seeds are similar to those found in some drugs, including heroin," attorney Zito points out. "Although it's very rare, some people have eaten poppy seed bagels, rolls, or muffins in such large quantities that they've tested positive for opiates."

If that happens to you, insist on having more sophisticated tests run. That can rule out the use of heroin, although it won't prove you were just eating poppy seeds. So, if you are subject to drug testing, be on the safe side and steer clear of poppy seed flavored food — at least, in large quantities.

What about your prescription medicines? Don't forget that drug tests may be positive as a result of legal prescriptions or over-the-counter medications. It's very important to advise the tester of any drugs you are taking.

Attorney James Zito warns that legal prescription drugs can also be a problem in the workplace, however. "Not only can they be abused, but some

drugs your doctor may prescribe can interfere with your ability to safely operate certain equipment."

"If that's the case, it's best to be open and honest with your employee
about the prescription drugs you're taking — before there's an accident or
problem."

Source:
Interview with James V. Zito, attorney-at-law, Lipshutz, Greenblatt, and King, Atlanta

AIDS testing: Can you be secretly tested?

If you have any risk factors for AIDS, you should be tested for the AIDS
virus.

But could you be tested without knowing it? When your doctor runs a battery of tests to check your general health, for instance, could he be checking
on your HIV status without telling you?

That's highly unlikely.

Although having your cholesterol level or blood sugar checked requires no
more consent than sticking out your arm to have blood drawn, testing for the
AIDS virus is different. True, it only requires a small blood sample — but the
social and personal consequences of having a positive HIV test are enormous.

In fact, in many states patients are required to give "informed consent"
before the test can be run. Some states have even legislated that patients must
be counseled about the possibility and consequences of an HIV infection and
AIDS before being tested as well as afterwards, if the test is positive.

If you donate blood, you may not know it — but you've already been tested for HIV. Blood banks routinely test for the AIDS virus and throw out any
blood that tests positive. The HIV-positive donor is notified but no one else
can be told about the test results. So, if you've given blood and no one's called
to tell you differently, you've tested free of HIV infection.

You can be forced to take an HIV test in some states, under special circumstances. For example, a health care worker who is taking your blood and
accidentally gets stuck with the needle can insist on knowing whether you
carry the AIDS virus.

Your doctor is not legally obligated to tell you if he or she is infected with
the AIDS-causing virus. Still, if you'd like to know your doctor's HIV status,
you do have the right to ask.

For more information on specific state and federal AIDS-related laws,
contact:

AIDS Policy Center of the Intergovernmental Health Policy Project
2021 K Street N.W.
Washington, DC 20052
(202) 872–1445

Source:
The Court T.V. Cradle-to-Grave Legal Survival Guide: A Complete Resource for Any Question You May Have
About the Law by American Lawyer Media, Little, Brown, and Company, l995

Can you be forced to take a lie detector test at work?

Your boss suspects someone is stealing from his inventory — and it looks like an inside job. Can he insist you take a lie detector test?

Probably not, thanks to the Federal Employee Polygraph Protection Act. Employers can't use lie detector tests to go on "fishing expeditions" just because they think something is amiss.

But when an employer begins an actual investigation of wrongdoing where money is involved — theft, embezzlement, sabotage, and other kinds of criminal activities — he can legally request some workers to take a polygraph test.

"For example, if there's a suspicion a cash drawer is short, the accounting department has to show there actually is money missing. Then they have to show that the person they want to take the lie detector test had access to the missing cash," says employment law specialist James Zito.

You can also be asked to take lie detector tests if your job involves nuclear power plants, public water supplies, or national security.

What happens if an employer follows the proper federal guidelines, asks a worker to take a polygraph test, and is told "no way"? You can be fired for refusing to take a test if you agreed to it when you were hired or if that's written in your employee handbook.

What happens if an employee fails a lie detector test? You can't be fired just because you failed the test. But you should get prepared to be investigated very closely.

Two more rules to remember: No employer can ask you to submit to a polygraph test before you are hired, unless you are applying for a job as a bank guard, police officer, train engineer, or any job where lots of money or people's lives are at stake.

If your employer tries to make you take a lie detector test without following the federal guidelines, he can be fined up to $10,000.

Source:
Interview with James Zito, employment law specialist, attorney-at-law, Lipshutz, Greenblatt, and King, Atlanta

No guarantee of e-mail privacy

With e-mail being used for everything from office get-togethers to contract negotiations, it's no surprise that some people are misusing it.

Make sure none of your e-mail messages include inappropriate comments or suggestive language. Courts are allowing e-mail to be used as evidence in harassment and discrimination suits. Sexual innuendoes, racial slurs, and other inappropriate comments used on e-mail systems are not protected under privacy laws. Plus, your employer has the right to read all your e-mail messages.

Also, remember that just because you deleted something from your computer does not mean it has been deleted from the system. Receivers of your e-mail messages may have printed them out, forwarded them to others, or saved them on their computer.

Source:
Supervisor's Guide to Employment Practices, Clement Communications, Concordville, Pa. (June 17 1996)

Taking your religion to work

Your faith is an important part of your life. So is your job. Fortunately, discrimination based on your religion is against the law.

You should never place your workplace over your beliefs, but you can avoid problems by knowing when you should separate the two.

▶ Find out your company's policy before displaying religious items — like a picture of a religious leader — in your office.

▶ Let your employer know upfront if a religious observance will interfere with your work. In most cases, you won't be fired. For example, if you are Jewish and your normal shift is Monday to Friday, you can't be fired if you refuse to work on Saturdays because that's the day you observe the Sabbath. However, if you knew when you were hired that you'd be asked to work on Saturdays — and you never spoke up about your religious beliefs — your employer can probably fire you.

What company management needs to know. Here's an example of a recent religion-in-the-workplace case that ended up in court:

An employee was told by his manager to stop quoting the Bible at staff meetings and using Scripture when talking to employees about their work habits. The worker was told he was a supervisor, not a minister.

The supervisor took his voluntary lunch-time prayer meetings out of the office building and moved them to a local library. But he did continue to use Biblical quotations occasionally when talking to employees.

His manager fired him. The reason? Concern that the supervisor's ardent religious faith might eventually pit employees who shared his beliefs against those who didn't.

The supervisor took his job loss to court — and won. The judge ruled an employee can't be fired just because the manager feared something might happen.

The bottom line for management: Restrictions you place on religious situations in the workplace should prohibit intimidating speech and discrimination or harassment based on religion. But you can't step over the line and interfere with a person's freedom of expression or religion.
Source:
Manager's Legal Bulletin (10:13)

Romance in the workplace: what to watch out for

It sounds simple enough: a man and a woman meet at work, start dating, maybe even fall in love and marry.

But in these days of sexual harassment suits, favoritism complaints, and complicated office policies, take a long, hard look before you leap into a workplace romance.

Find out the company rules before you start dating a co-worker. Many employers have policies on personal relationships. Some completely ban dating and marriage between employees. Others only have rules against husbands and wives working in the same department — or in positions where one can help or hinder the advancement of the other. These spousal policies can also be applied to couples who are living together but not legally married.

Favoritism. Employers who frown on love between employees aren't necessarily Scrooges — they may just be trying to avoid problems. After all, if a worker is promoted by a romantic partner, other employees may cry "favoritism."

Displays of affection. Workers who can't resist showing their affection for each other at work can also offend others. In fact, one employee in a company where several supervisors were unabashedly romancing employees won a lawsuit on the grounds that the romantic relationships had created a hostile working environment.

Nasty endings. Not all romances have fairy tale endings. When one person wants to break off a relationship and the other doesn't, you have a sure-fire recipe for complications at work.

What if one still-in-love employee harasses another with letters and calls? Or, after a lovers' spat, what happens if offensive remarks and arguments break out on company time? The recipient of unwanted attention could claim he or she was being sexually harassed.

Supervisors, beware of lawsuits. If you need to move someone to another department so a couple won't be working together, ask the couple to decide who will make the switch.

If you have to decide, make sure you stick to objective factors: Who has seniority, the best skills, and is most valuable to your company? Which person is most suited for jobs available elsewhere in your organization?

Don't make the mistake of forcing someone to transfer or quit a job because of a romance policy. You can be slapped with a sex discrimination suit.
Source:
Labor Relations Bulletin, Bureau of Business Practice, 1994

Telephone privacy: Don't tap into trouble

Your business has received bomb threats. So, without telling your employees, you've started to secretly record conversations on some of the security office telephones. Sound reasonable?

Not to the courts. In fact, when that exact scenario happened recently and a worker found out she had been recorded, she sued — and won.

Secretly tapping into private phone conversations violates the 1968 Federal Wiretapping Act. The law does allow some electronic communications to be intercepted in the ordinary course of business. But before you try to record any of your workers' telephone calls — no matter what the reason   consult an attorney and make sure you are obeying the law.
Source:
You and the Law, the National Institute of Business Management (25,1)

Whistle-blowing: when it's OK to tell company secrets

You're a loyal employee. You don't want to do anything to hurt your company. But you believe unsafe working conditions are risking the health of you and your co-workers.

What do you do?

To find out for sure if your workplace conditions are illegal or inappropriate, call the government agency that regulates your place of business. Ask for the safety guidelines that apply to your workplace.

Not sure who to call? Try your local Occupational Safety and Health Act office. If there isn't one, call the federal OSHA office in Washington, D.C. at 1-202-219-5000.

Under OSHA regulations, your employer must take all reasonable steps to make sure the workplace is safe. Some businesses, like hospitals and chemical manufacturing plants, have to follow extra, specific safety rules.

When you've determined your employer isn't following safety guidelines, take your evidence and concerns to your supervisor. Work with your employer to try and solve the problem within your company. If your employer fails to take action, your next step is to contact OSHA and file a formal complaint.

Can whistle-blowing cost you your job? If your claims of hazardous or illegal conditions turn out to be true, but you were fired for complaining about them, in some states you'll probably be able to get your job back. You'll also most likely collect back pay.

On the other hand, if you made accusations that proved false, you probably can't get your job back. That's a good reason to make sure you have your facts right and to help your company solve any problems internally before becoming a full-fledged whistle-blower.

Source:
The Court T.V. Cradle-to-Grave Legal Survival Guide: A Complete Resource for Any Question You May Have About the Law by American Lawyer Media, Little, Brown, and Company, 1995

SECRETS OF PERSONAL SUCCESS

Time-saving tactics

Pricing your time

Don't waste your dollar time on penny tasks. Let's say that you can save $10 by shopping at three different grocery stores, but it takes you an extra hour every week. Is it worth it? Probably not.

Full-time workers can easily figure out the value of their time. Add 40 percent to your salary to cover your fringe benefits. Divide that number by 52 to get your weekly salary. Then divide by 40 to get the hourly cost of your time.

Time is valuable for part-time and retired workers, too. Compare the value of time spent driving between stores to the value of time spent enjoying a hobby, visiting your grandchildren, or developing a home business to earn extra money.

Before you begin your next activity, ask yourself if it's really worth your precious time.

Source:
The A to Z of Time Management by Lynne Wenig, Allen & Unwin, St. Leonards, NSW 2065, Australia

Double your efforts

If you want to get more done in less time, try doing two things at once. Exercise while watching TV or planning your next dinner party. Listen to a book on personal money management while driving. Take reading material to keep you busy while you wait for doctor or hairstylist appointments. Sign letters or stuff envelopes during a meeting (OK this one with the meeting leader first.) Do calf raises or plan tomorrow's attire while you brush your teeth.

Source:
The A to Z of Time Management by Lynne Wenig, Allen & Unwin, St. Leonards, NSW 2065, Australia

Enjoy a quickie

Those little five-minute windows are big time wasters. They happen at home when we get ready for a lunch date too early and at work when we've switched off our computers at 4:55 in the afternoon. We waste these small time windows because, after all, we can't possibly accomplish anything in that short amount of time.

"Quickies" are tasks you can finish in five minutes or less. The next time you have a five-minute time window, spend it making a list of your personal quickies. Then, every time you have a few minutes on your hands, take out your list and write that thank-you note, make the telephone call, read the brochure, organize that file, or update your "to do" list.

Source:
The A to Z of Time Management by Lynne Wenig, Allen & Unwin, St. Leonards, NSW 2065, Australia

Thinking smarter

Self-help scams

P.T. Barnum knew what he was talking about when he said, "There's a sucker born every minute." And every unscrupulous seller since P.T. Barnum has attempted to make every buyer a sucker by preying on buyers' deep-seated desires and fears.

In this age of information where knowledge is power, everyone wants to be smarter, know more, and have healthier habits to live longer and take advantage of all this awesome information.

That's why subliminal self-help tapes are such a booming business. "Learn while you sleep." "Stop smoking the easy way," shout announcers and advertisements. With so much to do these days and so little free time, learning new stuff and breaking bad habits while you sleep seems like the perfect solution.

It isn't. It's only a good solution for parting you from your money without giving you anything in return, except perhaps a poor night's sleep.

Save your money, your sleep, and any other time you might be tempted to waste listening to subliminal self-help tapes. The only people these tapes help are the people who sell them.

Source:
The Owner's Manual for the Brain: Everyday Applications from Mind-Brain Research by Pierce J. Howard, Ph.D., Leornian Press, Austin, Texas, 1994

Easier learning

"You can't teach an old dog new tricks" is a saying that's been around forever, but it's just not true. In fact, the authors of *Forever Mind: Eight Ways to Unleash the Power of Your Mature Mind* say you can learn things better now than you did when you were younger. You've just got to figure out your personal learning style.

You've had a personal learning style since you were a child, but over the years you've probably gotten better and better at that one style of learning and worse at the other styles. Now, it's more important than ever to figure out how your mind likes to learn.

▶ Visual learners. You learn best by reading, looking at drawings or graphs, and taking notes. You probably find objects you've lost by visualizing where you last put them. After listening to a lecture or speech, it takes colorful descriptions to remember what you've learned. *Easiest learning techniques:* Reading, drawing, and making outlines or diagrams. (Find a challenging book at the library and read a chapter a day. Do a book report or write key phrases from the book on note cards you can study later.)

▶ Verbal learners. You talk to yourself when you learn something new. You may mutter out loud: "First, you slide this bolt in place. ... " You used to love to talk in class, and you like to read to people out loud. *Easiest learning techniques:* Workshops with a lot of participation required, discussion with others. (Get a reading group together or at least find a friend to share with. Putting what you've learned into your own words is a great learning tool for you.)

▶ Auditory learners. Listening is how you learn best. College lectures were easy for you. You probably like music. *Easiest learning techniques:* Listening to tapes or lectures. (Check out the tapes at your local library. You're lucky; you can learn while you drive.)

▶ Kinesthetic learners. You learn best by doing. You like to take things apart and put them back together again. *Easiest learning techniques*: Role-playing, hands-on projects. (You could learn yourself by teaching others. Demonstrating how something works is right up your alley.)

Source.
Forever Mind: Eight Ways to Unleash the Power of Your Mature Mind by Jacqueline Wonder and Priscilla Donovan, William Morrow and Co., New York, 1996

Don't be fooled by the 'scientists'

You weren't born yesterday. You know you can't believe everything you read in the newspapers. So you look for proof — scientific studies, research, public opinion polls. Unfortunately, businesses, the media, and politicians know exactly how to manipulate the "facts" and "data."

When you see a research study, look to see who sponsored the study.

You may have seen the recent study by the Cooper Institute for Aerobic Research. Its finding: White bread is nutritious and won't cause you to gain weight. The study sponsor was the maker of Wonder Bread.

Chocolate may actually prevent cavities, said a study by the Princeton Dental Resource Center. Of course, the Center is funded by Mars, the company that makes M&Ms and other chocolate candy.

When you read public opinion polls, look closely to see how questions are worded and who they chose to poll.

In a 1992 TV Guide, Ross Perot ran an ad with a question that read, "Should the President have the Line Item Veto to eliminate waste?" Yes, said 97 percent of the respondents. When the pollsters asked a random sample of people, "Should the President have the Line Item Veto, or not?" only 57 percent said yes.

Watch out, Alabama. A 1993 poll by the Southern Baptist Convention said 46.1 percent of Alabamans risk going to hell. And 2 percent of Americans may have been abducted by unidentified flying objects, says a 1991 Roper survey.

Remember that the media is out to sell information, even if it's bad information. Don't be a gullible consumer

Source:
Tainted Truth. The Manipulation of Fact in America by Cynthia Crossen, Simon & Schuster, New York, 1994

Communication skills

How to win an argument every time

Do you have a friend who always comes out ahead in any argument or debate? Your friend may have perfected one of the word-winning techniques that have been around for hundreds of years. In the early 1800s, the German philosopher Arthur Schopenhauer recorded 38 ways to win an argument in *The Art of Controversy*. Here are a few tactics you can use to get the upper hand in your next battle of bombast.

▶ Try to get your opponent to exaggerate his statements. The more general a statement, the easier it is to poke holes in it. (People tend to exaggerate both when they are flattered and when they are irritated, angered, or contradicted.)

▶ Use your opponent's beliefs against him. If your opponent is a staunch Republican, make sure your replies are based on right-wing principles.

▶ If your opponent is answering all your questions negatively, ask him to admit that the opposite of what you've been saying is true. That may confuse him completely.

▶ Find your opponent's words inconsistent with his actions. If he says television is stupid, ask him why he watches so much of it.

▶ Appeal to authority, especially to an authority your opponent respects. Being able to quote someone is always impressive, even if it doesn't make much sense. (If your conscience allows you, you can "create" a quotation that fits perfectly.)

▶ Admit that he's right, but say that it doesn't matter. For example: "That's all very well in theory, but it won't do in practice."

▶ Finally, if you think you're beaten, begin talking earnestly on a subject that is related to your argument. You may sidetrack your opponent into forgetting that he was ahead.

These seemingly simple methods worked for a brilliant philosopher. They can work for you, too.

Source:
Five Rings, Six Crises, Seven Dwarfs, and 38 Ways to Win an Argument: Numerical Lists You Should Know or Once Knew and Probably Forgot by John Boswell and Dan Starer, Penguin Books, New York, 1990

How to make a good first impression

Whether you're trying to make a good impression on the big boss or a bank loan officer, these seven steps will guarantee great results every time.

▶ Do a 30-second check before you make an entrance. Find a rest room and start at the top. Work your way down through all the critical points: Hair first, then teeth. If appropriate, look for smudged makeup and missing earrings. Straighten your scarf or tie. Check for lint, stains, open buttons, or unzipped zippers. Correct any problems. Now you're ready to put your best face forward.

▶ Practice good posture. Not only will you look 10 pounds lighter and 10 years younger, you'll project an instant impression of competence.

▶ Look the other person straight in the eye and smile. Maintain eye contact all the way through the handshake.

▶ Offer a quick, hearty, one-handed shake. Don't overdo it. One quick squeeze and one hand pump is plenty. If you're the host, you should initiate the handshake. If you're the guest, wait for the host to offer a handshake. If no handshake seems to be forthcoming, then extend your hand.

▶ Introduce yourself. As you're shaking hands, address the other person by name and then repeat your own. Example: "Mr. Johnson, I'm Carol Davies." If you need to introduce other people, remember the golden rule of introductions — introduce the most honored person first.

▶ Follow the other person's lead or style. People like other people similar to themselves. If the other person is calm and quiet, use smooth, slow gestures and speak with a volume similar to his. If someone shows excitement, it's also appropriate for you to be excited. Just attempt to make the person feel comfortable; don't make your imitation obvious.

Source:
Professional Presence by Susan Bixler, Perigee Books, New York, 1992

No clammy handshakes

Men and women, always stand for introductions, and always extend a hand. If you have clammy hands, spray them with antiperspirant once a day. Don't wait until the last minute — it takes at least a day for antiperspirant to work.

Another tip: At social events, you'll give a cold, wet handshake if you hold your beverage in your right hand, so keep the drink on the left.

Source:
At Ease ... Professionally: An Etiquette Guide for the Business Arena by Hilka Klinkenberg, founder of Etiquette International, Bonus Books, Chicago, 1992

10 ways to spot a liar

If you're like most people, at some point you've probably had the feeling that someone was lying to you. You just couldn't put your finger on what set off your internal alarms. Next time you have your reasonable doubts, run down the following checklist in your mind. If the person displays more than one of these signals, your suspicions are probably correct.

1. What the person says and how the person acts don't match up. Example: Your boss says she doesn't mind if you leave early, but she stalks off in a huff.
2. The person can't seem to maintain strong eye contact and looks everywhere but at you.
3. The person repeats the same information several times in an attempt to sound convincing.
4. The person's voice is higher-pitched and louder than normal.
5. The person's eyes shift constantly to the left.
6. The person's eye pupils become smaller. Smaller pupils are often an involuntary response by the body to an intentional lie.
7. The person swallows hard.
8. The person's face is red and sweaty.
9. The person speaks at a different rate of speed, often much faster than normal.
10. The person places a hand in front of his mouth while talking.

Once it becomes apparent that someone has a serious case of truth decay, you have several options:

First, determine how the lie will affect you. Is it just a face-saving device for the other person, or is it threatening you in some way?

If the lie compromises your position, sabotages your work, or puts you or your job at risk, confront the person directly. Let the other person know you don't think she is being straight with you and wait for a response.

Source:
Professional Presence by Susan Bixler, Perigee Books, New York, 1992

Handling silence with savvy

At some time or another, most of us have had the uncomfortable feeling of having said too much.

The problem lies in the fact that most people feel uncomfortable with silence, so they rush in to fill the void, often saying the first thing that comes to mind, which is often the least appropriate.

Here are some suggestions to help you handle silence with savvy:

▶ Don't feel that you have to immediately respond to any important question. The pregnant pause will give you time to prepare a polished reply. In the meantime, the other person may rush in to fill the silence with valuable information you may have otherwise missed.
▶ Don't fall for the fallacy that talking all the time makes you more important. The less you say, the more impact your words have when you do talk. And other people will appreciate an opportunity to share their views.

▶ Focus on the person who's talking. Don't think about what you want to say next. Acknowledge the other person with affirmative nods and don't interrupt. Complete attention to another person is also a simple way of showing respect and earning the other person's trust. Focused listening may take patience and practice, but the payoffs are worth it. The better listener learns more, and in these days of the information age, knowledge equals power.

Source:
Professional Presence by Susan Bixler, Perigee Books, New York, 1992

When you forget a name

You know the face. You know where you met him and who his father-in-law is. You just can't remember his name. Trouble is, he remembers yours and is coming to say hi. What do you do?

▶ Strike first. Walk up and say, "We met at last month's seminar. I'm ..." If you're lucky, the person will give his or her name.

▶ Honesty is a good policy. Simply ask the person's name again. Then repeat it several times so you won't forget again.

▶ Ask new acquaintances for business cards.

▶ If you're going to a business party or convention, try to get a guest list ahead of time. Just looking the list over should make some names stick in your mind.

Source:
Company Manners by Lois Wyse, McGraw Hill Book Co., New York, 1987

Positive thinking

Kicking a bad mood

Some days, even normally good-humored people wake up grouchy. Nobody knows why.

You have a choice: You can enjoy wallowing in your bad mood, or you can do something about it:

▶ Don't blame anyone else for your bad day. You certainly don't have to blame yourself, but it's nobody else's fault either.

▶ Don't keep your bad mood a secret. Find a button that expresses your mental state on bad days. Something like "Recent studies prove I don't have to be reasonable."

▶ Complain to your heart's content. Usually, if you tell someone else what a bad day you're having, life begins looking better.

▶ Make faces at yourself. Movie star Steve Martin once said that every morning he stands in front of the mirror and forces himself to laugh until the laugh comes naturally. (If this starts making you feel grouchier, stop!)

▶ Wear your Mickey Mouse underwear or put on your T-shirt backward.

▶ Check the list you've made of happy moments in your life. If you don't have one of these lists, get a pencil and a pad of paper ready. Anytime you have a happy memory or do something that brings you joy, write it down. This list can be hundreds of items long, and it can be a great blessing to you on sad days.

Source:
Lighten Up: Survival Skills for People Under Pressure by C.W. Metcalf and Roma Felible, Addison-Wesley Publishing, Reading, Mass., 1992

When the world revolves around you

Here are two sure signs that you are indeed the center of the universe:

1) Nothing is ever your fault. When you have a problem, you can always find someone else to blame. Things could have been perfect, if someone else hadn't screwed up.

2) Everything is always your fault. When you have a problem, you assume responsibility for everything. Things could have been perfect, if you had worked harder, done more, been nicer. ...

Fortunately, that church meeting you're in charge of next week isn't a conference on world peace, and the fight you had with your spouse wasn't World War III.

Source:
Lighten Up: Survival Skills for People Under Pressure by C.W. Metcalf and Roma Felible, Addison-Wesley Publishing, Reading, Mass., 1992

<u>Social strategies</u>

All about tipping

Do you figure the tip on a restaurant bill before or after tax? Do you tip your mail carrier at Christmas? What if you receive bad service?

For some people, a tip is a way to say thanks for the service; for others, it feels like highway robbery. No matter what your attitude toward tipping is, you're likely to have some questions on how it's normally done. Whether you take the advice or not, here's what the experts say:

Restaurant tipping

▶ Tips are figured on the pretax amount.

▶ Some people say the word tip comes from "to insure promptness."* Long ago, people tipped before the meal to ensure good service. These days, you only tip beforehand if you're hosting an important meeting and you want to make sure the service is perfect. Give $10 to the maitre d' for a party of four or more. At five-star restaurants, give $20. Make sure no one sees you give this tip.

► The standard restaurant tip is 15 to 20 percent. In rural areas, you can get away with 10 percent. At swanky establishments in big cities, 20 to 25 percent is expected. At the deluxe restaurants, the captain will receive 5 percent of the tip. He's the one who takes your order, cooks at your table, oversees the waiters, and sometimes gives you your bill.

► You don't have to tip the maitre d' unless you ask for a specific table or request special attention.

► Waiters don't necessarily prefer cash tips over tips added to charge slips. Either method is fine.

► When eating out with your boss, pay the bill and the tip unless the boss offers to pay.

► For bad service, leave a 10 percent tip (in the best restaurants) and complain to the management. Only skip the tip completely if you plan to never come back to the restaurant.

► Tip 15 percent of your liquor bill to the bartender and 10 percent of your wine bill to the wine steward.

► One easy way to figure a tip is to use the sales tax. If the tax is 5 percent, you can triple it for a 15 percent tip. If the tax is 8 percent, you can double it for a 16 percent tip.

► Tip $1 to doormen for summoning your car, to parking-lot attendants, and to coat room and restroom attendants.

Travel tipping

► At airports, tip the skycaps $1 to $1.50 per bag.

► Tip taxi drivers 10 percent of the meter if the amount is over $10. Tip 15 percent if several people are sharing the taxi. Tip hotel courtesy van drivers $1 to $2 if they help you with your luggage.

► At hotels, tip door attendants $1 to $2 for removing your luggage from the car, for getting a cab, or for handling your bags when checking out.

► Tip bellhops $1 to $2 per bag for taking your bags to your room and $1 to $2 for performing services such as delivering messages.

► You don't need to tip the messenger service or the concierge.

► If service is already included in the room service bill, add $1.

► Tip restroom attendants $1.

Personal care tipping

► Tip hairdressers and barbers 15 to 20 percent, unless they own the shop.

► Shampooers normally get a $1 to $2 tip.

► Tip 15 to 20 percent to your manicurist.

Holiday tipping

► The only hard and fast rule for holiday tipping is that you should give tip money to people you ordinarily tip during the year. You should give noncash gifts to those you wouldn't ordinarily tip.

► For the neighborhood baby sitter who sits occasionally, give $5. For someone who sits regularly, give $25.

► For day-care providers, give a small, inexpensive gift.

▶ For nannies and au pairs, give an extra $200 to $500 at the holidays. An appreciated gift is a round-trip airplane ticket to visit relatives.

▶ Tip a weekly house cleaner a day's wages.

▶ Tip hairstylists and barbers from $5 to $50. Women should usually tip more than men. For hair salon owners, a noncash gift such as a bottle of wine is more appropriate.

▶ For garbage collectors, tip $5 to $15 or perhaps give homemade cookies.

▶ For apartment building custodians, give $25 to $100 or a gift.

▶ Give newspaper delivery boys or girls $5 to $15. If you never see the deliverer and you get a tip envelope, you can give $5 to $10.

▶ For piano teachers and other instructors, give a gift equal to the cost of one hour of lessons.

* There is some disagreement about the origin of the word "tip." It probably comes from the 16th century English verb "tip," which means "to give unexpectedly." The English word comes from the German word "tippen," which means "to tap."

Sources:
At Ease ... Professionally: An Etiquette Guide for the Business Arena by Hilka Klinkenberg, founder of Etiquette International, Bonus Books, Chicago, 1992
Professional Presence by Susan Bixler, Putnam, New York, 1991
The Atlanta Journal/Constitution (Dec. 12, 1994, E1)
USAir Magazine (December 1995)

Saving dollars when dining out

▶ Call restaurants in your area and ask about specials. Many restaurants have the "early bird special," which gives you a discount if you dine before a certain hour.

▶ Experiment with a new restaurant at lunchtime when the prices are lower. If you don't like the meal, at least you won't be out the cost of a whole dinner.

▶ Look for coupons. Some restaurants, such as Red Lobster and Steak and Ale, regularly run $4 and $5 coupons in the newspaper.

▶ Planning a birthday celebration? Phone around first. Many restaurants offer free meals on your birthday, or at least a free dessert.

▶ Phone ahead when you're taking a child. Restaurants that don't have a child's menu may agree to give you a child's portion at a discount if you phone first.

▶ To get more for your money, order a complete meal instead of a la carte.

▶ Split an entree with your mate. You'll boost your romance and your budget.

▶ Drink water with your meal. For what you get, the beverage is one of the most expensive items on the menu. Often you can get pitchers of drinks for everyone instead of ordering by the glass. If you don't get free refills, ask for your beverage without ice to get more of it.

▶ Carry out your leftovers. You've paid for them so don't be embarrassed.

Source:
How to Pinch a Penny 'Til It Screams by Rochelle LaMotte McDonald, Avery Publishing Group, Garden City Park, N.Y., 1994

What to say at a funeral

Funerals are awkward, but they're a time when your friends need you most. If you don't know what to say, try:

▶ How sorry you were to hear the bad news.

▶ How much the deceased will be missed.

▶ How much you loved this person and what a personal loss it will be to you.

▶ How badly you feel for the person left behind.

▶ What a wonderful person the deceased was. Try to follow up with a story or anecdote.

Source:
Letitia Baldrige's Complete Guide to the New Manners for the 90's, Rawson Associates, New York, 1990

How to eat tricky foods

Not all foods fit nicely on a fork or spoon. Here are some tips on eating those hard-to-eat dishes.

Artichokes. Eat them with your fingers, one leaf at a time. Dip the leaf into a sauce and then scrape it between your teeth. Place the used leaf on the side of your plate. Eat the artichoke heart with a knife and fork.

Asparagus may be picked up and eaten with your fingers. The larger pieces may be cut up with a knife and fork.

Avocado. Sliced avocado may be eaten with a fork. Use a spoon to eat a halved avocado that is still in its shell.

Bacon is always eaten with the fingers.

Cheese. When cheese is served as an hors d'oeuvre, it should be spread on crackers with a knife. When cheese and fresh fruits are served for dessert, the cheese is cut and eaten with a fork.

Corn on the cob is always eaten with both hands.

Source:
Charlotte Ford's Guide to Modern Manners, Clarkson N. Potter, New York, 1980

<u>Successful</u> <u>parenting</u>

Better disciplining

Don't even try to sit down and reason with your child while he is misbehaving, even though it seems like the right thing to do. As smart as they may seem, children between ages 2 and 6 have a limited understanding of cause and effect and of other people's feelings.

When you talk to a young child when he misbehaves, he probably won't respond like you hope he will, plus you are rewarding his bad behavior by paying attention to him.

Instead, try these steps:

1) When the child misbehaves, give a short explanation or warning. Use one word for each year of the child's age. For example, say, "No hitting. Timeout," to a 3-year-old; then place him in timeout for hitting.

2) Give long explanations for punishment later, after you've both calmed down.
3) Think before speaking. Don't give a command or warning if you aren't willing to follow through with punishment.
4) If your child ignores your first warning, don't keep saying it! Move quickly to another type of punishment.

Words work better at getting your child to do something rather than stopping him from doing something. And words of praise work wonderfully well to reinforce good behavior.

Scientists who have studied children's behavior say that even if talking and reasoning with a child gets him to stop misbehaving, he'll probably be more likely than ever to misbehave again. For example, a teacher can tell a child in a classroom to "sit down," and he'll probably sit. But he is now more likely than ever to get out of his seat. After all, the child got the teacher's attention — and that's what he wanted more than anything.

Source:
Dr. Nathan J. Blum, Division of Child Development and Rehabilitation, Children's Seashore House, University of Pennsylvania School of Medicine, Philadelphia, writing in *Pediatrics* (96,2:336). Other study authors are Dr. George E. Williams of the Lincoln Pediatric Group, Dr. Patrick C. Friman of Father Flanagan's Boys' Home, and Dr. Edward R. Christophersen of The Children's Mercy Hospital at the University of Missouri-Kansas City.

How to make 'timeouts' work

You can't punish with a "timeout" unless you give your child plenty of "time-in." It just won't work.

"Time-in" means fun toys, praise, and lots of your attention. That's what your child should get when she's behaving well. Then you can punish with a timeout by taking those nice things away for a while.

If timeout is just an escape from a chore or from an angry parent, it's no punishment. It may just make bad behavior worse.

Source:
Dr. Nathan J. Blum, Division of Child Development and Rehabilitation, Children's Seashore House, University of Pennsylvania School of Medicine, Philadelphia, writing in *Pediatrics* (96,2:336). Other study authors are Dr. George E. Williams of the Lincoln Pediatric Group, Dr. Patrick C. Friman of Father Flanagan's Boys' Home, and Dr. Edward R. Christophersen of The Children's Mercy Hospital at the University of Missouri-Kansas City.

YOUR MONEY AND YOUR LOOKS

Common mistake when shopping for clothes

If you make a habit of buying clothes that don't reflect your personal style, the clothing retailers will love you, but your wallet won't.

If you are shopping for a special occasion, don't feel that you must alter your personality and style to suit the occasion. You'll make a better impression and have a better time if you play the role that comes most natural to you — being yourself.

If you don't have a flashy personality and you choose to wear a red leather miniskirt, it will look as if the skirt is wearing you instead of you wearing the skirt.

Instead, stick with the colors, lines, and shapes that suit you best. Play up your strengths. Decide what parts of yourself you like best, then find ways to make those areas stand out. For example, if you've got top-notch toes or strong shoulders, take every tasteful opportunity to show them off.

You can limit costly mistakes by trying new styles one at a time instead of attempting to change your whole wardrobe at once.

Source:
Dress Like a Million by Leah Feldon, Villard Books, New York, 1994

Buy designer clothes for half the price

Finally, there's no need to feel guilty about it. It's "in," accepted, even called "chic." It's buying second-hand. These days, even wealthy people are buying used items for half the original prices, and they feel good about it.

Sales are booming at resale stores such as Patti's ReSale House in Owensboro, Ky., and One More Time in Columbus, Ohio. Recently, you could find a wool J.H. Collectibles jacket for $45 at a resale shop in Dallas called Clothes Circuit.

At Play It Again Sports, you can buy used hockey skates for $30 to $50, instead of paying $55 to $300 for new skates, or buy a $30 soccer ball for just $10, or pick up a set of vinyl-covered dumbbells for half-price. Half-price, barely used exercise equipment, such as stair-climbing machines, are easy to find.

Thrift stores, pawn shops, and consignment shops are becoming more and more popular for bargain hunters. Don't miss out on great deals because of pride. If anyone catches you shopping resale, tell him you are concerned about the environment and support recycling in all its forms.

Source:
The Wall Street Journal (Dec. 19, 1995, B1)

10 ways to take home the best bargains from a thrift shop

▶ Decide if you're really a thrift store shopper. If you've got stamina, perseverance, patience, and a particularly good eye for quality, go for it. You're bound to find bargains. On the other hand, if you'd rather be doing anything but shopping, your luck may be limited.

▶ Know quality before you go. You can develop an eye for quality clothes by browsing through top-of-the line shops before you head for thrift town.

▶ Get ready to go a lot. You have to browse thrift shops regularly to catch the best bargains.

▶ Check out the quality and price range of a thrift shop by giving lamps, frames, and vases a quick once-over. If quality is good and prices are reasonable, clothes will probably follow suit.

▶ Dress for success. Wear clothes, such as a leotard or body suit and slip-on shoes, that will allow you to easily try on stuff you like, either with or without a dressing room.

▶ Choose classic over costume chic. Try to select styles with staying power.

▶ Buy only items in relatively good condition or that can be repaired easily.

▶ Look in out-of-the-way areas, such as drawers, boxes, and corner display cases. You're liable to luck up with real tortoiseshell combs, cuff links, or antique or novelty buttons, all of which can make great accessories for just the right outfit. Different buttons can really dress up your favorite finery.

▶ Glance through the men's section for suits, jackets, and baggy pants. Some women love to lounge around in a roomy, well made man's jacket, suit, or pants. However, you want the item to look nice, so if it doesn't fit well, have it altered. You'll still save a bundle over buying something new.

▶ Gently haggle if you have the heart for it. You may end up getting a better price on an already good deal.

Source:
Dress Like a Million by Leah Feldon, Villard Books, New York, 1994

For women: Best buys in men's department

Some of the best buys in women's clothes are found in the boys/young men's departments. The styles are the same but the prices are certainly a lot less. Look for sweaters, jackets, button-down shirts, t-shirts, sweat clothes, rain slickers, boxer shorts, and handkerchiefs.

Source:
Looking, Working, Living Terrific 24 Hours a Day by Emily Cho, G.P. Putnam's Sons, New York., 1982

How to look taller

Short women sometimes feel at a disadvantage in business or financial situations. When you need to present a powerful front, try these fashion tricks to make you look taller:

- Keep skirts at knee level. Midcalf hems make legs look shorter.
- Two words: vertical stripes.
- Straight unconstructed jackets look better than fitted ones.
- Dress with a 2/3 ratio — the proportion of your top (be it jacket or blouse) should be two-thirds longer than the skirt or pants.
- Harmonize the bottom part of an outfit. Wear skirt, hose and shoes in the same color scheme.
- Tunics and jumpsuits work wonders.

Source:
Chic on a Shoestring by Annette Swanberg and Leigh Charlton, Doubleday & Co., New York, 1984

Inside men's fashion

Whether you're trying to land a business deal or win a woman, avoid these fashion mistakes:

- Glasses. Never wear glasses that change tints.
- Neckties. Short neckties look silly. Make sure your tie extends down to the lower edge of your belt buckle.
- Fingernails. Keep 'em scrubbed. Dirty fingernails consistently turn off more women than any other aspect.
- Colognes. Heave-ho heavy colognes. For the most part, women hate them. They prefer a straight after-shave or a light cologne.
- Pens. Always carry a good pen.
- Trousers. Surprisingly, too short trousers are a common mistake among many men. Your pant legs should break slightly over your shoes.
- Socks. Make sure your socks are long enough so that when you sit down leg skin doesn't show.
- White shoes. Wave a fond farewell to your white dress shoes. The only exceptions are white tennis shoes for fun times and white bucks if you're shooting for a casual, Ivy League look.

A successful look is in the details — neat hair, well-trimmed mustache, ironed shirts, socks that don't sag, and polished shoes.

Sources:
Dress for Excellence by Lois Fenton with Edward Olcott, Rawson Associates, New York, 1986
New Dress for Success by John T. Molloy, Susan Warren Books, New York, 1988

A crash course in color combos just for men

You can't always rely on a salesperson to tell you when two colors clash. If you aren't certain what goes with what, here are some tips to help you cope.

For success in business, most experts recommend that you go with the three traditional suit colors: blue, gray, and tan. Choose blues and grays that range from medium to dark. Look for tans that range from light to medium.

You have more of a choice with shirt and tie colors. First, two general rules:

1. Your shirt should be lighter than your suit and your tie darker than your shirt.

2. The lighter your shirt and the darker your suit and tie, the more formal your look.

Now for specifics: Figure out your color type. If you have light hair, eyes, and skin color, you're considered light complexioned. You'll look good in colors that match your hair and eyes. Stay away from extremely pale-colored shirts. You'll looked washed out. Striped shirts in red, burgundy, dark blue, and green look good on you.

If you have black or brown hair, dark eyes, and olive skin, you're dark complexioned. You'll look good in shirts that contrast with your eye, hair, and skin colors, such as whites, pinks, creams, light blues, grays, or yellows.

Choose ties in rich, vivid tones of blue, red, or yellow. You can also wear elegant patterned ties.

If you're black, you'll look best in dark, Mediterranean colors.

If you have gray hair, add some pink or red-striped shirts to your wardrobe. They'll add warmth and vitality to your look.

You'll know a color is right for you if your eyes light up and look clearer. Your skin will also have a healthy glow. The wrong colors will make you look old, tired, turn your skin a sallow color, and bring out circles under your eyes and shadows around your mouth.

Generally, most men stick with the two-color combo — your tie repeats the colors in your shirt and suit. For example, say that you choose a dark gray suit and a white shirt with a burgundy hairline stripe. To tie the two colors together, select a burgundy tie with a small gray pattern.

Top off your look with these finishing touches:

▶ Wear socks that are darker than your pants. Black socks are always safe. For the truly color-blind, buy different-colored socks from different manufacturers, making sure each color has a distinctive toe stitch.

▶ Choose belts that repeat your shoe color, traditionally black or brown. Black shoes go with blue or gray suits; dark brown shoes with tan suits.

▶ Coordinate suspenders worn in place of a belt with your shirt or tie color.

For the one out of 11 men who are colorblind, get a friend to arrange your wardrobe, then write numbers on the labels with a permanent marker to note which clothes coordinate.

Source:
Dress for Excellence by Lois Fenton with Edward Olcott, Rawson Associates, New York, 1986

Hair replacement treatments: The bald facts

About 35 million men and almost 20 million women are bald or are going to be bald very soon. And apparently, most people don't really believe that "bald is beautiful" because the $1-billion-a-year hair replacement business is booming.

Despite the advance in treatments, there is still no surefire way to beat baldness, but you do have four basic options for handling your hair loss.

1. Have some hair surgically attached. This is the most expensive, as well as the most dangerous, way of handling hair loss. If your pocketbook survives the procedure (costs range from several thousand to as much as $60,000), you're liable to suffer from scarring, swelling, or infection.

   In the United States, you have three surgical options to choose from: flap surgery, scalp reduction, and transplant surgery. There is a special surgery which involves attaching hundreds of tiny hair anchors under your scalp, but the Food and Drug Administration (FDA) hasn't approved this procedure in the United States yet. You'll have to fly to France for this treatment.

   Flap surgery involves rotating a section of your scalp with hair to a neighboring section without hair. If the flaps don't hold, as they sometimes don't, you'll be left with ugly scars. Cost: $1,800 to $10,000.

   During a scalp reduction, the surgeon actually cuts away bald sections of your scalp and pulls sections with hair closer together. Cost: $1,800 to $10,000.

   Transplant surgery, the most common and widely accepted of the hair replacement surgical options, involves grafting sections of hair from the sides and back of a person's head (the areas where 75 percent of all hair grows) onto bald areas. Cost: $6,000 to $15,000.

   Make sure you thoroughly check out any surgeon you choose to use. You should talk to at least three or four different ones before you make a decision. You can get surgeon referrals from the American Hair Loss Council at 1-800-274-8717.

2. Wing it with a wig or other coverup. Options in this category range from spray-on hair to actual hair pieces. Spray-on hair, which simply colors your scalp the same color your hair used to be, costs about $30 a month.

   Hairpieces, or toupees or wigs, generally look better than spray-on hair, but you'll also pay more. They're easily attached in private, but they're often just as easily knocked off, sometimes in public. Cost: $2,000 to $3,000.

   To prevent embarrassing hair mishaps, you may opt to have hair woven or glued onto the existing hair you have left on your head. This type of hair won't come loose even if you decide to parachute from a plane, but you'll have to have this additional hair "adjusted" or "tightened" every few weeks as your natural hair grows. This service costs from $50 to $100 per session. Initial cost is about the same as for a toupee, but you'll have to invest in new hair (another $2,000 to $3,000) every two to three years.

3. Rub in some new hair. Hair replacement shampoos and lotions run the range of weird remedies, from tar-based to placenta-based. Most don't work. The only one that holds any promise at all is Rogaine, which can actually halt hair loss and may help you grow some new.

   This treatment works best for people in the beginning stages of hair loss. About 40 percent of the people who use Rogaine grow a little new hair. Only 10 percent grow thick, healthy, horselike manes. Cost: $30 for a month's supply.

If you stop using Rogaine two times a day for the rest of your life, you'll lose any new hair that you grew as well as any hair destined to fall out before you started the treatment. In addition, the main ingredient in Rogaine, minoxidil, causes heart problems in a few people.

4. Finally, if you can't beat 'em, join 'em. You decide bald really is beautiful and save yourself a lot of money and time. If you're ever tempted to change your mind, just remind yourself that Yul Brenner's or Demi Moore's sex appeal wasn't hurt when they didn't have hair.

Source:
Money (25,3:152)

Cheap and simple skin care

Who says the kitchen is only for cooking? It's also a great place to whip up some cheap and simple skin care solutions that will keep your skin looking great.

▶ Zap pimples with lemon juice. Use a cotton swab to apply to problem areas.

▶ Place raw, grated potatoes under your eyes to get rid of undereye bags and puffiness.

▶ Make an equal mix of cider vinegar and water to clean and tone your skin.

▶ Mix oatmeal with honey, milk, and water to make a good cleansing mask. Pat cream on face, and let sit for fifteen minutes. Rinse with warm water.

▶ Use a yogurt-based cleansing cream for oily skin. Mix 1 teaspoon of plain yogurt with half an egg yolk, 1/2 teaspoon of honey, and a pinch of corn-starch. Pat cream on face; leave in place for 15 minutes. Wash off with warm water. If you have normal to dry skin, use strawberry yogurt.

▶ Slough away dead skin with an equal crushed mixture of papaya and pineapple. Massage mixture into skin and leave on for 20 minutes. Remove with warm water.

These quick and easy home remedies will help you keep your skin looking great. In addition, you should remember to drink six to eight glasses of water a day to keep skin moist and supple. If you live in an extremely dry climate, consider sleeping with a vaporizer in your room.

Source:
Dress Like a Million by Leah Feldon, Villard Books, New York, 1994

Wrinkle creams that really work

With the slew of antiwrinkle creams flooding the market, it's hard to know which, if any, really work.

The new alpha hydroxy acid creams are a good bet. Made from the natural acids found in citrus fruits, apples, grapes, milk, and sugar cane, advertisers endorse these creams for everything from the bottom of your feet to the top of your head. Alpha hydroxy acids are recommended to firm up sagging skin, wipe out wrinkles, and help remove sun spots, blotchiness, and other types of skin discoloration.

AHAs work by speeding up your body's process of shedding dead skin cells, which means that your skin can renew itself more quickly. The moisturizing agents these creams contain, such as sunflower oil or almond extract, also help erase tiny wrinkles from your hands.

Even more important than an AHA however, is regular use of a sunscreen. If you use both together, put the AHA cream on first and then apply a layer of sunscreen. Some AHAs include sunscreen. Whatever form of sunscreen you choose, make sure it has a Sun Protection Factor (SPF) of 15.

And sunscreen is not just for the beach or outdoor activities. When driving, it's especially important to put some sunscreen on your face and the backs of your hands. You get more damaging sun exposure during that time than you might think.

Some tips when using alpha hydroxy acids

► At first, use AHAs only once a day. This will give your skin time to adjust. Also, you'll lessen any harmful effects that may occur if you have a reaction.

► An AHA level of less than 4 percent may not be effective. Keep track of what you are using and find a level — somewhere between 4–10 — that works for you without making your skin feel too tingly or tight. (Keep in mind that these products often do cause some stinging when first applied to the skin, but don't worry unless the feeling lasts more than 2–3 minutes or if you notice excessive blotching or redness.)

► Most cosmetics contain only a small amount of AHAs, so they ought not have any adverse effects.

► A note of caution: Although AHA products appear to be effective, they have yet to be sufficiently tested by the Food and Drug Administration. Because of their current popularity, however, the FDA hopes to have a set of guidelines outlined by the end of this year.

The best advice, for now, is to either check with a dermatologist or stick to products that contain AHA levels no greater than 8 percent. Monitor yourself, and if you have any adverse reaction to these products, either switch to a lower percentage of AHA or stop using them.

Source:
New Choices (34,3:19)

Let a student beautify you

You can get a good haircut, perm, or color treatment at a low price at your local beauty or barber school. Letting someone learn on your looks may not appeal to you, but most people are happy with their results. The beauty and barber school students will certainly give you the very best treatment they can. Check your yellow pages for these schools and call about their prices.

Source:
1001 Ways to Cut Your Expenses by Jonathan D. Pond, Dell Publishing, New York, 1992

BUYING ANTIQUES AND COLLECTORS' ITEMS

How to make sure your antique is really an antique

If you want an investment you can enjoy every day, consider antiques. Unlike modern furniture, antiques easily hold and usually increase in value. Plus, they add a certain charm and character to every home. Here are seven shopping suggestions from antique dealers themselves:

- ▶ Look for wood with a rich warm color, square corners and joints, and matching grain where planks of wood meet. If a piece generally looks good, don't be put off by a few cracks in the wood. That's a normal part of aging.
- ▶ Be on guard for fake or altered antiques. Some signs to search for include new nails in an old piece; a table top from one table screwed to the legs of a different table; antique sideboards with sawed off legs; varnishing stain on an unfinished part of the furniture, such as a drawer (sometimes used to make wood look older); name of a piano manufacturer on a panel of furniture (sometimes old, out-of-tune pianos are used to repair furniture); garden tables or chairs repainted gray or black to resemble Victorian cast iron. Real cast iron will be extremely heavy to lift.
- ▶ Shop at safe places, such as a vetted fair. The pieces offered at these fairs must meet the approval of the fair committee, which is made up of dealers and collectors who review each piece.
- ▶ Shop before sunup or do your dealing after dark at fairs and flea markets. Amateurs get the best bargains if they arrive at the same time the vendors start to set up or wait until almost closing time. Don't forget your flashlight. You'll probably need it.
- ▶ Find furniture that will meet your needs. A fine piece of furniture is not such a great investment if you can't get it through your front door into your house, if it's taller than your ceiling, or if you can't stand to sit on it once you get it home.
- ▶ Bargain for a better deal. Many dealers will agree to a 10 percent discount; some, 20 percent. But don't belittle the item, the shop, or the dealer or you're liable to have to say bye-bye to any bargain at all.
- ▶ Ask for a receipt that describes the item purchased, any repairs or restorations done, and the return policy. Be sure your receipt includes the dealer's name, address, and phone number.

Happy hunting!

Source:
The Wall Street Journal (Jan. 26, 1996, B10)

Antiques: Where to shop for what

Certain types of antiques are easier to find in some places than others. Generally, the thirteen original colonies and Ohio offer the finest antique furniture. Even in this area, certain regions have certain specialties. Here's where to find what:

New England: Shaker.

New York: American Art Deco.

South: Victorian. Some Empire in the Atlanta, Georgia, area.

Texas: Empire.

Source:
The Wall Street Journal (Jan. 26, 1996, B10)

Antiquing in England

England is still a hot spot for antiques due to the wealth of the nation in the 18th and 19th centuries. You'll find decorative artwork, period furniture, old silver, porcelain, carpets, jewelry, and other treasures.

The markets:

▶ Top end: Check King's Road or Pimlico in London. Outside London, the towns of Stow-on-the-Wold and Tetbury offer quality antiques.

▶ Mid- to high-range: Try Camden Passage or the Tower Bridge Road area in London. Outside London, Brighton and Harrogate also feature a variety of antique stores.

Many serious collectors plan their trips for June, the month of the Olympia Fine Arts Fair and the Antiques Fair in the Grosvenor Hotel on Park Lane.

Source:
The Wall Street Journal (Jan. 26, 1996, B10)

Buying antique jewelry for pleasure and profit

Technically, antique jewelry is over 100 years old. However, in popular usage, antique jewelry refers to any item made two to three generations previous to the present. Art Deco style items of the 1920s and 1930s balance on the border between antique and vintage.

In the U.S., you'll most commonly find antique jewelry from the Civil War, late Victorian, and turn-of-the-century eras. You can find older pieces in areas that were settled during Colonial times, such as parts of the South and the East coast.

If investing in antique jewelry sounds appealing to you, here are some tips that may help:

▶ Build up a wealth of practical knowledge before you begin buying. One good place to start is Rose Leiman Goldenberg's book *Antique Jewelry: A Practical and Passionate Guide* (Crown Publishers, 1976). You should be able to find this book at a local library.

► Attend antique shows. You'll find dealers who specialize in antique jewelry as well as those sellers who just keep a few jewelry pieces mixed in with their regular wares. If you're just starting out, stay with the dealers who specialize. They'll be better able to answer your questions in addition to generally carrying the highest quality pieces. You'll also usually find higher quality items at an exclusive show that charges admission than at a free show at a mall or flea market.

► Deal with a dealer you know and trust, especially if you don't have enough experience to trust your own judgment yet. Look for a dealer who has clean, neat displays containing a variety of items. Ask if the dealer belongs to any jewelry or antique associations. One who does may have to meet higher selling standards than one who does not. Reputable dealers will also provide you with a receipt, which describes your jewelry purchase in detail and notes its approximate age.

► Invest in a jeweler's loupe — a small magnifying glass with a magnification of at least 10 powers (written 10x on the loupe). You can find these devices at hobby shops, rock shops, scientific supply firms, and jewelry supply houses. To examine jewelry, hold the loupe about one inch from your eye. Hold the piece you're examining directly under the loupe. It will take practice to overcome the natural tendency to use a loupe like a magnifying glass.

► Closely examine, under natural light if possible, the workmanship of any piece you're considering. Check each gemstone for cracks, chips, or scratches.

► Examine metal for signs of wear, especially on rings. If the gold has rubbed off and you can see base metal underneath, this probably indicates that the piece is gold plated instead of real gold.

► Look for signs of repair, such as gray solder marks on the undersides of brooches or rings.

► Expect to see some signs of wear in antique jewelry. If you don't, ask the dealer for an explanation. Few signs of wear could mean the piece is a reproduction or that it has been polished, which some people say devalues antique jewelry.

If you're into antiques of any sort, you probably already know not to expect perfection. This applies to antique jewelry as well. If the piece was well loved, it's bound to show some signs of wear.

Source:
Buying Jewelry: Everything You Need to Know Before You Buy by Anne Bingham, HarperCollins Publishers, New York, 1989

Making money on trading cards

If you want to make money in the trading card market, forget about being simply a collector. In fact, you need to start by selling every card you now own. Don't expect to get catalog value for your cards. Just sell them.

Do some homework before you jump in the market. Study the price guides, subscribe to *Baseball America*, and, if you have a computer, buy card-collecting software such as The Card Collector from AbleSoft (Yorktown, Va.).

Once you've sold all your cards, get ready to buy undervalued cards you don't have, not to keep forever, but to sell later on.

To get top dollar, buy and sell complete sets. Dealers want complete sets because they mean less work and more money. You may be able to trade with someone to complete a set.

Ignore the price guides: Buy top quality. You want cards that meet the industry standard of *near mint* condition. Make sure you take a card out of its case and inspect it closely before you buy. Examine the corners; check for centering; make sure the print registration is right; even take a loupe and make sure the dot pattern isn't random. If it is, the card may be counterfeit.

Buy cards of Hall of Famers. These make up 90 percent of the market. Some great picks are: Ted Williams cards, Red Schoendienst cards, mid-grade '50s and '60s cards of Hall of Famers, tobacco hockey cards, Turkey Reds, Carlton Fisk cards, and stickers. Topps Double-headers, 3-Ds, Triple-headers, and other Topps are usually good buys, along with Donruss Pop-Ups, Opening Day sets, and All-Stars. More good deals to buy are Fleer boxed sets, Tiffany sets, minor-league team sets (the year they are issued), and lesser-known tobacco cards.

Set up at a show to sell your cards. You don't have to be a registered dealer. Walk the floors, find out what other dealers are asking for their cards, and sell your cards for 10 percent less. By setting up at a show, you may also be able to buy some older cards at a bargain price, like $2 or $5. (Never pay anywhere near the price listed in the catalog.)

Check the ads in the *Sports Collectors Digest*, and do what the dealers do. If the dealers are selling one player's card and offering to buy another, follow their lead.

Don't buy autographs. Just about everyone who wants a player's autograph has it.

Sell black-and-whites, exhibits, insert cards, cards made after 1989, Upper Deck cards, freebies, No. 1 draft picks, young pitchers, sportscasters, and politicians. Nobody wants them.

Buy football cards. The prices are down right now. And realize that people will never stop trading baseball cards. The future for basketball cards is less certain.

Sell Rookies of the Year the year after they win the Rookie of the Year award. The cards usually don't hold their value later.

Buy auction lots. Some of the best deals for small collectors have come out of big auctions. Look in the fancy catalogues for lesser known player's jerseys and cards buried behind the million-dollar treasures.

And finally, consider buying the book *101 Ways to Make Money in the Trading-Card Market* by Paul Green and Kit Kiefer, two top authorities on trading cards. They show you the way to financial gain, but remind you to have fun. After all, if you aren't having fun, "get yourself out of this market and into something like frozen pork bellies where you can really express yourself."

Source:
101 Ways to Make Money in the Trading-Card Market by Paul Green and Kit Kiefer, Bonus Books, Chicago, 1994

Making money on sports autographs

If you want to make money on a signature, don't hand a sports superstar one of his trading cards to sign. Trading card collectors want cards in mint condition. They consider cards "spoiled" by any marking, including an autograph.

Instead, take color photos and baseballs. Have a Sharpie permanent marker handy for your sports hero. The slick surface of many photos makes ballpoint pens useless. And you'll get a light and blurry signature from a felt-tip pen. Get a blue Sharpie to please the collector purists. Sharpie ink will bleed on baseballs, however.

Source:
Collecting Sports Autographs by Tom Owens, Bonus Books, Chicago, 1989

Know the limitations of limited-edition plates

Buy a plate because you love what it looks like, never because it is a "limited edition." However, if it's important to you to know that you're one of a select few with a certain plate, then make sure you're not being bamboozled by a plate producer.

Most producers limit plate editions by *year of issue*, by *number of firing days*, or by *absolute limitation*.

Absolute limitation means a producer will only make a limited number of a plate. For instance, the plate company Bing & Grondahl will only produce 15,000 *Christmas in America* plates.

Plates limited by year of issue can only be produced in a certain calendar year. After that year, the molds are destroyed. Many Christmas plates have this limitation.

But – number of firing days can simply be a limited edition scam. More plates are sold with this limitation than any other, but it's usually a meaningless advertising technique. The plate producer Royal Doulton says that if it limited any edition to 30 firing days, it would have enough time to create more than 3,000,000 plates.

Firing days don't even have to be consecutive, so a plate producer could have a 45-day firing limit and still be selling the same plate 10 years later. For four days a year, the producer could farm a popular plate out to a half-dozen plate decorators and produce millions of a particular edition.

Finally, never fall for that advertising line, "This is a strictly limited edition." Who knows what the plate producer means by that.

Source:
Everybody's Guide to Plate Collecting by Herschell Lewis and Margo Lewis, Bonus Books, Chicago, 1994

Coin collecting: How to make money buying rare coins

Whether you decide to get into rare coin collecting because you love holding a little bit of history in your hands or just because you're looking for new ways to diversify your investment portfolio or both, you can make a lot of money if you follow a few simple tips.

▶ If you aren't already fairly knowledgeable in this area, invest in some good coin-collecting books and learn all you can about the types of coins you're interested in buying.

▶ Find a friendly dealer and be friendly yourself. Don't do business with any dealer who won't respond to your friendly overtures and only seems interested in writing receipts for your purchases. Having a friendly relationship with your dealer will get you more good deals and more good advice than buying coins in a cold, businesslike manner.

▶ Trust your instincts. Don't do business with any dealer who seems dishonest or otherwise makes you uncomfortable. And don't buy a coin that looks ugly to you, even if it has the highest grading.

▶ Buy the best. High quality coins consistently get the best returns if you decide to sell. However, never sell a high quality coin when the coin market is in a slump. This is a good time to buy high quality coins though.

▶ Beware of waiting for magic numbers. If a coin you've been eyeing for a while keeps steadily decreasing in price, don't wait until some price guide reveals that the coveted coin has reached the magical number you have in mind. As soon as it's apparent prices are continuing to fall, talk to a dealer about the price you have in mind. You're likely to get it.

▶ Don't follow the crowd. If everyone else is buying, sell. If everyone else is selling, buy.

▶ Diversify your holdings. Your coin collection should not constitute more than 25 percent of your total investments. You should also apply the diversity principle to your coin collection itself. The most valuable collections of rare coins are those that contain different types of coins. Completing a certain set of coins still qualifies as a diverse holding because it contains different dates and mint-marks.

▶ Keep up your confidence in your coin collection. Some collectors get discouraged and give up during especially long slumps in the coin market. Just keep in mind that inflation always brings the coin market back, and coins make a good investment during a depression or in times of extreme prosperity.

▶ Remember that you can't predict the market. This is why you should usually never buy or sell a large quantity of coins at once. You're almost always better off buying or selling just a few coins at a time.

Source:
The Coin Collector's Survival Manual by Scott A. Travers, Bonus Books, Chicago, 1994

THE HEALTHY CONSUMER

Staying healthy without going broke

The money you shell out when you're sick can make you even sicker. Here's how to develop healthier spending habits:

You'll have fewer doctor's visits if you give the doctor as much information about your condition as possible. That way, he can make a better diagnosis and give you the proper medicine the first time. Take a list of questions to ask, and question anything you don't understand. You don't want to pay for visits you could have avoided if you'd made sure you understood each other the first time.

When you go for a second opinion, ask if you can use the same X-rays or relevant tests from the first doctor.

If you're taking a medicine for the first time, ask your doctor for free samples. You can make sure you are not allergic to the drug and that your system can handle it before you pay for a prescription you might not use.

Save money at the pharmacy by asking your doctor to write larger prescriptions for drugs you take regularly. You'll even save money if you have a prescription drug plan through your insurance. You may be able to get a three-month supply of your medicine at once and pay only one deductible. (Some insurance plans limit you to a 30-day supply while others even limit you to a two-week supply, but make sure you maximize your plan.)

If your doctor prescribes you a brand-name drug, ask your doctor or your pharmacist if you can have a generic drug instead. Drug companies don't have patents on generic drugs, so they are usually cheaper. In some states such as Georgia, the law states that a doctor must write *brand necessary* on the prescription if he wants you to get the brand instead of the generic.

Another way to save money on drugs is mail order. You mail your prescription to a pharmacy designated by your insurance company and receive your drugs through the mail later. Ask your insurance company or the benefits manager at your employer if mail order is available to you.

Follow all directions your doctor gives you about your medicine. You don't want to have to buy more just because you didn't follow directions right the first time.

Sources:
Interview with Dell Weaver, pharmacist, Atlanta
How to Pinch a Penny 'Til It Screams by Rochelle LaMotte McDonald, Avery Publishing Group, Garden City Park, N.Y., 1994

Better hospital care

Most people don't know it, but you can get justice (without pressing charges) if you think you've been mistreated in any way by a doctor or nurse in a hospital. Every hospital has a review process, one hospital nurse reveals. If you ask for an *incident report* to be filed against a medical caregiver, it will be filed.

Besides having a report filed against a nurse, you can complain through the hospital chain of command — first ask to speak to the *charge nurse*, then to the *director of nursing*, then to the *hospital manager*.

Source:
Interview with Suzanne Wilson, registered nurse, Upson County Hospital, Thomaston, Ga.

Hospital privacy

Does your insurance company only pay for a semiprivate hospital room? You may be able to get privacy without paying for it yourself. All you have to do is ask if any of the semiprivate rooms are unoccupied. The hospital staff will put you in an empty room if there's one available, but only if you ask for it.

If all the semiprivate rooms have an occupant, ask the hospital what it charges for private rooms. Being alone may be worth the extra $15 or so a day.

Source:
Interview with Suzanne Wilson, registered nurse, Upson County Hospital, Thomaston, Ga.

Hospital money savers

Refuse the hospital admission kit. Take your own supplies instead. If you accept the kit, you'll be charged around $12 for a hospital pillow and $8 for a water pitcher.

Take it with you when you go. If the hospital does slip a pillow under you, take it home afterwards. The staff will just throw away anything they use on you. Those wash basins are great for hand laundry.

Take your own prescription medicines. The hospital staff won't like it, but you can insist on using your own prescription eye drops, your own aspirin, etc. But don't take your own medicine without telling your doctor and nurse. You could have a drug interaction. For instance, you wouldn't want to take your own aspirin if your doctor is giving you Coumadin.

Ask when the hospital day starts. The exact time a 24-hour "day" begins can vary from hospital to hospital. If you can check in after a day starts or check out before another day begins, you can save money.

Try to limit your hospital stay to less than 24 hours. Many hospitals consider you an outpatient if you stay for less than 24 hours. Insurance companies often pay the entire bill for outpatient care instead of charging you a copayment.

Don't let the hospital issue you another pair of crutches if you or a friend has a set at home.

Never get any care in an emergency room that can be provided in a doctor's office. Emergency room care is expensive.

Ask to have your medicine *p.o.* **(by mouth) instead of** *I.M.* **(by shots) or** *I.V* **(intravenously).** Unless you can't keep your medicine down or there's some other reason you need shots or an I.V., take your medicine by mouth. It's a lot less expensive.

Provide your own blood. If you're having elective surgery, you may be able to store your own blood ahead of time.

Examine your final bill very carefully. Make sure you aren't charged for treatment and equipment you didn't receive.

Source:
Interview with Suzanne Wilson, registered nurse, Upson County Hospital, Thomaston, Ga.

Free health and weight loss classes

Instead of paying for Weight Watchers classes every week, go to free classes at your local hospital. Hospitals provide many educational freebies as a community service. Take advantage of free breast-feeding consultants, colostomy consultants, diabetes classes, and dietary consultants, especially during a hospital stay.

Source:
Interview with Suzanne Wilson, registered nurse, Upson County Hospital, Thomaston, Ga.

Less painful hospital stays

Picture yourself in the hospital after surgery, in severe pain, begging your nurse for medicine to kill the throbbing ache — because that's exactly where you'll be if you don't make other post-surgery arrangements.

It's not the nurse's fault. Most pain medicines are listed on your chart as *p.r.n.* That means "repeat as requested." You have to ask for it before you get it.

However, the nurse will usually give you your medicine on a regular schedule, every four hours or so, if you make it clear that's what you prefer. Or, you can ask for your medicine 20 minutes before you think you'll really need it.

Even better, ask for a *PCA (Patient Controlled Analgesia).* With this handy system, you can give the pain medicine to yourself.

If you aren't getting adequate relief, ask your nurse to see if your doctor can prescribe another painkiller. Medicines have different effects on different people.

One of the most common mistakes people make during hospital stays is waiting until they are in severe pain before asking for medicine. It's very rare to become addicted to a painkiller during a short hospital stay.

Besides, nurses say, it takes more medicine to relieve pain than to prevent it. So don't try to be a hero. Take the medicine you need, when you need it.

Source:
Interview with Suzanne Wilson, registered nurse, Upson County Hospital, Thomaston, Ga.

How to check out your doctor

According to Dr. Robert Derbyshire, a former president of the Federation of State Medical Boards, 10 percent of U.S. doctors are incompetent. Since choosing a doctor can sometimes mean the difference between life and death, you want to choose a good one. Here's how:

▶ Check him out through the American Medical Association's Physician Masterfile. This is a computerized database that tracks licensed medical doctors (M.D.s) and doctors of osteopathy (D.O.s) from medical school to retirement.

This database will tell you where the doctor went to school, when he graduated, if he's certified in any specialties, if any disciplinary action has ever been taken against him, states he's licensed in, and when he was licensed. For information from Masterfile, call 1-312-464-5000.

You may also want to check a two-volume directory called *10,289 Questionable Doctors*, published by Public Citizen. Your local library will probably have a copy or can assist you in locating one. This book provides a nationwide listing of doctors, dentists, chiropractors, and podiatrists who have been disciplined for poor health care and unethical or illegal activities.

If you're looking for a specialist to treat a specific problem, keep in mind that almost 30 percent of the doctors who call themselves specialists haven't been certified by a board of medical specialties. The ones who have are referred to as *diplomates* of the particular board which certified them.

To check out a specialist, call the American Board of Medical Specialties (ABMS) hot line at 1-800-776-2378. Although doctors of osteopathy have different specialty certification boards, they are sometimes certified by the ABMS. If your D.O. specialist isn't listed there, call the American Osteopathic Association at 1-800-621-1773.

Here are some other points to consider when selecting a doctor. If your doctor is a specialist, the *ABMS Directory* can answer many of these questions for you. If you belong to an HMO, the member services department should be able to give you this information.

▶ What hospitals is the doctor affiliated with? A doctor with no hospital affiliations could be a doctor to stay away from. It may mean his hospital privileges have been revoked, and other hospitals are avoiding him.

To find the very best doctor, look for a doctor on the attending staff of a prestigious hospital. But keep in mind that hospital reputations vary from specialty to specialty. A little-known hospital can sometimes have the best reputation in a certain field.

▶ Does your doctor serve on a medical school faculty? If he does and the school is reputable, this usually indicates a good treatment track record. You should still look for a doctor who is involved in direct patient care on a daily basis instead of spending most of his time in the classroom.

▶ Does your doctor keep up with the latest developments in his field? If you're searching for a doctor to treat a special condition, read some of the most recent research concerning your condition. Get your local librarian to help you locate research in reputable medical journals or call a research foundation that offers information about your particular condition, such as the American Academy of Allergy and Immunology. Ask your doctor about the studies you've read to see if he's kept up with the latest findings.

Feel free to ask your doctor any questions concerning his qualifications or your health. If he gets angry or exasperated, get another doctor.

Source:
Get the Facts on Anyone by Dennis King, Macmillan, New York, 1995

Problems with your doctor? How to file a complaint

Luckily, it doesn't happen very often. But sometimes a doctor's behavior or business practices are enough to, well, make you sick.

For example, what if your doctor's bill doesn't make sense to you? It seems far too high and you don't remember taking all those tests. When you contact the doctor's office for an explanation, your phone calls are never returned.

Or you ask your doctor to explain a medical diagnosis, and she becomes angry and sarcastic and huffs out of the room.

What can you do?

Report it.

According to the American Medical Association, you can file a complaint with your state or county medical association (listed in the phone book).

"When a patient calls us, we send them a form to fill out. They describe their complaint and sign it," notes Ginger Moore of the Medical Association of Georgia. "We request the patient's medical records from the doctor and let him or her know that this person has signed a grievance."

"If the dispute is over billing, the investigator may also contact the insurance company involved," Moore continues. "Sometimes procedures have simply been inaccurately coded."

A reviewer will speak to you and your doctor, and then bring all the facts before the grievance committee.

What happens if the doctor is found guilty of unethical or unprofessional behavior? It depends on how serious the charge is. A rude doctor may just get a letter advising him to control his temper and apologize to his patient, or the problem may be handed over the State Board of Medical Examiners, which can revoke medical licenses.

Source:
Interview with Ginger Moore, member, Medical Association of Atlanta Grievance Committee, Atlanta

Your right to your medical records

In many states, you have the legal right to see your medical records. Doctors and hospitals must give you (at your expense) all test results, diagnosis information, laboratory reports, X-rays, prescriptions, and any other medical information you ask for.

Not only do you often have the right to see your records, you should want to see them. Since your employer and your insurance company have access to them, you need to make sure they are accurate. An inaccuracy in your medical records may cause an insurance company to reject a claim you file someday.

Of course, even if you don't live in a state that gives you the legal right to your records, any doctor worth his salt will be eager to share your medical information with you. It's also a good idea to keep your own personal medical record at home.

Source:
Georgia Law (Section 31-33-1 — 31-33-6)

Body work: Treat yourself to a tuneup

"Body work" sounds like something your car needs after your grandson's bike smashes into the rear fender, but it's also a term for the therapeutic use of touch. Body work is more than massage: It's a total-body tuneup.

Dr. Andrew Weil, an authority in natural and preventive medicine, recommends four of his favorite types of body work.

Feldenkrais work is a gentle and effective system of floor exercises and massage. It is meant to retrain the central nervous system to find new pathways around blocked or damaged areas. To put it simply, Feldenkrais teaches you to move easier.

Here's an easy lesson: Turn your head slowly to the right until it stops. Face forward again, close your eyes, and imagine doing the same movement. Vividly imagine the movement becoming smoother and easier over 10 or 15 times. Now actually turn your head to the right. Has the movement improved?

Don't be concerned if a friend tells you she's "getting rolfed." Someone *is* "working her over," but in a good way. *Rolfing* is a firm massage. It can even be painful. You usually go through a series of massages, each focusing on a different part of the body. The idea is to break up tissues that have begun to stick together and grow rigid. The release of tension you feel can be very emotional.

A *shiatsu* masseuse uses her fingers only. She will use them at right angles to your body to improve your energy and blood circulation. That's called *tonification*. *Calming* is a gentle, rocking motion of the masseuse's fingers. *Dispersal* is a very active motion to distribute energy and break up blood blockages. This healing art is from Japan.

If you want to relax and feel good about yourself, try *Trager work*. The practitioner will gently rock, cradle, and rotate your body parts, releasing tense muscles and increasing your flexibility. Trager work has helped people with traumatic injuries, disabilities, polio, and other problems involving the nerves and muscles.

Some Trager practitioners will also teach you dancelike exercises to help you move more easily. One exercise is simply letting your arms drop freely to one side, and another is adding a shaking motion to your foot while you walk.

Sources:
Alternative Medicine: The Definitive Guide, The Burton Goldberg Group, Future Medicine Publishing, Puyallup, Wash., 1993
Nursing Times (89,46:38)
Spontaneous Healing: How to Discover and Enhance Your Body's Natural Ability to Maintain and Heal Itself by Andrew Weil, M.D., Alfred A. Knopf, New York, 1995

Chiropractic care helps 1 in 3

If you've been suffering with low back pain, you may be considering what a chiropractor could do for you. It's understandable — one in 20 Americans had chiropractic treatment last year. And according to one major study, most of them are happier with the outcome than people who were treated in traditional hospitals.

Your doctor may not think it's a great idea, though. Many traditional doctors think of chiropractors as quacks. After all, some chiropractors claim to be able to cure everything from bed-wetting to cancer.

How are chiropractors different from medical doctors? Chiropractors are the third largest group of health professionals, right behind doctors and dentists. Most chiropractic colleges offer four- and five-year degrees and require two years of previous college experience. While these standards are not as tough as those required for a medical degree, chiropractic colleges are accredited, and chiropractors must be licensed by the state. Unlike regular medical doctors, chiropractors are not allowed to prescribe medicine or perform surgery.

How does chiropractic work? Here's the theory in a nutshell: You have 33 individual bony vertebrae in your spinal column. Hundreds of nerves branch off the spine through openings in the vertebrae. Chiropractors believe that tiny misalignments in the vertebrae, called subluxations, can pinch these nerves. The body parts that are served by the nerves can't function correctly. By adjusting your vertebrae and eliminating the subluxations, chiropractors relieve the pressure on your nerves and allow your body to heal.

Does chiropractic help back pain? Yes. Studies have shown that chiropractic care relieves low back pain better than outpatient hospital care.

The people treated by chiropractors were also less likely to suffer a relapse. In a study that followed people over a three-year period, the people treated by chiropractors showed a 29 percent greater improvement in their symptoms than those treated by hospital therapists.

In another survey, people seeing a chiropractor were three times more likely to report that they were very satisfied than those who were being treated by a family doctor.

Can chiropractic also relieve headaches? Chiropractic can't help with all types of headaches, but it may help with tension headaches. Sometimes muscle spasms in the neck and shoulders cause tension headaches. Chiropractic therapy can help loosen and relax the muscles and allow your spine to move normally again.

Does chiropractic cure diseases and infections? Some chiropractors say that spinal adjustments are necessary for the health of every part of your body. They claim to be able to cure ear infections, allergies, bed-wetting, infantile colic, and asthma. However, there's no real scientific evidence to support these claims, and not all chiropractors agree with them.

How do I choose a chiropractor? If you decide to see a chiropractor, call your state's Chiropractic Board of Examiners before you make an appointment. (Look in your telephone book under state government.) They can tell you if the chiropractor is licensed, and whether or not people have complained about him or his practices.

Then call the chiropractor himself and ask questions. Does he only treat bone and muscle problems like back and neck pain? Is he willing to refer you to a doctor if necessary? Does he recommend long-term treatment?

How many treatments are necessary? Seven to 12 treatments per injury should be enough to relieve back pain. If you don't see an improvement in three weeks, chiropractic therapy may not work for you.

Chiropractic can be a safe, natural alternative to drugs or surgery for back pain. It may lead to a quicker, longer-lasting recovery for many people. Just remember to use caution when considering chiropractic care for any ailment, and don't hesitate to ask questions.

Sources:
American Health (11,3:41)
British Medical Journal (300,6737:1431 and 311,7001:349)
Canadian Medical Association Journal (152,3:329)
Health (7,4:45)
National Headache Foundation (Fall 1994)
The Atlanta Journal/Constitution (Dec. 18, 1995, B5)
The Western Journal of Medicine (150,3:351)

Top 10 healing herbs

When buying herbs, it's hard to know if you are getting anything in return for the money you shell out. With prescription drugs, at least you have hundreds of laboratory studies to tell you how the medicine should make you feel.

Some herbs have more proven track records than others. Based on centuries of experience plus scientific evidence, these herbs are likely to be true healers, experts say.

Chamomile — for indigestion
Echinacea — for boosting immunity
Feverfew — for migraine headaches
Garlic — for lowering cholesterol
Ginger — for nausea
Ginkgo — for circulation, especially to the brain
Hawthorn — for heart disease (consult your doctor before using)
Milk thistle — for liver damage (consult your doctor before using)

Saw palmetto — for enlarged prostate

Valerian — for sleep problems

Garlic, echinacea, chamomile, and ginkgo are also some of the most popular herbs. Other herbs people like to buy are ginseng, aloe vera, and goldenseal. Ginseng and goldenseal may be more likely to waste your money than give you any real benefits.

Sources:
Varro Tyler of Purdue University and Norman Farnsworth of the University of Illinois, cited in *Consumer Reports* (60,11:700)
HerbalGram (36:58)

The best time to use herbs

When you pay attention to your body, you learn that you have a certain run-down feeling before the cold symptoms furiously strike, you feel the itch before the cold sore erupts, and you have a vague sense of unrest before the infection takes hold.

That's the ideal time to use herbs, says Master Herbalist Debra St. Claire. In our Western society, we tend to use drugs and herbs to treat symptoms. With *ayurvedic medicine* (the oldest recorded healing system, originally from India), you use herbs to give your body strength and restore your imbalances before you get sick.

Once you're sick, you may need prescription drugs, which can interact dangerously with herbal treatments.

Using mild herbs in your food and drink is just one of the many ways you can keep your body free from tension, daily pain, and disease. And that may be the key to avoiding such killers as cancer and heart disease.

Source:
Healthy & Natural Journal (2,1:116)

Herbs vs. prescription drugs

Herbs and drugs aren't as different as you might think. Herbs are simply plants that are used to flavor foods or plants with medicinal value. And, the main ingredient in about a quarter of the prescription drugs sold in the United States comes from plants. For instance, the drugs Digoxin and Digitoxin come from the herb digitalis.

Drug companies know that plants can heal, and they would love to profit from selling herbs like ginger or garlic, but our government's Food and Drug Administration makes that almost impossible. The FDA began to lay down the law in the early 1900s when a series of deadly food and drug scandals rocked the United States. The final straw was the 1950s tragedy when the "safe" sleep aid thalidomide caused serious birth defects in thousands of children. At that time, the FDA passed a law that said drugs must be proven safe and effective before they are sold.

That sounds simple and fair, but to get through the FDA drug approval process, drug companies must spend years of research and millions of dollars to prove the safety and effectiveness of a drug. No drug company is going to spend that kind of money unless they can get a patent on a drug. A patent means nobody else can sell the drug, at least until the patent runs out.

Healing herbs can't be patented. Anyone can go out into his backyard and grow an herb. So, drug companies pinpoint the ingredient in the herb that has medicinal value, work with that ingredient in their laboratories to make it chemically unique and possibly more effective than before, then patent drugs made out of these "new" chemicals.

Selling a drug made out of an herb is profitable, but selling the herb itself as a medicine usually isn't.

Herbs can save you money, but use caution. Garlic seems to lower cholesterol as well as many prescription drugs, with fewer side effects. Garlic costs about 15 cents per day, compared with approximately $4 for a prescription drug. Some herbs for migraines cost cents a day instead of the dollars you'd spend on prescription drugs.

Herbs also give you more control over your health care. But since you are in control, you need to use extra caution to stay safe.

▶ Learn as much as you can about the herbs you plan to take. (The American Botanical Council has published English translations of excellent German descriptions of herbs. These reports combine historical traditional use with modern scientific information.)

▶ Buy herbs with labels that say they've been "standardized." That means the manufacturer has tried to get a consistent amount of the healing herb in each pill.

▶ Don't use more of an herb than experts recommend. You may even want to use lower-than-normal doses, especially if you are older.

▶ Pay attention to your body's reaction to the herbs you take. Know the symptoms of toxicity.

▶ Tell your doctor you are using herbs, especially if you also take prescription drugs.

Sources:
Medical Tribune for the Internist and Cardiologist (36,2:11)
The Honest Herbal by Varro E. Tyler, Ph.D., The Haworth Press, Binghamton, N.Y., 1993
The Journal of the American Medical Association (273,8:607)

Tip-offs to rip-offs

Unfortunately, experimenting with alternative medicine can be like leaping into murky waters filled with hungry piranhas. Don't be a victim of health fraud. Watch out for these red flags of fraud:

▶ A claim that the product works by a "secret formula."

▶ Ads in the back pages of magazines, phone solicitations, editorial-style newspaper ads, and 30-minute television commercials.

▶ A claim that the product is an amazing or miraculous breakthrough. Real medical breakthroughs are rare. Most alternative medical practices that work have been around for a while.

- ▶ Promises of easy weight loss.
- ▶ Guarantees of a quick, painless cure.

Steer clear of any alternative medicine doctor who wants you to quit seeing your regular doctor. He should want to work along with your regular doctor. Also, ask any practitioner of alternative therapy if he is certified.

Before you begin a treatment, try to find people who've gone through it already. Most people will be honest about their experience.

Be open-minded, but be wary, too.

Source:
FDA Consumer (29,5:10)

How to get unconventional cancer treatments for free

Every day, scientific researchers study new cancer treatments, searching for breakthroughs that really work to fight the growth and spread of tumors.

Every day, people with cancer search for treatments that haven't been proven in scientific laboratories, hoping against hope to find the miracle that will cure their disease.

These two groups can help each other. If you are interested in trying an unconventional, unproven treatment for cancer, don't go to a quack who claims to have a secret cure. Instead, ask your doctor if you are eligible to participate in a *clinical trial*.

Researchers use clinical trials to find out if promising new treatment methods really work. If you participate in one of these treatment studies, you (along with many others with cancer) will be given the new treatment and carefully watched. All your reactions will be written down and compared with others.

When the study is over, the researchers will gather all their findings, publish them in medical journals, and discuss them at scientific conferences. If the study results are positive, the unconventional experiment you were a part of may become a common treatment for millions of people who have cancer.

Participating in a trial is a safe way to try out unproven cancer treatments. Don't be bamboozled by people offering unconventional treatments who may either waste your money or, worse, waste the valuable time you need to take advantage of therapies that can really work.

When you're deciding whether to try an unproven remedy, take these steps:

- ▶ Ask a librarian to help you find out if the treatment has been reported in reputable scientific journals.
- ▶ Be wary of any treatment that is mainly dietary or nutrition therapy. Scientists don't believe right now that you can get rid of cancerous cells in your body simply by changing your diet.
- ▶ Watch out for treatments that supposedly have no side effects. Cancer treatments have to be powerful, so it's not likely that you'll find an effective therapy with no side effects.

If you're interested in participating in a clinical trial, ask your doctor to use PDQ (Physician Data Query) to get information for you. PDQ is a computer database of information from the National Cancer Institute.

You can also call the NCI's Cancer Information Service to request information about clinical trials. The staff will tell you about cancer-related services in your area. The toll-free number of the Cancer Information Service is 1-800-4-CANCER (1-800-422-6237).

By the way, you don't have to have cancer to take part in a clinical trial. People without cancer can contribute to medical science by helping researchers find new ways to stop the disease before it starts.

Source:
National Cancer Institute, Office of Cancer Communications, 31 Center Drive, MSC 2580, Bethesda, Md. 20892–2580

Seafood safety

Striving for a low-fat, nutritious diet, people are eating more fish these days than ever before. But seafood carries its own special set of risks. Some fish is contaminated with chemical pollutants, such as polychlorinated biphenyls (PCBs), mercury, and dioxin. Mercury comes naturally from the earth, but large amounts are also released into the atmosphere and ocean when wastes are burned. High levels of any of these chemicals could cause cancer.

Fish can also be contaminated with deadly bacteria, or histamine can grow on fish that isn't kept cool enough after it's caught. Histamine can cause scombroid fish poisoning, a disease which gives you allergylike symptoms that usually disappear on their own after a few days.

Fish should be a weekly part of a healthy diet, but only if you follow some precautions.

► Don't eat fish more than three times a week.
► Don't eat shark or swordfish more than once a week. More than that could give you mercury poisoning.
► Alternate between freshwater and saltwater fish.
► Eat smaller fish. It will have been exposed to chemical pollution for fewer years.
► Pregnant women should eat fish from inland waters only once a month. Toddlers, frail older people, and people with chronic or immune diseases shouldn't eat fish very often either.
► Three times a week should be the upper limit on tuna for children.
► Toxins collect in the fat, so get rid of as much fat as possible before cooking.
► Sportsmen who eat their catch may want to contact the nearest Environmental Protection Agency regional office to find out if they are fishing in polluted waters. You'll find EPA offices in Boston, New York, Philadelphia, Atlanta, Chicago, Dallas, Kansas City, Denver, San Francisco, and Seattle. Fishing is banned in some lakes and rivers, but even small, private lakes may not be safe. A lake near a farm or industrial area can be full of chemicals and fertilizers.

▶ Don't eat raw shellfish. The highest risk of a deadly infection comes from raw oysters and other shellfish. Raw oysters from the Gulf of Mexico can contain *Vibrio vulnificus* bacteria, which can cause diarrhea, serious illness, and even death. Cooking the oysters kills the bacteria. Oysters harvested between April and October are the most likely to be contaminated.

You shouldn't be afraid of seafood if you keep it cold, clean, and cooked. Enjoy the health benefits of fish often; just don't go overboard.

Sources:
Archives of Family Medicine (2,2:210)
FDA Consumer (28,7:5 and 29,6:2)
Medical Tribune (34,1:21 and 34,3:16)

Weak link between electromagnetic fields and cancer

Given a choice, most people wouldn't buy a house next to a power line. That's probably wise, but don't be too concerned about the dangers of electromagnetic fields (EMFs). The facts are:

▶ The latest studies of children and electrical workers have not been able to prove a connection between EMFs and cancer.

▶ Recent laboratory studies have not shown that EMFs cause cancerous changes in cells.

Unfortunately, in spite of study findings, some experts are still sitting on the "electrical" fence. They point out that exposure to EMFs hasn't been proven absolutely safe, either.

Most of the worry over EMFs stems from a few studies which link the magnetic fields with leukemia in children. Several other studies show a higher risk of cancer, such as brain cancer, in electric utility workers.

Recently, the world's largest group of physicists, The American Physical Society in Maryland, looked at more than 1,000 papers on EMFs and interviewed magnetic field experts. The Society concluded that fears over EMFs are groundless. They point out that the earth's magnetic field is about 500 milligauss, while a nearby power line can radiate fields of only five to 40 milligauss.

The Journal of the National Cancer Institute published a new study that said breast cancer was higher among women working in electrical jobs, but they also published an article pointing out all the problems in the study and calling the EMF/cancer link "unproven."

According to two groups of Scandinavian researchers who recently studied thousands of children, power lines don't pose a threat of childhood cancer.

Some health newsletters you may read try to scare you by claiming that the government is ignoring the dangerous possibilities of EMFs. The newsletters claim that the government of Sweden is regulating EMFs and relocating high tension power lines away from schools. Actually, Swedish officials have clearly stated recently that they are doing neither of these things.

Studies are still being done on EMFs, and researchers may prove someday that exposure to the electricity given off by power lines, appliances, computers, telephones, etc., is hazardous.

A lifetime of exposure to home appliances may turn out to be more dangerous than exposure to power lines. At a distance of one foot, home appliances can radiate magnetic fields from about one to 280 milligauss. However, studies linking home appliances to cancer have also had weak and inconsistent results.

Until we hear more from EMF researchers, it's better to be safe than sorry. There's certainly no need to panic about your exposure to electromagnetic fields, but there's no need to buy a house next to a power line, if you can avoid it.

Sources:
American Family Physician (4,2:928)
Cancer Biotechnology Weekly (May 29, 1995)
FAQs on Power-Frequency Fields and Cancer, Version: 3.3.2, Maintainer: jmoulder@its.mcw.edu, Last modified: Dec. 12, 1995
Journal of the National Cancer Institute (86,12:885,921)
Occupational Hazards (57,3:26)
Science News (147,20:308)
The Atlanta Journal/Constitution (Feb. 7, 1996, B3)

Hidden nursery hazard

Pregnant women living in a home built before 1978 should never, *never* strip paint or wallpaper in a future nursery unless they are absolutely sure that there's no danger from an old layer of lead paint.

Developing babies are extremely vulnerable to lead poisoning, and the government didn't ban lead paint until 1978. Paint manufacturers removed most of the lead in the 1950s. Test kits you can use at home will reveal the lead content of paint (and of water or pottery dinnerware.)

Source:
The Nontoxic Home and Office: Protecting Yourself and Your Family From Everyday Toxics and Health Hazards by consumer advocate Debra Lynn Dadd, Jeremy P. Tarcher, Los Angeles, 1992

Dry-cleaning health hazards

Did you know that the Environmental Protection Agency lists fumes from slightly damp dry-cleaned items as a common indoor air pollutant?

(Dry-cleaned items can be damp because dry cleaning isn't really dry. Clothes are washed with a detergent and a solvent that isn't absorbed by the fabric instead of with detergent and water.)

All you have to do to avoid the hazardous fumes is to remove the plastic covering immediately and hang the dry-cleaned item in an unoccupied room with windows open until the solvent evaporates. In cold weather, this could take up to a week for a large item. To speed up the process, put a space heater in the room, open the windows for ventilation, and close the door.

Another way to avoid the fumes is to avoid dry cleaning! Manufacturers sometimes put "dry clean only" on the labels to protect themselves from complaints when people wash an item incorrectly.

Linens and cottons can be washed in the washing machine, dried on medium heat, and taken out while still damp to prevent wrinkles. Even silk can be hand washed in very cold water with mild soap. Don't rub the silk, and let it drip dry. Wash big comforters, sleeping bags and down jackets in your bathtub with warm water and a mild soap instead of paying a fortune to your dry cleaner. Dry them on low heat in a tumble dryer.

Source:
The Nontoxic Home and Office: Protecting Yourself and Your Family From Everyday Toxics and Health Hazards by consumer advocate Debra Lynn Dadd, Jeremy P. Tarcher, Los Angeles, 1992

Walk your way to perfect health

Research has proven that just plain walking for 30 minutes a day provides long-lasting health benefits. And there are no fancy outfits, no weights, no classes to attend.

Look what walking can do for you:

▶ Burns calories at the rate of approximately 100 calories per mile.
▶ Improves digestion. Heartburn, gas, constipation — whatever you're troubled with, exercise is sure to help.
▶ Improves your mood. People who exercise regularly are less likely to be depressed. Several studies reveal that exercise helps lift depression as much as regular counseling does.
▶ Reduces your risk of high blood pressure, heart disease, diabetes, osteoporosis, and colon cancer.
▶ Improves your circulation.
▶ Helps relieve stress.

Find the time. Studies show that a lack of time is the number one reason American adults don't exercise. Break up your 30-minute walking routine into three 10-minute intervals. You'll receive practically the same health benefits as walking the 30 minutes all at one time.

Lose fat without dieting. Although your body weight may not change a lot at first, the composition of your weight will. Many people lose a noticeable amount of fat and gain lean body mass without even dieting.

Don't worry about speed. If you're an overweight beginner, don't worry about how hard or fast you walk. The important thing is to get up and get moving. Build up to a moderate-intensity workout, which translates to a walking speed of 3 to 4 miles per hour. Walking 30 minutes at this pace equals about two miles.

A higher intensity workout such as speed walking will naturally help burn fat and build muscle, and it may help suppress your appetite. But studies show that fat loss is more related to the amount of energy you use during exercise rather than the intensity of the exercise itself. So a low-intensity workout that lasts a long time can dramatically change the composition of your body.

Build up to a power walk. After two weeks of strolling, move up to the second stage known as striding. Striding is faster-paced and requires longer steps. Your heart rate will increase, and you'll begin to reap more health benefits. Although breathing will be harder, you should still be able to carry on a conversation with your walking partner without getting short of breath.

After three to four weeks of striding and the approval of your doctor, you can graduate to the third stage of walking known as power striding. This stage involves holding hand weights and vigorously pumping your arms. Pumping the weights builds up your shoulder and arm muscles. Legs, heart, lungs, arms, and shoulders — they all benefit from power striding.

Set your pace with music. To help you keep up a good pace, check out the cassette tape section at your local music store. You can buy tapes of music chosen specifically for walking. Music with 108 beats per minute keeps you walking at 3 mph. For "power walkers," you can even get tapes that go up to 175 beats per minute, which will keep you striding along at a brisk 5 mph.

Before hitting the open road, think about your feet! Choose safe and comfortable walking shoes, not running shoes. Because your feet have more contact with the ground during walking, you need the greater flexibility and smaller tread of walking shoes. Replace your walking shoes every four to six months. Worn-out shoes can lead to injury.

If you can't get motivated, recruit a friend to help you out. Things are always better in numbers, including exercise. Instead of meeting your friend at a restaurant, meet at the park for a walk. A friend provides encouragement and motivation. Besides, it's safer to walk with a partner.

Sources:
The Journal of the American Dietetic Association (95,6:661)
The Journal of the American Medical Association (273,5:402)

Choosing an exercise machine

If you prefer to exercise in the privacy and comfort of your own home, an exercise machine may be at the top of your wish list. But which one?

Stationary bikes, rowers, treadmills, step machines, and cross-country ski machines will all get your heart thumping, but in terms of getting the best workout, a treadmill may be your best bet.

Scientists recently rated different exercise machines according to how much energy exercisers expended, and the treadmill came out on top. When the average person thought he was exercising at a "somewhat hard" level on a treadmill, he was burning about 700 calories an hour. When the average person worked at a "somewhat hard" level on a stationary bike, he burned only about 500 calories an hour.

You can get a good workout on almost any exercise machine, but treadmills may make exercising a little less painful. You'll feel like you are working harder on a bike or a step machine, without getting any more benefits.

However, since an exercise machine won't do you any good if you don't use it, test out machines until you find one that you enjoy using. If you prefer cycling to walking or running, a stationary bike might be a better choice for you than a treadmill. On the other hand, if you don't like biking outdoors, you probably won't enjoy it inside, either.

Price is always a consideration. Exercise machines come in a wide variety of price ranges, and the most expensive won't necessarily give you a better workout. Try buying a used machine at first, at least until you find one you like.
Source:
The Journal of the American Medical Association (275,8:1424)

Get the right kind of fiber

Fiber is the indigestible parts of plants, and it comes in two types — water-soluble fiber and water-insoluble fiber. Some foods have both kinds of fiber, but most foods are higher in one than the other. It's important to eat both kinds.

Insoluble fiber is the clear winner when it comes to reducing your risk of constipation and colorectal cancer. Insoluble fiber doesn't dissolve in water. It passes through your digestive system pretty much unchanged from the way it went into your mouth.

The fiber draws and holds water in your intestines, which makes the stool soft, bulky, and easy to eliminate. And, since you don't digest fiber, the food goes through your system much more quickly, reducing the possible harmful effects of wastes staying in the intestines longer than necessary.

You'll find the most insoluble fiber in wheat bran, vegetables, and whole-grain wheat breads and cereals.

The cheapest and probably best source of insoluble fiber is raw, unprocessed wheat bran, which is one of the few high-fiber foods that really does call to mind those ugly images of rough, gritty, tasteless foods. But you can easily cover it up by mixing it with your cereal, hot or cold, or baking it into low-fat muffins or breads. It also adds an interesting texture to thick soups and stews.

Soluble fiber lowers cholesterol and even raises the good HDL cholesterol.

As little as three grams per day of fiber from oat bran or oatmeal can be effective. There are 7.2 grams of soluble fiber per 100 grams of dry oat bran, and five grams of soluble fiber per 100 grams of dry oatmeal. (Read labels to check the number of grams in a serving.)

Other sources of soluble fiber are barley, beans, peas and many other vegetables. Corn fiber is a good cholesterol reducer. It lowered cholesterol 5 percent in a recent study. The researchers used 20 grams of corn fiber a day. You'd be hard pressed to eat that much in a day (one serving of corn has three grams of corn fiber), but every little bit helps.

Pectin (a soluble fiber found in fruits such as apples and prunes) and psyllium (the fiber you'll find in many breakfast cereals and bulk laxatives) seem to lower cholesterol even better than oat bran.

One fiber does double duty. Psyllium is a soluble fiber, but it's an oddity. The bacteria in your stomach don't break it down as quickly as other soluble fibers, so it also works like an insoluble fiber to increase stool bulk and prevent constipation. A good food source of psyllium is Kellogg's Bran Buds. To get the best cholesterol-lowering results from products containing psyllium, mix the fiber with your food instead of taking it between meals.

Add about 10 grams of fiber to your diet a day until you regularly eat 20 to 35 grams of fiber daily. Take care to introduce extra fiber into your diet gradually. Adding too much fiber too quickly could cause more constipation, gas, and bloating.

Make sure you drink plenty of water as you increase the amount of fiber. If you don't, the fiber may just make the problem worse.

Sources:
Inside Tract: Maintaining Your Digestive Health, Glaxo Institute for Digestive Health, West Caldwell, N.J.
Journal of the American Dietetic Association (93,12:1446)
Journal of the National Cancer Institute (87,7:477)
Nutrition and Cancer (19,2:213 and 19,1:11)
The Lancet (344,8914:39)
The Physician and Sportsmedicine (22,7:15)

How to be a wise caffeine consumer

Caffeine is just as addictive as cocaine, scientists are saying these days.

"Uh-oh," you're probably muttering. "Now the health police are after my last indulgence, my morning coffee!" You needn't worry — much. If you're healthy, you don't have to give up caffeine.

Caffeine, unlike cocaine, is fairly harmless. However, too much caffeine can make you jittery, anxious and headachy, give you a stomachache or interfere with your sleep. Withdrawing from a caffeine addiction can be extremely painful, so it's smart to know how much caffeine you're getting every day.

How much is too much? Almost every person in America takes in caffeine in one form or another every day. Most coffee lovers drink about three and a half cups a day.

A five-ounce cup of automatic drip coffee contains about 103 milligrams (mg) of caffeine. (That's *cup*, not mug. Mugs hold 10 ounces, or up to a whopping 206 mg of caffeine.) Most experts recommend you get no more than 250 to 450 mg of caffeine per day, depending on your weight, age, and general health.

Overdoing it. Too much caffeine can cause abnormal heart rhythms or raise blood pressure, especially in people who aren't used to the jolt. It can affect cholesterol levels slightly, but recent research has suggested that any rise in LDL ("bad") cholesterol that it causes is offset by an equal rise in HDL ("good") cholesterol.

Drinking more than two cups of coffee a day can cause calcium loss, increasing the chance of osteoporosis and hip fracture. Coffee lovers, especially women, should drink a glass of milk a day to offset coffee's effect on bones.

Caffeine can also hinder the absorption of certain kinds of iron, including iron from supplements. If you're anemic, don't take your iron with your morning coffee!

And if you are pregnant or soon plan to be, it's best to avoid caffeine. Heavy use can increase the risk of miscarriage or low birth weight. It may also make you less fertile.

Caffeine and other drugs. Caffeine can intensify the effects of some stimulants, common cold remedies, and hormones. It can cause extremely high blood pressure when combined with certain antidepressants. Make sure your doctor or pharmacist knows how much caffeine you drink.

Cold turkey ... er, coffee. Someone who consumes a lot of caffeine can find quitting, or even cutting back, rough going. Flulike symptoms, insomnia, jangling nerves, and a nasty headache are frequent consequences. Withdrawal symptoms usually start within 18 to 24 hours, but can begin earlier. In fact, the "lift" your morning cup of coffee gives you may be simple relief from early withdrawal symptoms. If you need to cut down, do it gradually.

Now for the good news. Caffeine's stimulating effect can be useful. It can improve mental and physical performance, make a dull task go faster and help with fatigue on long drives. In military combat, it can keep soldiers alert and save lives.

It helps some pain relievers work more efficiently, and research has shown it to "rev" the metabolism slightly. Dieters always appreciate even a slight metabolism boost.

The trick to healthy coffee consumption is balance and constancy. Since it is possible to develop a tolerance for caffeine, it's best not to get too much. Be aware that caffeine "hides" in unexpected places, and you may be consuming much more than you know. Read labels, and check the caffeine chart below.

Let's say you want to limit yourself to no more than 350 mg of caffeine per 12-hour day. Suppose you like to have a mug of coffee in the morning and a cup after lunch. You're already near 309 mg — almost your limit. You could have a chocolate cupcake and a cup of hot tea, at 35 mg, for your total of 344, but no more coffee.

Or ... you *could* make that lunch cup decaf and "bank" about 103 mg — enough for a double cappuccino later. However, if you took Excedrin for a headache that day, you're a little over your limit, so better make that after-dinner coffee decaf. (But you could still have the chocolate cupcake.)

Moderation, as in most things, is the key.

In an age of "don'ts," isn't it nice to know that you can have your coffee — and eat your cake, too?

Sources:
American Family Physician (47,5:1262)
Food Safety Notebook (4,9:88)
Medical Tribune (33,5:19)
The Journal of the American Medical Association (266,8:1070 and 267,6:811)
U.S. Pharmacist (17,12:34)

The caffeine calculator

Beverages	Milligrams Caffeine
Coffee, brewed (6 oz. cup)	103
Coffee, instant (6 oz. cup)	65
Coffee, decaf (6 oz. cup)	2
Cocoa, hot (5 oz. cup)	5
Tea, brewed, (5 oz. cup)	30
Coca-Cola (12 oz. can)	46
Mountain Dew (12 oz. can)	54

Sources:
Bowes and Church's Food Values of Portions Commonly Used, HarperCollins, New York, 1989
Physicians' Desk Reference for Nonprescription Drugs, Medical Economics Data Production, Montvale, N.J., 1993

SECURITY AND SAFER LIVING

Car phone accidents: Hang up and drive

Steer clear of drivers with car phones, especially if they appear to be over age 50.

Car phone drivers have been put to the test, and what you suspected all along is true. People talking on car phones don't respond as quickly to what's happening on the road, putting themselves and other drivers at risk for accidents. And the older you are, the more the phone conversation distracts you.

In the study, 150 people sat behind the wheel of a car set up in a research lab and watched a video of highway traffic. When drivers over 50 were distracted by a car phone conversation, their response rates to traffic situations decreased by one-third. Younger drivers had trouble when the conversation got intense.

Ideally, you should only use car phones in emergencies or when you're parked. Undoubtedly, you should never negotiate a heated business deal on the highway.
Source:
Accident Analysis and Prevention (25,3:259)

Smarter home security

Approximately one out of 12 homes gets burglarized every year. Have you had a couple of break-ins in your neighborhood lately? If so, don't rush out and buy a security system. You may be reacting emotionally to the break-ins, making you a vulnerable target for burglar alarm salesmen. Consider your purchase logically:

1) A system you install yourself may cost $500 or more. A professionally installed system may cost from $1,000 to $3,000.
2) The average loss from burglary is around $526.
3) At least part of that loss is usually covered by insurance.
4) Alarm systems are a hassle. You have to set them as you leave; disarm them when you come home; and be prepared for false alarms. If you have a lot of false alarms, you can be fined by your police station.

Still want an alarm? Here are some buying guidelines:

▶ Don't lease anything. You don't want the system to be a liability when you sell your house.
▶ Shop for price. With alarm systems, you don't necessarily get what you pay for.

- ▶ Consider buying a wireless do-it-yourself system.
- ▶ If you get a monitored home security system, get smoke and fire monitoring, too.
- ▶ Call your local police or sheriff's department for suggestions.

You can protect your home without an alarm. Burglars are looking for easy targets. In fact, the typical thief is a young male who often lives within a couple of miles of your home. He wants a home he can enter and exit quickly and quietly.

Is your home an open invitation to a burglar?

- ▶ If your door hinges are on the outside, replace those hinges with nonremovable hinges.
- ▶ You need deadbolt locks with a one-inch throw, but you need extra protection if you have breakable glass within 40 inches of the lock. Either have nonbreakable glass installed or get double cylinder deadbolts.
- ▶ Do not rely on a chain lock to allow you to see visitors before you open the door. A wide-angle lens peephole is easy to install.
- ▶ Sliding glass doors and windows can easily be lifted up and out of the tracks. To prevent this, insert a screw from the inside through the door or window frame and into the section that doesn't move. Have small screws poke down from the top track so that they almost touch the door or window.
- ▶ Place a piece of wood into the bottom track of the sliding glass door or window when you lock it. Even better, buy a swinging metal rod called a Charlie Bar to attach to your sliding glass door.
- ▶ Many windows are easy to open even when locked. If you can, drill a hole that slopes downward through the top of the bottom window into the bottom of the top window. Put a nail in this hole.
- ▶ Install outside lighting.
- ▶ Trim any bushes or trees that would allow someone to creep close to your house without being seen.
- ▶ Put a big dog dish by your back door. Only a big, mean dog would need a big dog dish, right?

Source:
How To Protect Your Home, American Association of Retired Persons, 601 E Street, N.W., Washington, D.C. 20049

No. 1 crime fighter

Appreciate your friendly, nosy neighbors. They may have already stopped a robber from burglarizing your home.

Before you buy deadbolt locks or a security system for your home, get to know your neighbors: It's the single most effective way to reduce crime in your neighborhood. Even better, start a neighborhood watch group.

Learn each other's routines and be suspicious when something seems out of the ordinary. If you see someone you don't know in the neighborhood, write down the person's description and the car's license number, and call the police.

Exchange home and work phone numbers with your neighbors. Consider drawing a diagram of the neighborhood and labeling each house with the house number, owner's name, and phone number.

Tell a neighbor when you will be away from home. Leave a number where you can be reached, and ask him to collect your mail, newspaper, and other deliveries. You can do the same for him.

Get the neighborhood together for regular meetings, and ask a police officer to attend. He can tell you about local crime trends and what you need to do about them.

You'll be glad you made the effort to be neighborly when the next crime wave hits town.

Source:
How To Protect Your Neighborhood, American Association of Retired Persons, 601 E Street, N.W., Washington, D.C. 20049

How to buy a home safe that will really protect your valuables

Too many times people buy convenient, fireproof portable safes, expecting them to protect their valuables from fire and theft. For fire, they work well. For thieves, they do too. So well, in fact, that all a thief has to do is carry (or roll — some safes have wheels) your convenient little safe right out the door when you're not home.

Now that you know never to buy a portable safe if you'd like for your valuables to stay at home where they belong, here are three other tips on choosing a safe:

▶ Look at a safe's Underwriters Laboratories (U.L.) rating. The better the rating your safe has, the lower your insurance rates will be. Before you buy, check with your insurance company to see if they require a minimum U.L. rating on a safe before they'll provide protection for items you plan to store inside.

▶ Buy burglar resistant, not fire resistant. Select a steel safe with a high quality lock. To protect your valuables from fire, buy a separate fire resistant safe that will fit into your burglar resistant safe.

You can buy safes that provide protection against both fire and theft, but they are extremely expensive. You may actually come out cheaper purchasing the two safes separately. Shop around.

▶ Bolt your safe to the floor. This makes it more difficult for a burglar to carry off a small or light safe.

Source:
The Coin Collector's Survival Manual by Scott A. Travers, Bonus Books, Chicago, 1994

The best weapon to own

The weapon of choice for college students and others who need extra protection is not a dangerous firearm, a hard-to-use knife, a club or stun gun (which require you to be close to your attacker), or an often useless personal alarm. The weapon you need is an aerosol chemical irritant. And police officers say pepper sprays are more powerful than Mace.

Mace doesn't always work against people who are drunk, on drugs, or mentally ill. Pepper sprays are absorbed into the skin quicker, they make the eyes and skin feel like they're on fire, and they seem to work against all attackers.

Pepper sprays can reach 10 or more feet, and they cost between $4 and $20. Look for products containing at least 5 percent oleoresin capsicum. The canister should say that it's nonflammable and it doesn't freeze.

Buy at least three canisters — one to practice with, one for beside your bed, and one to carry in your purse, pocket, or on a key chain. Practice aiming at a small point on a shopping bag. Find out how far away you can be when you spray. Be sure you're upwind of your target!

Keep your spray handy at all times. Just seeing you carrying a canister in your hand may keep any attackers away.

Source:
Crime at College: The Student Guide to Personal Safety by Curtis Ostrander and Joseph Schwartz, New Strategist Publications, Ithaca, N.Y., 1994

How to avoid dangerous situations

The best way to avoid danger is to keep your wits about you at all times. Don't make these mistakes:

Fumbling for your keys. Always have them ready when you walk to your house or car. Think it's a good idea to put your name or address on your key chain in case you lose it? Guess again. A criminal could easily use your lost keys to get into your home.

Ignoring someone who seems to be following you. Playing it cool isn't smart. Look at the person, then cross the street. You don't want him to think he can surprise you with an attack.

Being a hero. If you arrive home and notice anything out of the ordinary, don't go inside. You don't want to stop a burglary in progress. Leave immediately and call the police from a neighbor's phone.

Being a nice guy. Don't let anyone, even a girl or a sick person, into your house to use the phone. Remember, a girl could have an armed man waiting around the corner.

Hitting the emergency stop button on the elevator. This could trap you between floors with your attacker. Hit as many floor buttons as you can.

Running a red light when you think someone is following your car. That could be dangerous. Instead, do an old police trick. Take three right hand turns in a row. If the car behind you does the same, lock your doors and drive to a police or fire station or crowded area.

Stopping at a deserted rest area. Remember, that's where Michael Jordan's father was murdered. Countless other people have also had their last and final rest at deserted rest areas. Stop at restaurants and gas stations.

Another highway safety tip: Buy a sign for your front or rear car window that says "Call police." Except for cellular phones, that's your safest bet if your car breaks down on the road. Turn on your flashing lights, fly a white hand-kerchief from your antenna, put your hood up, and remember, don't get out of the car if someone besides the police stops to help you.
Source:
Crime at College: The Student Guide to Personal Safety by Curtis Ostrander and Joseph Schwartz, New Strategist Publications, Ithaca, N.Y., 1994

How to avoid losing a child while traveling

A lost child alone in a strange place — that image triggers every parent's worst nightmare. You can calm those fears by taking advance precautions and making smart choices if you do lose sight of a child while traveling.

Before you go out, do your homework:

▶ Pin a paper with your hotel name inside the child's pocket.

▶ Never dress your child in clothes that show his name.

▶ Carry a recent photo of your child in your wallet, and be able to give a good description of what he's wearing.

While you're out sightseeing:

▶ Agree on a meeting place if you are separated. Many theme parks have a lost and found area that serves as a good home base.

▶ Another great survival skill: Make sure the children know to call 911 or ask for help from a uniformed guard or police officer.

▶ If you do lose sight of your youngster, stay for 20 minutes where the child was last seen. Ask vendors in the immediate area if they have seen the child, and send someone else to ask authorities for help.

The final step when you can't find your child is to file a missing persons report with the local authorities.
Source:
Travel Holiday (September 1993)

Best ways to get rid of confidential papers

Almost everybody has some, even the sweet old lady down the street — those confidential papers with secrets you'd just as soon nobody else ever see. Confidential curios include everything from old love letters to canceled or unused checks, credit card receipts and statements, tax returns, bank state-ments, old bills, and paid-off loans.

Even though you don't want anyone else to see them, you'd still like to dispose of outdated confidential clutter without worrying about unfriendly snoops sneaking through your garbage to see what kind of trash they can dig up on you.

Resourceful snoops can dig up quite a lot with your bank account and credit card numbers, including your current bank account and credit card account balances, your credit limits and money market account information, among other things. Many times they won't even have to speak to anyone directly. With a touch-tone phone, they can access the information through an automated account information system.

Don't fool yourself by thinking you're protected from this kind of invasion of privacy just because you have to give your mother's maiden name before you yourself can access any of your account information. For the determined snoop, that information wouldn't be all that hard to come by.

Snoops who scoop up some of your old bills out of the trash can also easily find out if you're in difficult financial straits by calling up electric, gas, and telephone companies to find out if you are currently or have recently been behind on your payments. They can also find out how much you owe and if you use or have used the deferred payment option.

And don't think you can rely on the courts for protection either. Most courts rule that once you place your garbage on the street for pickup, you abandon property rights. This means if someone digs something out of your trash that could put you in a bad position or lead to a lawsuit, you probably won't get any protection for your trash from the courts.

California is an exception. There, it's against the law to look in anyone's garbage until it's being dumped in the garbage truck. Usually, you can consider your secrets safe with the Sanitation Department. They see so much paper trash, they really couldn't care less.

To protect yourself from snoops with malice in mind, make confidential papers you trash absolutely inaccessible. This means running confidential papers through a paper shredder or burning them. If neither of those options is very convenient for you, here are a few others.

▶ Bleach them. Place papers in a large bucket filled with water and laundry bleach. Let them soak for a day or until all ink and images disappear. Drain off excess water and dispose of the soggy papers with the regular trash.

▶ Flush 'em. Tear papers into tiny pieces and flush down the toilet. You only want to use this method for small amounts of paper. Otherwise, you could jam the john and end up with an expensive visit from the plumber.

▶ Make those papers so stinky snoops can't stand it. Place confidential papers in a sealed plastic bag with leftover chicken or fish. Let bag sit out and ripen for a few days, then toss in the trash. The stench will scare off the most unscrupulous snooper.

Sources:
Complete Trash: The Best Way to Get Rid of Practically Everything Around the House by Norm Crampton, M. Evans and Company, New York, 1989
Get the Facts on Anyone by Dennis King, Macmillan, New York, 1995

Defrauding a fake: How to expose an impostor

If you ever suspect that someone is not who he says, you can track down the real truth by following his paper trail.

People with false identities usually create them by a method they call paper tripping. With a little luck and some fact digging, you can trip them up with their own system.

A paper tripper creates a false identity based on the birth certificate of a dead person. He will search through old newspapers, looking for a person who died as an infant or child who once grown would probably have had the same characteristics as the impostor, such as sex, race, eye color, and same date of birth if possible. The fake tries to track down and obtain a copy of the dead person's birth certificate.

Getting a copy of the birth certificate isn't as hard as it might sound because many applicants for birth certificates aren't required to show proof of identity. Also, many places don't maintain cross-registers of birth and death certificates.

Check personal records. Your first clue that a person may be paper tripping is that his personal records only go back a few years.

Secret code cracks Social Security numbers. Your second clue is that the impostor's Social Security number does not fit with numbers assigned to his age group. The fourth and fifth numbers on a Social Security card can sometimes give you an idea of when a card was issued. For example, you might be suspicious if your 50-year old boyfriend has an area number that was assigned to his state only in the last decade.

Most people don't know it, but the first three numbers of your Social Security number reveal the state you were living in when the number was assigned to you. A Social Security number gives you a place to start when you are checking out someone's background.

Nowadays, Social Security numbers are assigned to you by age 2. Before 1977, they were assigned when you applied for one, usually around age 13.

You can find a person's Social Security number through voter's registration records, driving records, mortgage paperwork on file at the county records department, and through other public records such as a summons or a child support order.

For more detailed instructions on using a person's Social Security number to check his background, go to your local Social Security Administration Office and ask to take a look at their *Program Operations Manual System (POMS)*. This will tell you how to spot a SSN issued before 1972. Also helpful is The National Employment Screening Services' *Social Security Number Guide*.

Of course, a person can request a new SSN anytime during his life. However, a real person will have a paper trail before the new SSN was issued. An impostor won't.

Request a driver's license abstract. Your third clue might be that a person received a driver's license for the first time at an age older than usual. You can check this out by contacting the Department of Motor Vehicles in the impostor's state and requesting a license abstract. Most will search for you for a fee of $3 and a turnaround time of two weeks. If the driver has requested his records not be made public, you may have trouble getting this information if you are not a bill collector or a business seeking to verify information.

Birth and death records are revealing. To help you expose an impostor, it will also be helpful to check the central death index in the state in which the individual claims to be born. You may find that the impostor is using the identity of someone who has been dead for many years.

Many paper trippers try to assume the identity of a person who was born in one state and died in another, so that any future correlation of a state's birth and death records won't expose them as an impostor. However, this is often hard to do, so some impostors have to choose a person's identity who lived and died in one state. This makes them much easier to expose.

You can also obtain your own copy of the birth certificate and try to track down any remaining relatives of the deceased person that the impostor is impersonating. Get them to help you expose the impostor.

Sometimes your search is much easier because the impostor you're tracing is really lazy. He either stole a Social Security card or purchased one to use for a short while. This makes him easy to track. Simply access an on-line Social Security database to get the real address of the person the Social Security card belongs to.

Some people even forge Social Security cards. Again, check a Social Security database. This will tell you if their SSN has even been assigned or if it has, to whom it really belongs, living or dead.

Sources:
Get the Facts on Anyone by Dennis King, Macmillan, New York, 1995
When In Doubt, Check Him Out: A Woman's Survival Guide for the '90s by Joseph J. Culligan, licensed private investigator, National Association of Investigative Specialists Hall of Fame member, Hallmark Press, Miami, 1993

TRAVEL DOLLARS AND SENSE

Best luggage buys

Discount stores advertise soft-sided luggage because it's inexpensive, but for a suitable suitcase that won't wrinkle your clothes or crumple in a crisis, go for hard-sided luggage. It will also better protect breakables.

Some other nice features to look for: plentiful, inside and outside pockets to help you organize; ultra-light plastic frames for easier carrying; locks; wheels that won't tip; and retractable pull handles.

Good brands: Delsey Club, Samsonite, Boyt, Travelpro, and Lark. For the best deal, watch for discounts at specialty luggage stores.

Source:
New Choices (34,4:92)

5 tips for cheaper, more convenient travel

▶ Take advantage of airlines' policy of providing special meals to those who request them. You'll often feast on better fare than if you just settled for whatever they happen to be serving that day. Some alternatives that airlines offer include vegetarian, kosher, all-fruit, all-seafood, low-calorie, Hindu, and Moslem entrees.

▶ Save 50 percent on airfare by not purchasing your usual unrestricted-fare ticket. Instead, buy two round-trip tickets that require a Saturday night stay and use only the outbound part of each.

▶ Check your bags at the boarding gate to avoid a trip to the baggage carousel. You can usually pick them up as you exit the airplane.

▶ Reserve the smallest car the rental office offers. You've got a good chance they'll have to upgrade you to a more expensive car for free because they're out of small ones. Even if they have some small cars left, you can often upgrade cheaper in person than you can reserve a larger car in advance.

▶ Keep your guests' tab to a minimum at an expensive restaurant by taking the lead and ordering a low-cost meal. Your guests will often follow your example.

Source:
202 Tips Even the Best Business Travelers May Not Know by Christopher McGinnis, Irwin Professional Publishing, 1994

For cheap international air fare, travel as a courier

Does a $100 round-trip ticket to Europe sound too good to be true? It's possible, if you're willing to pack light and do a little work along the way. Flying as a courier is an inexpensive way to see the world.

International express-delivery companies have found it's cheaper and quicker to send packages as passenger baggage rather than air cargo. Sending their own employees adds to the cost, though, so they hire you to sit in the airplane seat. You may not be able to take any luggage, since that space is occupied by the freight you're escorting, but you will save between 50 and 85 percent of the ticket price. Recent bargains include round-trip tickets to the Orient for $200, Europe for $99 to $199, and South America for $150.

Forfeiting part (if not all) of your baggage allowance is the biggest drawback of being a courier. You have to be able to stuff at least a week's worth of clothes into a carry-on bag. Also, if you tend to change your travel plans often, being a courier is not for you. Once you commit to a courier job, there's no backing out.

Having a flexible schedule is a good idea, but not a necessity. Most couriers book their flights weeks or months in advance. Where you go is up to you. There are several companies around the country that post travel opportunities. The first person to sign up for the flight gets the trip. If you're not particularly concerned about your destination, companies offer drastically lower prices to couriers who make runs on short notice.

Generally, courier flights depart from New York, Los Angeles, or Miami, though some fly out of Chicago or Washington, D.C. Among the most common destinations: London, Frankfurt, Hong Kong, Tokyo, and Paris. (You're just as likely to travel to Sydney, Tel Aviv, or Singapore, though.) Typically, you'll spend at least seven days wherever you end up, although some tickets give you a 10-, 14-, or 21-day vacation.

Once you arrive and deliver the manifest (a list of the items traveling with you) to the person meeting you at the airport (for your safety and the company's, you're not allowed to touch the baggage), you're on your own. Food, lodging, and other expenses come out of your pocket.

Traveling as a couple is possible, but somewhat difficult. Companies typically only need one courier per flight. You and your spouse may have to take separate flights, perhaps even a day apart.

If you're worried about the material you would be escorting, don't. Air courier companies deal in legitimate freight that they expect customs to examine thoroughly. You are not personally liable for the baggage. If your concern persists, though, ask the company what precautions they take on your behalf, such as bonding and insurance.

Source:
Interview with Byron Lutz, editor, *The Shoestring Traveler* (a division of the International Association of Air Travel Couriers), Lake Worth, Fla.

Stretch your travel dollar: Ask the right questions

It's hard to find answers to your travel problems if you don't know even know the right questions! But you can travel more comfortably and cheaply if you make the right request. You can even save money on items you purchase abroad.

These traveler's tips can help:

Planes — The early bird sometimes gets the best deal, but you won't always get the cheapest seat by making your reservation far in advance. Airline prices rise and fall with demand, and tickets often go on sale after you have made your reservation.

Be sure to ask if you can re-book your ticket later in case prices drop. Often you can re-book even restricted and discounted seats. It may cost you $25–$50 to re-book, but you can save twice that much on a sale ticket.

In addition, you don't have to pay first class prices to get more room. When you buy your ticket, ask to be seated on an aisle, a window or by the emergency exit doors. And ask for a boarding pass, which locks in your seat assignment. Another option is to check in early and ask to be put on a waiting list for a better seat.

Trains — It used to be that you only had two choices when you bought a train ticket in Europe: Either you bought a ticket for each individual train trip or you bought a Eurail-pass good for unlimited travel all over Europe.

But what if you have three weeks of vacation and you only want to wander around France? Ask about new options that allow train travelers to save money by choosing from almost 100 different kinds of tickets, including national passes.

Prices for these rail passes go up on January 1 each year, but your pass is good for six months. So if you plan to travel during the spring, you can save money by buying your ticket in December.

Automobiles — It pays to keep a clean driving record if you plan to rent a car during your travels. Many rental agencies run a check on your driving record when you reserve a car, and they may refuse to rent to you if you've had too many accidents or speeding tickets.

Of course, you can take the chance of renting on the spot when you arrive at your destination, but you'll lose discounts you might get for booking ahead. When you call to reserve a car, ask if past violations will hurt your chances.

Taxes — Most western European countries charge a value- added tax (VAT) of 15 to 25 percent on goods bought for use in that country. Americans who buy items in Europe for use in the United States do not have to pay these taxes and can request a refund. Ask your travel agent or the store's clerk about the paperwork required for these refunds.

Tax tip — Unfortunately, Americans do have to pay taxes on rental cars and hotel rooms whether they travel to New York or Europe. If you don't want any surprises on your credit card bill, always ask for the price quote to rent a hotel room or rental car to include taxes. State and local taxes can add up to 25 percent to your bill.

Source:
National Geographic Traveler (March/April 1994)

ATM cards are your best bet for currency exchange

You've gone abroad, and you need some cash. You reach for your traveler's checks and head for the nearest currency exchange center, right? Not so fast.

An automated teller machine (ATM) may be a better choice, especially if you want to avoid the 12 percent commission you'll often pay at a currency exchange center plus the 1 percent you pay to buy traveler's checks. Currency exchange centers may advertise a great exchange rate, but may secretly charge outrageous service fees.

Two competing systems, CIRRUS and PLUS, now link banks in countries around the world directly to banks in the United States. For example, if your home bank is linked by CIRRUS to banks in Europe, you can use your ATM card at any automated teller showing a CIRRUS logo. You will be withdrawing cash from your own checking account in the United States at a favorable exchange rate, and you'll avoid extra charges.

The CIRRUS system even offers an 800 number, 1-800-4-CIRRUS (1-800-424-7787) you can call to find the ATM nearest you. These ATMs work just like the ones at home except you have to select English as the language of your transaction.

Even using a credit card for cash is not as economical as using an ATM abroad. The money you withdraw using your Visa or MasterCard is actually a cash advance, and you will pay 1.5 percent interest on every pound, franc, or escudo, even if you pay your bill on time.

Another advantage to using an ATM for your traveling money — if your card is stolen, no one else knows your personal information number, and no surprise withdrawals will be waiting for you when you come home.

You may want to travel with a few traveler's checks, just in case you can't get to an ATM every time you need cash, but your ATM card is your best bet for cash these days.

Source:
The Wall Street Journal (March 17, 1994)

Find lower air fares on the Internet

Exploring the Internet could save you hundreds of dollars on your next trip. American Airlines offers cheap seats to "Net surfers," if they know where to look. Point your browser to American's home page at http://www.amrcorp.com/aa_home and sign up for the "Net SAAver" Fares mailing list.

Each week you'll get an e-mail which lists dozens of ultra-low fares. (How does Dallas to Mexico City for $170 round trip sound?) When you get the mail, be ready to go. You'll have to leave three days after receiving the e-mail and you can only stay three or four days.

Source:
American Airlines home page

Losing sleep won't save you money

Red-eye flights may leave you feeling a little sluggish, but the sleepiness is worth the money you save, right? Wrong.

While late-night and early morning departures may have meant big discounts 20 years ago, they don't offer significant savings anymore. The deregulation of the airline industry brought about a number of new carriers. With all the competition, fares have gone down and evened out. You might save a few dollars if you fly at 3 a.m., but unless you're going to be up at that hour anyway, why bother?

Your best bet is to plan in advance. Book your flight 21 days in advance and plan to stay over on a Saturday. Those two steps will save you up to 70 percent of what you would pay if you were to walk up to the gate the day you planned to fly.

There are some exceptions, of course. Red-eye flights to Las Vegas are often deeply discounted. And TWA and America West Airlines offer some late-night deals. Otherwise, you're better off in bed.
Sources:
Interview with Ginger Beverly, partner, Decatur Travel Agency, Decatur, Ga.
Interview with Chris Smith, account manager, World Travel Partners, Atlanta

Another reason to hate Mondays

Planning a trip? Don't leave on Monday. That's the day you're likely to pay the most for an airline ticket.

Airlines often raise their fares by $5 to $10 dollars over the weekend, hoping other carriers will match the increase. If no one does, the prices return to normal. Also, Monday is the busiest day of the week for business travelers. With fewer empty seats, there's no reason for the airline to offer discounts. Wait until Tuesday or Wednesday to fly. That's when you'll find the best deals.
Sources:
Interview with Ginger Beverly, partner, Decatur Travel Agency, Decatur, Ga.
Interview with Chris Smith, account manager, World Travel Partners, Atlanta

Airline discounts aren't always money savers

If you want to get a really good buy on airline tickets, you should look beyond bargain airfares.

Sometimes, airlines offer ticket prices lower than supposed sale fares. Many times these tickets are for the same routes with the same restrictions.

Especially during the slower travel months of March and April, airlines are liable to heavily advertise supposed sale fares to tempt leisure travelers. Often sale fares are really overstated.

In other words, you aren't really getting a bargain. If you closely compare fares or have your travel agent do it for you, you can often find a cheaper fare than the sale price.

It's typical these days for airlines to post a fairly high regular discounted fare, then advertise huge savings on that price despite what other bargains may be buried in their reservation computers.

The truth is, many airlines have adopted a department store philosophy — "if it's not discounted, it won't sell," and offer reduced fares on many routes year-round.

Just be on your guard when you see an airline advertising a sale. And be sure to ask for the lowest available price, not just the sale price. You might get a better bargain.

Source:
The Wall Street Journal (March 11, 1996, B1)

5 ways to avoid annoying airline delays

► Plan your trip outside peak travel times. The busiest airport hours are between 6 a.m. and 9 a.m. and after 4 p.m. Friday, Sunday, and Monday are the most hectic travel days.

► Try to book a nonstop flight. These days, many major airlines match the prices of smaller carriers who make connecting flights.

► If you must take a connecting flight and you're traveling in winter, ask to be routed through a fair-weather hub, such as Atlanta, Dallas/Fort Worth, Houston, Las Vegas, or Phoenix instead of an airport where weather is often unpredictable, like Chicago or Denver.

► When making a connecting flight, ask if you can be routed through an airport with a moving sidewalk, such as Atlanta, Chicago's O'Hare, Dallas/Fort Worth, Seattle/Tacoma, or Tampa. It takes longer to travel through airports using shuttle buses than those with moving sidewalks. Once your flight attendant has announced your connecting gate number, check the airline's in-flight magazine for an airport map to see how far you have to go.

► Sign up for the airline's frequent flier program when you book your flight. Not only will you become eligible to earn free miles, you're less likely to be bumped from your flight.

Source:
New Choices (34,9:87)

How to bargain your way to a better hotel price

If you want to save thousands of travel dollars, all you have to do is master one simple skill — learn to bargain for a better price on your hotel room.

If the thought of bargaining makes you uncomfortable, just remember that a hotel owner is better off renting a room at a low price than not renting a room at all. You may also want to comfort yourself with the thought that you can conduct these negotiations with dignity.

Most smart hotel owners recognize this fact themselves and have authorized front desk clerks to do whatever it takes to move a room on a slow night. Here are some tips that may help you get a better deal on your next hotel room:

Use insider's language to show you are shopping. For example, ask if the hotel offers a corporate rate or a commercial rate. Offer the name of the company or corporation you work for and say you believe your company normally gets a special rate at this hotel.

Whether your company actually gets a discount or not isn't really important. You're just letting the hotel management know in a discrete way that
you're looking for a discount, and if they aren't prepared to give it to you,
you'll look somewhere else.

Ask for a reduced rate based on your status or occupation. For example, if you're a student, a teacher (even a Sunday School teacher), a travel
agent, etc., ask for that reduced rate. Travel agent and writer Arthur Frommer
is usually able to cut his hotel costs in half by calling his hotel of choice from
the airport and asking for a travel agent's discount. Not once in over 30 years
of travel has he actually been asked to prove he is a travel agent.

Call first. You may want to phone a number of hotels and ask for a discount over the phone. It's a bad mistake to show up in a hotel's lobby looking
tired and burdened with baggage. They'll figure you're desperate and probably won't give you that lower rate. A clerk will try harder to satisfy the savvy
shopper over the phone than he will the road-weary traveler standing in his
front lobby.

Ask for off-season discounts. No matter how hard you try, you won't be
able to get a good bargain if you're traveling during a peak tourist time. Either
go and expect to pay full price or wait until prime time is over and save yourself a pretty penny.

Examples: Prices at hotels in business centers such as New York, Chicago,
and Philadelphia are sky-high during the week, but when weekends come and
all the business travelers go home, prices plummet. If you're planning a stay
in one of these places on a Friday, Saturday, or Sunday, you can get a good bargain if you try.

In resort spots like Atlantic City or Las Vegas, you won't get a bargain on
weekends, but you can get a bargain if you show up during the first of the week.

Schedule your trip during a slow travel time, and write ahead to your hotel
of choice asking for a discount. For example, write that you are planning a trip
for a certain date, but only if you can get a room for $45 a night. The proba-
ble reply will be that such a room is yours for the taking.

Have a definite price range in mind. For example, say, "I'm looking for
a room that costs no more than $35 per night," even if you know the hotel usu-
ally charges $65.

Don't call the hotel's 800 number. The people who answer those calls
don't have the authority to give you a reduced rate, so chances are you won't
get one. Call the hotel directly and ask to speak to someone in management. If
they know that you're only going to stay at their hotel if you get a reduced rate,
and they need the business, you're likely to get that reduced rate.

Expect the first quote you get to be high. Hotels typically begin by quoting
their top price. Once you tell them this price is too high, they'll often come down.
Source:
The New World of Travel by Arthur Frommer, Prentice Hall, New York, 1990

Playing to win in the frequent flier game

You don't have to jet to Fiji to get where you want to go in the frequent flier game — ordering a bouquet of flowers, investing in a money market fund, or renting a car can boost your point total just as fast. But frequent flier rules keep changing and getting the most for your travel dollar can be tough. Winning players follow these guidelines:

▶ Focus on your favorites: Choose one regional airline and one domestic airline with international routes. Be aware that mileage requirements vary and that points expire after a certain time with some carriers.

▶ Don't toss that frequent flier statement in the trash! All airlines offer summer and winter promotions that score extra miles, and special deals that encourage you to fly in off times pop up constantly.

▶ When you think you have earned enough miles for a free trip, call your airline's frequent flier line to redeem your mileage. Many airlines will handle all the flight arrangements over the phone, and others will send you certificates good for free travel.
When you call, have alternate travel dates in mind. All airlines restrict the number of free tickets per flight, and some black out dates when frequent flier tickets cannot be used at all.

▶ If you fly at least 25,000 miles per year, ask your airline for elite status. Road warriors with elite status board first, receive the best service, and are actually awarded more miles for taking the same trip that the average frequent flier takes.

▶ Most airlines have multiple business partners: hotels, credit cards, car rental firms, phone companies, even florists. By using the services of these partners, you can double and even triple the miles you win.

▶ If your airline allows, you can apply your accumulated mileage to upgrade your ticket to business or first class.

▶ Watch for new markets and segment sales. When airlines open routes into new markets, you can get better prices and sometimes earn bonus miles.
What is a segment sale? Suppose you are traveling round trip from New Orleans to New York with a plane change in Atlanta — you would gain credit for four segments. In one recent promotion, eight segments earned a free domestic ticket. Airlines use segment sales to lure travelers away from heavily booked direct flights.

▶ Some foreign carriers have entered alliances with U.S. partners, allowing you to apply your mileage to the frequent flier program of either airline.
Drawbacks: Foreign airlines usually require a much higher mileage total for a free flight, and many award frequent flier miles only to those who purchase full price tickets.

▶ Suppose your airline goes under — do your frequent flier miles fly away forever? Not necessarily. Chances are a surviving airline will honor your miles. But if you are concerned about losing free flights, you can insure your frequent flier miles. Randy Petersen of *InsideFlyer* has joined Lloyd's of London to offer frequent flier insurance.

▶ A final option for the travel weary — make someone's dreams come true by sharing your frequent flier miles with a friend or relative or donating them to someone in need. Some airlines accept donated miles and provide tickets to nonprofit organizations.

No matter which program you choose, take time to know the rules for the airline you fly with. You'll be ahead of the game.

Source:
Fortune (Feb. 22, 1993)

Credit cards speak louder than cash when it comes to renting cars

If you want to rent a car, make sure you have what it takes — a credit card.

It may seem strange, but in the rental car market credit cards speak louder than cash.

Rental industry officials defend their credit card policy, citing the rise in the number of stolen rental cars. Credit cards offer a way for companies to track rental car customers.

If you don't have a credit card, you may still be able to rent a car, but it could be a long, drawn out process, taking anywhere from one day up to six weeks.

Source:
The Atlanta Journal/Constitution (May 22, 1995, E1)

Learn the rules before you rent a car abroad

The car rental office you visit in Europe might look the same as the one back home, but you're on their turf now, and you may find that the rules are different. In fact, Americans provide U.S. car rental agencies in Europe with less than 10 percent of their business these days; therefore, these agencies do not necessarily cater to tourists.

To guarantee that you have a positive experience renting a car in Europe and get no surprises on your final bill, try these renter's rules:

▶ Reserve your car through a U.S. travel agent for a better rate. Find out whether you will need an international driver's license and ask for a written confirmation of your reservation, including the rate you will pay in the local currency.

A word of advice: Don't be surprised if you get a small car with a manual transmission and no air conditioning. Most agencies will not promise to provide a larger, more comfortable car.

▶ Be aware that gasoline costs as much as $5.00 per gallon abroad and sales tax on your rental can be much higher than you are used to paying in the United States. If you rent a car in Italy, for example, get ready to pay 19 percent sales tax!

▶ Know exactly what accident and liability coverage your credit card or auto insurance will provide for your foreign rental car. Some companies will require that you buy rental insurance and theft coverage in addition to any coverage you have.

▶ Ask about local regulations. You might have to pay a surcharge if you rent at an airport. Another problem: If you rent a car in Florida, you can drop it off in Georgia, right? It doesn't work that way in Europe.

Cars rented in one country usually cannot be returned in another. So if you rent in one country, don't plan on leaving that car in another country unless you are willing to pay a hefty fee for the cost of returning the car to its country of origin.

▶ Try to learn about the local customs wherever you are. For example, when you leave a car with an agency in Berlin, don't leave the key in the ignition — Germans consider that bad manners.

Some car rental agencies abroad are located in garages and other locations equally confusing for tourists, and their hours can be even harder to figure. Imagine waiting to return a car in Venice, where one rental agency closes for lunch from 11:30 a.m. to 3:30 p.m.!

▶ Confirm the terms of your agreement. Ask about business hours, confirm the rate you will be paying, and keep all your papers.

Make sure that you understand the terms of any special deal you accept. Your agency may define a week as five days while you assume it means seven days.

When you return your vehicle, ask the agent to verify that you have not damaged the car and get a copy of your final bill right then and there.

Of course, it's not possible to foresee all the travails of traveling, but a little planning and a few careful questions can at least help you know what to expect. After all, when it comes to renting a car abroad, the best surprise is no surprise.

Source:
The Wall Street Journal (Dec. 10, 1993)

Distance yourself from travel scams

▶ Watch out for postcard, letter, or phone offers claiming you've won a free trip or can get discounts on hotels and airfares. These so-called great deals usually don't disclose the hidden costs involved, such as deposits, surcharges, excessive handling fees, or taxes.

▶ Be wary of offers that require you to purchase a product to get a trip that's "free" or "two-for-one." You'll end up paying for the "free" trip or more for the product than the trip is worth, and the two-for-one deal might be more expensive than if you had arranged a trip yourself by watching for airfare deals.

▶ Use caution and common sense when considering travel offers which ask you to redeem vouchers or certificates from out-of-state companies. Their offers are usually valid only for a limited time and on a space-available basis. The hotels are often budget rooms and very uncomfortable. The company charges you for the trip in advance, but there are no guarantees that it will still be in business when you're ready to take the trip.

▶ Check the reputation of any travel service you use, especially travel clubs offering discounts on their services in exchange for an annual fee. Contact your state or local consumer protection agency or Better Business Bureau.

▶ Request copies of a travel club's or agent's brochures and contracts before purchasing your ticket. Don't rely on oral promises. Find out about cancellation policies and never sign contracts that have blank or incomplete spaces.

▶ Never give your credit card number to a club or company with which you're unfamiliar or which requires you to call 900 numbers for information.

▶ Don't feel pressured by requests for an immediate decision or a statement that the offer is good only "if you act now." Don't deal with companies that request payment in advance or that don't have escrow accounts where your deposit is held.

▶ Research cut-rate offers, especially when dealing with travel consolidators who might not be able to provide your tickets until close to your departure date.

▶ Protect yourself by using a credit card to purchase travel services. If you don't get what you paid for, contact the credit card issuer. You may be able to get the charges reversed. Keep in mind that you only have 60 days to dispute a charge.

Source:
1994 Consumer's Resource Handbook, United States Office of Consumer Affairs, Washington, D.C.

Common con games played on 'foreigners'

Crafty currency exchange. Be very, very careful conducting currency exchanges with unauthorized dealers. Often, money-changers who offer you a better deal are the only ones who get a bargain. That's because they take your real money and replace it with counterfeit local currency or currency that's no longer circulating.

You also risk a run-in with the police when you use unauthorized currency exchangers. Local police (or even people pretending to be police) often pose as money-changers to try and involve international travelers in an illegal transaction. They'll demand "a little something" for their silence.

Save yourself the trouble. Deal with authorized money-changers only.

Bogus baggage handler. Be careful who you let carry your baggage. Even people dressed as porters and wearing the customary cap and uniform sometimes aren't who they say they are. Trust your instincts, and never let the bag containing your essentials, such as passport, medications, tickets, etc., leave your possession.

Broken taxi meter. A torn-up taxi meter is a common excuse for charging travelers outrageous fares. This rip-off runs rampant in countries where taxi fares are not well regulated. Your best protection is to set a firm taxi fare for your destination before you ever get in the cab.

Credit card swap. This is one swap you'll want to sidestep. After using your credit card to make a purchase, sometimes a seller will try to scam you by giving you back an expired or stolen credit card that's no longer usable. To save yourself the indignity of having your credit card stolen from right under your nose, always check to make sure the credit card you get back is yours. Destroy all carbons completely.

Fast cash sale. If some deal seems too good to be true, it probably is. Hurriedly conducted sales on foreign soil often leave a confused consumer with poor quality goods or change that's no longer being circulated and no one to complain to. The seller quickly disappears.

Source:
A Personal Safety Guide for International Travelers by Edward L. Lee II, Falls Church, Va.

Save yourself from street crime — any time, anywhere

- ▶ Leave your gold and other expensive-looking jewelry at home. If you wear it on your trip, you'll only identify yourself as a naive traveler who'd make a good target.
- ▶ Rely on your ATM card or traveler's checks when you need money. You should never carry large amounts of cash or credit cards you don't plan to use.
- ▶ Consider purchasing a money belt or fanny pack. These cases help protect your passport, traveler's checks, credit cards, etc., from being stolen, especially if you tuck the case inside your pants or stuff it under your shirt. If the hotel you're staying in has a safe, leave your passport there and only carry a photocopy of the first inside page with you.
- ▶ Separate your cash into small bills and large bills and keep them in separate sections of your purse or wallet. This will help you avoid flashing around lots of money when you make a purchase and possibly identifying yourself as a potential target for pickpockets.
- ▶ Walk in the middle of a sidewalk whenever possible. Walking too close to a building or a road makes you a better target for a thief.
- ▶ Stand a few feet back from the curb when you're waiting to cross a street. Motorcycle muggers sometimes speed by and grab an unwary traveler's camera or purse.
- ▶ Protect your purse by carrying it close to your body with the latch facing inward and the zipper closed. Your best bet is to carry money and identification in a small pouch you can easily carry in a front pocket. Use your purse only for those items that can be easily replaced, such as sunglasses and makeup.
- ▶ Carry your wallet in a front pocket. Wallets carried in back pockets are potential targets for pickpockets.
- ▶ Elude a suspicious person following you by crossing the street or changing directions. Mixing in with other passersby will often protect you from a personal threat. Never walk or jog alone at night or in the early morning.
- ▶ Use caution if you choose to carry some sort of self-defense product, such as mace. These items may not be legal in some countries. Also, if you aren't trained or prepared to use these protective devices, they may be used

against you. Your best bet is a passive type of self-defense protector, such as a portable siren, a whistle, or Dye-Witness, a semi-permanent dye which momentarily immobilizes your attacker and gives you time to get away. For the next seven days, your attacker will sport a distinctive green stain, making him easily identifiable.

▶ Never resist a robber. You can usually replace lost valuables, but you only get one life.

Source:
A Personal Safety Guide for International Travelers by Edward L. Lee II, Falls Church, Va.

How to get a passport in a hurry

Need a passport fast? Here's how to get one in five working days.

Apply in person at the nearest passport agency. Bring your airline tickets or travel itinerary, two 2x2 identical passport photos, proof of U.S. citizenship (previous passport or certified birth certificate) and proof of identity (previous passport, valid driver's license, government ID, etc.), the $65 application fee ($55 for a renewal), and a good reason for putting a rush job on your passport.

You can also apply for a rushed passport by mail. Simply bring all the required items to your local court or post office. Be sure to note your date of departure on your application. Request that the application be sent to the passport agency via an overnight delivery service. Include a self-addressed, prepaid envelope for the overnight return of your passport.

If the overnight service you choose won't deliver to a post office box, mail your application to:

Mellon Bank
Attn: Passport Supervisor 371971
3 Mellon Bank Center, Rm. 153–2723
Pittsburgh, PA 15259–0001

If you need more information about emergency passport services, contact the Miami Passport Agency at (305) 536–4681.

Source:
Passports: Applying for Them the Easy Way, Department of State Publication 10049, Bureau of Consular Affairs, 1993

Ski industry does a snow job on consumers

If you normally scan the newspaper ski reports or tune in your favorite radio or television station for snow conditions, here's some not-so-heartening news.

Those ski reports run the risk of being less than accurate. Snow measurements are questionable, and resorts commonly use fancy phrases to gloss over actual conditions. For example, icy slopes might be described as "packed powder" or "frozen granular."

Ski resorts don't deny that they spiff up actual snow conditions. They consider these reports part of the competitive edge they need to have to make a profit during the three-month snow season.

If you're planning a ski trip anytime soon, just keep in mind that many ski reports are a slick advertising trick of the ski industry. Ask yourself what those glittering and glossed over phrases really mean. There usually is a grain of truth somewhere. When you really think about it, "frozen granular" really couldn't mean much else but ice.

On the other hand, if you want an accurate report, try one of the on-line reporting services such as America Online or Internet. You can access up-to-date weather information. Even better, the chat lines and message boards carry firsthand condition reports from skiers themselves.

You may also want to consider fax reports like "The Skier's Edge" or radio programs such as CRN International Inc's. "Ski Watch." Neither of these sources is sponsored by the ski industry.

Source:
The Wall Street Journal (Feb. 17, 1995, B13)

Insiders travel tip: the party towns

You'll feel like a true outsider if you travel without this inside information. Some cities have a reputation for providing a party atmosphere.

Whether you would like to travel to a party town or hate parties and just want to know which places to avoid, here are the seven towns which surfaced at the top of a survey conducted by Weissman Travel Reports.

1. New Orleans, La. Of course, Mardi Gras (celebrated a full week before Lent begins on Ash Wednesday) is the big one, but you can find a party just about any other time as well.

2. Amsterdam, Netherlands. You'll find that bars and nighclubs abound in this hopping town.

3. Rio de Janeiro, Brazil. If you love to party, Rio's annual Carnival, celebrated during the four days before Ash Wednesday, will be your cup of tea. You'll see lavish costumes side by side with the scantily clad.

4. Las Vegas, Nev. If you play your cards just right, this rip-roaring trip could be compliments of the house.

5. Newcastle, England. This is a trip for people who love pubs. In Newcastle, they go on endlessly.

6. Vienna, Austria. Party lovers have a ball during ball season. About 300 balls are staged between New Year's Eve and the beginning of Lent. The grandest ball of all is the Vienna Opera Ball.

7. Key West, Fla. Anything is a cause for celebration, including each evening's sunset, where visitors and town folk alike gather on the pier to applaud one of nature's most majestic moments. For the ultimate in Halloween fun, don't miss their annual Fantasy Fest.

Sources:
Fodor's South America, Fodor's Travel Publications, New York, 1994
The Atlanta/Journal Constitution (Aug. 6, 1995, K1)